CATH

MW00438903

PRACTICES
Christian Initiation of Adults

Fr. John J. Pasquini, Th.D.

Copyright ©2015
John J. Pasquini

An Ecce Fides Publication

Instituti ratione, fides, et cultura

Right to reproduce or transmit in any form or by any means, electronic or mechanical, including photocopying, recording, or by any information storage and retrieval system, is granted with full permission of the copyright holder as long as the copyright owner is acknowledged as the holder of the copyright and the author of the work.

Citations come from the following primary and secondary sources, unless otherwise cited: Greek and Latin translations are from Migne, *Patrologia Graeca,* the *Patrologia Latina* and the *Liber Pontificalis*: Jurgens, William A. ed. and trans. *The Faith of the Early Fathers.* 3 vols. Collegeville: The Liturgical Press, 1970: Quasten, Johannes. *Patrology.* 4 vols. Westminster, Md.: Newman Press, 1962-63: *The Christian Centuries.* 5 vols. Edited by Louis Rogier. New York: Paulist Press, 1978: *The Christian Faith: Doctrinal Documents of the Catholic Church.* Edited by J. Neuner and J. Dupuis. New York: Alba House, 1990: *The Apostolic Fathers: The Loeb Classical Library.* 2 vols. Edited by G.P. Goold and translated by Kirsopp Lake. Cambridge: Harvard University Press, 1998: Chadwick, Henry. *The Early Church: The Story of Emergent Christianity from the Apostolic Age to the Foundation of the Church of Rome.* New York: Penguin Books, 1990.

Bible citations are from the *New American Bible Revised Edition,* unless otherwise cited. Used with permission.

Appendices have been previously validated as free of doctrinal error by the original publishers of the sections within the appendices, *Ecce Fides* (Paul Cardinal Poupard), *Light, Happiness and Peace* --Catholic Spirituality (Alba House), copyright John Pasquini.

Lesson plans have been deemed free of error in faith and morals:

Nihil obstat
Right Reverend Archimandrite Glen J. Pothier, JCL, DTh
Adjutant Judicial Vicar
Censor deputatus
Memorial of the First Martyrs of the Holy Roman Church
June 30, 2015

Imprimi potest
✠ Most Reverend Gerald M. Barbarito, DD, JCL
Bishop of Palm Beach
Memorial of the First Martyrs of the Holy Roman Church
June 30, 2015

The *Nihil obstat* and *Imprimi potest* are ecclesiastical declarations that a book or pamphlet is free of doctrinal or moral error. No implication is contained therein that those who have attested to this agree with the contents, opinions, or statements expressed.

Printed in the United States of America

TABLE OF CONTENTS

INTRODUCTION

Inspired by the call to a *New Evangelization* within Christianity, *Catholic Beliefs and Practices* is a scripture, catechism, history, spirituality and apologetics based work which seeks to introduce Christians into the beauty of the Catholic faith. Although this book is primarily intended for those who are seeking to enter into the Catholic Church through the *Rite of Christian Initiation of Adults* (RCIA), it is also an ideal book for renewing one's faith in Catholic Christianity, or for coming to a better appreciation and understanding of Catholic Christianity.

The text is divided into 27 lesson plans, which makes it idyllic for small group learning.

The appendices are intended for personal exploration and reference. They are directed towards one's ongoing faith journey.

1

THE AWAKENING

People are hungry for God. People are hungry for love. Are you aware of that? Do you know that? Do you see that? Do you have eyes to see? Quite often we look but we don't see. We are all passing through this world. We need to open our eyes and see.

Mother Teresa, *One Heart Full of Love* (Ann Arbor: Servant Publications, 1984), 11.

When one's eyes are open to the reality of God, then one can be said to be awakened. There is a point in life where one is faced with the reality that there is something which is beyond the self and the here and now, something which transcends the limits of one's being. This moment is a moment of choice. Does one seek to explore and enter into this mystery of that which is not limited to the self or does one repress the experience? The choice made is the choice that will help govern one's life.

What attracts you to God?

One is awakened and moved to follow the ways of grace by being enlightened to the presence of God. Traditionally, people have been attracted to God in the following ways:

Meaning and Purpose

People are often awakened or attracted to God because God gives them a sense of meaning and purpose in life (cf. Dt. 6:24-25). One recognizes that one must be more than some complex organism that is born, lives, struggles, and dies in emptiness. Life in many ways would be a farce if that were so. Life would be inevitably on the edge of disintegration. There must be more to life than mere existence, than mere survival.

Life needs purpose and meaning, a purpose and meaning that transcends the here and now.

God provides this purpose and meaning, for he is the source and summit of all meaning and purpose.

Truth

Many are attracted to God because he is Truth (cf. 1 Jn. 4:6). Such people seek truth in life, no matter where they may find it. Such people find great comfort in God because he is the goal of their quest, truth itself. Hence, life becomes for such individuals a delving into the mysteries of God, which consumes the entirety of their lives and gives them their ultimate joy.

Good

Some people find God by seeing the good around them. Malcolm Muggeridge, a world-renowned reporter for the BBC, was such a person in many respects. It was in seeing the good that was in the heart of Mother Teresa of Calcutta that he was able to find Christ. In Mother Teresa he saw Jesus Christ, and his life would never be the same again. God is good, and those who have found authentic goodness have found God (cf. Rm. 12:2).

Beautiful

Many are attracted to God because they see in the beauty of creation the handprint of God. For them all of creation echoes the beauty and providence of God. To find authentic beauty is to find the source of all beauty, God (cf. Wis. 13:3).

The Four Ways

While it is true that most people will find an affinity for one of the above ways in which we are attracted to God, all the above ways should be a part of one's attraction to God.

The spiritual journey is a chase after the heart of God, and this entails continual growth and maturity into the ways of God.

Reflections
What attracts you to God?
Where do you see God?
How does your belief in God impact your life?

Homework
Review *Appendix 3: Books of the Bible.* What do the themes from the books of the Bible teach you about God?

2

WAYS OF KNOWING GOD: NATURAL REVELATION (Cf. CCC 1-50)

The Bible teaches:

> Ever since the creation of the world, [God's] invisible attributes of eternal power and divinity have been able to be understood and perceived in what he has made (Romans 1:20).

Natural revelation is that knowledge about God which can be acquired through the natural gift of reason. By examining the world one can see signs of God's handprint in creation.

The following are examples of "convincing and converging" arguments in favor of belief in God:

Argument from Change and Causes

> The first and most obvious way [to prove the existence of God] is based on change [and causes]. We see things changing. Anything that changes is being changed by something else.... This something else, if itself changing, is being changed by yet another thing; and this last change by another. Now we must stop somewhere, otherwise there will be no first cause of the change, and, as a result, no subsequent causes.... We arrive then at some first cause of change not itself being changed by anything, and this is what everybody understands by God.

There must be a beginning to change, and we call this beginning to change, this being not brought about by change, God.

Argument regarding Existence Itself

> The [argument from existence] is based on what need not be and on what must be.... Some of the things we come across can be but need not be, for we find them springing up and dying away, thus sometimes in being sometimes not. Now everything cannot be like this, for a thing that need not be, once was not; and if everything need not be, once upon a time there was nothing. But if that were true there would be nothing even now, because something that does not exist can only be brought into being by something already existing. If nothing was in being nothing could be brought into being, and nothing would be in being now, which contradicts observation. Not everything therefore is the sort of thing that needs not be; some things must be, and these may or may not owe this necessity to something else. But just as a series of causes must have a stop, so also a series of things which must be. One is forced to suppose something which must be, and owes this to nothing outside itself; indeed it itself is the cause that other things must be. This is God.

Something cannot come from nothing. Something can only come from something. Since we live in a world that exists, something had to make it exist. Since everything that exists in our world has a source for its existence, then the world must have a source for its existence. We call this source, without a prior source for existence, God. God put the world into existence.

Argument from the Natural Law

> [Another argument for the existence of God] is based on the guidedness of nature. Goal-directed behavior is observed in all bodies obeying natural laws, even when they lack awareness. Their behavior hardly ever varies and practically always turns out well, showing that they truly tend to goals and do not merely hit them by accident. But nothing lacking awareness can tend to a goal except it be directed by someone with awareness and understanding.... Everything in nature, therefore, is directed to its goal by someone with understanding, and this we call God.

An arrow cannot hit its target without a bow propelling it. A bow needs an archer to pull the chord that propels the bow. An archer has awareness of what his goal is—hitting the target. If he did not have an awareness of what he was doing or an awareness of his goal, he would not be able to hit the target.

The sciences like math, physics, astronomy, chemistry, biology etc., are directed by laws and by goals. These laws of nature are meant to understand why things do the things they do. The whole scientific method presupposes laws, goals, and/or ends. Without these laws we would be blind to nature. Nature would be unpredictable and chaotic.

God is the intelligent being, the archer that pulls the bow that propels the arrow to its goal, its target. God is the intelligent being of the intelligent design of creation.

Design implies a designer. God is the designer of creation.

Argument from Gradation

> [A way to prove the existence of God] is based on the gradation observed in things. Some things are better, truer, more excellent than others. Such comparative terms describe varying degrees of approximation to a superlative.... Something therefore is the truest and best and most excellent of things, and hence the most fully in being.... Now when many things possess some property in common, the one most fully possessing it causes it in the others.... Something therefore causes in all other things their being, their goodness, and whatever other perfection they have. And this is what we call God.

How do we know what is better, truer or more excellent unless we can distinguish between levels or gradations of goodness, truth, excellence, etc.? Anything that has gradations must have a perfection, a superlative, from which all lesser gradations can be observed.

What is this superlative?

What is best described as the fullness of goodness, truth, beauty, excellence or any other superlative?

Everything of human origin is flawed. God is by definition perfect, the Superlative! The gradation of observed things points to the existence of God.

In Conclusion

There are many arguments for the existence of God. The above arguments were simplified for our purposes. The point being made is that Catholics believe that God can be known by the natural light of human reason.

Reflections

What argument for the existence of God do you prefer? Do you know any other arguments?

What moves you to believe in God by means of your reasoning abilities?

Homework

Catechism of the Catholic Church (CCC)
Numbers 27-49

(Arguments are quoted from Thomas Aquinas, *Summa Theologiae: A Concise Translation*, ed. and trans. Timothy McDermott, Westminster: Christian Classics, 1989.)

3

WAYS OF KNOWING GOD
DIVINE REVELATION
(PART ONE)
(Cf. CCC 50-133)

Sacred Scripture (The Bible)

The Bible is the inspired Word of God. It is useful for "teaching, refutation, correction, and for training in righteousness so that one who belongs to God may be competent, equipped for every good work" (2 Tim. 3:16-17). The Word of God awakens souls, sanctifies, enlightens, nourishes, comforts, refreshes, builds up, helps combat temptations and sins, and changes lives. It fosters virtue and forms consciences. It helps to bring about meaning and purpose in life, bringing happiness even amidst the sufferings of life. It nourishes faith, hope and love. It nurtures humility, prudence, temperance, fortitude, charity, generosity, joy, peace, patience, gentleness, goodness, perseverance, modesty, wisdom, and friendship with God.

The Bible (also referred to as the Scriptures) helps us grow in harmony with God, neighbor, creation, and the self. It makes us Christ-like, and helps us to continue Christ's work in the world.

The Scriptures make us authentically and abundantly human. The Word of God guides us in living life fully, abundantly, and everlastingly.

<u>The Formation of the Bible</u>

The Bible is the Word of God, but it is the Word of God

because the Holy Spirit guided the Catholic Church in determining it to be such.

In the early Church there was no set Bible. In fact, there were many false works and writings floating around claiming authenticity. Furthermore, many of the works we accept as part of the New Testament today were not fully accepted into the canon of the Bible until the fourth century. For example, Eusebius, the greatest Church historian of his time, writing around the year 324 AD, pointed out that the epistles of James, Jude, 2 Peter, 2 and 3 John and the epistle to the Hebrews as well as the book of Revelation were still being deliberated over for admission into what would become the Bible.

This is where Sacred Tradition (the life of the Holy Spirit working through apostolic succession within the Church) comes in. It is the apostles and their successors, the bishops, who guided the Church in the ways of the faith. It is only through the guidance of the popes and the bishops in union with them that a Bible started to take shape.

A list of works of what would become the Bible was approved by Pope Damasus I in 382 and reaffirmed by Pope Innocent I in 411. This list of the books of the Bible would become approved at the Councils of Hippo (393 AD), Carthage III (397 AD) and Carthage IV (419 AD). And it would not be till the Council of Trent in 1546 that the Bible would be officially considered complete.

The formation of the Bible over centuries should not be a source of concern for us since the "Chosen People" of the Old Testament lived without any written Scriptures for centuries. The Hebrew Scriptures were the product of the writing down of Sacred Tradition—God working in the life of the People of God.

The Bible is the Word of God, but it is the Word of God because the Holy Spirit guided the Catholic Church in determining it to be such.

The Church has always venerated the divine Scriptures just as she venerates the body of the Lord, since, especially in the sacred

16

liturgy, she unceasingly receives and offers to the faithful the bread of life from the table both of God's word and of Christ's body. She has always maintained them, and continues to do so, together with sacred tradition, as the supreme rule of faith, since, as inspired by God and committed once and for all to writing, they impart the word of God Himself without change, and make the voice of the Holy Spirit resound in the words of the prophets and Apostles. Therefore, like the Christian religion itself, all the preaching of the Church must be nourished and regulated by Sacred Scripture. For in the sacred books, the Father who is in heaven meets His children with great love and speaks with them; and the force and power in the word of God is so great that it stands as the support and energy of the Church, the strength of faith for her sons, the food of the soul, the pure and everlasting source of spiritual life. Consequently these words are perfectly applicable to Sacred Scripture: "For the word of God is living and active" (Heb. 4:12) and "it has power to build you up and give you your heritage among all those who are sanctified" (Acts 20:32; see 1 Thess. 2:13).

Dei Verbum, 21

Sacred Tradition

The Word of God is found in Sacred Tradition. Luke reminds us that his Gospel is the writing down of what had been handed down {by Tradition} to him (Lk. 1:1-4). The apostle John reminds us that there are not enough books in the world to describe what Jesus did (Jn. 20:30; 21:25) and that often when he communicated with his own disciples he did not use pen or ink, but spoke face to face (2 Jn. 1:12; 3 Jn. 1:13). Paul, Timothy, and Jude remind us strongly to hold firm to the traditions that have been handed down by word of mouth {Tradition} and by letter {Scripture} (1 Thess. 2:13; 2 Thess. 2:15; 1 Cor. 11:2; 2 Tim. 1:13; 3:14; Jude 1:17).

When we as Catholics speak of Sacred Tradition we are not talking about human traditions, such as those alluded to in Matthew 15:3; 6-9 or Colossians 2:8, rather what we are pointing to is tradition with a big T--Traditions that were handed down to the Church by Jesus and his apostles (Lk. 1:1-4; 10:16; Jn. 21:25; Acts 2:42; 1 Cor. 15:3, 11; 2 Thess. 2:15; 2 Tim. 2:2).

The passing on in an *oral form* the words and deeds of Jesus is called Sacred Tradition. The writing down (in letter or other literary form) of Sacred Tradition is called Sacred Scripture—the Bible.

Sacred Tradition conveys the entirety of the Word of God as transmitted through the preaching, in word and deed, of Christ to the apostles. Sacred Scripture came from Sacred Tradition and needs Sacred Tradition to assure its certainty about all revealed truths.

Sacred Tradition and Sacred Scripture enlighten and communicate with each other. Both flow from the same divine well-spring (what we call the deposit of the faith).

The *deposit of the faith* is that which Jesus transmitted by word and example to his apostles for our salvation—that is, the faith and morals necessary for our salvation. With the death of the last apostle, John, the *deposit of the faith*, the fullness of Revelation, was closed or made complete.

In order to know the true Word of God as found in Sacred Tradition and Sacred Scripture, we need one more gift from God, the Church, and in particular, the teaching office of the Church—the Magisterium.

The Magisterium

The task of giving an authentic interpretation of the Word of God (often referred to as the deposit of the faith), whether in its written form or in the form of Tradition {in word and deed}, has been entrusted to the teaching office of the Church, the Magisterium—the successors of the apostles in union with the successor of the apostle Peter.

Since private interpretation can often lead to mistakes, the Church is needed to authentically interpret the faith. As 2 Peter 3:16 states: *"There are certain things hard to understand, which the unlearned and unstable distort, as they do also the other scriptures, to their own destruction."*

In Acts 15 of the Bible, at the Council of Jerusalem, we see the magisterium in action. A conflict arose in the early Church concerning Gentile converts. Should they first convert to Judaism through circumcision and then follow the Jewish dietary laws or should they be admitted into the Church without the need to follow these regulations.

Paul was the leader of the opposition who believed that under the new law of Christ there was no need for circumcision or the dietary laws. In 49 AD Paul and some of his associates journeyed to Jerusalem to confer with the apostles, and in particular with the head of the apostles, Peter. After much discussion, Peter and James ruled that Gentile converts would not be required to observe the Jewish regulations.

Even the great apostle Paul recognized the need for a Magisterium, a teaching office, an interpreting office. Even Paul recognized the need for seeking the Church's advice and approval for the correct interpretation of the Scriptures and God's will.

Originally the teaching office was made up of the apostles, the first bishops, in union with Peter, the first pope (Acts 15:1-35). With every succeeding generation the successors of the apostles, the bishops, in union with the successor of Peter, the pope, were (and continue to be) given charge of protecting the faith from errors.

The Bible reminds us of the importance of listening to the Church, the Pillar of Truth (1 Tim. 3:14-15; Mt. 18:17-18; Lk. 10:16) in its authority to teach (Mt. 28:20) to interpret the Scriptures (Acts 2:14-36; 2 Pet. 1:20-21; 2:1; 3:15-17) and to bind and loose, to include or exclude from the Church (Mt. 18:18; Acts 15:28:29).

The Magisterium—the teaching office of the Church--is not superior to the Word of God but is its servant. Under the power of the Holy Spirit, the Magisterium can only transmit that which is found in the deposit of the faith.

Sacred Tradition, Sacred Scripture, and the Magisterium are inseparable realities. All three are necessary to assure the proper transmission of the faith, the proper understanding of the Word of God.

Vincent of Lerins (ca. 450) in his *Commonitoria* (2,1-3) beautifully illustrates the need for Sacred Tradition, Sacred Scripture, and the teaching office of the Church (the Magisterium) when seeking the authentic word of God.

> With great zeal and closest attention...I frequently inquired of many men eminent for their holiness and doctrine, how I might, in a concise and, so to speak, general and ordinary way, distinguish the truth of the Catholic faith from the falsehood of dissenting teaching. I received almost always the same answer from all of them, that if I or anyone else wanted to expose the frauds and escape the snares of the dissenters who rise up, and to remain intact and sound in a sound faith, it would be necessary, with the help of the Lord to fortify that faith in a [pertinent] manner: first, of course, by the authority of the divine law; and then, by the Tradition of the Catholic Church. Here, perhaps, someone may ask: 'If the canon of the Scriptures be perfect, and in itself more than suffices for everything, why is it necessary that the authority of ecclesiastical interpretation be joined to it?' Because, quite plainly, Sacred Scripture, by reason of its own depth, is not accepted by everyone as having one and the same meaning. The same passage is interpreted by others so that it can almost appear as if there are as many opinions as there are men. Novatian explains a passage in one way, Sabellius another, Donatus in another; Arius, Eunomius, Macedonius in another; Photinus, Apollinaris, Priscillian in another; Jovinian, Pelagius, Caelestius in another.... [Without reference to the Tradition as expounded and taught by the apostles and their successors, the bishops, there would be no way of knowing the true meaning of the Scriptures.] (Jurgens, vol. 3).

The "Bible only" approach to divine revelation is unbiblical and contrary to Sacred Tradition--which we are commanded to hold onto (2 Thess. 2:14-15). The "Bible only" approach is a "human" tradition or invention of the sixteenth century which is contrary to the deposit of the faith (Matt. 15:3, 6-9; Col. 2:8).

Christianity was not built on the Bible; The Bible came from the Church. The Church was first!

Reflections

All Christians accept the New Testament in its entirety as put together by the Catholic Church. What insights do St. Augustine's words *"I would not believe in the Gospel, had not the authority of the Catholic Church already moved me"* give you in regards to the formation of the Word of God?

Does it not make sense that the Church that put the Bible together infallibly in the fourth century would be the Church with the gift of interpreting it most accurately? And what does this say about all Church teaching in faith and morals?

What problems do you see with the "Bible only" approach to the Word of God?

Why do Catholics have more books in the Old Testament?

In the sixteenth century, seven books and parts of two other books of the Old Testament were dropped by Protestant Reformers—1 and 2 Maccabees, Sirach, Wisdom, Baruch, Tobit, Judith and parts of Daniel and Esther (These books and passages are often referred to as deuterocanonical books and passages). These books (or parts of them) were dropped because they came from the Greek Septuagint version of the Scriptures, a version of the Scriptures that the Protestant Reformers did not agree with.

The Catholic Church accepts these books and passages because Jesus and the apostles accepted them. The apostles often quoted from the Septuagint version of the Scriptures, thereby affirming its importance and validity. For example, when we compare Matthew 1:23 with Isaiah 7:14 we notice that Matthew is quoting from the Septuagint version of the Scriptures. Another example can be found in Luke's Gospel. Luke chapter 1:5 to chapter 3 is entirely constructed with reference to the Septuagint version of the Bible.

As you look at the New Testament footnotes you will find the abbreviation for the Septuagint, LXX, throughout. The New Testament quotes the Old Testament approximately 650 times, and in the majority of those instances, the quotations are taken from the Septuagint version of the Old Testament which contains the books and passages that Protestants eliminated.

The point is that if the Old Testament Septuagint was good

enough for the apostles, and the early Church, it is good enough for us Catholics.

Homework
Catechism of the Catholic Church (CCC)
Numbers 50-108

Homework Prayer Exercise—Getting to Know Jesus
Step One
Read the Gospel of John, chapter 1.

Step Two—Selecting a Section
Read the Gospel of John, chapter 1:1-18. Read the footnotes. Collect the facts. What is being said? What is going on?

Step Three
Meditate on the passage. What is God saying to me in this passage from the Bible? Is there something in my life that God wants to talk to me about?

Step Four
Pray to God. Share your feelings and thoughts with him.

Step Five—Taking Action
What do I feel and think God wants me to do? What is he calling me to do?

4

WAYS OF KNOWING GOD
DIVINE REVELATION
(PART TWO)
Interpreting the Scriptures
(Cf. CCC 50-133)

As Catholics we seek to understand the Scriptures in the way they were meant to be understood. We allow the Scriptures to say what they want to say (*Exegesis*) as opposed to making them say what we want them to say (*Eisegesis*).

Many people take a particular belief system and then go to the Scriptures and try to find justification for their belief system by forcing a completely foreign interpretation into a particular Scripture passage.

We should never fear the Lord. Let him speak to us the way he intended.

As Catholics we seek to comprehend the *intent* of the inspired authors in their writings. We also try to comprehend the various *senses* in which the Scripture passages were written. Finally, we seek to understand the Scriptures in light of the same *Spirit* in which the inspired writers wrote them.

The Intent

The following provides a helpful guideline regarding author intent:

1) What condition was the author confronting?
2) What was the culture of the area like?
3) What literary genres or styles were common at the time?
4) What modes of feeling, narrating, and speaking were

common at the time?

For example, the book of Revelation addresses a Church under persecution by either Nero or Domitian. The sacred author is seeking to encourage the faithful to persevere in Christ amidst great trials and tribulations. "Hold on," "stand fast," victory is at hand for those who remain loyal to God.

The author uses symbolic and allegorical language characteristic of apocalyptic or resistance literature. Apocalyptic literature makes use of visions, animals, numbers, and cosmic catastrophes in a coded language with the express purpose of instructing the faithful in times of difficulty. The very nature of apocalyptic literature--which enjoyed great popularity amongst the Jews and Christians during the first two centuries—was ideal for conveying a secret message to Christians that could not be readily understood by the enemies of Christianity.

The Senses

In terms of the senses of Scripture, the following are important to keep in mind.

1) What is the literal meaning of the text?
2) What is the spiritual sense of the text?
3) What is the allegorical sense?
4) What is the moral sense?
5) What is the anagogical sense?

In the "passion and resurrection narratives" (Mt. 26f; Mk. 14f; Lk. 22f; Jn. 18f) we have the literal reality that Jesus Christ suffered, died, and rose from the dead.

In terms of the spiritual sense of these narratives we recognize that Christ's death and resurrection was for our salvation—that in Christ we are born to eternal life. We also recognize, amongst other insights, that Christ's death made all suffering redemptive.

In terms of the allegorical sense, Jesus can be seen as the

"New Moses." Moses freed the people of God from slavery and brought them to the edge of the "promised land" "flowing with milk and honey." In a much more powerful manner, Jesus, as the new and greater Moses type or figure, freed us from the slavery of sin and brings us into the eternal bliss of heaven. Likewise, the crossing of the Red Sea by Moses is seen as being symbolic of baptism as well as a sign or type of Christ's victory over death.

As for the moral sense that can be acquired through a reading of these narratives, the insights are unending. The moral sense is intended for, as Paul states, "our moral instruction" (1 Cor. 10:11). Jesus reminds us that being moral entails the seeking and fulfilling of the will of the Father (cf. Mt. 26:39).

The anagogical sense of the passion and resurrection narratives focus on realities and events in terms of their eternal significance. The resurrection of Jesus is a sign to us that we too, in him, will likewise rise and be brought into eternal glory after the end of our earthly journey. The anagogical sense is intended to guide us toward eternal life with God in heaven.

The four above senses are beautifully summarized by a medieval couplet that states: "The Letter speaks of deeds; Allegory to faith; The Moral how to act; Anagogy our destiny."

The Spirit

In terms of interpreting the Bible in light of the Spirit in which it was written we pursue the following rules:

1) How is the Bible understood within the Tradition it came out from? If an interpretation of a particular passage makes a person conclude that Jesus was only a phantom or spirit, then one cannot accept this as being an authentic Tradition of the Church. One must reject this interpretation as not being faithful to the life of the Holy Spirit in the Church as taught by the successors of the apostles.

2) How is the passage of the Bible understood in terms of a coherence of truths? All the doctrines of the Church must fit together like a puzzle. You cannot have one belief contradicting another belief. There can only be one coherent truth.

3) How is a particular Scripture passage understood within the context of the whole Bible? Each Scripture passage is like a piece of a puzzle that depicts a picture. One piece of the puzzle is insufficient for understanding and recognizing what is being portrayed by the whole of the puzzle. One needs all the pieces, or at the very least, the core pieces. The same can be said of the Scriptures. One passage needs to be understood within the context of the whole of the Scriptures for a true interpretation of the Word of God.

This prevents the use of a technique used by many fundamentalists and pseudo-Christians called "proof-text" arguing. Let us use an example: In one passage of the Bible Jesus says "Blessed are the peacemakers" (Mt. 5:9), yet in another he says, "I have not come to bring peace, but division" (Lk. 12:51). This may seem a contradiction but it is not. Jesus is pointing out that in the process of being a peacemaker one will inevitably come up against obstacles which could inevitably lead to division. When the one text is understood in terms of the other, both make perfect sense in terms of the Christian way of life. But if one passage is taken without the other passage, confusion can occur regarding Jesus' true teaching.

Another example of the need to interpret a particular Scripture passage within a coherent and historically accurate context within the whole of the Bible is seen in Jesus' words on the cross: "My God, my God, why have you forsaken me" (Mt. 27:46). At first glance this makes Jesus appear as a man on the verge of despair. Yet when this passage is taken within the context of the whole of the Scriptures we see that the contrary is true. Far from being an echo of despair, the words "My God, my God, why have you forsaken me" are an affirmation of Jesus' identity as the Savior and Messiah. "My God, my God, why have you forsaken me" are the first words of Psalm 22 of the Old Testament which foretell of the passion and triumph of the Messiah (While it is true that Jesus suffered the pangs of abandonment, he did not despair.). If I were to say "Our Father, who art in heaven" everyone would know that I was reciting the first words of the "Our Father"; likewise when Jesus said "My God, my God, why have you forsaken me" the Jewish people would have been fully aware that Jesus was making reference to Psalm 22. He was reminding them that he was the fulfillment of Psalm 22--that he was the Savior and Messiah!

If one took Matthew 27:46 out of context, one could end up with a distorted vision of Jesus.

Jesus teaches us to "turn the other cheek," (Mt. 5:39) but also reminds us that we are "our brother's keeper" (cf. Gen. 4:9). Both passages need each other for a proper interpretation.

Seeking to understand the Scriptures the way they were meant to be understood is at the heart of the Catholic Church's approach to the Word of God. We as Catholics seek to understand the intent, the senses, and the spirit of the Scriptures.

Our Language is Inadequate

As human beings we speak as humans do; consequently, we will always be limited in our attempts to describe God, a God far beyond the limits of our minds.

Since our knowledge of God is limited, our language about him is equally so. We can name God only by taking creatures as our starting point, and in accordance with our limited human ways of knowing and thinking. All creatures bear a certain resemblance to God, most especially man, created in the image and likeness of God. The manifold perfections of creatures - their truth, their goodness, their beauty all reflect the infinite perfection of God. Consequently we can name God by taking his creatures' perfections as our starting point, "for from the greatness and beauty of created things

27

comes a corresponding perception of their Creator." God transcends all creatures. We must therefore continually purify our language of everything in it that is limited, image bound or imperfect, if we are not to confuse our image of God --"the inexpressible, the incomprehensible, the invisible, the ungraspable"-- with our human representations. Our human words always fall short of the mystery of God. Admittedly, in speaking about God like this, our language is using human modes of expression; nevertheless it really does attain to God himself, though unable to express him in his infinite simplicity (CCC 39-43).

Reflection
What dangers do you we face when we interpret the Bible in a literal, fundamentalistic way?

Can you see that even when using the above guidelines, we still need a teaching office—the Magisterium?

Homework
Catechism of the Catholic Church (CCC)
Numbers 109-141

Homework Prayer Exercise—Getting to Know Jesus
Step One
Read the Gospel of John, chapter 2.

Step Two—Selecting a Section
    Read the Gospel of John, chapter 2:1-12. Read the footnotes. Collect the facts. What is being said? What is going on?

Step Three
    Meditate on the passage. What is God saying to me in this passage from the Bible? Is there something in my life that God wants to talk to me about?

Step Four
    Pray to God. Share your feelings and thoughts with him.

Step Five—Taking Action
    What do I feel and think God wants me to do? What is he calling me to do?

5

THE TRINITY
(Cf. CCC 198-741)

The Trinity: Father, Son, Holy Spirit

> Christians are brought to future life by one thing...that they recognize that there is a oneness, a unity, a communion between the Son and the Father, and that there is a oneness, a unity, a communion, albeit a distinction, between the Spirit, the Son, and the Father.
>
> Justin Martyr (ca. 148 AD), *Legat. Pro Christ*

In the story of creation, in Genesis 1:26, we read: "Then God said: 'Let *us* make man in *our* image, after *our* likeness." In Genesis 3:22 we read: "Then the Lord God said, 'See, the man has become like one of *us*...'"

Who is this *us*? Who is this *our*?

In the Hebrew Scriptures, the Old Testament, God is referred to as YHWH (often pronounced Yah-weh) and Elohim. Elohim is translated into English as God, and YHWH is translated as LORD. What is of particular interest is that Elohim is a plural noun for God. The name Elohim indicates a oneness yet a plurality. Therefore, Elohim indicates a oneness yet a plurality in God. For the Christian, there is one God in three *Persons* or means of expression; there is a "oneness," yet a *plurality*. The Hebrew Scripture's, the Old Testament's, name for God attests to the *plurality* of *Persons* in the one, indivisible God!

At the baptism of Jesus in the Jordan we hear: "When Jesus had been baptized he at once came up from the water, and suddenly the heavens opened and he saw the Spirit descending like a dove and coming down on him. And suddenly there was a voice from heaven, 'This is my Son, the Beloved; my favor rests on him'" (Mt. 3:16f). At his baptism the Trinity was manifested to the world: The voice is the Father, Jesus is the Son, and the image of the dove is the Holy Spirit.

At the Transfiguration Jesus is manifested in the midst of a cloud casting a shadow: "A bright cloud covered [Moses, Jesus, and Elijah] with a shadow, and from the cloud came the voice which said, 'This is my beloved Son in whom I am well pleased. Listen to him" (Mt. 17:5). The voice is that of the Father, the beloved one is Jesus, and the cloud covering Jesus with a shadow is the Holy Spirit (Note that throughout the Hebrew Scriptures, particularly in Exodus, Numbers, and Deuteronomy, a cloud or a shadow represents God's presence).

Before Christ's ascension he reminded his apostles to go throughout the world and baptize in the "name of the Father, and of the Son, and of the Holy Spirit" (Mt. 28:10). Notice Jesus says to baptize in the "name" (singular) and not the "names" (plural) "of the Father, and of the Son, and of the Holy Spirit. There is one God, yet three Persons or means of expression within that one God.

In the Gospel of Luke and the Acts of the Apostles, the sacred writer emphasizes the theme that in the Hebrew Scriptures the Father was most apparent, in the Christian Scriptures, the New Testament, Jesus became the center of attention, and in the acts of the early Church, the presence of the Holy Spirit is the main character. Obviously all three Persons of the Trinity are present in each, yet the revelation of the Trinity took place through a process of revelation.

The word *Trinity* is first recorded in the writings of Theophiles (ca. 169), the bishop of Antioch, to describe the mystery of One God in three Persons--Father, Son, and Holy Spirit. And according to the ecclesiastical writer Tertullian, by the year 211, the signing of oneself with the *sign of the cross*, with the sign of the Trinity, had become a well-established custom of the Christian faithful.

"YHWH is the true God and there is no other" (Dt. 4:35). God is One and has One nature (cf. Is. 40:25-28; 43:10-13; 44:6-8; 1 Chron. 17:20; Mk. 12:29; 1 Cor. 8:4-6). There are three Persons in One God--the Father, the Son, and the Holy Spirit. There is no confusion, change, division, or separation between the Persons of the Trinity. The Father cannot be confused with the Son or the Holy Spirit; the Father does not change into the Son or the Holy Spirit; and you cannot separate or divide the Father from the Son and the Holy Spirit. What is said of one Person is said of all.

The three Persons, however, are distinct in their relations of origin: The Father eternally generates, the Son is eternally begotten (Jn. 1:1-4f) and the Holy Spirit eternally proceeds from the Father and the Son (cf. Jn. 15:26).

The Son

> I will redeem you with outstretched arms and with mighty acts of judgment.
>
> God (Exodus 6:6)

At Jesus' birth the prophet Isaiah is quoted (Mt. 1:23: Is. 7:14): "'Behold a virgin shall be with child and bear a son, and they shall name him Emmanuel," which means God is with us.'" Jesus is "God [who] is with us." "In Christ the fullness of deity resides in bodily form" (Col. 2:9). He is the "I AM" of the burning bush (Ex. 3:14) as attested to by the apostle John (Jesus makes use of the words "I AM" in reference to his divinity at least 11 times in John's Gospel alone). Jesus is, as Thomas proclaims, "my Lord and my God" (Jn. 20:28). In the Hebrew Scriptures the title "LORD" refers to YHWH, to Adonai, to God. In the New Testament, the name "Lord" or "LORD" always refers to God! In John 20:16 Mary Magdalene calls the risen Christ by the title "Rabbouni" which was often a title used to address God. Likewise, the phrase "to him be glory forever," which is often used to address Jesus (2 Tim. 4:18; 2 Pet. 3:18; Rev. 1:6; Heb. 13:20-21), is a phrase that was usually reserved

31

to God alone (cf. 1 Chron. 16:38; 29:11; Ps. 103:31; 28:2). And in Titus 3:5 Jesus is referred to as "God our savior." The Old Testament God is likewise referred to as savior: "It is I the Lord; there is no savior but me." The Old Testament "savior" and the New Testament "savior" are one and the same, since there is "no savior but [God]" (Is. 43:11). Can anyone doubt that Jesus is Lord and God? Can anyone doubt that whoever has seen Jesus has seen the Father (Jn. 14:9)?

The Son of God that existed from all eternity became incarnate some 2000 years ago. He assumed a human nature (Mt. 1:21; Lk. 2:7; Jn. 19:25). The Son is one Person, the second Person of the Trinity, with two natures, a human nature (like us in all things but sin) and a divine nature. He is fully human, fully divine, and there is no confusion, change, division or separation between his two natures (cf. Mt. 3:17; 9:6; Mk. 1:1; 8:31; Lk. 1:32; 19:10; Jn. 1:34; 3:13-14; 8:46; Rm. 1:3; 2 Cor. 5:21; Heb. 4:15; 1 Pet. 2:22).

Jesus has a divine will and a human will. His human will is in complete conformity with his divine will (Mt. 11:25; Mk: 36; Lk. 2:49; Jn. 4:34; Phil. 2:8).

Jesus assumed a human, rational soul (Phil. 2:7f). In his human nature Jesus grew in "wisdom and stature" (Lk. 2:52). In his human nature Jesus had the "fullness of understanding of the eternal plan he had come to reveal" (Mt. 13:32). Jesus emptied himself of all knowledge and power not necessary for our salvation (Phil. 2:6-11) so that he could teach us how to be authentically human.

Jesus is the Creator of all things (Jn. 1:3; Col. 1:16f; Heb. 1:2), the Lord of Glory (1 Cor. 2:8), the King of kings (Rev. 17:14; 19:16), the Alpha and Omega (Rv.1:7f). He preached the Kingdom (Mt. 3:2; Mk. 1:15; Acts 2:38). He was immune from sin (Jn. 8:46; 2 Cor. 5:21; Heb. 4:15). He died for all (Jn. 3:16f; Heb. 4:15) and rose from the dead (Mt. 12:39f; Acts 1:22; Rom. 4:24; 1 Cor. 14:4) and will come again to judge the living and the dead—a uniquely divine prerogative according to Hebrew theology (Mt. 19:28; 25:31; Jn. 5:22; Acts 10:42).

The Holy Spirit

"Peter said, 'Ananias, why has Satan filled your heart so that you lied to the Holy Spirit....You have not lied to human beings, but to God'" (Acts 5:3-4).

The Holy Spirit is the third Person of the Trinity and is the source of Holy works. His divinity and consubstantiality or oneness with the Father and the Son is attested to throughout the New Testament (i.e., Jn. 14:16-18; 14:23; Acts 5:3f; 28:25f; 1 Cor. 2:10f; 3:16; 6:11, 19f; 1 Pet. 1:1-3; Ep. 4:4-6). As the third Person of the Trinity, he proceeds from the Father and the Son: "When the Advocate comes whom I will send you from the Father, the Spirit of Truth that proceeds from the Father, he will testify to me" (Jn. 15:26).*****

Through the operation of the Holy Spirit we are made aware of the Incarnation (Mt. 1:28, 20; Lk. 1:35), the mysteries of the Church (1 Cor. 2:10), the forgiveness of sins (Jn. 20:22-23), the justification and sanctification of souls (1 Cor. 6:11; Rom. 15:16), and the charity of God (Rm. 5:5).

The Holy Spirit is the Spirit of truth (Jn. 14:16-17; 15:26). The Spirit strengthens our faith (Acts 6:5), dwells within us (Rom. 8:9-11; 1 Cor. 3:16; 6:19) and guides our works (Acts 8:29). The Spirit gives us a supernatural life (2 Cor. 3:8) with supernatural gifts (1 Cor. 12:11).

The gifts of the Spirit are wisdom, understanding, counsel, fortitude, knowledge, piety, and fear of the Lord (wonder and awe) (cf. Isa. 11:1-2). The fruits of the Spirit are love, joy, peace, patience, kindness, generosity, faithfulness, gentleness, and self-control (Gal. 5:22-23).

Many attempts have been made to understand the mystery of the Trinity. Some attempts to describe the Trinity include that of a married man and father: The man is himself, a husband, and a father. Another analogy is that of the three states of water—water as liquid, as gas, as solid ice. St. Patrick used the example of the shamrock by pointing out that there is only one shamrock, yet three petals. St. Ignatius of Antioch (ca. 107) used the example of three notes making one musical sound. Many saints have used the example of the sun—it has an image (round), heat, and light.

Despite the fact that the above analogies all fall short of explaining the great mystery of the Trinity, they still help us in striving to grasp that which is beyond our grasp.

God is mystery and will always be mystery. And it is because he is mystery that we will always be attracted to HIM.

"May the grace of the Lord Jesus Christ and the love of God [the Father] and the fellowship of the Holy Spirit be with all of you" (2 Cor. 13:13).

****In regards to the procession of the Holy Spirit, the Catholic churches prefer the saying that "The Holy Spirit proceeds from the Father and the Son." The Orthodox churches prefer to say that the Holy Spirit proceeds from the Father," or that he "proceeds from the Father through the Son." Given the correct understanding of the Trinity, all the above expressions are acceptable.

Reflection

What analogy do you prefer in describing the Trinity? And how does it fail in describing the Trinity when we consider that the three Persons of the Trinity are One--without any *confusion, change, division or separation* between the Persons?

When you pray, what Person of the Trinity do you call upon most often?

Which Person, or means of expression, of the Trinity gives you the most comfort?

Homework

Catechism of the Catholic Church (CCC)
Numbers 199-315; 422-480; 512-747

Homework Prayer Exercise—Getting to Know Jesus

Step One
Read the Gospel of John, chapter 3.

Step Two—Selecting a Section

Read the Gospel of John, chapter 3:22-30. Read the footnotes. Collect the facts. What is being said? What is going on?

Step Three

Meditate on the passage. What is God saying to me in this passage from the Bible? Is there something in my life that God wants to talk to me about?

Step Four

Pray to God. Share your feelings and thoughts with him.

Step Five—Taking Action

What do I feel and think God wants me to do? What is he calling me to do?

6

THE CHURCH
(Cf. CCC 748-933)

For as in one body we have many parts, and all the parts do not have the same function, so we, though many, are one body in Christ and individually parts of one another. Since we have gifts that differ according to the grace given to us, let us exercise them: if prophecy, in proportion to the faith; if ministry, in ministering; if one is a teacher, in teaching; if one exhorts, in exhortation; if one contributes, in generosity; if one is over others, with diligence; if one does acts of mercy, with cheerfulness (Romans 12:4-8).

The Church was founded by the words and actions of Jesus Christ (1 Cor. 3:11).

The Church is one, but made up of two components, one human, one divine, one visible, one spiritual. The Church is a hierarchical society and the mystical body of Christ (Acts 6:2-6; 14:23; 1 Tim. 3:8-13; 1 Cor. 12:4-11; Eph. 4:11-13).

People in the Church are part of a "royal priesthood, a holy nation" (1 Pet. 2:9; 1 Tim. 2:1).

All are called to enter the Church. All are called to enter into the life of the People of God by faith and baptism (1 Cor. 3:9, 10, 16; Lk. 12:32; Jn. 10:3-5, 11).

The Church is the Body of Christ which is sustained by the Spirit and the sacraments. Through the Spirit and through the sacraments the Church is established and nourished (1 Cor. 12:12f, 27; Rom. 12:5; Eph. 1:22f).

In the one Body of Christ, the Church, there is a diversity of members and roles or functions. All are linked together in such a way as to make a solid, strong force for the proclamation of the Gospel (Mt. 18:17f; 28:18-20; Lk. 10:16; Jn. 14:16f, 26; 16:13; 20:21; Eph. 4:11f).

"The Church is this Body of which Christ is the head: she lives from him, in him, and for him; he lives with her and in her" (1 Cor. 12:12f, 27; Rom. 12:5; Eph. 1:22f) (CCC 807).

The Church is Christ's Bride for which he gave his life. He continually purifies her and makes her our mother (2 Cor. 11:2; Eph. 5:25, 27, 29; Rev. 19:7).

The Church is the Temple of the Holy Spirit, from which flows all the gifts and charisms (1 Cor. 3:9, 10, 16; Acts 13:2, 4).

The Church is *one* in that she has one Lord, one faith, one baptism, one body, one Spirit, and one hope (Eph. 4:5).

The Church is *holy* for the Father is the author of the Church, the Son the bridegroom, and the Spirit the giver of life-sustaining holiness. Yet despite this reality, the Church is "the sinless one made up of sinners" (CCC 867). The Church is made up of saints and sinners each struggling along the journey of faith (Acts 13:2, 4; 20:22, 28; Jn. 14:16f).

The Church is *catholic* in that she proclaims the fullness of the faith throughout the world. "She bears in herself and administers the totality of the means of salvation (CCC 868)," and therefore is missionary in nature (Eph. 4:11, 12).

The Church is *apostolic* in that she is built on the foundations of Christ's chosen apostles and their successors, with the successor of Peter as the head. Christ governs the Church "through Peter and the other apostles, who are present in their successors, the Pope and the college of bishops" in communion with him (CCC 869-870) (Mt. 18:19; Mk. 16:15; Lk. 24:46; Jn. 15:16, 27; 20:21).

The Church of Christ "subsists" in the Catholic Church. "Nevertheless, many elements of sanctification and of truth are found outside its visible confines" (LG 8).

Salvation is possible for those outside the explicit, visible confines of the Church. Those who *through no fault of their own*, and *moved by grace*, who have not grasped the reality of the explicit expression of the faith are also open to salvation.

How do we understand "Outside the Church there is no Salvation" (CCC 846-848)?

Joseph of Arimathea…was a disciple of Jesus, though a *secret* one… (Jn. 19:38).

Joseph of Arimathea was an anonymous follower of Christ. What lesson can we learn from him?

The Catholic Church affirms that Christ is the way and the truth and the life and that no one goes to the Father except through the Son (Jn. 14:6), and consequently through his Body, his Bride, the Church. All salvation therefore comes from Christ and his Body the Church (1 Cor. 12:12f; 2 Cor. 11:2; Rom. 12:5; Eph. 1:22f; 5:25, 27; Rev. 19:7).

The Church, however, makes it adamantly clear that there are those who "through no fault of their own" will be saved.

Those who, through no fault of their own, do not know the Gospel of Christ or his Church, but who nevertheless seek God with a sincere heart, and, **moved by grace**, try in their actions to do his will as they know it through the dictates of their conscience those too may achieve eternal salvation (LG 16).

Given the above teaching we must ask ourselves, "How do we reconcile these two positions of the Church?"

The key is found in the quoted passage's key phrase "moved by grace." One who is authentically holy is one who has the gift of grace at the core of his or her being. And since Christ is another word for grace, Christ consequently is the source of salvation for a person of authentic holiness, whether that person is explicitly aware of it or not. Such a person is saved by Christ who is the way and the truth and the life (Jn. 14:6). The soul of such a person is one in which *implicit* faith is being experienced. Such a soul makes one a member of the Mystical Body of Christ, the Church.

Another way of saying this is that the soul may know Christ, but the head, the mind, may not be aware of the one who is working within him or her.

This reality finds a most beautiful expression in Matthew 25:

When the Son of Man comes in his glory, and all the angels with him, he will sit upon his throne, and all the nations will assemble before him.... [He will then say] 'Come, you blessed by my Father inherit the kingdom prepared for you from the foundation of the world; for I was hungry and you gave me something to drink, I was a stranger and you welcomed me, I was naked and you gave me clothing, I was sick and you took care of me, I was in prison and you visited me.' Then the righteous will answer him and say, 'Lord, when did we see you hungry and feed you, or thirsty and give your drink? When did we see you a stranger and welcome you, or naked and clothe you? When did we see you ill or in prison, and visit you? And the king will say to them in reply, *'Amen. I say to you whatever you did for one of these least brothers of mine, you did to me.'*

But what about the necessity of baptism? The Church from the earliest of times has recognized three forms of baptism: baptism by water; baptism by desire; and baptism by blood. Since grace, Christ, is in the soul of a person *who through no fault of his or her own* has not grasped the explicit proclamation of the Gospel, that person, because he or she is *moved by grace*, is understood as having accepted a baptism by means of desire at an implicit level. In other words, if such a person had been fully aware of the Gospel message in its explicit form, then that person would have gladly been baptized by a baptism of water.

So people from other religions (i.e., Jews, Muslims, Buddhists, Hindus, etc.) can be saved if they are holy; that is, moved by grace (another word for Christ) to live a life that can be viewed as a continual "yes" to God. They are saved anonymously or implicitly by Christ who is the way and the truth and the life and by his Church, his Body, his Bride (1 Cor. 12:12f; 2 Cor. 11:2; Rom. 12:5; Eph. 1:22f; 5:25, 27; Rev. 19:7). They are baptized by their desire into Christ's life, death and resurrection.

If this is so, some may argue, "What's the point in evangelizing?" Evangelizing is not diminished by recognizing holiness in others. In fact, it is made easier, for the mystery of Christ is already within that person at an implicit level waiting to be nourished intellectually. In other words, missionary work, evangelizing, makes a person recognize (in his or her mind) the Jesus that is already at work in his or her soul (heart).

One's State in Life

The Church is made up of the laity and those called to serve as sacred ministers. Within the laity and those called to sacred ministry are those dedicated to the consecrated life, a life of poverty, obedience, and chastity (1 Cor. 12:13, 27; Gal. 3:27; Acts 2:38).

Lay persons have a unique role of proclaiming the Gospel amidst a world often engulfed in secular humanism. They are called to express the priesthood of the faithful, by virtue of their baptism, in their personal, social, family, and ecclesial lives. They are called to be witnesses of Christ in the very heart of the world amidst all its circumstances (Acts 19:6; 8:17; Heb. 6:2; 2 Cor. 1:21f; Eph. 1:13).

The successors of the apostles, the bishops, have the authority to act in the person of *Christ the Head*.

The successor of St. Peter is the visible head of the Church, just as St. Peter himself was in the early Church. The successor of St. Peter, the Pope, is the head of the college of bishops, the Vicar of Christ, and the Pastor of the universal Church on earth (Mt. 10:2; 16:18f; Lk. 22:31f; Jn. 21:15; Gal. 2:7f).

The other bishops, as successors of the apostles, are "the visible source and foundation of unity in their own particular churches," dioceses (CCC 938).

"Helped by the priests, their co-workers, and by the deacons, the bishops have the duty of authentically teaching the faith, celebrating divine worship, above all the Eucharist, and guiding their churches as true pastors. Their responsibility also includes concern for all the churches, with and under the Pope" (CCC 939).

Those dedicated to the consecrated life by a professed life of poverty, chastity, and obedience (i.e., monks, nuns, religious order priests, religious brothers, religious sisters) are called to serve God and the world in the most intimate of ways in accordance with the unique giftedness of these evangelical counsels.

Why is apostolic succession so important?

The people of God always knew of the importance of spirit-filled successors to their leaders. When Moses' earthly journey was approaching its end, Moses went to Joshua and called the spirit of God upon him by the "laying on of hands" (cf. Ex. 34:1-12). Thus Joshua succeeded Moses in leading the people of God.

In a similar yet more tragic manner, after the death of Judas, the apostles sought out a successor to replace Judas. Two men were proposed to succeed Judas, Barsabbas and Matthias. The apostles prayed and then cast lots. The lot fell on Matthias. Matthias, after the "laying on of hands," then became the successor of Judas and took his place alongside the eleven (Acts 1:15-26).

Paul mentions how he "laid the foundation" for others, successors, to build upon (1 Cor. 3:10). Paul mentions Silvanus and Timothy as being ordained to the office of apostle and thus having apostolic authority (cf. 1 Thess. 1:1; 2:6,7; 2 Tim. 1:6). Other examples of passing on the teaching authority of the apostles through apostolic succession and the "laying on of hands" can be seen and implied in Acts 14:23, Acts 20:28, 1 Corinthians 12:27-29, Ephesians 2:20; 4:11, and 1 Timothy 3:1-8; 4:13-14; 5:17-22.

Apostolic succession is that reality that allows the Church of today to be connected to the faith of the Church of 33 AD. Each Catholic bishop in the world can trace his authority from bishop to bishop all the way back to the apostles themselves.

The apostles did not live in a vacuum. They walked and talked with people and in turn they appointed men to take their place as bishops in guiding their communities, and these bishops were in turn succeeded by other bishops in the same line of succession (cf. Acts 1:15-26; i.e., Matthias succeeded Judas in the office of apostle).

In this way the deposit of the faith would always be protected. The faith of Christ would always be kept pure. Without apostolic succession, Christianity would be a mist of confusion.

Clement of Rome (88 AD), Peter's friend and successor as the fourth pope, makes it quite clear how important apostolic succession is:

> Our apostles knew through our Lord Jesus Christ that there would be strife for the title of bishop. For this cause, therefore, since they had received perfect foreknowledge, they appointed those who [were properly chosen], and afterwards added the codicil

that if they should fall asleep [die or retire], other approved men should succeed to their ministry *(Letter to the Corinthians,* 44, trans. Lake).

Apostolic succession assures the passing on of the true and authentic Christian faith.

The successors of the apostles in union with the successor of Peter form the teaching office of the Church—the Magisterium. When they teach *as successors* in union with the successor of Peter, they teach infallibly in faith and morals.

Reflections

What dimension of the Church do you find particularly attractive?

What is the importance of apostolic succession in your view?

Do you know any anonymous or implicit Christians? How could you evangelize them?

Homework

Catechism of the Catholic Church (CCC)
Numbers 748-870

Homework Prayer Exercise—Getting to Know Jesus

Step One
Read the Gospel of John, chapter 5.

Step Two—Selecting a Section
Read the Gospel of John, chapter 5:19-29. Read the footnotes. Collect the facts. What is being said? What is going on?

Step Three
Meditate on the passage. What is God saying to me in this passage from the Bible? Is there something in my life that God wants to talk to me about?

Step Four
Pray to God. Share your feelings and thoughts with him.

Step Five—Taking Action

What do I feel and think God wants me to do? What is he calling me to do?

7

THE POPE
(Cf. CCC 815-816; 834; 882; 879; 891; 937; 2034-2035)

Peter, the Rock upon which Jesus built his Church!

> [Jesus said,] "Who do men say that the Son of man is?"... Simon Peter replied, "You are the Christ, the Son of the living God." And Jesus answered him, "Blessed are you, Simon Bar-Jona! For flesh and blood has not revealed this to you, but my Father who is in heaven. And I tell you, you are Peter, and on this rock I will build my church, and the powers of death [of hell] shall not prevail against it. I will give you the keys of the kingdom of heaven and whatever you bind on earth shall be bound in heaven, and whatever you loose on earth shall be loosed in heaven" (Mt. 16: 13-19, RSV).

In the naming of the apostles, Peter is always named at the head of the list (Mt. 10:1-4; Mk. 3:16-19; Lk. 6:14-16; Acts 1:13). Of all the apostles Peter is named 195 times in the New Testament, whereas the next most often mentioned apostle, John, is only mentioned 29 times. Peter is the one who usually spoke as the representative of the apostles (Mt. 18:21; Mk. 8:29; Lk. 9:32; 12:41; Jn. 6:69). (The Bible emphasizes Peter's authority and special role by phrases such as "Simon Peter and the rest of the apostles" or simply "Peter and his companions" (Lk. 9:32; Mk. 16:7; Acts 2:37).) It is to Peter that an angel is sent to announce the resurrection of Jesus (Mk. 16:7). It is to Peter that the risen Christ appears to before appearing to the other apostles (Lk. 24:33-35). It is Peter that leads the apostles in selecting the replacement for Judas with Matthias (Acts 1:15-26). It is Peter who was called upon to strengthen his brothers in the faith (Lk. 22:31-32). Peter is the one who preached to the crowds at Pentecost as the leader of the apostles (Acts 2:14-40) and received the first converts (Acts 2:41). It is Peter who performed the first miracle after the resurrection (Acts 3:6-7) and it is Peter who inflicted the first punishment on the disobedient, on Ananias and Sapphira (Acts 5:1-11). It is Peter who excommunicated the first heretic, Simon Magnus (Acts 8:21). It is Peter who led the Church's first council, the Council of Jerusalem, and encouraged the baptism of the Gentiles (Acts 10:46-48). It is Peter who pronounced from the council the first dogmatic decision (Acts 15:17). And it is to Peter that Paul journeyed to make sure his teachings were in line with his (Gal. 1:18). And finally, it was to Peter alone that Jesus told, before his Ascension into heaven, to nourish the faithful in the faith (Jn. 21:15-17), even though the other apostles were present in their midst.

There is only one Church that can trace itself back to Peter and thus to Jesus--the Catholic Church. Peter was the first pope, followed by Linus, Anacletus, Clement, and so forth. This line of succession continues to our present pope (see appendix 4).

Popes have always exercised supreme authority in honor and jurisdiction in Christianity. From Peter to the current pope, the Church has always recognized this reality.

The second pope Linus (67-76) developed the clergy in Rome. Anacletus (76-88) was consulted regarding the proper consecration of bishops, and Clement (88-97) was called upon to squash the disobedience of the Corinthians. Alexander I (105-115) issued the decree that unleavened bread was to be used for consecration; Sixtus I (115-125) decreed the praying of the *Sanctus* and Telesphorus (125-136) the praying of the *Gloria*. Pius I (140-155) issued the decree regarding the proper date for the celebration of Easter. Hyginus (136-140) was asked to squash the heresy of Gnosticism, Anicetus (155-166) the heresy of Manichaeism, Soter (166-175) the heresy of Montanism, and Victor I (189-199) the heresy of Adoptionism.

Damasus I (366-384) chose which books would be in the Bible and which would not. The popes have led the way for 2000 years.

Whenever the Church sought guidance, it always looked to the successor of Peter, the pope. This pattern continued and continues uninterrupted to this very day! Vatican I would officially affirm this pattern under the doctrine of Papal Infallibility.

At the Council of Chalcedon (451) Pope Leo's letter regarding Christ's two natures was read. After Leo's affirmation that Christ was fully human, fully divine, without any confusion, change or division amongst his natures, the bishops sprang to their feet and proclaimed: "Peter has spoken through Leo." The successor of Peter had led the bishops and all the Christian faithful to the truth.

The Holy Father, the pope, is important because he is the successor of the apostle Peter who was entrusted with the keys to the Kingdom and who was entrusted to lead the Church (Mt. 16:18f). In rabbinic terminology the ability to "bind and loose" (cf. Mt. 16:18f) is equated with the authority to decide what is allowed or forbidden by the law (moral and faith issues) as well as the authority to include and exclude individuals from a community.

Thus, the pope is in charge of leading the Church. All are to be obedient to him in faith and morals and in respect. He is infallible in and by himself in the areas of faith and morals when he speaks *ex cathedra*; that is, when (1) he speaks on faith and morals, (2) on behalf of the universal Church, (3) from the authority or "chair" of Peter, and (4) with a clear affirmation that what he is about to proclaim is to be held infallible. All the above conditions are necessary for an infallible statement.

The pope also speaks infallibly in an "ordinary" manner when he affirms a teaching that has always been held by the Church (i.e., the evil of abortion).

Bishops share in this infallibility in faith and morals when they teach in union with the pope a teaching that is intended to be understood as an infallible teaching.

There is an old motto that says, "Where Peter is, there is the Church!" We as Catholics hold to this belief.

> There is one God and one Christ, and one Church, and one Chair founded on Peter by the word of the Lord. It is not possible to set up another altar or for there to be another priesthood besides that one altar and that one priesthood. Whoever has gathered elsewhere is scattering…. If someone does not hold fast to this unity of Peter, can he imagine that he still holds the faith? If he deserts the chair of Peter upon whom the Church was built, can he still be confident that he is in the Church?
>
> Cyprian of Carthage (ca. 251), *De Ecclesiae Unitate* (cf. 2-7)

Reflections

What were your thoughts regarding the pope prior to your becoming acquainted with the Catholic Church?

Do you have a favorite pope, and if so, who?

Homework

Catechism of the Catholic Church (CCC)
Numbers 871-945

Homework Prayer Exercise—Getting to Know Jesus

Step One
Read the Gospel of John, chapter 6.

Step Two—Selecting a Section
Read the Gospel of John, chapter 6:41-60. Read the footnotes. Collect the facts. What is being said? What is going on?

Step Three
Meditate on the passage. What is God saying to me in this passage from the Bible? Is there something in my life that God wants to talk to me about?

Step Four
Pray to God. Share your feelings and thoughts with him.

Step Five—Taking Action

What do I feel and think God wants me to do? What is he calling me to do?

The term "pope" finds its origins in the Greek "pappas," "father." Priest continue to be referred to as "Father" to this day. The Latin version of "pappas," "papa," would eventually be rendered "pope" in the English speaking world. Today, "pope" is exclusively used for the bishop of Rome, the successor of St. Peter.

8

COMMUNION OF SAINTS
(Cf. CCC 946-959)

What do we mean by the communion of the saints?

Scripture points out that the saints are first and foremost in heaven with Christ before the general resurrection (2 Macc. 15:11-16; Mk. 12:26-27; Lk. 23: 43; 2 Cor. 5:1, 6-9; Phil. 1:23-25; Rev. 4:4; 6:9; 7:9; 14:1; 19:1, 4-6). God is the God of the living, and not the dead (Mk. 12:26-27).

The thief on the cross turns to Jesus, repents, and is reminded that he will be in paradise with him that very day (Lk. 23:43). In Hebrews 12:1 we are reminded that we are surrounded by a cloud of heavenly witnesses. The Old and New Testaments remind us that the martyrs are in the hand of God (Rev. 6:9-11; 20:4; Wis. 3:1-6). The *Didache* affirms: "The Lord will come and all his saints with him."

The Scriptures point to the fact that the faithful on earth are in communion with the saints of heaven (1 Cor. 12:26; Heb. 12:22-24), and that they assist us by their intercessory prayers (Lk. 16:9; 1 Cor. 12:20f; Rev. 5:8). For example, the Scriptures point out that "in his life [Elisha] performed wonders, and after death, marvelous deeds" (Sir. 48:14). Even after death, Elisha was interceding for us and bringing us "marvelous" things. In Tobit 12:12 we see how an angel offers the prayers of the holy ones to God. In Revelation 5:8 we read: "Each of the elders [in heaven] held a harp and gold bowls filled with incense, which are the prayers of the holy ones [being brought to God].

The communion of saints is one of the most precious gifts that God has given us (cf. 1 Cor. 12:24-27). For the Catholic there is no "until we meet again." For the Catholic, relationships never end. The communion we share with each other here on earth (1 Cor. 12:24-27) is one that extends into purgatory and heaven. Our relationships change, but they continue into eternity. How comforting to know that we are able to help people by our prayers when they are being purified (2 Macc. 12:45). How comforting it is to know that from heaven they are interceding for us in our time of need in the presence of God (cf. Rev. 5:8; 1 Cor. 12:20f; Heb. 12:22f).

Christ is the One True Mediator, but we and the saints in communion with us have been gifted with sharing in that one mediation.

> On the third day there was a wedding in Cana in Galilee, and the mother of Jesus was there. [2] Jesus and his disciples were also invited to the wedding. [3] When the wine ran short, the mother of Jesus said to him, "They have no wine." [4] [And] Jesus said to her, "[How] does your concern affect me? My hour has not yet come." [5] His mother said to the servers, "Do whatever he tells you." [6] Now there were six stone water jars there for Jewish ceremonial washings, each holding twenty to thirty gallons. [7] Jesus told them, "Fill the jars with water." So they filled them to the brim. [8] Then he told them, "Draw some out now and take it to the headwaiter." So they took it. [9] And when the headwaiter tasted the water that had become wine, without knowing where it came from (although the servers who had drawn the water knew), the headwaiter called the bridegroom [10] and said to him, "Everyone serves good wine first, and then when people have drunk freely, an inferior one; but you have kept the good wine until now." [11] Jesus did this as the beginning of his signs in Cana in Galilee and so revealed his glory, and his disciples began to believe in him (Jn. 2:1-11).

The above passage shows how Mary interceded for the couple. We can intercede for others too!

Examples of Intercessions

The following are a few examples of American saints that have interceded for people. These miracles were associated with their canonizations.

Elizabeth Ann Seton
Through the intercession of Elizabeth Ann Seton, Anne Theresa O'Neill was cured in 1959 of acute lymphocytic leukemia. Carl Kalin was cured of fulminating rubeola meningo-encyphalitis in 1963. Sister Gertrude Korzendorfer was cured of inoperable pancreatic cancer in 1935.

John Neumann
Through the intercession of John Neumann, eleven year old Eva Benassi was cured on her deathbed of acute peritonitis. Michael Flannigan was diagnosed at the age of six with cancer and given six months to live. He was cured in 1963.

Frances Xavier Cabrini
Through her intercession, Peter Smith, blinded by an accident, recovered his sight in 1921.

Katherine Drexel
Her intercession is attributed to the healing of Amy Wall and Robert Gutherman in 1974. Both were cured of deafness.

Kateri Tekakwitha
Jake Finkbonner, an eleven year old Indian boy, was healed in 2006 of a flesh-eating bacteria.

Anyone in heaven is a saint. The Church, however, chooses prominent holy people to serve as examples of holiness for us. Saints remind us that we too are called to be saints, to be in heaven--that we too, from heaven, will be able to intercede for the good of others.

> As I stand upon the seashore, a beautiful sailing ship is in my view. I watch and watch until the sea and sky meet, and then she is gone. Where? Gone from my sight, that is all! And just as she is gone in my sight, she becomes visible in the site of others on the other side of the world. That is what dying is all about.
> Letter found on the body of Colonel David Heinz

Worship vs. Veneration

Only God is due worship (Mt. 4:10; Lk. 4:8; Acts 10:26)! Saints and angels are venerated. If we can honor our mother and father (Ex. 20:12), why can we not honor the saints? Peter, James, and John venerated Elijah and Moses in the event of the Transfiguration (Mk: 9:4). Joshua fell prostrate before an angel (Jos. 5:14), Daniel fell prostrate before the angel Gabriel (Dan. 8:17), Tobiah and Tobit fell to the ground before the angel Raphael (Tob. 12:16). If these great ones could venerate angels and saints, why can't we?

Sharing in Christ's Mediation

We as Catholics recognize there is only one mediator, Jesus Christ (1 Tim. 2:5). We recognize that Christ is the one mediator, but that he has gifted us and the saints with the ability to engage in that one mediation. As Paul states: "Be imitators of me, as I am of Christ" (1 Cor. 11:1; also 1 Thess. 1:6-7; 2 Thess. 3:7) In other words, do what I do as I do what Christ does. Isn't this participating in Christ's mediation? By being a Christian, by being an example of Christ, one shares in Christ's mediation.

The Scriptures remind us of the importance of praying for one another, of interceding for one another (1 Thess. 5;25: Heb. 13:18-19; Mt.5:44; Lk. 6:28; etc.). Praying for one another is an act of mediation.

Finally, Paul reminds us that "we make up what is lacking in the sufferings of Christ" (Col. 1:24). If this is so, then to be a Christian means that we are by nature sharers in Christ's one mediation. He unites our sufferings to his!

Angels, In Communion with Us

Angels are heavenly body-less pure spirits (Heb. 1:7). They are created beings who are in communion with us (Heb. 12:12). They pray for us and bring our prayers to God (Rev. 8:4; Zech. 1:12; Tob. 12:12). They are in charge of conveying God's directives and protecting and caring for humanity (Gn.

24:7; 48:16; Heb. 1:14; Mt. 18:10). Each person has a guardian angel.

Angels do not have bodies, but are often depicted in the Bible as having bodies. This depiction in the Bible allows us to see and understand what would not ordinarily be seen or understood.

Reflections

What do you like most about the doctrine of the "communion of saints"?

What benefit does your going to heaven have on your family and friends and on all the needy on earth? Does this encourage you to be holy?

What brings you the most comfort in regards to the existence of angels?

If you have a favorite saint, who is it? Choose a saint name for your baptism and/or your confirmation? Share the name (s) you have chosen with us next week.

Homework

Catechism of the Catholic Church (CCC)
Numbers 946-962

Homework Prayer Exercise—Getting to Know Jesus

Step One
Read the Gospel of John, chapter 7.

Step Two—Selecting a Section
Read the Gospel of John, chapter 7:37-44. Read the footnotes. Collect the facts. What is being said? What is going on?

Step Three
Meditate on the passage. What is God saying to me in this passage from the Bible? Is there something in my life that God wants to talk to me about?

Step Four

Pray to God. Share your feelings and thoughts with him.

Step Five—Taking Action

What do I feel and think God wants me to do? What is he calling me to do?

9

MARY
(Cf. CCC 484-507; 963-975-773; 829; 2030)
(PART ONE)

Spouse of the Holy Spirit, Mother of God?

Look, the virgin shall conceive and bear a son, and they shall call him Emmanuel, which means "God is with us" (Mt. 1:23).

The greatest cosmic event to ever have occurred, an infinite being, God, becoming through Mary, a finite being, occurred in the Incarnation.

Mary is unique for she is the spouse of the Holy Spirit. When we examine the phrase "to overshadow" as used in the Annunciation scene in Luke 1:35 we cannot but be made cognizant of the spousal relationship between Mary and the Holy Spirit. Jewish rabbis knew that the phrase "to overshadow" when used in the context of conception was a euphemism for a spousal relationship (*Midrash Genesis Rabbah* 39:7; *Midrash Ruth Rabbah* 3:9). The Holy Spirit "overshadowed" Mary (cf. Lk. 1:35). Thus, Mary entered a spousal relationship with the Holy Spirit.

No other human being can make the claim of being the "spouse of the Holy Spirit!" And as "spouse of the Holy Spirit," Mary is the Mother of the God who "is with us," (Mt. 1:23). When Mary visited Elizabeth, Elizabeth responded: "And how does this happen to me that the mother of my Lord (God, YHWH) should come to me" (Lk. 1:43)? Upon recognizing the resurrected Jesus, Thomas would say, "my Lord (YHWH) and my God (Elohim)" (Jn. 20:28).

Mary is the Mother of the *Lord*, the Mother of YHWH, the Mother of *Elohim*, the Mother of *God*.

Mary is what the ancient Church called the "theotokos," the "God-bearer." In fact, this title for Mary was so common that the anti-Christian emperor Julian the Apostate (361-363 AD) would mock Christians for its "unremitting use."

At the Council of Ephesus (431), in seeking to understand more profoundly the mystery of Christ, the Council Fathers could hear the crowds outside the walls chanting "theotokos, theotokos, theotokos!" This was no coincidence. For to truly understand Jesus, the crowds, under the power of the Spirit, knew that one needed to understand Mary.

Thus, it is no accident that the identity of Jesus and the identity of Mary would be clarified together. Mary always points to her Son!

The Council Fathers (i.e., bishops) reaffirmed Jesus as being fully human, fully divine without any confusion, change, division or separation between his two natures (cf. Mt. 3:17; 9:6; Mk. 1:1; 8:31; Lk. 1:32; 19:10; Jn. 1:34; 3:13-14; 8:46; Rm. 1:3; 2 Cor. 5:21; Heb. 4:15; 1 Pet. 2:22). Mary therefore could not be the Mother of Jesus "only," or the Mother of God "only." To separate Jesus' divinity from his humanity would be to make Jesus into two distinct persons. Yet Jesus is one Person, the second Person of the Trinity, the Son of God, with two inseparable natures--a human and a divine nature (cf. Mt. 3:17; 9:6; Mk. 1:1; 8:31; Lk. 1:32; 19:10; Jn. 1:34; 3:13-14; 8:46; Rm. 1:3; 2 Cor. 5:21; Heb. 4:15; 1 Pet. 2:22).

All mainline Christians accept this logic, despite some feeling uncomfortable with the title *Mother of God*. Interestingly, the first Protestants such as Luther, Calvin, Zwingli, and Henry VIII all used the title *Mother of God* with affection.

The Council Fathers at Ephesus affirmed what Pope John Paul the Great would affirm so many years later: One must study at the "school of Mary" if one is to truly understand the mystery of Christ. No one knows Christ better than Mary. No one can introduce us to a profound knowledge of his mystery better than his mother. No one knows a son more than a mother.

Let us always seek to grasp the mysteries of Mary, for as we do, we will discover the wonders of her Son.

> Mother of God listen to my petitions; do not disregard us in adversity, but receive us from danger.
>> Second Century Papyrus, Or. 24, II.

The facts are:
1) All mainline Christians affirm that Mary is the mother of Jesus.
2) All mainline Christians affirm that Jesus is God.
3) All mainline Christians affirm that Jesus has two inseparable natures—a human nature and a divine nature.
4) Therefore, all mainline Christians, no matter how uncomfortable, recognize that Mary is the Mother of God. To deny this reality is to distort who we all agree Jesus is and who we all agree is the Triune God.

Mary is the woman that the Holy Spirit chose as his spouse, the woman who Jesus chose as his mother.

Note: It is important to remember that the Son of God always existed. Mary did not. Mary did not exist prior to the Son of God. Mary is the "Mother of God" in the sense that God became incarnate, came into the world, in flesh, through her.

The Immaculate Conception

In the year 306 AD we read in Ephraeim's *Nisbene Hymn* (27, 8) the following:
> You alone and your Mother
> Are more beautiful than any others;
> For there is *no blemish* in you,
> *Nor any stains or sins* upon your Mother

Full of Grace

The Immaculate Conception is the teaching which affirms that Mary was redeemed by Jesus from the very moment of her conception. She was preserved from *original sin* and personal sin by Jesus, her Redeemer and Savior.

This teaching has always been part of the deposit of the faith and can be seen through the logical philosophical implications that flow from Luke 1:28. Mary is *kecharitomene*; that is, she is "full of grace." She is full of grace because of Christ and thus if one is full of grace one cannot have the stain of *original sin* or the stain of any personal sin. Jesus was "full of grace" (Jn. 1:14) and thus without sin, and because of Jesus, Mary was like her Savior without sin, "full of grace."

New Temple, New Ark of the Covenant

Mary is the pure Temple in which the Savior came to dwell in. In Luke 1:35 the angel of the Lord states: "The power from the Most High will overshadow (*episkiazein*) you." The phrase "to overshadow" is the same one used to describe how the cloud of God's glory came to overshadow the Ark of the Covenant (Ex. 40:35; Num. 9:18, 22).

Like the Ark Mary carried the presence of God (cf. Ex. 40). The Ark is the most holy object in all the Old Testament! The Ark was to be made immaculate, "perfect in every detail" to allow that which is perfect to "fill it" (Ex. 25; 40:5). Not only did the Ark have to be perfect, it had to be kept free from all impurity and profanation (In 2 Samuel 6:6-7 Uzzah was struck dead for simply touching the Ark). For Luke, and thus for us, Mary was the pure Ark, the pure Temple, that held the divine presence, the Son of God, Jesus.

When comparing the Greek and Hebrew imagery used for the Ark of the Covenant (Ex. 25:20; 40:35; Num. 9:18, 22) and the scene of the Annunciation (1 Chr. 28:18; Lk. 1:35f), one cannot but see—when read in their original languages--the powerful and unquestionable parallel.

The Ark was to be made perfect, immaculate for God to dwell within. Mary was created immaculate, "full of grace," "without sin" so that Emmanuel, the "God who is with us," Jesus, could dwell within her.

The Ark carried the *written* Word of God; Mary carried the *living* Word of God. Ambrose writing around the year 390 said of Mary:

> The Ark contained the Ark of the Tables of the Law; Mary contained in her womb the heir of the Testament. The Ark bore the Law; Mary bore the Gospel. The Ark made the voice of God heard; Mary gave us the very Word of God. The Ark shown forth with the purest of gold; Mary shown forth both inwardly and outwardly with the splendor of virginity. The gold which adorned the Ark came from the interior of the earth; the gold with which Mary shone forth came from the mines of heaven.

Now one may argue by saying: "How can Mary have been saved prior to the crucifixion and how is it that she had no *original sin* or personal sin on her soul?"

Is Abraham in heaven? Is Isaac in heaven? What about Moses, Judah, Jeremiah, and all the holy men and women of the Old Testament? Are they in heaven? Of course they are, yet they lived before the Incarnation of the Son of God and lived before the crucifixion (Lk. 16:22; 1 Pet. 3:18f). In Genesis 5:24 and Hebrews 11:5 we read how Enoch was "taken up" to God in heaven. And in 2 Kings 2:1, 11, we are told how Elijah was taken up to heaven in a whirlwind.

Christ's salvific event, his dying for our sins on the cross, was not limited to one time period. Jesus' salvific event engulfed all of history. It engulfed that which is beyond the limits or confines or boundaries of space and time. Thus Mary being preserved from the stain of *original sin* and personal sin is not so hard to grasp in this context. Jesus' salvific event in history and on Calvary affected all who have ever lived and affects all who will ever live.

Mary needed a Savior: "My spirit rejoices in God my savior" (Lk. 1:47). All need the Savior Jesus Christ!

The New Eve

Mary is the New Eve as Jesus is the New Adam. In the Garden of Eden the devil, a fallen angel, brought the words that would lead to death. At the Annunciation, the angel Gabriel would bring the words that would lead to life through Mary. Eve disobeyed God and brought about the fall of the human race. Mary obeyed God and helped to bring about the redemption of the human race. Eve was a poor disciple and poor mother, Mary, the New Eve, was the perfect disciple and perfect mother. Jesus, the New Adam, was without sin; Mary, the New Eve, by virtue of her son, is likewise without sin! Mary, which means "excellence" or "perfection," truly lived up to her name.

The Old Testament Eve was the mother of the human race in the order of nature. Mary, the mother of Jesus, is the New Eve, the new mother of the human race in the order of grace.

The "woman" (cf. Jn. 2:4; 19:26)

Mary is the "woman" of Genesis 3:15, who with her son, will crush the serpent's head; she is the "woman" at Cana that gives birth to Jesus' first miracle, who gives birth to the "new wine," the new age of life and grace, the new covenant; she is the "woman" at the foot of the cross at Calvary, the "skull-place," where the serpent's head is crushed. Mary is the "woman" who obeys God as opposed to the "woman" who disobeyed God in the Garden. Mary is the "woman" who wages war against the dragon, the serpent, the devil (cf. Rev. 12).

Jesus is the "new Adam," the "new man," Mary is the "new Eve," the "new woman."

When Jesus refers to Mary as "woman," he is reminding the people of her role in salvation history.

The Assumption

Even though your most holy and blessed soul was separated from your happy and immaculate body, according to the usual course of nature, and even though it was carried to a proper burial place, nevertheless it did not remain under the dominion of death, nor was it destroyed by corruption. Indeed, just as her virginity remained intact when she gave birth, so her body, even after death, was preserved from decay and transferred to a better and more divine dwelling place. There it is no longer subject to death but abides for all ages.

John Damascene (ca. 645)

The teaching of Mary's Assumption into heaven is the belief that Mary after the course of her earthly life was assumed body and soul into heaven.

Jesus was "full of grace" (Jn. 1:14) and "without sin" (Heb. 4:15). Jesus ascended body and soul into heaven (Lk. 24:50-53). Mary, being the perfect disciple, the perfect imitator of her son, the perfect model of the Church, the one who knew her son more than any other creation of God, would be granted the gift of imitating her Savior, her son, by being "full of grace" and without sin. And at the end of her earthly journey, she would imitate her Savior, her son, by going into heaven body and soul. (The difference being, Jesus *ascended* into heaven, and Mary was *assumed* by her Son into heaven.).

The fact that Mary was assumed into heaven should not be a shocking idea for the Christian. After all, in Genesis 5:24 and Hebrews 11:5 we read how Enoch was "taken up" to God. And in 2 Kings 2:1, 11, we are told how Elijah was taken up to heaven in a whirlwind. If Enoch and Elijah were taken up to God, why would we have trouble believing that the Mother of Jesus, the Mother of the Savior would be taken up, assumed, into heaven.

When we look to the historical evidence regarding those who were close to Jesus we notice that their bones were and are venerated and held in places of honor in churches throughout the world. Yet no mention has ever been made about the bones of Mary and no mention has ever been made about the veneration of her bones anywhere.

Mary knew no decay, for she was free from original sin and concupiscence. As Psalm 16:10 reminds us: [the beloved will not] know decay." The beloved blessed Mary knew no decay.

She was assumed body and soul into heaven.

[Because of concupiscence, the lingering wound of original sin that remains after baptism, we are separated from our body upon death, to be reunited with it, in an immortal form, at the final judgment—a topic we will later discuss. Mary, because of her Savior, Jesus, had no concupiscence].

Just as the Ark of the Covenant was to remain intact, the New Ark of the Covenant, Mary, was to remain intact, Body and Soul!

It is interesting to note that August 15 has always been reserved by Lutherans and Anglicans as a day for Mary. In recent years, Anglicans have allowed their followers to believe in the Assumption; they concluded that this belief was in perfect conformity with the Scriptures. Likewise, some branches of Lutheranism allow for the belief in the Assumption--as a matter for personal devotion.

Reflections

Share your thoughts on the Immaculate Conception and Mary. Do you see why Catholics love her so much?

What does Mary's assumption into heaven teach us about our life, death, and afterlife?

Homework

Catechism of the Catholic Church (CCC)
Numbers 487-511

Homework Prayer Exercise—Getting to Know Jesus

Step One
Read the Gospel of John, chapter 8.

Step Two—Selecting a Section
Read the Gospel of John, chapter 8:12-20. Read the footnotes. Collect the facts. What is being said? What is going on?

Step Three

Meditate on the passage. What is God saying to me in this passage from the Bible? Is there something in my life that God wants to talk to me about?

Step Four

Pray to God. Share your feelings and thoughts with him.

Step Five—Taking Action

What do I feel and think God wants me to do? What is he calling me to do?

10

MARY
(Cf. CCC 484-507; 963-975-773; 829; 2030)
(PART TWO)

Ever-Virgin

Mary remained a virgin throughout her life. She had no other child than Jesus.

Catholics believe in the perpetual virginity of Mary. The title "ever-virgin" has always been a title for Mary from antiquity. If she had given birth to anyone else other than Jesus, that ancient title would have ceased to exist.

Even the pillars of all modern mainline Protestant denominations affirm Mary's perpetual virginity. Martin Luther wrote:

> It is an article of faith that Mary is Mother of the Lord and still a virgin…. Christ we believe, came forth from a womb left perfectly intact (*Works of Luther*, 6, 510).

Ulrich Zwingli wrote:

> I firmly believe that Mary, according to the words of the gospel, as a pure Virgin brought forth for us the Son of God and in childbirth and after childbirth forever remained a pure, intact Virgin (Zwingli *Opera,* v. 1, 424).

The first Protestants believed in the perpetual virginity of Mary.

In the Scriptures and in history we never find the appellation "Mary's children." If Mary would have had children, the title "Mary's children" would certainly have been found somewhere in history. When Jesus was found in the temple at the age of twelve by Mary and Joseph, the context of the scene makes it quite clear that Jesus was Mary's only child (Lk. 2:41-51). In Mark 6:3 we are reminded that Jesus is the "son of Mary" and not "a son of Mary."

So how do we respond to quotes such as those found in Matthew 12:46, Mark 3:31-35; 6:3, John 7:5, Acts 1:14, in 1 Corinthians 9:5 and Galatians 1:19 that mention brothers (and sisters) of Jesus. And how do we respond to the Greek word *adelphoi* (brothers) which means "from the womb."

First, our English word for "brother" comes from the root "from the same parents." Yet we use the word brother or brothers more broadly (i.e., "brothers in arms").

Secondly, when interpreting the Scriptures we need to understand the term "brother" in the same way the people during Jesus' time understood the term. (*Remember our rules on Bible interpretation?*) When we do this, the use of the term "brother" becomes clarified.

In the ancient Jewish culture of Jesus' time, there was no word for cousin, uncle, or close relative. The word "brother" was used for all such appellations. In the Old Testament, or what we refer to as the Hebrew Scriptures, brothers and sisters are often meant to refer to close relations. Brothers and sisters in Semitic usage can refer to nephews, nieces, cousins, half-brothers, half-sisters, etc. (cf. Gen. 13:8; 14:14-16; 29:15, Lev. 10:4, etc.). For example, when we look at the original Hebrew texts and even the better English translations we find the following: Lot is described as Abraham's brother, yet Lot is the son of Aran (cf. Gen. 14:14). Lot was Abraham's nephew. Jacob is called the brother of Laban, yet Laban is his uncle (Gen. 29:15). When we look to Deuteronomy 23:7-8 and Jeremiah 34:9 we notice the appellation "brothers" is used in terms of a person who shares the same culture or national background. When we look to 2 Samuel 1:26 and 1 Kings 9:13 we notice that brother is used in terms of a friend. When we look at Amos 1:9 we see that "brother" is used in terms of an ally.

The New Testament makes it quite clear that this is the appropriate understanding of brothers and sisters in reference to Mary. For example, James and Joseph are called "brothers of Jesus," yet in examining the Bible we see that this is impossible, for James and Joseph "are sons of another Mary, a disciple of Christ," whom Matthew significantly calls "the other Mary," Mary the wife of Clopas (Jn. 19:25) (Mt. 13:55; 28:1; cf. Mt. 27:56). In the Acts of the Apostles, Peter in addressing the "one hundred and twenty brothers" [adelphon] (Acts 1:15f), was certainly not addressing one hundred and twenty blood-brothers! In Acts 22:7 fellow Christians are called "brothers," "adelphon," and the Jewish leaders are called "brothers," "adelphon." The Greek word adelphoi has a broad meaning as does the English understanding of the word. In fact, in the ancient world it had an even broader meaning!

It is not an unusual or an odd practice to call people who are not related to us as brothers or sisters. Even today in many Protestant denominations people like to refer to themselves as brothers and sisters in the faith. Yet they are not real brothers or real sisters. They are close friends within the Body of Christ. As Jesus himself mentions we are "all brothers" (Mt. 23:8).

Other examples of the use of brothers in a non-familial sense can be seen in the following: In Romans 14:10, 21, we read, "Why then do you judge your brother?" "It is good not to...do anything that causes your brother to stumble." In 1 Corinthians 5:11 we read, "I now write to you not to associate with anyone named a brother, if he is immoral, greedy...." In 2 Corinthians 8:18 we read, "We have sent to you the brother who is praised in all the churches for his preaching of the gospel." In 1 Thessalonians 4:6, we read, "Do not take advantage or exploit a brother." In 1 John 3:17 we read, "If someone who has worldly means sees a brother in need and refuses him compassion, how can the love of God remain in him?" In 1 John 4:20 we read, "If anyone says, 'I love God,' but hates his brother, he is a liar." And on and on the pattern goes. In fact, Paul makes use of the appellation "brothers" in 97 scriptural verses. Every letter in the Bible written by the apostle Paul begins with his addressing the faithful as "brothers."

The word "brother" in the New Testament is used over 105 times and the word "brothers" is used more than 220 times.

Firstborn

In Luke 2:7 Jesus is described as the "firstborn." In the English language firstborn implies the birth of other children; in Jesus' time "firstborn" had no such implication. For example, in the Old Testament Psalm 89:27 David is referred to as the "firstborn," yet he is the eighth son of Jesse (1 Sam. 16). In the Old Testament book of Genesis (43:33), we read about Joseph as being referred to as the "firstborn." Yet this cannot be understood in the modern sense of firstborn since Joseph was one of the youngest children of the Patriarch Jacob (He was the firstborn of Rebecca but not Leah). In the book of Exodus, Moses reminds the Pharaoh, because of his obstinacy "every firstborn in the land of Egypt shall die" (Ex. 11:5). Obviously, no implication for second-born children can be inferred. The firstborn son had to be redeemed within forty days (Ex. 34:20). There would be no way of knowing if other children would be born after!

The term "firstborn" is primarily a legal term, a term indicating rights and privileges (i.e., Gn. 27; Ex. 13:2; Nm. 3:12-13;; 18, 15-16; Dt. 21:15-17). For example, the term "firstborn" often referred to a child that was responsible for opening the womb of a woman, without any further implication (Ex. 13:2; Nb. 3:12). Sometimes it referred to someone as being special, as being sanctified (Ex. 34:20). According to the Law of Moses, all firstborn Jewish children were to be presented in the Temple and offered to God in thanksgiving (cf. Lk. 2:22f). This very fact did not mean that the parents of this firstborn child, presented in the Temple, were assured of having a second-born child or any other children!

The term "firstborn" was a very important legal title in regards to rights and privileges. Upon the death of the father, the firstborn became the head of the family, inherited the majority—a double portion—of the family's goods, and was consecrated to God's service.

Until

Some like to refer to Matthew 1:25 where the ancient Greek compound word *heos-hou* is translated in many English Bibles as "until," rather than "when" (as in the *New Jerusalem Bible*). They infer that the word "until"—as found in many English Bibles--in the phrase "until she bore a son" implies children after the birth of Jesus.

Again, taking into account our study on Bible interpretation, we must look at the way this compound word was understood in the time of Jesus. No implication can be made regarding marital relations by the use of the compound word. It was a common compound word of the period which had no further implications regarding future events, including future births. For example, in Luke 1:80 John the Baptist was called by God to remain in the desert "until the day of [the Messiah's] manifestation to Israel." Yet John remained in the desert after the Savior's manifestation to Israel and even after Jesus himself began baptizing in the Jordan—only with John's capture by Herod's men, did he cease to be in the desert. In Acts 25:21 Paul was to remain imprisoned "until" (*heos-hou*) he was sent up to Caesar. Yet the Acts of the Apostles (cf. 28:20) show Paul remaining in custody even after his meeting with Caesar. In the Septuagint version of Isaiah 46:4 God says: "I am until you grow old." Did God cease to exist when Isaiah grew old? No. When God the Father spoke to his Son saying, "Sit on my right hand until I make your enemies your footstool," he certainly was not implying that the Son would no longer sit on his right hand once his enemies were restrained? In 2 Peter 1:19 Peter reminds the faithful to remain dutiful to

God "until (*hous-hou*) the day dawns and the morning star rises in your hearts." If "until" had further implications, then Peter would be saying that once the morning star rises we can forget about God.

The word "until" has no further implications in the Greek of Jesus' time. The purpose of verse 25 was to emphasize that Joseph was not in any way responsible for the birth of Jesus—that Mary gave birth to a child without having sexual relations. It is for this reason that some Bibles, like the New Jerusalem Bible, to avoid confusion, translate *hous-hou* as "when": *"Joseph took his wife into his home; he had not had intercourse with her **when** she gave birth to a son; and he named him Jesus."*

The Korban Rule

The most powerful argument however for the perpetual virginity of Mary is found at the foot of the cross.

> When Jesus saw his mother and the disciple there whom he loved, he said to his mother, "Woman, behold your son." Then he said to the disciple [John], "Behold, your mother." And from that hour the disciple took her into his home (Jn. 19: 26-27, NAB).

It makes absolutely no sense for Jesus to give his mother over to the apostle John if a brother or brothers or sister or sisters were around. Wouldn't you entrust your mother to a brother or sister? *And would a mother abandon her own children so as to become the mother of another?* As Athanasius of Alexandria (ca. 295) states:

> If Mary had had other children, the Savior would not have ignored them and entrusted his Mother to someone else; nor would she have become someone else's mother. She would not have abandoned her own to live with others, knowing well that it ill becomes a woman to abandon her husband and her children. But since she was a virgin, and was his Mother, Jesus gave her as a mother to his disciple, even though she was not really John's mother, because of his great purity of understanding and

because of her untouched virginity (*De virginitate, in Le Museon* 42: 243-44).

The above is especially true because Jesus condemned and invalidated the Korban Rule (cf. Mt. 15). The Korban Rule allowed people to bypass the taking care of their parents by the offering up of a sacrificial offering to God. Jesus demanded that widows be entrusted to the care of a living child. They could not circumvent this obligation through an offering.

With no blood-relations, Jesus entrusts Mary into his apostle's care.

Mary is the "ever-virgin" as the Church has from the beginning of time always called her.

> There is no child of Mary except Jesus...
> Origen (ca. 250)
> Commentary of John I:4;
> PG 14, 32; GCS 10, 8-9.

How much should we love Mary?

Pope Benedict XVI, in his ecumenical discussions, has found that more and more Protestants are turning back to Mary, for they recognize that a Christianity without Mary is a Christianity that is lacking the feminine dimension of human life.

Blessed Mother Teresa of Calcutta was about to give a talk at a conference when a young woman rushed to her side and mentioned that one of the hot topics at the conference dealt with the issue of Mary and how much we should love her. Some were arguing that we were showing too much love for her, others argued we were not showing enough love for her. The debate went back and forth with no resolution in sight. Mother Teresa looked at the messenger and said that she need not worry. She would take care of the dilemma. Mother Teresa proceeded to the stage and began to address the impasse in a very simple fashion. She said: "You want to know how much to love Mary? I'll tell you. Love her *no more* or *no less* than Jesus loved her." Wow! How can we poor creatures ever equal the love of Jesus? We can never love Mary too much, for she always leads us to her Son.

Let us not forget that Jesus was obedient to Mary at the wedding feast of Cana and in the Temple.

Let us never forget Mary's special place in history. Remember to honor Mary is to honor her son, Jesus, for it is Jesus who gave Mary all her privileges. To deny Mary's privileges is to deny Jesus' will and work on behalf of Mary! In honoring Mary we are being obedient to God's will of honoring her; Mary's privileges were given by God and not man. Let us be obedient to the Scriptures which remind us that "all generations will call me blessed" (cf. Luke 1:48).

We as Christians are members of the Body of Christ, the Church (1 Cor. 12). Mary is the Mother of the Head of the Body, Jesus. So Mary is our mother too! She is the Mother of the Church, Christ's Body!

Reflections

Can you understand why Catholics call Mary "blessed" as the Bible reminds us to call her (Cf. Luke 1:48)? Why would you call her "blessed"?

Do you agree with Pope Benedict that a Christianity without Mary is a Christianity that lacks an important feminine dimension that only Mary can provide?

If you were near death, would you entrust your mother's care to a friend or to a brother, sister, cousin, or other family member? If you were a mother, would you abandon your children to be taken care of by a friend of one of your children? Does this argument from Athanasius of Alexandria--writing approximately 100 years before the Bible was put together-- appeal to you as a proof of Mary's Perpetual Virginity? Or do you prefer another argument for her Perpetual Virginity?

How is Mary our mother too? How does the scene at the foot

of the cross help you in understanding Mary's role as the mother of all Christians?

Does Blessed Mother Teresa of Calcutta's explanation on how much we should love Mary help you in loving Mary?

Homework
Catechism of the Catholic Church (CCC)
Numbers 963-975

Homework Prayer Exercise—Getting to Know Jesus
Step One
Read the Gospel of John, chapter 9.

Step Two—Selecting a Section
Read the Gospel of John, chapter 9:1-12. Read the footnotes. Collect the facts. What is being said? What is going on?

Step Three
Meditate on the passage. What is God saying to me in this passage from the Bible? Is there something in my life that God wants to talk to me about?

Step Four
Pray to God. Share your feelings and thoughts with him.

Step Five—Taking Action
What do I feel and think God wants me to do? What is he calling me to do?

11

THE LAST THINGS
(Cf. CCC 1020-1050)

Providence

There are some Christians who believe in a strict form of predestination. This can be traced to the early Protestant reformers. They believed that God had predestined some people to heaven and some people to hell.

According to this view, people do not possess free will in responding to God's grace. People are either members of the elect or members of the damned. This extreme view of predestination was rejected by the Catholic Church.

True love implies freedom. One loves because one makes a decision to love. A Catholic makes a decision to love God in response to God's showering grace. Strict predestination is rejected by the Catholic Church.

The Catholic Church believes in God's providential will. Providence can be seen as a reality somewhere in between extreme predestination and extreme free will. That is, providence is somewhere in between a strict predestination where some are predestined from conception to heaven or hell, and an extreme understanding of free will where God has no say in the world or salvation.

Providence is the belief that God has a predestined plan for the world. Yet within this predestined plan is the exercise of free will. God knows all, including the free will decisions that we will make, and these free will decisions that God knows in advance, are part of his plan. Grace is sufficient to fulfill God's will.

Particular Judgment

At death one experiences a particular judgment by Christ where one's soul is judged and receives its eternal recompense according to its faith and works. The soul goes to its reward or punishment awaiting the second coming of Christ, the end of time, where Christ will re-unite the soul with an immortal body.

If a person dies in God's grace, his friendship, then that person will enjoy eternal bliss in heaven.

If a person dies in God's grace and friendship, yet has been imperfectly purified during life's journey, then that person undergoes a purification after death in purgatory. If one rejects the offer of grace during one's lifetime, then one will receive eternal damnation. (cf. Wis. 3:1f; Eccl. 8:6-8; 11:9; 12:14; Sir. 11:28f; 16:13-22; 2 Macc. 12:43-46; Lk. 16:19-31; Heb. 9:27; 10:30-31).

Hell

Hell is eternal damnation. Hell's principle pain consists of eternal separation from God, and thus eternal separation from happiness and the fulfillment of the longing of one's heart (cf. Mt. 25:41; 2 Thess. 1:9).

Purgatory

On the next day [after the battle with Gorgias]...Judas [Maccabee] and his men went to take up the bodies of the fallen and to bring them back to lie with their kindred in the sepulchers of their ancestors. Then under the tunic of each one of the dead they found sacred tokens of the idols of Jamnia, which the law forbids the Jews to wear. And it became clear to all that this was the reason these men had fallen. So they all blessed the ways of the Lord, the righteous judge, who reveals the things that are hidden; and they turned to supplication, praying that the sin that had been committed might be wholly blotted out. The noble Judas exhorted the people to keep themselves free from sin, for they had seen with their own eyes what had happened as a result of the sin of those who had fallen. He also took up a collection, man by man, to the amount of two thousand drachmas of silver, and sent it to

Jerusalem to provide for a sin offering. In doing this he acted very well and honorably, taking account of the resurrection. For if he were not expecting that those who had fallen would rise again, it would have been superfluous and foolish to pray for the dead. But if he was looking to the splendid reward that is laid up for those who fall asleep in godliness, it was a holy and pious thought. *Therefore, he made atonement for the dead, so that they might be delivered from their sin* (2 Macc. 12:39-46, NRSV).

The Jewish feast of Chanukah is a commemoration of this battle and the cleansing of the temple that followed this event. This is a passage that would have been in the hearts and minds of all the apostles.

In this passage we see how Judas Maccabee identifies the reason for the deaths of many of his soldiers: they had sinned by wearing amulets associated with the false gods of Jamnia.

Upon recognizing this, Judas does something critically important: he prays for the forgiveness of his dead soldiers' sins; he takes up a collection for an expiatory sacrifice, and seeks atonement so that those who died in battle due to sin might be freed from sin.

This passage is the most powerful proof for purgatory in all of the Scriptures. If one dies, one either goes to heaven, purgatory, or hell. If one goes to heaven, one has no need for one's sins to be blotted out, since one is enjoying eternal paradise. If one is in hell, then all the prayers in the world cannot release one from hell since hell is eternal (Mt. 25:41; 2 Thess. 1:9). Hence, if sin can be blotted out after death, then there needs to be a place for purification; that place is called purgatory.

The Bible makes reference quite often to a "cleansing fire" (i.e., cf. 1 Pet. 1:7; Wis. 3:1-6). This cleansing fire is a purging fire, where God's fiery love "burns" away the soul's impurities, where one is "saved, but only through fire" (1 Cor. 3:1-16). The Bible also testifies to the reality of paying debts, as in the case of the Judge who reminds us that we "will not be released until [we] have paid the last penny" (Mt. 5:21-26; also 18:21-35; Lk. 12:58; 16:19-31; 1 Pet. 3:19; 4:6). In other words, we will not be released until every sin, every word, is accounted for (Mt. 12:36).

Historically, prayers for the dead have always been a part of the Hebrew and Christian tradition. In the Jewish Orthodox culture, prayers for the dead were common. At the time of Jesus, prayers for the dead in the Jewish faith were said in temples and synagogues on feasts such as Passover, Booths, and Weeks. Jews to this very day still utter the "Mourner's Kaddesh" after the death of a person for the purification of that person's soul.

Graffiti in the catacombs of Rome from the first three centuries of Christianity, when the Church was under persecution, attests to this common practice. In the first century catacombs we read: "Sweet Faustina, may you live in God." "Peter and Paul, pray for Victor."

It is not until the Protestant Reformation that prayers and sacrifices for the dead become seriously challenged.

Pure logic attests for the need of a place called purgatory. We are reminded to be "perfect as [the] heavenly Father is perfect" (Mt. 5:48). We are called to "strive for that holiness without which one cannot see God" (Heb. 12:14). In Revelation 21:27 we are told that "nothing unclean shall enter heaven." Heaven is a place of perfection where "nothing impure" can enter (Rv. 21:27). If this is so, then one who dies in sin must be purified. In Hebrews 12:33 we are reminded that the "spirit of the just are made perfect;" that is made perfect to enter into heaven. If anything impure were to enter into heaven, then heaven would no longer be a place of purity for it would have been tainted with impurity. Pure water, for example, if it is contaminated with a chemical, is no longer pure water. Likewise, heaven, if it is contaminated with imperfection, is no longer a place of perfection.

Another interesting clue to purgatory is seen in 1 Corinthian 15:29-30 where people where baptizing themselves for their dead loved ones. This very practice--albeit a wrong practice--points to early Christianity's recognition that there had to be something more than just heaven or hell. There had to be a place where the efforts of the living on earth could have an impact on those in the afterlife. We call this place purgatory.

Another fascinating example is that of Jesus preaching to the "dead" after the crucifixion (1 Pet. 3:18-20: 4:6): Clearly Jesus was cleansing, purging them through his preaching in order to free them to enter into heaven.

Hence from a Scriptural point of view and from a philosophical point of view, derived from the Scriptural understanding of heaven, purgatory is a reality of Christianity.

In purgatory one is assured of heaven, but is in need of being purified to enter into the realm of perfection. In purgatory a man gains, as Gregory of Nyssa (ca. 379) states, "knowledge of the difference between virtue and vice, and finds that he is not able to partake of divinity until he has been purged of the filthy contagion in his soul by the purifying fire" (*Sermones*, 1).

How sad it must be for those who cannot pray for their deceased loved ones. There is no greater sense of psychological closure than to pray for one that has passed away. That is why Paul asked for mercy on the soul of his dead friend Onesiphorus in 2 Timothy 1:16-18. He knew his prayers would release him from that place of purification--purgatory. (If Onesiphorus was in heaven he would be in no need of prayer, and if he was in hell no amount of prayer could release him. Therefore, Onesiphorus was in purgatory where Paul's prayers could be effective.).

Temporal punishment?

Some have made the argument that when God forgives, he forgives, and therefore there is nothing to be made up, or accounted for, or paid off. They therefore deny the reality of purgatory and the reality of temporal punishments. The above makes it quite clear that there is such a thing as purgatory, but let us address the issue of temporal punishment.

Temporal punishment refers to earthly punishments that flow from sin. A sin may be forgiven, but the punishment due for that sin is either made up for, or accounted for, or paid off in this life or in the life to come (cf. Mt. 5:26; 12:36; 1 Cor. 3:15; Rev. 21:27). As Catherine of Genoa explained, "We either do our purgatory here on earth or in the afterlife."

The Bible is replete with examples of temporal punishment. But let us look at just one: In 2 Samuel 12:13-18 we see the consequences of David's sin of adultery with Bathsheba and David's subsequent killing of her husband Uriah. Even though David's sins were completely forgiven, there was still a temporal, earthly, punishment associated with his sins. Though forgiven, he was still punished.

David paid a heavy price for his sin, but he also changed as a person because of the temporal punishment that was inflicted upon him. David would become one of the Bible's great saints.

The Funeral Mass

Catholics should make sure that they have a Funeral Mass upon death. In fact, it is one of the greatest gifts one can give to a departed loved one. The Mass helps to purify the deceased person of sin and temporal punishment. It reminds the living that they are in communion with their loved one who has died in Christ. The Mass is the ultimate prayer for a loved one who has passed away.

> In the Eucharist, the Church expresses her efficacious communion with the departed. Offering to the Father in the Holy Spirit the sacrifice of the death and resurrection of Christ, she asks to purify his child of his sins and their consequences, and to admit him to the Paschal fullness of the table of the Kingdom. It is by the Eucharist thus celebrated that the community of the faithful, especially the family of the deceased, learn to live in communion with the one who "has fallen asleep in the Lord," by communicating in the Body of Christ of which he is a living member and, then, by praying for him and with him (CCC 1689).

Heaven

Upon a holy, graced death, or after release from purgatory, heaven is experienced.

Heaven is eternal life with God. It is a communion of life and love with God and all the saints and angels. It is a state of perfect happiness, the fulfillment of the deepest longings of the heart.

Final or Last Judgment

> The "Last Judgment" is God's triumph over the revolt of evil, after the final cosmic upheaval of this passing world. Preceded by the resurrection of the dead, it will coincide with the second coming of Christ in glory at the end of time, disclose good and evil, and reveal the meaning of salvation history and the providence of God by which justice has triumphed over evil (CCC, *Glossary*, p. 884).

At the end of time, the second coming, the *parousia*, Christ will re-unite the bodies of all who have died with their souls. For those still living at his second coming the final or last judgment will judge the entirety of the person, body and soul, at that moment. Upon judgment, the body will be glorified or made immortal.

The resurrected body is an immortal body, not an ordinary body—a body not bound by the restraints of space and time.

Those whose souls are in hell will be reunited with their bodies, in an immortal form, at the final judgment and spend eternity in hell.

Those whose souls are in heaven, will be reunited with a glorified body and spend eternity with God.

Those whose souls are in purgatory will be cleansed from purgatory and reunited with a glorified body to spend eternity with God. (cf. Jn. 5:22; Mt. 25:31-46; Rev. 6:14-17).

At the final or last judgment each person's "relationship with God will be laid bare." The final or last judgment "will reveal even to its furthest consequences the good each person has done or failed to do during his earthly life...." (CCC 1039; Cf. Jn. 12:49).

New Heaven, New Earth (cf. Rev. 21)

At the end of time, the entire material universe will be transformed in a manner that is a mystery to us now. We await the unraveling of this mystery where we will live with God forever (Rom. 8:19-23; Eph. 1:10; 2 Pet. 3:13; Rev. 21:1-2; 14-5; 9; 27).

An Aside
Premillennialism, Postmillennialism, Amillennialism and the Rapture

Revelation 20 and 1 Thessalonians 4:15-17 are among the most fascinating passages in Scripture in that they have been interpreted in such radically different ways. The primary reason for this is the confusion over the placing of the thousand year reign, the rapture, and over the sense in which these passages were meant to be understood.

Premillennialism

Premillennialism holds that after the period of the Church there will be a time of tribulation that will be followed by Christ's Second Coming, the binding of Satan, and the resurrection of the faithful who have died in Christ. Christ and the risen faithful will reign on earth physically for a thousand years. This will be followed by another period of tribulation, albeit short, the Final Judgment and the rapture of the faithful into heaven. The creation of a new heaven and a new earth will follow.

The Catholic Church has always rejected this view.

Postmillennialism

Postmillennialism holds to the idea that after the period of the Church, Satan will be bound, and a thousand year reign will follow, followed by the rapture into heaven of the living faithful before the period (or during the middle) of the tribulation. The people left on earth will await the Second Coming of Christ, the resurrection of the dead, the Final Judgment, and the creation of a new heaven and a new earth.

84

The Catholic Church rejects Postmillennialism.

Amillennialism—Catholicism's View

Catholicism rejects both Premillennialism and Postmillennialism—and their variations. It believes in what is called Amillennialsim. It holds that Revelation 20 is a symbolic passage and that the thousand year reign is a symbolic term for the period from Christ's salvific act on the Cross to the time of Christ's Second Coming (the number 1000 is used in the Scriptures to refer to a long, but indeterminate time, a time known only by God). Christ's Second Coming will be preceded by a short tribulation period. Jesus' return will be followed by the resurrection of the dead (Acts 24:15), the Final Judgment (Mt. 25:31; 32; 46; Jn. 5:28-29; 12:49) and the creation of a new heaven and a new earth (Rom. 8:19-23; Eph. 1:10; 2 Pet. 3:13; Rev. 21:1-2; 14-5; 9; 27). How this transformation of a new heaven and a new earth will take place and how it will look like or when the Second Coming will occur is a mystery.

The Second Coming is the end of time as we know it!

The Catholic Understanding of the Rapture

And what is the Catholic understanding of the rapture as found in 1 Thessalonians 4:15-17? At the second coming of Christ, the dead will be resurrected, the Final Judgment will take place, and those faithful who are still alive when Christ returns—and after the Final Judgment--will go with the resurrected faithful to be with Christ forever.

Reflections

What part of purgatory gives you comfort?

From our section on the communion of the saints, what can we do for those in purgatory?

Homework

Catechism of the Catholic Church (CCC)
Numbers 992-1060

Homework Prayer Exercise—Getting to Know Jesus

Step One
Read the Gospel of John, chapter 10.

Step Two—Selecting a Section
   Read the Gospel of John, chapter 10:1-21. Read the footnotes. Collect the facts. What is being said? What is going on?

Step Three
   Meditate on the passage. What is God saying to me in this passage from the Bible? Is there something in my life that God wants to talk to me about?

Step Four
   Pray to God. Share your feelings and thoughts with him.

Step Five—Taking Action
   What do I feel and think God wants me to do? What is he calling me to do?

12

LITURGY
(Cf. CCC 1069-2655)

When the hour came, he took his place at table with the apostles. He said to them, "I have eagerly desired to eat this Passover with you before I suffer, for, I tell you, I shall not eat it [again] until there is fulfillment in the kingdom of God." Then he took a cup, gave thanks, and said, "Take this and share it among yourselves; for I tell you [that] from this time on I shall not drink of the fruit of the vine until the kingdom of God comes." Then he took the bread, said the blessing, broke it, and gave it to them, saying, "This is my body, which will be given for you; do this in memory of me." And likewise the cup after they had eaten, saying, "This cup is the new covenant in my blood, which will be shed for you (Luke 22:14-20).

Liturgy is the Church's public worship of God in all its rites and ceremonies.

Liturgy involves a whole person's being, including his or her intellect, senses and emotions.

Liturgy involves aesthetic and artistic expressions and actions directed toward the love of God through the spoken word, gestures, symbols, music, and so forth.

The actions involved in liturgy require the participation, according to their unique roles, of all the people of God.

The leaders of liturgy are those instituted with sacred orders.

The purpose of the liturgy is to give honor and glory to God, to build up the faith, and to teach and instruct the faithful in the ways of God.

The liturgy is primarily centered on the seven sacraments, which are by nature for the good of the whole Church. The seven sacraments are baptism, confirmation, Eucharist, penance, anointing of the sick, holy orders, and matrimony.

Non-sacramental liturgical expressions include the *Liturgy of the Hours*, blessings, sacramentals, etc.

Sacraments vs. Sacramentals

"Sacramentals are sacred signs by which spiritual effects are signified and are obtained by the intercession of the Church (Canon 1166)." They differ from the sacraments in that the grace which is obtained through the use of the sacramental is obtained through the intercession of the Church and not through the action itself. Some of these sacred signs or sacramentals include holy water, medals, rosaries, statues, scapulars, relics as well as actions such as blessings and exorcisms.

Relics

A relic is that which is from a saint or associated with a saint and is intended for the spiritual enrichment of the faithful. There are three classes of relics. A *first class relic* is one that is part of a saint's body. A *second class relic* is one that is a part of the clothing of the saint or something that was used or belonged to the saint during his or her lifetime. A *third class relic* is one that a saint has touched, such as a piece of cloth or other object.

Relics are placed in shrines, reliquaries, and placed in altar stones during the consecrations of church altars.

Relics are intended to stir a person's devotion to living a Christ-like life. They are reminders that living the Christian life is not impossible. If others have been able to live it, we likewise can be comforted in the fact that we too can become saints.

Relics are often associated with miracles. In the Bible we read in 2 Kings 13:21: *"Once some people were burying a man... They cast the dead man into the grave of Elisha, and everyone went off. But when the man came in contact with the* bones of Elisha, he came back to life and rose to his feet." In Acts 5:15-16 we read, *"[People] carried the sick out into the streets and laid them on cots and mats so that when Peter came his shadow could fall on one or another of them...and they were all cured."* In Acts 19:11-12 we read, *"So extraordinary were the mighty deeds God accomplished at the hands of Paul that when face cloths or aprons that touched his skin were applied to the sick, their diseases left them and the evil spirits came out of them."*

A relic is that which is from a saint or associated with a saint and is intended for the spiritual enrichment of the faithful.

Statues
In Exodus 20:4-5 we read:

> You shall not make for yourself an idol, or any likeness of what is in heaven above or on the earth beneath or in the water under the earth. You shall not worship them or serve them; for, I the Lord your God, am a jealous God... (NASB).

Given the above quote, why do Catholics and other Christians have statues and art work in their places of worship?

Again, when we interpret the Bible we need to interpret it within the context of the whole Bible. When taken in the context of the whole, this passage refers to worshiping a "graven image" as a god. In other words, worship which is only due to God is being given to a man-made object.

In Exodus 25:18-22 we read where God spoke to Moses and instructed him to do the following:

> [You] shall make two cherubim [angels] of gold; of hammered work shall you make them, on the two ends of the mercy seat. Make one cherub [angel] on the one end, and one cherub [angel] on the other end. The cherubim [angels] shall spread out their wings above, overshadowing the mercy seat with their wings, their faces facing one another. Toward the mercy seat shall the faces of the cherubim be (RSV).

Isn't this a graven image? There it is right in the Bible! God had commanded the making of statues. In Numbers 21:8-9 we read how God commanded Moses to "make a bronze serpent and mount it on a pole." In the fabrication of the tent cloth covering the "Dwelling," the artisans were commanded to embroider cherubim on the cloth (Ex. 26:1). In the building and furnishing of the Temple (1 Kings 6:23-28; 7:23-45) images and carved figures were copious—images of cherubim, trees, flowers, oxen, lions, pomegranates, and so on.

What is forbidden by the commandment expressed in Exodus 20:4-5 is the worship of anything which is not God. Only God is due worship.

In many ancient pagan cultures it was thought that after a statue of a god was made, the god would come to dwell within or around the object created. So pagans would worship the object for they believed their god was dwelling in the object.

As Catholics, and as most Christians today recognize, we do not see statues or any object as worthy of worship. Statues and other forms of art are simply reminders of the true God we worship. Statues and art help us to move our hearts to love the true God that is not found in any statue or work of art.

In the ancient world of Judaism and Christianity, images, icons, and statues were the books of those who could not read. The ability to read was primarily the domain of the well-to-do, the clerics, the aristocrats and the scholars.

In Christianity, preachers would often point to stained-glass windows, icons, frescoes and all forms of art to help the faithful understand the message of the Gospel. Churches were "visual libraries" for the faithful in a time when people could not read.

Sacramentals move our senses to that which is holy.

Liturgical Seasons

The Church has several liturgical seasons that help us to renew our commitment and fervor for our faith. Advent, which begins in December, is the beginning of the Church year. It has a two-fold character: Advent is a reminder of Christ's first coming, his Incarnation. It is also a reminder to all the faithful that Christ will come again at the end of time to judge the living and the dead. Advent is marked by joyful and heartfelt expectation. The liturgical color violet is used in Advent as a reminder of the coming of the Savior of the world, the King of kings, the Lord of lords. It is also a reminder for the Catholic to renew his or her fervent commitment to Christ.

Advent is followed by the season of Christmas, which begins in December and usually ends with the feast Epiphany in January. Christmas is the memorial of Christ's birth. Epiphany is the commemoration of the manifestation of Christ to the whole world as symbolized by the three Gentile magi (Mt. 2:1-12). The liturgical color of white is used during Christmas as a symbol of light, purity, innocence, joy and glory.

Ordinary time follows the Christmas season. Ordinary time is devoted to the mystery of Christ in all its fullness. Green is the liturgical color that is used. Green is the natural color of life and renewal in nature and therefore points to the hope of life eternal.

Lent follows this first period of ordinary time. Ash Wednesday is the beginning of Lent, where one is reminded to "turn away from sin and to be faithful to the Gospel." Lent is a season of preparation where catechumens and all the faithful are being prepared for the celebration of Easter, the commemoration of the death and resurrection of Christ. It is a time of penance and a time for renewing one's baptismal vows. The liturgical color of violet symbolizes melancholy and somberness and is used as a symbol for the Lenten experiences of penance and renewal.

Holy week is the week before Easter. It is marked with the specific remembrance of Christ's passion, death, and resurrection.

The three days before Easter are known as the Paschal Triduum, which begins with the Mass of the Lord's Supper.

These three days recall Christ's institution of the sacraments of the Eucharist and holy orders, and Jesus' passion, death and resurrection. The liturgical color during this period alternate between white, red, and violet, red symbolizing the shedding of blood.

The Easter season ends with the feast of Pentecost. Pentecost commemorates the great outpouring of the Holy Spirit on the disciples (Act 2:1-41), and their empowerment to preach the Gospel to the ends of the world. The liturgical color of red is used during Pentecost: Red signifies the Holy Spirit who came upon the disciples like flames of fire.

After Pentecost the second season of ordinary time begins. Again, green is the main liturgical color. The end of ordinary time is marked by the feast of Christ the King. White is the liturgical color for Christ the King. White is the symbol for purity.

Rose may be worn during Gaudete, "Rejoice" Sunday (Third Sunday of Advent) and Laetare "Rejoice" Sunday (Fourth Sunday of Lent). It symbolizes joy in the midst of a penitential season.

The Heart of liturgy

The sacraments are at the heart of the liturgy.

For the Catholic sacraments are efficacious. That is, they produce what they signify. A sacrament imparts grace to the individual (Acts 2:38; 8:17; 19:4-7; 1 Pet. 3:19-22). Baptism

The seven sacraments of the Church are foreshadowed in a powerful manner in the Hebrew Scriptures, in the Old Testament signs and symbols of the covenant--baptism replacing circumcision, anointing of the sick replacing the ancient anointings, consecrating or ordaining priests by the laying on of hands replacing the consecration of kings and Levitical priests, and the institution of the Eucharist as sacrifice and presence replacing the Old Testament sacrifices of lambs and the Passover re-presenting.

92

The sacraments that initiate one into the Church are the sacraments of baptism, confirmation, and Eucharist. The sacraments dedicated to healing are the sacraments of penance (often referred to as reconciliation) and the anointing of the sick. The sacraments dedicated to service are holy orders and matrimony.

How is God present in the Liturgy as the "Bread of Life"?
--He is present in the proclamation of the Word
--He is present in us as Temples of the Holy Spirit
--He is present in the neighbor who is created in the image and likeness of God
--He is present in the community of faith, the Church—"where two or three are gathered in my name there I am"
--He is present in the minister
--He is present in the sacraments, and most fully in the Eucharist

Reflections
What kind of spiritual art moves your heart to love God?

Do you see any advantage to having liturgy, organized public worship?

Homework
Catechism of the Catholic Church (CCC)
Numbers 1066-1211

Homework Prayer Exercise—Getting to Know Jesus
Step One
Read the Gospel of John, chapter 11.

Step Two—Selecting a Section
Read the Gospel of John, chapter 11:38-44. Read the footnotes. Collect the facts. What is being said? What is going on?

Step Three

Meditate on the passage. What is God saying to me in this passage from the Bible? Is there something in my life that God wants to talk to me about?

Step Four

Pray to God. Share your feelings and thoughts with him.

Step Five—Taking Action

What do I feel and think God wants me to do? What is he calling me to do?

13

TOUR OF THE CHURCH

What's What, and Who's Who

The <u>sanctuary</u> is the elevated portion of the church where the Mass takes place.

The <u>sacristy</u> is the room where the sacred vestments, vessels, and other items used in the celebration of the liturgy are stored and prepared.

The <u>*sacrarium*</u> is a sink and drain in the sacristy that flows directly into the earth instead of sewage. It is used for the respectful disposing of holy water, blessed ashes, the water used to rinse out altar linens, and for the purification of the chalice and paten.

The <u>tabernacle</u> is the place where the Eucharist is reposed for adoration.

The <u>altar</u> is the sacred table on which the sacrifice of the Mass is offered to God.

The <u>ambo</u> is the lectern from which the readings are proclaimed. Lay persons, called lectors, read or proclaim the Old Testament and New Testament readings. The Gospel is restricted to the deacon, priest or bishop to read or proclaim.

The <u>presider's chair</u> is the chair reserved for the bishop or the priest during Mass.

The ambry is the cabinet where the three holy oils blessed by the bishop at the Chrism Mass are held:

- Sacred Chrism is oil used after baptism, during confirmation, in the ordination of priests, and in the consecration of bishops.
- Oil of the Sick is used for the anointing of the sick (Jas. 5:14).
- Oil of Catechumens is used in preparation for baptism, signifying the call to repentance and conversion.

The chalice is the cup which holds the wine that becomes the precious Body and Blood of Christ (under the appearance or species of wine).

The paten is the golden or silver "plate" that holds the bread that becomes the Sacred Body and Blood of Christ (under the appearance or species of bread).

The ciborium is a vessel with a lid that is used for the distribution and reservation of the Eucharist.

The pyx is a small, closing vessel or container that is used to bring the Eucharist to those who cannot come to the church, particularly the ill.

The monstrance is an ornate vessel used to display the Eucharist for public adoration and Benediction.

The ablution cup is a small container of water that sits near the tabernacle or on the credence table for the priest or Eucharistic ministers to cleanse their fingers--in a holy manner--after the distribution of Holy Communion. Any particle dissolves into the water.

The credence table is a side table used to prepare the altar for Mass.

The cruets hold the wine and the water used at Mass.

The lavabo dish is used for washing the priest's hands. The lavabo towel is the towel which the priest dries his hands.

Holy water is water that has been blessed, and serves as a reminder of baptism and of the supernatural life of God's grace.

The aspersorium is a bucket used to carry holy water for sprinkling. The aspergillum is the sprinkler for casting holy water on people, places, or objects.

The corporal is a square cloth placed on the altar beneath the chalice and paten. It is folded after Mass so as to catch any particles of the Eucharist that may have accidentally fallen. It is purified in the *sacrarium*.

The purificator is a small rectangular cloth used for wiping the chalice.

The pall is a hard, cardboard-like square cloth used to cover the chalice.

The thurible is used for carrying and burning incense. The incense boat holds the incense before it is placed in the thurible for burning.

The processional cross hearkens back to the days of the Roman army when the standard-bearer would carry the insignia of a particular legion into battle. We carry the insignia of Christ the Victor into spiritual battle.

The crucifix is a cross with the figure of Christ upon it.

The Paschal candle is a candle that is prepared and blessed every year at the Easter Vigil. This candle stands near the altar during the Easter Season and near the baptismal font during the rest of the year. It also stands near the casket during the funeral rites.

The tabernacle lamp is a red candle that burns near the tabernacle when the Eucharist is present.

The Stations of the Cross are fourteen pieces of art attached to the walls of the Church that remind people of Jesus' journey from condemnation to burial.

Vestments

The alb is a white robe worn by a priest, bishop or deacon. In some places, it is also worn by others, such as servers or lectors. It symbolizes purity of heart as well as the white garment given in baptism. It also symbolizes the clothing worn during Jesus' time.

The cincture is a rope-like chord that is worn around the alb, if the alb does not fit closely to the body. It symbolizes chastity. It also symbolizes the chord used to scourge Jesus at the pillar.

The stole is a long strip of fabric worn around the neck. It matches the color of the liturgical day. Priests wear the stole around the neck and over the breast. Deacons wear the stole diagonally from the left shoulder to the right side. It symbolizes Jesus' carrying of the cross.

The chasuble is worn by the priest over his other vestments. It symbolizes the yoke of Christ and the outer garment Jesus wore. In ancient times, it was worn as a winter "coat."

The dalmatic is the vestment of the deacon. It seems to have developed in Dalmatia, hence the name. Unlike the chasuble, the dalmatic has sleeves.

The surplice is a short white garment worn over a cassock, usually a black robe-like garment.

The cope is a cape-like vestment that may be worn during processions and liturgical celebrations outside of Mass.

Ministry of the Altar

Altar servers are servers who assist the priest and deacon at the altar.

Extraordinary ministers of Holy Communion are delegated lay persons who assist in distributing Communion in times of necessity.

Liturgical Books

The Roman Missal (Sacramentary) is the book containing the ceremonial instructions and prayers for the celebration of the Mass.

The Book of the Gospels is the liturgical book from which the Gospel reading is proclaimed by the deacon or priest.

The Lectionary is the book containing the biblical readings arranged for the celebration of Mass.

Gestures

Standing signifies respect and readiness, such as during the Gospel reading. It is also the normal posture when singing or when praying in common.

<u>Genuflection</u> is made by bending the right knee to the ground. One genuflects when entering or leaving the church or when passing in front of the tabernacle.

<u>A profound bow</u> is made to the altar whenever one passes in front of it.

<u>Kneeling</u> signifies the adoration of God and humility before him. Kneeling is the proper posture for the congregation during the Eucharistic Prayer and after the *Agnus Dei,* the *Lamb of God.*

<u>Striking the breast</u> is done during the *Penitential Rite* to signify sorrow for one's sins.

Homework Prayer Exercise—Getting to Know Jesus

Step One
Read the Gospel of John, chapter 12.

Step Two—Selecting a Section
Read the Gospel of John, chapter 12:44-50. Read the footnotes. Collect the facts. What is being said? What is going on?

Step Three
Meditate on the passage. What is God saying to me in this passage from the Bible? Is there something in my life that God wants to talk to me about?

Step Four
Pray to God. Share your feelings and thoughts with him.

Step Five—Taking Action
What do I feel and think God wants me to do? What is he calling me to do?

Liturgical Vestments and Vessels

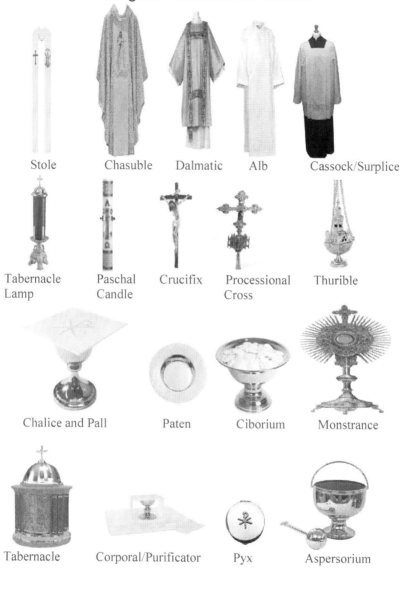

Stole	Chasuble	Dalmatic	Alb	Cassock/Surplice
Tabernacle Lamp	Paschal Candle	Crucifix	Processional Cross	Thurible
Chalice and Pall		Paten	Ciborium	Monstrance
Tabernacle	Corporal/Purificator		Pyx	Aspersorium

Cruets	Lavabo	Ambry	Ablution Cup

14

SACRAMENT OF BAPTISM AND CONFIRMATION
(Cf. CCC 1213-1274; 1285-1314)

Being "born again" (Jn. 3:3-5)

> Baptism is God's most beautiful and magnificent gift…. We call it gift, grace, anointing, enlightenment, garment of immortality, bath of rebirth, seal, and most precious gift. It is called gift because it is conferred on those who bring nothing of their own; grace since it is given even to the guilty; baptism because sin is buried in the water; anointing for it is priestly and royal as are those who are anointed; enlightenment because it radiates light; clothing since it veils our shame; bath because it washes; and seal as it is our guard and the sign of God's Lordship.
>
> Augustine of Hippo, *Letter to Jerome*
> (Oratio 40, 3-4: PG 36, 361C)

In the Old Testament, the reality of baptism was prefigured in Ezekiel 36:25-27:

> I will sprinkle clean water upon you to cleanse you from all your impurities, and from all your idols I will cleanse you. I will give you a new heart and place a new spirit within you, taking from your bodies your stony hearts. I will put my spirit within you and make you live by my statutes, careful to observe my decrees (NAB).

Jesus taught Nicodemus that one must be born again by *water* and the *Spirit* to be saved (Jn. 3:5), not by the Spirit *only*, but by *water* and the *Spirit*.

For the Catholic, to be baptized is what it means to be "born again." Baptism is a sacrament with real power and it is a sacrament which is necessary for salvation, for it is by baptism that we are "born again" by *water* and the *Spirit* (Jn. 3:5; Mk. 16:16). God "saved us through the bath of rebirth and renewal by the Holy Spirit, whom he richly poured out on us through Jesus Christ our Savior, that we might be justified by his grace and become heirs in hope of eternal life" (Titus 3:5-7).

In baptism one enters into Christ's life, death and resurrection (cf. Rom. 6:3-4). One puts on Christ in baptism (Gal. 3:27). Baptism cleanses one from *original sin*, personal sin, and the punishment for sin (Mk.16:16; Jn. 3:5; Acts 2:38f; 22:16; Rom. 6:3-6; Gal. 3:7; 1 Cor. 6:11; Eph. 5:26; Col. 2:12-14; Heb. 10:22).

Psalm 51:7 states: "In guilt was I born, and in sin my mother conceived me." In baptism one becomes a new creation in Christ and a partaker in the divine nature (2 Pet. 1:4). One becomes a member of the Church as an adopted child of God (cf. 1 Cor. 12-13; 27). One becomes a Temple of the Holy Spirit (Acts 2:38; 19:5f) with an indelible mark or character on the soul which enables one to share in the priesthood of Christ and in his passion (Mk. 10:38f; Lk. 12:50).

Original Sin and Concupiscence
Original Sin

The Book of Genesis is a theological account teaching us that God is the ultimate source of being. He created the world and people out of nothing. He created them good.

Genesis is an account of freedom and the cost of using freedom in a negative manner. It is an account of human individuals who chose to rebel against God and sought to live without God. By their sin they forever distorted the nature of the world. We call this distortion *original sin*.

Concupiscence

Original sin distorted the harmony of creation and damaged the relationship between God and humanity. The second Person of the Trinity, the Son of God, came into the world and cleansed or healed it of this damage, this original sin. While the sin was forgiven in Christ, concupiscence remained—an inclination toward disharmony.

Human beings, through the gift of baptism in Christ, in God, are capable of an intimate, personal, saving relationship with God, and are capable of experiencing eternal life with God in heaven. Yet despite this, because of the wound of original sin, a human being is still inclined and tempted toward that original rebellion; that is, human beings are inclined toward the temptations of evil, the temptations against right reason. We call this concupiscence. The spiritual journey becomes a battle against concupiscence.

***Baptism wipes away original sin, but concupiscence remains.

Baptism of Infants

The very nature of baptism impels the faithful to have their infants baptized. As Irenaeus explained in *Against Heresies* (cf. 2, 22, 4) (ca. 180): "Jesus came to save all for all are reborn through him in baptism—infants, children, youths, and old men." To deny a child baptism is to deny a child the precious gifts of baptism. How contrary to God's will (Mt: 19:14; Lk. 18:15-17): "Let the children come to me, sayeth the Lord."

St. Hippolytus of Rome (ca. 215) argues: "Baptize first the children; and if they can speak for themselves, let them do so. Otherwise, let their parents or other relatives speak for them" (*Apostolic Tradition*, 21). The ecclesiastical writer Origen in 244 AD wrote: "The Church received from the apostles the tradition of giving baptism to infants" (*Commentary on Romans*, 5:9).

In terms of Bible quotations with reference to infant baptism let us examine the following quotes: Acts 16:15, 33 and 1 Corinthians. 1:16. In these quotations we see that whole families were baptized. Given the culture of the ancient world, this most likely implied the baptism of infants. How can whole households not have any infants, any children? (The average household of ancient Greece and Rome averaged seven people).

In Acts 2:38-39 we read a direct account of where Peter

baptized adults and children: *"Peter said to them, 'Repent, and be baptized every one of you in the name of Jesus Christ for the forgiveness of your sins; and you shall receive the gift of the Holy Spirit. For the promise is to you and to your children and to all that are far off, every one whom the Lord our God calls to him.... (RSV)."*

Many argue that one must be old enough to accept the faith: No one, not even your parents, they argue, can stand in for you. This might sound appealing but it is contrary to the Scriptures. God often bestowed spiritual gifts on peoples because of the faith of others. The centurion's faith brought about the healing of his servant (Mt. 8:5-13); the Canaanite's woman's faith brought about the healing of her daughter (Mt. 15:21-28); and in Luke 5:17-26 a crippled man is healed by the persistent faith of his friends. A parent's faith bestows the gifts of baptism upon their children.

Paul in Colossians 2:11-12 reminds us that baptism replaces circumcision for the Christian. In the Old Covenant, the Old Testament, one became a member of the people of God through circumcision on the eighth day. In the New Covenant, the New Testament, one becomes a member of the people of God through baptism as early as possible! For the Christian baptism is the replacement for circumcision (Col. 2:11-12). If Jewish parents would covenant with God on behalf of their eight-day old children through the command to circumcise their children, then Christian parents covenant with God on behalf of their children through the command to baptize. How could people deny children entrance into the covenant, into the people of God? As Jesus said: "Let the children come to me for the Kingdom of God belongs to such as these" (cf. Mk. 10:14; Lk. 18:15).

And as alluded to above, the fact that "whole households" were baptized in the New Covenant makes absolute sense since "whole households" were circumcised in the Old Covenant (Gen. 17:12-14), including house-born slaves and "foreigners acquired with money." Children were circumcised under the Old Covenant, and under the New Covenant they were baptized.

In Judaism a child had no say as to whether he was circumcised or not! On the eighth day he became a part of the people of God by virtue of the will of his parents and the act of circumcision. The same applies with the baptism of children! And just as in the Old Testament, when one reached the age of reason and could reject the gift received as an infant, one could likewise, in the New Testament times, reject the gift of baptism upon reaching the age of reason. The gift is given to be affirmed or rejected, to be nourished or to be allowed to die.

Baptism by blood and desire for adults and infants

Sacred Scripture and Sacred Tradition refer to three forms of baptism for salvation. The first form is sacramental baptism by water and the Spirit: Jesus send his disciples throughout the world to baptize in the name of the Father, and of the Son, and of the Holy Spirit (Mt. 28:19-20).

The other two forms are referred to as *baptism by blood* and *baptism by desire*. The Church has always maintained that those who suffer death for the sake of the faith before having been baptized are baptized by their blood, by their death in, for, and with Christ. The fruits of the sacrament of baptism are given to the person even though they did not receive the sacrament. Similarly, those who die before being baptized and yet desired baptism in their lifetime likewise receive the fruits of the sacrament without receiving the sacrament itself. Those who are moved by grace and may not be explicit Christians are equally considered as having been baptized in a baptism by desire. And children who die before baptism are baptized by the desire of the parents or the mystical body, the Church.

The Scriptures point to the salvation of the Holy Innocents by Herod (cf. Mt. 2:16-18): The infants that were massacred died for Christ and therefore can be considered to have been baptized by their blood. On the cross of Calvary, the good thief, Dismas, called for mercy and received God's forgiveness and salvation. He certainly could not have come down off the cross to be saved in a water baptism. He was saved and baptized by his desire (Lk. 23:42-43).

In Summary
Baptism
--cleanses the soul of original and personal sin
--makes one an adopted child of God
--opens the gates of heaven for the baptized person
--incorporates one into the Church
--bestows gifts of the Holy Spirit
--bestows sanctifying grace (the grace that makes us holy)
--gives the theological virtues of faith, hope and love
--leaves an indelible mark on the soul
--helps one to serve in Christ's roles of priest, prophet, and king

SACRAMENT OF CONFIRMATION

There are different kinds of spiritual gifts but the same Spirit; there are different forms of service but the same Lord; there are different workings but the same God who produces all of them in everyone. To each individual the manifestation of the Spirit is given for some benefit. To one is given through the Spirit the expression of wisdom; to another the expression of knowledge according to the same Spirit; to another faith by the same Spirit; to another gifts of healing by the one Spirit; to another mighty deeds; to another prophecy; to another discernment of spirits; to another varieties of tongues; to another interpretation of tongues. But one and the same Spirit produces all of these, distributing them individually to each person as he wishes (1 Cor. 12:4-11).

Completing Baptism
Confirmation perfects baptismal grace. In Acts 19:5-7 Paul "lays his hands" on the recently baptized invoking the Holy Spirit, thereby confirming them. Likewise, in Acts 8:14-17 Peter and John "lay their hands" on the converts of Samaria,

for as the Bible says: "the [fullness of the] Spirit had not come upon any of them; they had only been baptized in the name of the Lord Jesus" (Acts 8:16). Peter and John were confirming, perfecting, what had begun at baptism in the converts of Samaria.

Once confirmed we are strengthened by the Holy Spirit to be powerful witnesses of Christ's self-communicating love to the world. We become strengthened members in the mission of the Church, the proclamation of the Gospel. Like baptism, a sacred mark or seal is imprinted on the soul, forever changing it (cf. 2 Cor. 1:21-22; Eph. 1:13). In Acts 1:6-8 we see how, despite being baptized previously, the apostles received the gift of the Holy Spirit to be witnesses to the world.

In receiving this sacrament by a bishop or a delegated priest, one is empowered in making a commitment to profess the faith and to serve the world in word and deed as a disciple of Christ (Acts 19:5-6; 8:16-17; Heb. 6:1-2; 2 Cor. 1:21-22; Eph. 1:13).

Gifts of the Spirit

The gifts of the Holy Spirit are essential to the spiritual growth of the person and are essential for salvation. The gifts of the Spirit transform hardened hearts into docile hearts-- hearts ready for God's engulfing presence.

Knowledge, understanding, wisdom, counsel, piety, fortitude, and fear of the Lord are the traditional gifts of the Spirit (Is. 11:2f). The gift of knowledge helps one to understand God's creation; the gift of understanding helps one to delve into the sphere of truth; the gift of wisdom, the highest of the gifts, aids one to perceive the divine; the gift of counsel helps one to direct one's actions according to God's will; the gift of piety, aids one in proper worship; the gift of fortitude, helps one fight off the fears that confront one in the works of God, and the gift of fear of the Lord protects one from falling into disorderly temptations.

Confirmation completes baptism, and prepares one to be a disciple of Jesus Christ.

In Summary
Confirmation
--completes baptism (it seals and strengthens one's baptismal call)
--strengthens the gifts of the Holy Spirit
--leaves an indelible mark on the soul
--empowers one to be a witness for Christ and a more committed member of the Church.

Reflections
What is the greatest gift of baptism in your opinion?

What, in your view, are some obligations of a confirmed Catholic?

Homework
Catechism of the Catholic Church (CCC)
Numbers 1212-1321

Homework Prayer Exercise—Getting to Know Jesus
Step One
Read the Gospel of John, chapter 13.

Step Two—Selecting a Section
     Read the Gospel of John, chapter 13:31-35. Read the footnotes. Collect the facts. What is being said? What is going on?

Step Three
     Meditate on the passage. What is God saying to me in this passage from the Bible? Is there something in my life that God wants to talk to me about?

Step Four
     Pray to God. Share your feelings and thoughts with him.

Step Five—Taking Action

What do I feel and think God wants me to do? What is he calling me to do?

15

SACRAMENT OF EUCHARIST
THE MEDICINE OF IMMORTALITY
(Cf. CCC 1322-1405)

Mass as Presence and Sacrifice

Catholics have a Mass because Jesus instituted the Mass and the early Church always had a Mass.

> When the hour came, he took his place at table with the apostles. He said to them, "I have eagerly desired to eat this Passover with you before I suffer, for, I tell you, I shall not eat it [again] until there is fulfillment in the kingdom of God.... Then he took the bread, said the blessing, broke it, and gave it to them, saying, "This is my body, which will be given for you; do this in memory of me." And likewise the cup is the new covenant in my blood, which will be shed for you (Lk. 22:14-20, RSV).

In John's Gospel chapter 6:53-57 we read:

> Truly, truly, I say to you, unless you eat the flesh of the Son of man and drink his blood, you have no life in you; he who eats my flesh and drinks my blood has eternal life, and I will raise him up at the last day. For my flesh is food indeed and my blood is drink indeed. He who eats my flesh and drinks my blood abides in me, and I in him. As the living Father sent me, and I live because of the Father, so he who eats me will live because of me. (RSV).

And in Paul's letter to the Corinthians we read:

> For I received from the Lord what I also handed on to you, that the Lord Jesus, on the night he was handed over, took bread, and, after he had given thanks, broke it and said, "This is my body that is for you. Do this in remembrance of me." In the same way he

took the cup, and after supper, said, "This cup is the new covenant in my blood. Do this, as often as you drink it, in remembrance of me." For as often as you eat this bread and drink this cup, you proclaim the death of the Lord until he comes (1 Cor. 11:23-26, NAB).

In the Old Testament, the Hebrew Scriptures, sacrifices of lambs, bulls, goats, and other animals were offered in the temple for the forgiveness of sins. Today, this sacrifice takes place in the mystery of the Mass, the bloodless sacrifice of the Lamb of God, Jesus Christ, at the altar of every Church, the New Temple of God. (It is no coincidence that John's Gospel has Jesus die at the exact time that the Jewish Temple sacrifices were taking place. It is Jesus who is the true Lamb, the true sacrifice. Jesus is the true Lamb that takes away the sins of the world).

When the Jews were preparing for the Passover into the Promised Land, they offered up a paschal lamb and afterwards consumed the lamb, the victim, for strength for the journey (Ex. 12:1-20). This prefigures the Eucharistic sacrifice where Jesus, the Lamb of God, was offered up for our sins and then eaten sacramentally for the spiritual nourishment necessary to enter into the Promised Land of Heaven.

The Mass, the Last Supper, is a *re-presenting*, or making present of what took place once and for all at Calvary (Heb. 7:27; 9:12, 25-28; 10:10-14). Just as the Passover meal made present to those who participated in it the Exodus events, the Mass in a fuller way makes present what happened at Calvary.

At every Mass we are truly at the foot of the Cross with Mary, Mary Magdalene, and John. We are truly present sacramentally at Calvary.

The Mass of Ages

When we look at history, the Mass is a well-established reality for Christians. At first Christians celebrated Mass in their homes and with time they moved into public worship spaces, but the fundamental structure always remained the same.

Justin Martyr, known by the "friends of the apostles," wrote to the emperor Antoninus Pius in 150—only fifty years after the death of the apostle John--about the long-standing practice of Christian worship as inherited from the apostles.

On the day we call the day of the sun, [Sunday] all who dwell in the city or country gather in the same place, for it is on this day that the Savior Jesus Christ rose from the dead.

The memoirs of the apostles and the writings of the prophets are read, as much as time permits [This is the Liturgy of the Word where the lector and clergy read the Old Testament and New Testament Readings].

When the reader has finished, he who presides over those gathered admonishes and challenges them to imitate these beautiful things [This is the homily].

Then we all rise together and offer prayers for ourselves...and for all others, wherever they may be, so that we may be found righteous by our life and actions, and faithful to the commandments, so as to obtain eternal salvation [These are the petitions or the prayers of the faithful, including prayers for the deceased in purgatory].

When the prayers are concluded we exchange the kiss [This is the sign of peace].

The faithful, if they wish, may make a contribution and they themselves decide the amount. The collection is placed in the custody of the one who presides over the celebration to be used for the orphans, widows, and for any who are in need or distress [The collection].

Then someone brings bread and a cup of water and wine mixed together to him who presides over the brethren [This is the "presentation of the gifts"—water, wine, bread].

He takes them and offers praise and glory to the Father of the universe, through the name of the Son and of the Holy Spirit and for a considerable time he gives thanks (in Greek: eucharistian) that we have been judged worthy of these gifts *[This is the Eucharistic Prayer which is directed to the Father, through the Son, and in the Spirit]*.

When he has concluded the prayers and thanksgiving, all present give voice to an acclamation by saying: "Amen"
[This is the acclamation by the faithful].

When he who presides has given thanks and the people have responded, those whom we call deacons give to those present the "eucharisted" bread, wine, and water and take them to those who are absent (Apol. 1, 65-67; PG 6, 428-429) *[This is communion, and the dismissal]*.

In explaining the mystery indicated by the word "eucharisted," Justin states in his *First Apology* (65) the following:

We call this food Eucharist...since Jesus Christ our Savior was made incarnate by the word of God and had both flesh and blood for our salvation, so too, as we have been taught, the food which has been made into the Eucharist by the Eucharistic prayer set down by Him, and by the change of which our blood and flesh is nourished, is both the flesh and the blood of that incarnated Jesus.

Justin further goes on to say:

None is allowed to share in the Eucharist unless he believes the things which we teach are true...for we do not receive the Eucharist as ordinary bread and ordinary wine, but as Jesus Christ our Savior.

What was celebrated during the time of the apostles, and during the time of Justin in 150 AD, is what we celebrate today.

During Mass we are present at the Last Supper and at Calvary. During the Mass we enter into the entire Mystery of Christ, the source and summit of all. We enter into his life, death, and resurrection. We are forgiven on Calvary and given the *medicine of immortality*, the Eucharist, the Body, Blood, Soul, and Divinity of the glorified, resurrected Christ.

In Summary

The Eucharist is the source and summit of Church life.

In the Eucharist, the Church is united to Christ's sacrifice of praise and thanksgiving offered, once and for all, on the cross to the Father.

The Eucharistic sacrifice pours out and floods the Church with grace.

Christ, under the species or appearances of bread and wine, is the offering of the Eucharistic sacrifice for the salvation of all.

The Eucharist is offered in reparation for the sins of the living and the dead in purgatory.

In the Eucharist venial sins are forgiven, and one is aided in preserving oneself in grace from falling into serious sin. Strength is given to enter into the life of union with God and to deal with life's trials and tribulations.

The Eucharist brings about a unity and communion between a person and the Church on earth and in heaven.

The Eucharist is the presence of the glorified, resurrected Christ—not dead flesh. It is, as St. Ignatius of Antioch, the disciple of the apostle John, explained, the "medicine of immorality and the promise we shall live forever."

Transubstantiation

Catholics believe in the doctrine of Transubstantiation. Transubstantiation *"indicates that through the consecration of the bread and the wine there occurs the change of the entire substance of the bread into the substance of the Body of Christ, and of the entire substance of the wine into the Blood of Christ—even though the appearances or "species" of bread and wine remain"* (CCC 1376, *Glossary*, p. 902).

Reflections

Share your insights, feelings, or thoughts regarding the Eucharist.

How to Receive Communion

You can receive communion on the tongue or on the hand-- place one hand over another, both palms up. Always receive in the presence of the priest or Eucharistic minister.

When to Leave

Many Catholics leave Mass early. They do so for many reasons, but the main reason is due to a lack of knowledge. They fail to recognize the importance of the final blessing. The final blessing is Christ's blessing that strengthens one to go in the power of peace to love and serve the Lord.

Homework

Catechism of the Catholic Church (CCC)
Numbers 1322-1419

Homework Prayer Exercise—Getting to Know Jesus

Step One
Read the Gospel of John, chapter 14.

Step Two—Selecting a Section
Read the Gospel of John, chapter 14:1-14. Read the footnotes. Collect the facts. What is being said? What is going on?

Step Three
Meditate on the passage. What is God saying to me in this passage from the Bible? Is there something in my life that God wants to talk to me about?

Step Four
Pray to God. Share your feelings and thoughts with him.

Step Five—Taking Action
What do I feel and think God wants me to do? What is he calling me to do?

16

SACRAMENT OF PENANCE
AND
ANOINTING OF THE SICK
(Cf. CCC 1422-1484; 1499-1525)

The forgiveness of serious sin, or what we call mortal/deadly sin (1 Jn. 5:17) requires the authority of the priest as an authoritative, power-filled representative of God and of the community. When we look at the Scriptures (Mt. 18:18; 16:19; Jn. 20:21-23) it becomes obvious that God entrusted his apostles with the gift of forgiving sins. In the words of the apostle John:

> Jesus said to [the apostles], "Peace be with you. As the Father has sent me, even so I send you." And when he had said this, he breathed on them, and said to them, "Receive the Holy Spirit. *If you forgive the sins of any, they are forgiven; if you retain the sins of any, they are retained (Jn. 20:21-23, RSV).*

Jesus didn't say "Now go out into the world and tell people to confess their sins directly to God and he will forgive everyone's sins." Rather he said, *"If **you** forgive the sins of any, they are forgiven; if **you** retain the sins of any, they are retained."* Jesus empowered the apostles to forgive sins in his name and he passed this authority through apostolic succession to bishops and priests.

Jesus has an important reason for giving us the sacrament of penance. When we sin we harm our relationship with God, the community, and we do damage to ourselves (cf. Lk. 15:21). That is because when we sin we break the commandments that Jesus fused together, the love of God and the love of neighbor as ourselves (Mt. 22:37-40).

Since sin damages our relationship with God, our relationship with ourselves, and our relationship with others, it needs to be healed in all three dimensions.

The priest—as a member of the human race--therefore is a representative of God and of the community and he brings Christ's healing and the community's healing, as the Body of Christ, to the sinner. That is why God chose the apostles, the first bishops, the first priests, to forgive sins.

When Jesus said to Peter, "Whoever sins you bind shall be bound, and whoever sins you loose shall be loosed" (cf. Mt. 16:18f), he was saying--within the Judaic and Hebrew understanding of the terms "bound" and "loose"--whoever you exclude from your communion will be excluded from communion with God and whoever you receive into your communion God will receive into his. Reconciliation with God is inseparable from reconciliation with the Church (cf. 1 Cor. 12:12f; Rom. 12:5; Eph. 1:22f; 1 Cor. 3:9, 10, 16; 1 Thess. 1:4; 1 Tim. 3:5, 15) (CCC 1445).

Paul reminds the faithful that he has been entrusted with the "ministry of reconciliation" (2 Cor. 5:18-20); James reminds us, within the context of the sacrament of anointing, that the presbyter, the priest, administers Christ's forgiveness (Jms. 5:14-16).

God knew that a human person acting in the Person of Christ, *in persona Christi capitas*, or as Another Christ, *alter Christus* (cf. Mt. 10:40; Lk. 10:16; Lk. 25:47), could bring the only true healing that people needed. People need to hear from someone they are forgiven.

Ignatius of Antioch (ca. 107), the disciple of the apostle John, recognized the importance and absolute necessity of confession to a priest when he said: "The Lord...forgives all who repent, if their repentance leads to the unity of God and the council of the bishop" (*Philadelphia*, 8, trans. Lake).

In Cyprian of Carthage's *Letter to the Clergy* (ca. 250) [cf. 16

(9), 2] Cyprian writes: "Sinners may come to confession and, through the imposition of hands by the bishop and priests, may receive re-admittance into the life of the Church." And in his letter to *The Lapsed* (ca. 351) (28) Cyprian writes: "I beseech you, brethren, let everyone who has sinned confess his sin while he is still in this world, while his confession is still admissible, while satisfaction and remission made through the priests are pleasing before the Lord."

The sacrament of penance is a healing sacrament.

The spiritual effects of the sacrament of penance are beautifully summarized in the *Catechism of the Catholic Church* (1496):

> -*reconciliation with God by which the penitent recovers grace*
> -*reconciliation with the Church*
> -*remission of the eternal punishment incurred by mortal sins*
> -*remission, at least in part, of temporal punishments resulting from sin*
> -*peace and serenity of conscience, and spiritual consolation*
> -*an increase of spiritual strength for the Christian battle*

Priests who hear confessions may never reveal nor use any information they have acquired through confession.

Temporal Punishment

Temporal punishment refers to earthly punishments that flow from sin. A sin may be forgiven, but the punishment due for that sin is either made up for, or accounted for, or paid off in this life or in the life to come (cf. Mt. 5:26; 12:36; 1 Cor. 3:15; Rev. 21:27). The Bible is replete with examples of temporal punishment. For example, in 2 Samuel 12:13-18 we see the consequences of David's sin of adultery with Bathsheba and David's subsequent killing of her husband Uriah. Even though David's sins were completely forgiven, there was still a temporal, earthly, punishment associated with his sins. Though forgiven, he was still punished.

David paid a heavy price for his sin, but he also changed as a person because of the temporal punishment that was inflicted upon him. David would become one of the Bible's great saints.

An Aside: Indulgences

The *Catholic Encyclopedia* describes indulgences in the following manner:

> [Indulgences are granted for the remission] of the temporal punishments for sins, and therefore the giving of satisfaction owed God for one's sins. Indulgences are granted either after the sacrament of Penance or by perfect contrition. Indulgences are either plenary (when all punishments are remitted) or partial (when only part of that punishment is remitted). Plenary indulgences demand that one be free of all venial sin, but partial indulgences do not require this.
>
> Indulgences can only be gained for oneself or for those in purgatory, but not for other living human beings. Indulgences are derived from the treasure of merits of the saints, from Christ Himself or from His Mother (*Catholic Encyclopedia*, ed. Peter M. J. Stravinskas, Huntington: Our Sunday Visitor, Inc., 1991, 509).

Jesus expiates sins (1 Jn. 2:2) and therefore his body, the Church, which is inseparable from its head, also expiates sins (Rom. 12:4-8)-- for one cannot decapitate the head from the body. When we put these two quotes together (1 Jn. 2:2 and Rom. 12:4-8) with Paul's insight in Colossians 1:24 that states that we make up in our sufferings "what is lacking in the afflictions of Christ on behalf of the body, which is his Church," then we can see how the Church can possess a spiritual reservoir of satisfaction for the good of others, for the expiation of sins. Nothing spiritual is ever wasted; it always finds a home!

SACRAMENT OF ANOINTING OF THE SICK

In the Bible, in James' letter, chapter 5 verses 13-15, we read:

Is anyone among you sick? He should summon the presbyters [priests] of the church, and they should pray over him and anoint [him] with oil in the name of the Lord, and the prayer of faith will save the sick person, and the Lord will raise him up. If he has committed any sins, he will be forgiven (NAB).

The sacrament of anointing confers a special grace on those suffering from illness or old age. It is a sacrament that can only be administered by a bishop or a priest—because it is tied to the forgiveness of sins.

Its power is in the unifying of a person's sufferings with the Passion of Christ. It brings God's healing and loving presence upon the person.

At times the healing is spiritual, at times it is emotional or physical: God brings about in the person whatever is best for a person's eternal destiny, for his or her salvation (cf. Jms. 5:13f).

For souls predisposed, and not able to make a complete, integral confession, it brings the remission of sin and temporal punishment due to sin. In the words of the *Rite for the Pastoral Care of the Sick*, n. 6, the sacrament "provides the sick person with the forgiveness of sins and the completion of Christian penance," for souls properly disposed. If the person recovers, however, the formal use of the sacrament of penance is necessary for the forgiveness of sins.

For those near death, the priest is granted the right to proclaim an *apostolic pardon* or *blessing*: "Through the holy mysteries of our redemption may almighty God release you from all punishment in this life and in the life to come."

Viaticum
Viaticum often follows, for those who are sufficiently conscious, the sacraments of penance and the anointing of the

sick. Viaticum is the giving of Holy Communion for those about to die. It is the reception of the Eucharist, the "medicine of immortality," the "promise that we shall live forever" (Ignatius of Antioch). Viaticum means "with you on the way," and therefore is often referred to as the "food for the journey" into heaven.

The sacrament of the anointing of the sick is called the *Last Rite* when it is the last rite or sacrament that a person receives before dying.

In Summary
Anointing of the sick
--provides grace
--strengthens one to deal with the temptations and anxieties associated with death
--gives patience and strength to deal with suffering
--sometimes restores health
--forgives sins and fulfills penance for the predisposed and incapacitated

Reflections
What appeals to you regarding the sacrament of penance? What do you fear?

What appeals to you regarding the sacrament of anointing of the sick?

Going to Confession
Celebrating the Sacrament of Penance

Enter the confessional.

Penitent:
"In the name of the Father, and of the Son, and of the Holy Spirit."
"My last confession was (give time since last confession)."

Confess your sins and the number of times you committed them—as best as you can remember. Withholding serious sin, or what one perceives as mortal sin, makes the confession ineffective.

Priest gives penance:
He may give as a penance some prayer or prayers or some act or acts of charity. Then he will instruct the penitent to pray the act of contrition.

Penitent prays act of contrition:
O my God, I am sorry for my sins with all my heart. In choosing to do wrong and failing to do good I have sinned against you whom I should love above all. I firmly intend with your help to do penance, to sin no more, and to avoid whatever leads me to sin. Our Savior Jesus Christ suffered and died for our sins, in His name, my God, have mercy.
(Other acts of contrition may also be used).

Priest grants absolution:
God, the Father of mercies, through the death and resurrection of his Son has reconciled the world to Himself and sent the Holy Spirit among us for the forgiveness of sins; through the ministry of the Church may God give you pardon and peace, and I absolve you from your sins in the name of the Father, and of the Son, and of the Holy Spirit.

Dismissal
The priest dismisses the penitent with the following words, or words similar to them: "The Lord has freed you from sin. Go in the peace of Jesus Christ."

Homework
Catechism of the Catholic Church (CCC)
Numbers 1422-1532

Homework Prayer Exercise—Getting to Know Jesus

Step One
Read the Gospel of John, chapter 15.

Step Two—Selecting a Section
Read the Gospel of John, chapter 15:1-1-17. Read the footnotes. Collect the facts. What is being said? What is going on?

Step Three
Meditate on the passage. What is God saying to me in this passage from the Bible? Is there something in my life that God wants to talk to me about?

Step Four
Pray to God. Share your feelings and thoughts with him.

Step Five—Taking Action
What do I feel and think God wants me to do? What is he calling me to do?

17

SACRAMENT OF HOLY ORDERS
(Cf. CCC 1536-1589)

Let the bishop be ordained after he has been chosen. When someone pleasing to all has been named, let the people assemble on the Lord's Day with the presbyters [priests] and with such bishops as may be present. All giving assent, the bishops shall impose hands on him, and the presbytery shall stand in silence (2). When the presbyter is to be ordained, the bishop shall impose his hand upon his head while the presbyters touch the one to be ordained....(8). When a deacon is to be ordained the bishop alone shall lay his hands upon him (9).

Hippolytus of Rome (ca. 200)

The sacrament of holy orders is an indispensable part of the Church. Without it the Church could not trace itself back to apostolic times, and therefore back to Christ.

As in Old Testament times (cf. Ex. 19:6; Num. 18:1-7), the Church makes a distinction between the common priesthood of all the faithful (1 Pet. 2:9) and the ordained, ministerial priesthood. For the Christian, all participate in the priesthood of Jesus Christ by virtue of their baptism.

The Levitical priesthood would be replaced by Jesus by his own priesthood and his own priests. Through the providential mystery of God the ancient Temple where sacrifices were performed by the Levitical priests was destroyed in 70 AD by the Romans, never to be rebuilt! Thus the new priests would be the priests of the New Covenant, the priests according to the order of Melchizedek, priests who act in the person of Jesus Christ himself.

The priesthood conferred by the sacrament of holy orders

is one that is specifically designated for teaching, leading worship, and meeting the pastoral needs of the people. Holy orders confer an indelible spiritual mark on the soul.

The most important of the holy orders is that of the bishop because he serves as the visible head of the local or particular church (cf. 1 Tim. 3:1-7; Titus 1:7). Every bishop in the world can trace himself from one bishop to another bishop all the way back in time to an apostle. Consequently, bishops have the fullness of the priesthood and are crucial in protecting the true faith. The preeminent of the bishops is the pope, since he is the successor of the leader of the apostles, Peter.

The next order is the order of presbyter or what we commonly call the priest (cf. 1 Timothy 5:17f). He is a "prudent-coworker" and extension of the bishop. He receives his authority from the bishop, and teaches in power because of his tie to the tree of apostolic succession.

The final order is that of the deacon who likewise is attached to the bishop, but who is entrusted primarily with works of charity (cf. Acts 6:1-7; 1 Timothy 3:8-13).

Holy orders were instituted by Christ (Lk. 22:19; Jn. 20:22f), conferred by the imposition of hands by an apostle or his successor (Acts 6:6; 13:3; 14:23), and give grace (1 Tim. 4:14; 2 Tim.1:6-7).

Archbishop-Cardinal

Archbishops and Cardinals are bishops—albeit one can be a Cardinal without being a bishop. An archbishop governs his own diocese and presides over the bishops of a well-defined district. Cardinals are prelates that are part of the Roman Curia which helps the pope in governing the universal Church.

Why celibate priests?

Why do Catholics of the Roman rite have unmarried priests?

Jesus was not married. The priest acts in "the person of Christ the Head," and as "another Christ" (cf. Mt. 18:18-19; 2 Cor. 5:18-20).

Furthermore, Jesus taught that celibacy was a gift for the sake of the kingdom of God:

Some are incapable of marriage because they were born so; some, because they were made so by others; some, because they have renounced marriage for the sake of the kingdom of heaven. Whoever can accept this ought to accept it (Mt. 19:12, NABRE).

We see the gift of celibacy and the blessedness of celibacy in Paul's writings in the Scriptures. Paul himself was celibate (cf. 1 Cor. 7:8). Let us reflect on 1 Corinthians 7:32-35:

I should like you to be free of anxieties. An unmarried man is anxious about the things of the Lord, how he may please the Lord. But a married man is anxious about the things of the world, how he may please his wife, and he is divided (NAB).

Virginity and celibacy are commended in 1 Corinthians 7:8-9, 36-40, and 1 Timothy 5:9-12. In in Matthew 22:30-32 and Mark 12: 25-27 we are reminded that those in "heaven neither marry nor are given in marriage." The priest, as a sign of contradiction, is a reminder of what our ultimate future in heaven will be like.

Given what has been said, the Church does recognize that celibacy is a discipline and not a doctrine of the faith. That is why some Catholic priests from the Eastern rites are married.

The Roman rite has chosen to keep the practice of celibacy. While it is true that many of the early popes and bishops were married, and in fact most of the apostles were married, with the exception of Paul and John, the Church has always had two currents of priestly life, one which incorporated celibacy into the priesthood, and one which incorporated marriage. Both are currents that have existed from the beginning. Ignatius of Antioch, a disciple of the apostle John, (ca. 107) reminds his clergy in his letter to Polycarp (5): "If anyone can live in a celibate state for the honor of the Lord's flesh, let him do so without ever boasting." Tertullian (ca. 200) in *The Demurrer Against the Heretics* (40, 5) states that the Lord has "virgins and celibates" in his service.

Why "Father"?

Why do we call priests "Fathers"? The Bible says that we are to call no man "Father" (Mt. 23:9).

A priest is referred to as "Father" because the early apostles referred to themselves as "Fathers." When we look at Paul's *First Letter to the Corinthians* (1 Cor. 4:15-17) and John's *Epistle* (1 Jn. 2:12f) we see that these two apostles perceived and named themselves as "Fathers." As the apostle Paul states: "I became your father in Christ Jesus through the gospel" (1 Cor. 4:15). And in 1 Corinthians 17 the apostle Paul refers to his friend Timothy as his "beloved and faithful son in the Lord."

Paul never shied away from referring to others and himself as a father. In Acts 22:1 Paul addresses the Jerusalem Jews as "brothers and fathers." In Romans 4:16-17 Paul calls Abraham "the father of us all." In 1 Thessalonians 2:11 Paul reminds the Thessalonians that he has "treated each one as a father treats his children," and in 1 Timothy 1:2 and Titus 1:4 he calls Timothy, "my true child in faith and Titus "my true child in our common faith." In Paul's letter to Philemon 1:10 he encourages the community to accept Onesimus when he states: "I urge you on behalf of my child Onesimus, whose father I have become in my imprisonment, who was once useless to you and me but is now useful to both you and me."

In Acts 6:14 and 7:2 Stephen, the first martyr of the Church, calls the Jewish leaders "fathers." And in Hebrews 12:7-9 we are reminded that we have earthly "fathers" to discipline us.

Is this a contradiction? No. Jesus in Matthew 23:9 is pointing out that we have one ultimate Father, one ultimate source of being and teaching. God is the ultimate Father. He is also pointing out that the title "Father" can be abused when the person who bears the title does not bear it worthily.

Paul and John are not pointing to the same understanding of "Father" as is seen in Matthew's Gospel. They are primarily pointing to a spiritual fatherhood in the sense of spiritual guides who proclaim the Gospel by their lives and works.

Christ placed Paul, John and all the apostles as spiritual guides to the ultimate Father, God. In turn, all those with authentic authority may bear the name of 'Father" as understood by Paul and John. Thus, priests, by means of the gift of holy orders, serve as spiritual guides for their communities. They serve as spiritual "fathers."

The term "pope" finds its origins in the Greek "pappas," "father." Priest continue to be referred to as "Father" to this day. The Latin version of "pappas," "papa," would eventually be rendered "pope" in the English

130

speaking world. Today, "pope" is exclusively used for the bishop of Rome, the successor of St. Peter.

In Summary
Holy orders
--confer power and grace, enabling the recipient to lead, teach, and sanctify people
--imprint an indelible mark on the soul

There are three orders:
 -*Bishops* have the fullness of the priesthood and thus fulfill all priestly duties. As bishops they ordain priests and deacons and other bishops and lead the local church, the diocese.
 -*Priests* act on behalf of the bishop as spiritual leaders. They celebrate and participate in the sacraments of baptism, Eucharist, confirmation, penance, anointing of the sick, and matrimony. They are also entrusted with the preaching of the Gospel.
 -*Deacons* can baptize, give communion, preach, and perform marriages outside of Mass. They are primarily called to do works of charity.

Reflections
What are your thoughts regarding holy orders?

How could you see bishops or priests as "spiritual fathers"?

Do you see an advantage in having celibate priests?

Homework
Catechism of the Catholic Church (CCC)
Numbers 1536-1600

Homework Prayer Exercise—Getting to Know Jesus
Step One
Read the Gospel of John, chapter 16.

Step Two—Selecting a Section

Read the Gospel of John, chapter 16:16-24. Read the footnotes. Collect the facts. What is being said? What is going on?

Step Three

Meditate on the passage. What is God saying to me in this passage from the Bible? Is there something in my life that God wants to talk to me about?

Step Four

Pray to God. Share your feelings and thoughts with him.

Step Five—Taking Action

What do I feel and think God wants me to do? What is he calling me to do?

18

SACRAMENT OF MATRIMONY
(Cf. CCC 1601-1658)

How can I ever express the happiness of a marriage joined by the Church, strengthened by an offering, sealed by a blessing, announced by angels, and ratified by the Father? How wonderful the bond between two believers, now one in hope, one in desire, one in discipline, one in the same service! They are both children of one Father and servants of the same Master, undivided in spirit and flesh, truly two in one flesh. Where the flesh is one, one also is the spirit.

Tertullian (ca. 155-240)
Ad uxorem, 2, 8, 6-7: PL 1, 1412-1413

Jesus infused his very presence into the wedding feast at Cana (Jn. 2:1f) and forever changed the mystery of marriage.

In Matthew 19:5-6 we read: "A man shall leave his father and mother and be joined to his wife, and the two shall become one flesh. They are no longer two, but one flesh. What God has joined together, no human being must separate." Just as Christ's union with his Body, the Church, cannot be separated (Eph. 5:22-32), likewise the union between husband and wife, a union which mirrors the relationship between Christ and his Church, cannot be separated.

Christ elevated marriage to the level of a sacrament by the gift of grace, the gift of his very self. The reality of a man who gives himself completely, without doubt, without reservation, fully to his wife, and a wife who gives herself completely, without doubt, and fully to her husband can only come about by the supernatural gift of grace. It is only in this way that two can really become one (Mt. 19:3-6; Mk. 10:6-9).

Because of this unity to which God calls a couple, marriage must be holy, indissoluble, open to life, and according to the natural order (Mt. 19:5; Mk. 10:7f; Eph. 5:22-32; 1 Thess. 4:4; 1 Tim. 2:15; Gn. 38:9-10; Lv. 20:13). Marriage must mirror Christ's love for his own Bride, the Church (Eph. 5:25, 31-32). It must mirror God's covenant with his people (cf. *Song of Songs*).

Because of the above reality, marriage is that which must be blessed by the Church. As Ignatius of Antioch (ca. 107), the disciple of the apostle John, states:

> It is right for men and woman who marry to be united with the bishop's approval. In that way their marriage will follow God's will ... (*Letter to Polycarp*, 5).

Marriage is that precious gift where spouses are called to aid each other on the journey towards holiness. Marriage is a vocation directed toward the salvation of spouses and the perpetuation of the mystery of Christ and his Church to the world.

What about same-sex unions?

The Catholic Church sees homosexual acts as contrary to Sacred Scripture, Sacred Tradition, and as *"contrary to the natural law." "They close the sexual act to the gift of life. They do not proceed from genuine affective and sexual complementarity."* (CCC 2357).

A person's orientation is not sinful. It is the act that is wrong.

Apart from the individual quotes from Scripture (i.e., Romans 1:26-27), the very theology of the Old and New Testaments forbid homosexual acts. The underlying theology of God's love for his people in the Old and New Testament is based on the complementarity of the sexes and on the natural law which underlies this complimentarity (Genesis 1 illustrates how the complimentarity of the sexes reflects God's inner unity).

Men and women are physically and psychologically different, and it is in this distinction that the complementarity between a man and a woman make the prospect of two becoming one through total self-donation possible (cf. Gen. 2; Mt. 19:3-6; Mk. 10:6-9). The theology of Genesis and the entire Pentateuch as well as the theology of the Wisdom and Prophetic books of the Bible are all based on the underlying theology of the love of God for his people in the form of the love of a man for a woman in their distinct natures. In fact, there is *no way* of understanding the Scriptures without understanding the relationship between the sexes! There is no way of understanding Jesus, the Bridegroom, united to his Church, his Bride.

Having stated the above, the Church reminds us of the following:

[Homosexuals] must be accepted with respect, compassion, and sensitivity... These persons are called to fulfill God's will in their lives and, if they are Christians, to unite to the sacrifice of the Lord's Cross the difficulties they may encounter from their condition.... Homosexual persons are called to chastity. By virtues of self-mastery that teach them inner freedom, at times by the support of disinterested friendship, by prayer and sacramental grace, they can and should gradually and resolutely approach Christian perfection (Cf. CCC 2358-2359).

A person's orientation is not sinful. It is the act that is wrong.

What is an annulment or declaration of nullity (in regards to two baptized persons)?

People often refer to annulments as the Catholic version of divorce. Nothing could be remoter from the truth!

A Catholic annulment does not deny that a civil, worldly or paper marriage existed. But what an annulment does assert is that this civil union was not a sacramental union, a marriage elevated by God's blessing. In other words, it was a civil marriage between two baptized persons that was never elevated to the level of a sacramental marriage.

How can this be? The answer lies in what makes a sacramental marriage: The key to a valid sacramental marriage is based on the consent between two baptized people. Two people must enter into marriage freely and without any natural (i.e., pathological or psychological) or ecclesiastical hindrance (i.e., outside the proper form required by the Church).

It is important to recognize that a marriage under its proper form is always presumed to be sacramental, no matter what pathological or psychological factors may be present in the marriage. If a couple remains together, grace is keeping it together in all likelihood. However, if at one point the marriage breaks up, then the Church can investigate, upon the request of a spouse or spouses, whether the consent at the time of the wedding was possibly invalid, whether a couple or one of the spouses lacked the capacity for making a true and valid consent.

The determination of the validity of the consent between spouses at the time of their wedding is left to professionals in various fields, including canon lawyers and judges.

One might ask: "How do we justify an annulment in terms of Scripture?" After all, doesn't the Bible say, "A man shall leave his father and mother, and he shall cling to his wife, and the two shall become one" (Eph. 5:31); "they are no longer two but one flesh" (Mk. 10:8); and "what God has joined no man must separate" (Mk. 10:9; cf. 16:18; 1 Cor. 7:10-11).

If there are marriages that God has joined together, there must necessarily be some marriages or unions which God has not joined together. Likewise, the reality of two becoming one in marriage implies that one must in fact have the free will and capacity to live this reality of oneness! Hence, from a purely philosophical point of view, some marriages are not sacramental marriages, that is, marriages elevated to the level of a sacrament since they are not joined by God's blessing nor are they blessed with the ability of two people becoming one.

Scripture supports these philosophical conclusions when it refers to "unlawful marriages," marriages prohibited by God (cf. Acts 15:20; 15:29; Mt. 19:5-9; cf. Lev. 18).

It is in part for this reason that John the Baptist was beheaded. John condemned the unlawful, invalid relationship between King Herod and Herodias, the wife of Herod's brother Philip (Mt. 14:3-12).

An annulment is a recognition of a non-binding, non-sacramental union. It is based on Scripture and the natural philosophical conclusions that flow from the Scriptures.

Why do non-Catholics need annulments (a declaration of nullity)?

A marriage by two properly baptized Protestants is presumed to be a sacrament by the Catholic Church. Those who divorce civilly and would like to marry in the Catholic Church would thus require a declaration of nullity.

Natural marriages (non-sacramental marriages) are between two unbaptized persons or between a baptized person and a non-baptized person. Those who divorce civilly and would like to marry in the Catholic Church would require a declaration of nullity. Natural marriages are seen "as a covenant in which a man and a woman establish between themselves a partnership for the whole of life...which is ordered by its nature to the good of spouses [their complimentarity] and the procreation and education of offspring" (cf. can. 1055). An annulment recognizes in what is referred to as natural marriages that one lacked the proper consent in regards to this covenant.

Natural Family Planning vs. Contraceptives

> The innate language that expresses the total reciprocal self-giving of husband and wife is overlaid, through contraception, by an objectively contradictory language, namely, that of not giving oneself totally to the other. This leads not only to a positive refusal to be open to life but also to a falsification of the inner truth of conjugal love, which is called upon to give itself in personal totality....The difference, both anthropological and moral, between contraception and recourse to the rhythm of the cycle...involves in the final analysis two irreconcilable concepts of the human person and of human sexuality.
>
> *Familiaris Consortio*, 32

Many hormonal contraceptives, such as the "pill," Norplant, Depo-Provera, RU-486 and Ovral are at times abortifacients; that is, they can at times be abortion-causing. Similar effects are also apparent in the use of intrauterine devices such as Lippes Loop and the Copper-T 380A. Contraceptives are not self-giving, other-centered, or open to life. They are contrary to the natural law.

Those who use contraceptives have a high divorce rate, 50 to 60 percent. Those who practice natural family planning have a less than 10 percent divorce rate. Those who practice natural family planning respect the innate language that expresses the "total reciprocal self-giving of husband and wife."

Every diocese offers courses in natural family planning. The internet as well offers natural family planning courses. Contact your local diocese for details.

In Summary
The sacrament of matrimony or marriage
--is between two baptized people
--grants special graces that enable couples to fulfill their duties as spouses and parents
--grants couples the grace to be united in Christ indissolubly
--makes a couple a sign of Christ's love for his Church and for the world

Pray as a Couple and as a Family
There is an old cliché that says, "A family that prays together stays together." One way every family can pray together is before and after each meal.

Prayer before Meals
Bless us, O Lord, and these your gifts which we are about to receive from your bounty through Christ our Lord. Amen.

Prayer after Meals
We give you thanks almighty God, for all your gifts, who live and reign, now and forever. Amen.

Family Prayer
    Almighty and loving God, teach us to always see the best in each other. Protect us, guide us, and help us in all our needs, through Christ our Lord.

Reflections
What aspects of the Church's teaching on marriage do you find most appealing?

What is most appealing to natural family planning?

Homework
Catechism of the Catholic Church (CCC)
Numbers 1601-1666

Homework Prayer Exercise—Getting to Know Jesus
Step One
Read the Gospel of John, chapter 17.

Step Two—Selecting a Section

Read the Gospel of John, chapter 17:1-26. Read the footnotes. Collect the facts. What is being said? What is going on?

Step Three

Meditate on the passage. What is God saying to me in this passage from the Bible? Is there something in my life that God wants to talk to me about?

Step Four

Pray to God. Share your feelings and thoughts with him.

Step Five—Taking Action

What do I feel and think God wants me to do? What is he calling me to do?

19

GRACE AND JUSTIFICATION
(Cf. CCC 142-175; 1703-1707; 1987-2016)

If I speak in human and angelic tongues but do not have love, I am a resounding gong or a clashing cymbal. And if I have the gift of prophecy and comprehend all mysteries and all knowledge; if I have all faith so as to move mountains but do not have love, I am nothing. If I give away everything I own, and if I hand my body over so that I may boast but do not have love, I gain nothing.

Love is patient, love is kind. It is not jealous, is not pompous, it is not inflated, it is not rude, it does not seek its own interests, it is not quick-tempered, it does not brood over injury, it does not rejoice over wrongdoing but rejoices with the truth. It bears all things, believes all things, hopes all things, endures all things.

Love never fails. If there are prophecies, they will be brought to nothing; if tongues, they will cease; if knowledge, it will be brought to nothing. For we know partially and we prophesy partially, but when the perfect comes, the partial will pass away. When I was a child, I used to talk as a child, think as a child, reason as a child; when I became a man, I put aside childish things. At present we see indistinctly, as in a mirror, but then face to face. At present I know partially; then I shall know fully, as I am fully known. So faith, hope, love remain, these three; but the greatest of these is love (1 Cor. 13:1-13, NABRE).

The Dignity of the Human Person

Christ ...in the very revelation of the mystery of the Father and of his love, makes man fully manifest to himself and brings to light his exalted vocation (GS 22).

The human person has been created in the "image and likeness of God" (cf. Gen. 1:27). This image and likeness to God is seen in a person's expression of his or her powers of the intellect, will, and freedom. And in Christ, the Savior and Redeemer, the divine image is ennobled and most perfectly manifested.

The human person is gifted with an immortal and spiritual nature. The human person is the only act of creation that God willed for its own unique sake. From the very moment of conception, the human person is born to eternal life.

The human person has been endowed with the gift of freely seeking, perceiving and loving the good and the true. This is a gift that is found at the very core of the person. It is a natural law that has been embedded into the core of a person's conscience.

The Fall

At the beginning of time humanity had a choice to live with God or live without him (cf. Gen. 3:1-24). The choice to live without God caused a wound, a wound that would forever affect human nature. This wound would come to be known as *original sin*, a sin of such a great nature that it destroyed the possibility of eternal life with God and happiness.

God would not allow humanity to remain separated from eternal life with him. He sent his only begotten Son to restore us to new life (2 Cor. 5:17). Sin was forgiven by the merits of Christ.

Yet even though the deep, penetrating cut of original sin was cleansed by the blood of Christ on the cross, a scar persisted, a scar called *concupiscence*. Thus, scarred, but not destroyed, human nature is forever tempted and inclined, on this earthly journey, toward evil, rebellion, and error.

Thus, human nature is involved in a spiritual battle, a battle between good and evil, light and darkness (cf. Jn. 1:5; 8:12; 12:35). It is a spiritual battle, however, that is fought with the gift of God's grace that was restored to us in Christ Jesus.

The gift of grace is that gift that enables one to become a child of God (cf. 1 Jn. 5:1). A person, through the merits of

Christ and the gift of grace, is able to grow in the spiritual and moral life.

Grace

The Christian is one who responds to live life in love, the love of God, neighbor, and self (cf. Lk. 10:27). The Christian is one who is moving toward total authenticity, toward total and full *human-ness*. The Christian is radically oriented to respond to one's ultimate destiny of union with the self-communicating God of love. The spiritual journey is a call to be awakened, purified, and illuminated to one's true nature. The spiritual life is a call to reality, to see reality as it truly is and to see one's own self as one truly is.

Grace is the fundamental reality of the spiritual journey. Grace is a participation in the life of God, which justifies, sanctifies, glorifies, and makes one a co-heir with God (cf. Jn. 1:12-18; 17:3; Rom. 8:14-17; 2 Cor. 5:17-18; 2 Pet. 1:3-4). Grace is the gift of God himself—the giver is the gift. Grace is a supernatural, gratuitous, and perfecting gift and favor that is present—existentially present—at the very core of the person waiting to be accepted or rejected in freedom. When a person truly seeks to understand his or her very core, he or she is bound to end up finding grace, finding God.

Habitual Grace

Habitual grace or sanctifying grace is that gift of the Holy Spirit that gives an individual the capacity to act in accordance with the demands of faith, hope and love. It is with the person, unless rejected by mortal sin.

Actual Graces

Flares of grace, divine touches, wounds of love, darts of love are often what are referred to as actual graces. An actual grace is a gift, a special flare or moment of God's self-communicating that enables a person to act in a salutary, beneficial, curative, and holy manner. Often this flare of grace is experienced as an interior impulse, attraction, inspiration, illumination, or interior light. At times it is experienced as a special moment of strength, courage or endurance. At other times it arouses good thoughts and feelings that seem to come from nowhere.

Grace and Nature

We are body and soul (cf. 1 Thess. 5:13; Mt. 10:28). This reality has a profound impact on the spiritual life. If a person's body is healthy, psychologically and physically, grace has a much more profound impact on the spiritual life of the person, depending on the person's free-will response to God's self-communication. If, however, the body is ill, psychologically or physically, then the spiritual life is subject to difficulties in its progress. Likewise, if the person's spiritual life is weak, then a person's body is more apt to be subject to all kinds of psychological and related physical ailments—for we were created and meant to live with, in, and for God.

One, therefore, is called to nurture nature and grace. If one's bodily existence is ailing, one should seek all the medical attention within one's capacity (i.e., medication, treatment, counseling, etc.) (cf. 1 Tim. 5:23). If one's spiritual life is unhealthy, one must seek spiritual knowledge and a deeper conversion so as to promote a healthy, holistic experience of life.

What about the cross? It is true that at times, despite all the medical attention one may have access to, the body bears incurable wounds. This is the mystery of the cross and the mystery of grace. Despite it all, Christ, the *Great Physician*, takes the weaknesses and wounds of a person and elevates them into strengths: Who better to understand a person's weakness than one who is weak?

Grace builds upon nature, and heals and elevates it to new heights (cf. 2 Cor. 12:10).

> The quality of holiness is shown not by what we say but by what we do in life.
>
> Gregory of Nyssa (d. 394)
> PG 46, 262

While it is true that we are justified by faith (Acts 13:39; Rom. 1:17; 3:20-30; 4:5; Gal. 3:11); we are not justified by faith alone (Jms. 2:14f). Let us look at what the Bible says:

> What good is it, my brothers and sisters if you say you have faith but do not have works? Can faith save you? If a brother or sister is naked and lacks daily food, and one of you says to them, 'Go in peace, keep warm and eat your fill,' and yet you do not supply for their bodily needs, what is the good of that? So faith by itself, if it has no works, is dead.
>
> But someone will say, 'You have faith and I have works.' Show me your faith apart from your works, and I by my works will show you my faith. You believe that God is one; you do well. Even the demons believe and shudder. Do you want to be shown... that faith apart from works is barren? Was not our ancestor Abraham justified by works when he offered his son Isaac on the altar? You see that faith was active along with his works, and faith was brought to completion by the works. Thus the scripture was fulfilled that says, 'Abraham believed God, and it was reckoned to him as righteousness,' and he was called the friend of God. You see that a person is justified by works and not by faith alone.... For just as the body without the spirit is dead, so faith without works is also dead (Jms. 2:14-24, 26, NRSV).

In Matthew 7:21 we read: "Not everyone who says, 'Lord, Lord,' will enter the kingdom of heaven, but the one who does the will of my heavenly Father."

And in Matthew 25:41-46 we read:

> [Jesus] will say to [those] on his left, 'Depart from me, you accursed, into the eternal fire prepared for the devil and his angels. For I was hungry and you gave me no food, I was thirsty and you gave me no drink, a stranger and you gave me no welcome, naked and you gave me no clothing, ill and in prison, and you did not care

for me. Then they will answer and say, 'Lord, when did we see you hungry or thirsty or a stranger or naked or ill or in prison, and not minister to your needs?' He will answer them, 'Amen, I say to you, what you did not do for one of these least ones, you did not do for me. And these will go off to eternal punishment, but the righteous to eternal life (NAB).

It is true that we are **not** saved by our works (Eph. 2:8-9). The Church has always believed this. In fact, the heresy of Pelagianism which argued that one could work out one's salvation was condemned in the fifth century.

Salvation for Catholics implies faith and works. Authentic faith always implies the fruits of that faith, works. And authentic holy works always implies a source for those holy works, faith. Faith and works therefore cannot be separated.

The Scriptures reminds us that "if I have all the faith in the world, but am without love, I gain nothing" (cf. 1 Cor. 13:1-3). It is for this reason that the Scriptures remind us that we will be rewarded according to our works: "None of those who cry out, 'Lord Lord, will enter the kingdom of God but only the one who does the will of my Father in Heaven" (Mt. 7:21). "If you wish to enter into life, keep the commandments" (Mt. 19:17-18). "The one who holds out to the end is the one who will see salvation" (Mt. 24:13). "Work with anxious concern to achieve your salvation" (Phil. 2:12). "The just judgment of God will be revealed when he will repay every man for what he has done" (Rom. 2:6). "He will receive his wages in proportion to his toil" (1 Cor. 3:8). "It is not those who hear the law who are just in the sight of God; it is those who keep it who will be declared just" (Rom. 2:13). "[We are saved' by faith, which expresses itself through love" (Gal. 5:6). "[We are] created in Christ Jesus to lead the life of good deeds" (Eph. 2:10).

Saint Paul says, "I do not run like a man who loses sight of the finish line. I do not fight as if I were shadowboxing. What I do is discipline my own body and master it, for fear that after having preached to others I myself should be rejected" (1 Cor. 9:27).

Faith operates through love, a work (cf. Gal. 5:6). We will receive our reward from God according to our grace- filled works (Rm. 2:6).

Let us not be presumptuous. Let us follow Paul's teaching which reminds us to "work out...[our] salvation with fear and trembling" (Phil. 2:12).

Authentic faith implies authentic works, and authentic holy works implies authentic faith. Without grace, without faith, without God, there is no authentic merit.

Is salvation assured?

"Are you saved?" is a question that is often posed by non-Catholics. As Catholics we can say that at this moment I am saved (cf. Rom. 8:24; Eph. 2:5, 8; 2 Tim. 1:9; Tit. 3:5), but because of the gift of free will, I can in the future deny Christ and lose the salvation that was gifted to me (cf. Phil. 2:12; 1 Pet. 1:9; Mt. 19:22; 24:13; Mk. 8:3-5 Acts 15:11; Rom. 5:9-10; 13:11; 1 Cor. 3:15; 5:5; Heb. 9:28).

Basing itself on the correct interpretation of the Scriptures and the constant teaching of the Church, the Church has always affirmed that salvation is conditional. Catholics believe that one's salvation is dependent on one's constant "yes" to God's grace, to God's call. To say that one is assured of salvation by one act, as some argue, is to essentially say that once one has proclaimed Jesus as Lord and Savior, one's free will has been lost, since one cannot reject God from that point on.

The question must be asked in such a case: "How can one truly love God if one is assured of salvation?" Love implies a free will. Love is a decision, a free decision. Love is a continual "yes" to love. To deny free decisions and future free decisions is to eliminate the capacity to love God—and the capacity to love anyone or anything.

As Catholics, we argue that our salvation is dependent on the state of our mortal soul at the moment of our death (cf. Mt. 25:31-46). A person who dies in the friendship of God, in a state of grace, is granted the rewards of heaven with God and the saints and angels. The person who dies in mortal sin (1 Jn. 5:16-17) will reap what they have sown, eternal separation from God.

For Catholics there is a distinction made between redemption and salvation. Jesus has redeemed the world by his blood; he has restored our friendship with God. But redemption is not the same as salvation.

Salvation presupposes redemption, but is distinguishable from redemption. Christ opened the gates of heaven for us, delivered us from sin, and restored humanity to the life of grace by the redeeming act on the Cross. We in turn must respond to the redemption won for us. We must respond to the engulfing grace he has released upon us (Phil. 1:6; Heb. 13:20-21). The gates are open, but one must choose to enter through those gates. One must accept the grace. One must accept salvation.

If salvation is assured why would we have to be careful and pray for strength against temptations (Mt. 26:41; Mk. 14:38; Lk. 22:46; Gal. 6:1)? Why would one have to train oneself like an athlete for fear of losing one's salvation (1 Cor. 9:27)? If salvation is assured, why do we need to "persevere" (Mt. 24:13; 2 Tim. 2:12)? If salvation is assured, why would we need to do penance (Mt. 3:8; Acts 2:38; 8:22; 2 Cor. 7:10)? If salvation is assured why would we need to be judged by the Lord (1 Cor. 4:4-5; 2 Cor. 5:10)? If salvation is assured why would we be concerned about being paid "according to our works" (Rom. 2:6) or being paid according to our "conduct" (Mt. 16:27)? If salvation is assured, why would we need to "remain in his kindness" for fear of being "cut off" (Rom. 11:22)? If salvation is assured, how can one be in the process of "being saved," or "perishing" (2 Cor. 2:15)? If salvation is assured, why are we called to "test ourselves" and fear the failing "of the test" (2 Cor. 13:5)? If salvation is assured, why must we "work out our salvation with fear and trembling" (Phil. 2:12)? If one is assured of salvation, why bother with religious duties and moral obligations (cf. 1 Tim. 3:8)? If salvation is assured, why bother follow in Jesus' footsteps (1 Pet. 2:21)? If salvation is assured, why acknowledge our sinfulness (1 Jn. 5-10). If salvation is assured, why bother to follow the commandments (1 Jn. 2:1-11; Jn. 14:21; Mt. 19:17)? If salvation is assured, why is crying "Lord, Lord" insufficient for entering the kingdom of heaven (Mt. 7:21)? If salvation is assured how do we explain these words from Jesus: "If anyone wishes to come after me, he must deny himself and take up his cross daily and follow me. For whoever wishes to save his life will lose it and whoever loses his life for my sake will save it" (Lk. 9:23-24).

If one was assured of salvation, then faith would not have a future goal? Hope would be meaningless! Yet Peter reminds the faithful to persevere during times of trial for they are achieving in this process "faith's goal, salvation" (cf. 1 Pet. 1:6-9). Or as Paul states: "I continue my pursuit toward the goal, the prize of [salvation]" (Phil. 3:14).

One must avoid the sin of presumption, the sin that boasts in a false sense of assured salvation (Jms. 4:13-16). One must remember the words of Paul who reminds us to "work with anxious concern to achieve one's salvation" (Phil. 2:12), and to let no one "think he is standing upright...lest he fall" (1 Cor. 10:12).

In Summary--Justification (CCC 1987-1995)

Justification is the process by which a person is made holy. Justification or "making just" flows from the free gift of grace. Grace provides the person with the possibility of entering into the Paschal Mystery--Jesus' life, death, resurrection and ascension. Consequently, grace justifies a person. It makes one a "new creation" in God (cf. Rom. 3:22; 6:3-4, 8-11; 1 Cor. 12; Jn. 15:1-4). It brings about salvation.

Jesus continually offers us grace. He continually offers us the remission of sins and the freedom from enslavement to sin. He continually offers us the renewal of our interior and exterior being through the continual offer of forgiveness, reconciliation, healing and faith, hope, and love. *And what is required of us?* We must say "yes" to this offer by our words and actions, by our whole being; we must be a "yes" to God by our response to his free gift of grace.

Evolution and the Catholic Church

There are basically three competing theories to describe the creation or evolution of man and woman. Some argue for the theory of *creationism* which maintains that God created humanity without the necessity of an evolutionary process. There is the theory of *atheistic evolution* which maintains that human life evolved from lower forms to higher forms by a random process. Finally, there is the theory of *theistic [God-guided] evolution*, the belief that God created the world out of nothing and that he guided an evolutionary process in such a way that the first *immortally souled* human beings were created by him through an evolutionary process.

One, as a Catholic, can believe in a form of *creationism*—in its Catholic form of understanding--or one can believe in *theistic [or God-guided] evolution*—in its Catholic form. One cannot however believe in atheistic evolution, for it denies God's creative power and his providential will.

One may wonder how the belief in *theistic [God-guided] evolution* can be believed in terms of the account of creation in the book of Genesis. Remember our *Interpretation of Scriptures* class: Genesis is not a history textbook. All one needs to do is to compare Genesis 1 with Genesis 2:4f: Here, within the first two chapters of Genesis, you find two different accounts of creation. In chapter one, "man" is created near the end of the creation process; in chapter two, "man" is created near the beginning of the creation process. Chapter one emphasizes, among other things, that the human person is the summit of creation; Chapter two emphasizes, among other things, that God entrusted creation to humanity's stewardship.

The Book of Genesis is a theological account teaching us that God is the ultimate source of being. He created the world and people out of nothing. He created them good. It is an account of freedom and the cost of using freedom in a negative manner. It is an account of two people, Adam and Eve, who chose to rebel against God and sought to live without God. By their sin they forever distorted the nature of the world. It is also a story of hope, the hope for a future savior: Christ would be that savior, the one who would come to save the world from the damage that was caused by the Fall, the *original sin* of Adam and Eve.

Genesis is the Word of God told to a people thousands of years ago about the eternal truths of God, a God of mercy and love, a God of second chances.

Consequently, one, as a Catholic, can believe in a form of *creationism* or one can believe in *theistic [God-guided] evolution* as understood by the Church.

Reflections

What does it mean to be created "in the image and likeness of God"? What are the implications of this reality when dealing with other persons?

What does the gift of grace tell you about God's love for us?

Do you see God's grace working in yourself or others? If so, how?

How does God's grace teach us that we are not alone on this earthly journey?

Homework
Catechism of the Catholic Church (CCC)
Numbers 1949-2051

Homework Prayer Exercise—Getting to Know Jesus
Step One
Read the Gospel of John, chapter 18.

Step Two—Selecting a Section
    Read the Gospel of John, chapter 18:33-40. Read the footnotes. Collect the facts. What is being said? What is going on?

Step Three
    Meditate on the passage. What is God saying to me in this passage from the Bible? Is there something in my life that God wants to talk to me about?

Step Four
    Pray to God. Share your feelings and thoughts with him.

Step Five—Taking Action
    What do I feel and think God wants me to do? What is he calling me to do?

20

THE MORAL LAW
(Cf. CCC 1950-1974; 2031-2046)

The Moral Law

The moral law is that which guides a person on the spiritual journey. There are three kinds of moral laws, all of which are interrelated, and all of which find their source of being at the core of the person (cf. Phil. 2:12-13).

Natural Law

Natural law finds its impetus in God's wisdom and the immutable gift of reason. The goal of the moral law is life in Christ (cf. Rom. 10:4).

> The natural law is written and engraved in the soul of each and every man, because it is human reason ordaining him to do good and forbidding him to sin.... But this command of human reason would not have the force of law if it were not the voice and interpreter of a higher reason to which our spirit and our freedom must be submitted.
>
> Leo XIII, *Libertas praestantissimum*

> The natural law is nothing other than the light of understanding in us by God; through it we know what we must do and what we must avoid. God has given this light or law at creation.
>
> *St. Thomas Aquinas*
> *Dec. praec.* I

Through the natural law one practices that which is good and attends to one's eternal destiny, one's salvation. The natural law promotes the dignity and the rights and duties of the person.

Revealed Law

Divine revelation, which is found in the Sacred Scriptures and Sacred Tradition, reveals that which is in the heart. It aids, enlightens, and clarifies the natural moral law, which sin can often cloud. The moral law finds its fulfillment in the law of love.

Ecclesiastical Law

The laws or precepts of the Church nourish and strengthen a person's ability to perceive and follow the innate natural law. The emphasis on these laws is on attending Mass on a regular basis, receiving communion, seeking reconciliation, fasting and abstaining from meat on appointed days, joining in the missionary efforts of the Church, and so on.

The Moral Virtues

A holy person is a virtuous person (cf. Wis. 8:7; Phil. 4:8). A holy person is a virtuous person who seeks "to be like God"; that is, to be in the image and likeness to which he or she was originally created in (cf. Gen. 1:27). Therefore, in order for one to comprehend the path that grace draws one toward, one needs to comprehend the virtues. There are two types of virtues, the acquired moral virtues and the infused moral virtues.

Acquired Moral Virtues

The acquired moral virtues are acquired by the repetition of acts under the direction of the light of *natural right reason*. Grace is not required to acquire these natural virtues.

For example, by the natural light of human reason and discipline one can learn to be just, temperate, courageous, and prudent.

Infused Moral Virtues

Infused moral virtues require a person's response to grace.

Through a person's response to grace, the acquired virtues, which are guided by right reason, can be elevated to a level that surpasses the limits of right reason and discipline alone. Only God can empower or endow a person with infused moral virtues, for they are by nature supernatural acts of grace. These virtues are directed toward a person's supernatural last end and consequently are essential for eternal life.

For example, justice, temperance, prudence, and courage can be elevated to supernatural levels, levels beyond the natural capacity of the human person's ability. The lives of the martyrs illustrate the supernatural, infused virtues of courage and love.

There are some virtues, such as faith, that can only be acquired by grace, by being infused.

The Relationship between Acquired and Infused Moral Virtues

Holiness at whatever level requires the proper interaction of the acquired and infused moral virtues. The proper interaction of the acquired moral virtues and the infused moral virtues make for the perfect spiritual person. In such a case, all of a person's life, in all its aspects, is in perfect harmony, like five fingers on a hand.

The Theological Virtues (cf. 1 Cor. 13:13)

The theological virtues of faith, hope, and love empty a person of all that is not for the honor and glory of God and fills such a person with God's self-communicating, cleansing presence.

The human virtues are grounded in the theological virtues (cf. 2 Pet. 1:4), which enable a person to be animated, informed, and enlivened in Christ. Faith frees the intellect to soar into realms of knowing it had never before experienced (Is. 55:8-9). It penetrates the deep mysteries of God that are beyond the natural and rational boundaries. Hope empties the memory of the unhealthy, worldly passing allurements that seek to compete with the bliss that comes from God. Love unburdens the will and the heart of all that is false and fleeting and helps one to cling to that which is of God. In faith, hope, and love one moves toward union with God, toward peace, happiness, and light.

The Evangelical Counsels

The evangelical counsels are poverty, chastity, and obedience. They lead to spiritual perfection and the healing of moral wounds. Poverty is empowered by the theological virtue of hope, chastity by the theological virtue of love, and obedience by the theological virtue of faith. The counsels, thus, render to God what is due to him.

The evangelical counsels take on a special meaning for those in religious life and holy orders. They, in a unique manner, point to life in heaven. *Poverty* points to the reality that in heaven we will have no need; *celibacy* points to the fact that in heaven there will be no marrying; and *obedience* points to the fact that our eternal destiny will be consumed with being in perfect harmony with our Creator.

Reflections

How do you see the moral life? Some see it as following a roadmap to happiness. Some see it as being an "owner's manual" on how to be authentically human. How do you see it?

Homework

Catechism of the Catholic Church (CCC)
Numbers 1749-1775; 1803-1845

Homework Prayer Exercise—Getting to Know Jesus

Step One
Read the Gospel of John, chapter 19.

Step Two—Selecting a Section

Read the Gospel of John, chapter 19:17-30. Read the footnotes. Collect the facts. What is being said? What is going on?

Step Three

Meditate on the passage. What is God saying to me in this passage from the Bible? Is there something in my life that God wants to talk to me about?

Step Four

Pray to God. Share your feelings and thoughts with him.

Step Five—Taking Action

What do I feel and think God wants me to do? What is he calling me to do?

21

CONCIENCE
(Cf. 1776-1794)

Freedom, Responsibility, and Personal Becoming

At the core of a person's nature or essence, intrinsic to him or her, is that person's freedom. Freedom is the means by which a person primarily becomes something. One is so free that one has within oneself the capacity to take control of one's basic nature. A person is able to determine what he or she is and what he or she is to be. Therefore, at the heart of the definition of the person is the reality that the person is one who is open to becoming and achieving.

The person endowed with grace is on a journey—whether he is aware of it or not—toward the perfection of Christ, the God-man, the fully divine, fully human being. By seeking the God that dwells within, one can find one's true human potential, and one's true happiness, and by seeking to find one's full humanity, one can find the divine working within us.

The Limitations of Human Freedom

> By deviating from the moral law man violates his own freedom, becomes imprisoned within himself, disrupts neighborly fellowship, and rebels against divine truth (CCC 1740).

Human freedom is not absolute. It is limited and subject to errors. It is limited in that it demands obedience to the natural law that resides at the core of every person, and it is subject to error in that it is subject to the slavery and blindness that is associated with sin.

The Christian is called to live a life in imitation of Christ. The Savior who saved us from the slavery of sin is the one that all are called to imitate, for in this imitation is found the ultimate in liberation and freedom (cf. Gal. 5:1; Jn. 8:32; 2 Cor. 17; Rom. 8:21). In the grace of Christ one is educated and nourished in the ways of authentic freedom.

Moral Conscience

> Deep within his conscience man discovers a law which he has not laid upon himself but which he must obey. Its voice, ever calling him to love and to do what is good and to avoid evil, sounds in his heart at the right moment.... For man has in his heart a law inscribed by God.... His conscience is man's most secret core and his sanctuary. There he is alone with God whose voice echoes in his depths.
>
> *Gadium et Spes, 16*

A person entrusted with this innate moral law is obliged to be faithful to this moral law in choosing what is right and just. Conscience is that gift that enables the faithful to recognize and follow the moral law. In so doing one recognizes the ultimate in truth, truth itself, God himself, Christ himself.

> Conscience is a messenger of him, who, both in nature and in grace, speaks to us behind a veil, and teaches and rules us by his representatives. Conscience is the aboriginal Vicar of Christ.
>
> *John Henry Newman*

Conscience directs a person to conversion and to hope. It enables one to recognize the evil one has done and to consequently ask for God's forgiveness. Conscience also helps one recognize the good and the power of hope. It directs one away from evil, unhappiness, despair, and moves one toward happiness, peace, and light.

The Formation of Conscience

One has a moral obligation to form one's conscience in accordance to right reason and the will of God. It is a life-long task. The following are some general guidelines for the proper formation of one's conscience:

- Reflection, self-examination, and introspection make up the ground level of an informed conscience.
- Absorption in the Word of God (Ps. 119:105) and Sacred Tradition (the life of the Holy Spirit within the Church) serve as the blood of life for the conscience.
- The authoritative teachings of the Church that flow from Sacred Scripture and Sacred Tradition are essential (cf. 2 Thess. 2: 15).
- Reading the spiritual masters and the advice of good spiritual directors are extremely helpful in putting all the above into a concise vision of reality that corresponds to the innate reality at the core of a person's being.

A well-formed conscience engenders freedom and peace of heart.

Determining a Well-Informed Conscience

There are essentially two key guides that help to determine if one has a well-informed conscience:
1) A good end does not justify an evil means.
2) Do unto others as you would like done unto you (cf. Mt. 7:12; Lk. 6:31; Rom. 14:21; 1 Cor. 8:12; Tob. 4:15).

An Uninformed Conscience

> Like all things human, even [the] conscience can fail to...[perceive] illusions and errors. It is a delicate voice that can be overpowered by a noisy, distracted way of life, or almost suffocated by a long-lasting and serious habit of sin.
>
> *Pope John Paul II*

There are two main reasons for an uninformed conscience:

1) The propensity toward laziness is at the heart of those who fail to seek a well-informed conscience.
2) A sinful life often blinds one to recognize the truth and often deadens a person's conscience.

> The more correct conscience prevails, the more do persons and groups turn aside from blind choice and try to be guided by objective standards of moral conduct.
>
> *Gadium et Spes. 16*

An Examination of Conscience

An examination of conscience is a powerful way of keeping one's conscience informed and open to the working of grace.

The following is a general method of examining one's conscience: One must first begin by praying to God for enlightenment. One must then ask oneself the following key questions: "Who am I as God sees me? What is happening in my life at this moment? How is God working in me? How is evil working in me? What is God asking of me? What would Jesus do in my situation?" From these key questions flows a profound examination of conscience.

The Ten Commandments and their implications are highly recommended when examining one' conscience. See Chapter 23.

Voting with a Catholic Conscience

What is it that makes one a great citizen? A holy citizen. A holy citizen seeks to protect and preserve the good and seeks to overturn evil. A holy citizen seeks to do what Jesus would do! But in order to know what Jesus would do, we need to, in fact, know what Jesus did and continues to do in his body, his bride, the Church.

A good and holy citizen must be familiar with the Church's teachings, whether one is dealing with immigration, refugee assistance, international peace and justice, healthcare, workers' rights, conscience protection, education, the environment, the nature of marriage, parental rights, stem cell research, euthanasia, the death penalty, abortion, etc. A wonderful place to find answers to these pressing questions is in the *Catechism of the Catholic Church*—which is the summary of the Church's consistent teachings on faith and morals as given to us by the successors of the apostles, the bishops, in union with the successor of Peter, the pope.

Having said this, some parishioners inevitably and understandably come and ask, "Who am I to vote for when so few candidates share all of the Catholic Church's teachings?"

It is here that we seek to vote according to a hierarchy of values. At the top of the list is the protection of the sanctity of human life and the human family. All other rights flow from these rights. For example, the right to "cheap or free healthcare" implies that there is someone alive to receive it! Likewise, the common good of a society implies that marriage and the family function as a school of values and morals, a school of holy citizenship. If the family implodes, so does society!

When in doubt, fear not! Christ did not leave us as orphans. He has blessed us with his life, his Church. Let us pray, reflect, study and seek to be obedient to the successors of the apostles in union with the successor of Peter, the pope. In doing so, we can be assured of our role in fulfilling the obligations of holy citizenship.

Reflections
How does one's conscience guide a person to be happy?

What is the danger of not having an informed conscience?

How has conscience helped you in the past?

Homework
Catechism of the Catholic Church (CCC)
Numbers 1730-1748; 1776-1802

Homework Prayer Exercise—Getting to Know Jesus
Step One
Read the Gospel of John, chapter 20.

Step Two—Selecting a Section
Read the Gospel of John, chapter 20:11-18. Read the footnotes. Collect the facts. What is being said? What is going on?

Step Three
Meditate on the passage. What is God saying to me in this passage from the Bible? Is there something in my life that God wants to talk to me about?

Step Four

    Pray to God. Share your feelings and thoughts with him.

Step Five—Taking Action

    What do I feel and think God wants me to do? What is he calling me to do?

22

SIN
(Cf. CCC 396-412; 1846-1869)

Original and Personal Sin

Original Sin

The Book of Genesis is a theological account teaching us that God is the ultimate source of being. He created the world and people out of nothing. He created them good.

Genesis is an account of freedom and the cost of using freedom in a negative manner. It is an account of human individuals who chose to rebel against God and sought to live without God. By their sin they forever distorted the nature of the world. We call this distortion *original sin*.

Concupiscence

Original sin distorted the harmony of creation and damaged the relationship between God and humanity. The second Person of the Trinity, the Son of God, came into the world and cleansed or healed it of this damage, this original sin. While the sin was forgiven in Christ, concupiscence remained—an inclination toward disharmony.

Human beings, through the gift of baptism in Christ, in God, are capable of an intimate, personal, saving relationship with God, and are capable of experiencing eternal life with God in heaven. Yet despite this, because of the wound of original sin, a human being is still inclined and tempted toward that original rebellion; that is, human beings are inclined toward the temptations of evil, the temptations against right reason. We call this concupiscence. The spiritual journey becomes a battle against concupiscence.

***Baptism wipes away original sin, but concupiscence remains.

Personal Sin

Sin is a personal act in which reason, truth, and right conscience are offended. It is a failure to live up to the command of love of God and neighbor caused by a perverse attachment to that which is not for the honor and glory of God. It is an act of self-infatuation, disobedience (Gen. 3:5) and hatred toward God (Ps. 51:4). It wounds the nature of the human person, the nature of solidarity, and the nature of the eternal law.

Kinds of Sin

Sin comes from the heart, from the very core of the person's being (cf. Mt. 15:19-20). The two main kinds of sins are sins of commission and sins of omission. Sins of commission are sins in which a person takes an active part in. Sins of omission are sins that involve actions that are omitted in fostering the glory and honor of God. These are sins committed by people who keep quiet when evil is being done. People who do nothing to put an end to abortion or euthanasia, for example, commit serious sins of omission. Failing to stop gossip, vulgarity, and so forth, are other forms of sins of omission.

Gravity of Sin

> If any one sees his brother committing what is not a mortal sin, he will ask, and God will give him life for those whose sin is not mortal. There is sin which is mortal.... All wrongdoing is sin, but there is sin which is not mortal (2 Jn. 5:16-17).

There are mortal/deadly sins and there are venial/non-deadly sins. Mortal sins involve the loss of sanctifying grace and love. It is a radical rejection of God, a radical turning away from God. Dying in mortal sin leads to hell. On the other hand, venial or non-deadly sins do not deprive one of heaven. In venial sin love remains, though it is offended and damaged.

In order to commit a mortal sin one needs to take into account the following conditions:

1) The sin must be one that involves a *grave matter*. Traditionally grave matter has been associated with the gross violation of the Ten Commandments.
2) Full knowledge and deliberate consent is needed in the committing of the sin.
3) Unintentional ignorance (not feigned ignorance or hardness of heart) diminishes or removes the seriousness of the sin (i.e., unintentional ignorance can be caused by pathological disorders, inordinate feelings and passions).

Venial sin is sin that does not meet the above requirements. Venial sin weakens love, disorders affections for created things, hinders virtuous progress, and disposes one toward mortal sin by damaging the conscience. Yet venial sin does not break a person's covenant or friendship with God. It does not deprive one of sanctifying grace nor of heaven.

Communal Nature of Spirituality

The love of God and the love of neighbor are inseparable realities. To authentically love God one must authentically love one's neighbor, and to authentically love one's neighbor one needs to authentically love God.

The communal nature of spirituality promotes the common good of society, which promotes the defense of the fundamental rights of persons, the development of spirituality, and peace and security. Any form of sinful inequality is condemned.

Sin and Mercy

All people fall short of the perfection of Christ and therefore sin is a cancer that engulfs this world (cf. 1 Jn. 8-9). Yet despite this sad reality, God's mercy never leaves a person. Even a mortal sin does not withdraw from the core of the person God's divine mercy, for if it did, there would be no possibility of repentance, forgiveness, and conversion.

The Seven Capital Sins and Their Vices

The capital sins are commonly found in the early stages of the spiritual journey. They are often mortal, but not always. A person, as a consequence of original sin, is susceptible to capital sins and their vices. A capital sin leads one to separation from God and all kinds of sins. They also lead from lesser sins to more serious sins.

The following is a brief description of the seven capital sins and what is often born of them: The capital sin of envy gives birth to hatred, slander, calumny, detraction, and joy at the misfortune of others. Anger leads to disputes, fits of passion, insults, blasphemy, rudeness, haughtiness and contempt. Vanity leads to disobedience, boasting, hypocrisy, unholy rivalry, discord, and stubbornness. Sloth (or acedia) gives rise to malice, rancor, discouragement, cowardliness, spiritual apathy or stagnation, forgetfulness of spiritual obligations, and the seeking after forbidden things. Avarice gives rise to disloyalty, treachery, fraud, deceit, perjury, harshness, hardness of heart, and an excessive desire for acquiring and maintaining things. Gluttony leads one to engage in improper jokes, coarse, loutish behavior, impurity, foolish conversation, and stupidity. Lust gives rise to spiritual blindness, poor judgment, impetuous or rash decisions, fickleness, instability, capriciousness, self-infatuation, and an inordinate attachment to this present life.

Jesus is fully human and fully divine. Jesus, being fully human, and having no sin, teaches us what it means to be fully human. To be fully human is to be without sin. Sin diminishes our humanity.

Reflections

How does sin diminish our humanity? In other words, how do the above capital sins and their vices make us less human?

How does sin make us and those around us unhappy?

Homework

Catechism of the Catholic Church (CCC)
Numbers 1846-1948

Homework Prayer Exercise—Getting to Know Jesus

Step One
Read the Gospel of John, chapter 21.

Step Two—Selecting a Section
    Read the Gospel of John, chapter 21:15-19. Read the footnotes. Collect the facts. What is being said? What is going on?

Step Three
    Meditate on the passage. What is God saying to me in this passage from the Bible? Is there something in my life that God wants to talk to me about?

Step Four
    Pray to God. Share your feelings and thoughts with him.

Step Five—Taking Action
    What do I feel and think God wants me to do? What is he calling me to do?

23

TEN COMANDMENTS
(Cf. CCC 2084-2550)

The Ten Commandments
1. *I am the Lord your God: you shall not have strange gods before me.*
2. *You shall not take the name of the Lord your God in vain.*
3. *Remember to keep holy the Lord's Day.*
4. *Honor your father and your mother.*
5. *You shall not murder.*
6. *You shall not commit adultery.*
7. *You shall not steal.*
8. *You shall not bear false witness against your neighbor.*
9. *You shall not covet your neighbor's wife.*
10. *You shall not covet your neighbor's goods.*

The Ten Commandments and their implications for Catholics (cf. Exodus 20:2-17)
1. The first commandment forbids acts of voluntary doubt (the disregarding or refusing to believe as true what God has revealed), incredulity (the refusal to assent to truth), heresy (the denial of truth), apostasy (the rejection of the Christian faith), schism (refusal to submit to the Catholic Church), despair (ceasing to hope in salvation), presumption (the counting on one's own capacities for salvation), indifference (the failure to appreciate or care in God's goodness), ingratitude (the refusal to return love for love), lukewarmness (a

hesitation in responding to God's love), spiritual sloth (refusing the joy that comes from God), hatred of God (denying God's goodness), idolatry (divinizing worldly "things" such as power, pleasure, race, country, etc.), sacrilege (profaning things and persons of God), atheism (the denial of God's existence), and agnosticism (a refusal to affirm or deny the existence of God). Occult beliefs and practices such as superstition, divination, magic and sorcery are also forbidden.

2. The second commandment demands a respect for the sacredness of the Lord's name. Acts of blasphemy (asserting words or thoughts of hatred, reproach, or defiance against God), the taking of oaths (the superficial misuse or lack of respect for God's name), false oaths (swearing to take God as a witness to something that is not true), and perjury (making a promise under oath with no intention of keeping it) are sinful.

3. The third commandment is a summons to keep the Lord's Day a holy day. It demands the faithful attendance at Sunday Mass, and an attitude of profound worship. It is a time to spend with God and to abstain from any work that distracts from authentically consecrating Sunday as a precious day of love of God and love of neighbor. One seeks comfort, but one also seeks to be challenged to grow.

4. The fourth commandment demands the authentic honoring of father and mother. Children owe just obedience, respect, gratitude, assistance, and the repaying of love for love to their parents. Parents have the responsibility of caring for their children's physical and spiritual needs, fostering a vocation, and teaching

them to serve and follow God above all. The family forms the foundation for societal and ecclesiastical life.

5. The fifth commandment is an affirmation of the dignity of life. Being created in the image and likeness of God, the human person is sacred from conception to natural death. Murder is a violation of the dignity of the person and the creator. Teachings flowing from the fifth commandment include the following:

   a. Recourse to the death penalty is not forbidden in societies that have no means to protect the common good. If non-lethal means are available to defend and protect the common good, then such means must be used. In modern societies, therefore, the death penalty should be "very rare" or practically "non-existent" (*Evangelium Vitae*, 56).
   b. Indirectly bringing about a person's death, such as exposing someone to mortal danger without grave reason, is sinful.
   c. Direct abortion is an attack on the "image and likeness of God," a direct attack and killing of a human person. Formal cooperation in an abortion constitutes an act penalized by automatic excommunication.
   d. The human embryo is to be treated from conception as a person to be defended, cared for, and healed like any other human person. Embryonic as opposed to adult stem cell research, artificial insemination, contraception, and cloning are prohibited since these acts often lead to the death of life at its earliest stages, and in the case of embryonic stem cell research always destroy the embryo.
   e. Direct euthanasia, the putting to death of the handicapped, sick, or dying is not permitted. Palliative care is permissible and encouraged (i.e., using medications to alleviate pain, even if the medication has the indirect consequence of shortening life).
   f. Discontinuing "over-zealous" medical treatments is permissible. The normal care of the person consists of

prolonging life by ordinary means as opposed to extraordinary means. To put it more succinctly, the ordinary and obligatory means of prolonging life involve "all medicines, treatments, and operations which offer a reasonable hope of benefit for the patient and which can be obtained or used without excessive expense, pain, or burden" (Pius XII, *Discourse on Doctors*, 1957). This is often understood to mean that proper nutrition (including intravenous feeding) and hydration are not to be withheld. In terms of those means of treatment which can be discontinued: "All medicines, treatments, and operations, which cannot be used or obtained without excessive expense, pain, or other burden [can be refused]." In other terms, when therapy no longer benefits the person, "letting go" is ethically justifiable. To disconnect a respirator when a person has reached the point of no return is ethically acceptable and appropriate.

g. Suicide and assisting in suicide is morally forbidden. It is a violation of the just love of self, neighbor, and God. Psychological issues, anguish, grave fear of hardship, suffering or torture can diminish the responsibility for the act.

h. One has a moral obligation to care for one's health and the health of others.

i. Given that wars are sadly inevitable, recourse to war is permissible when the following conditions are met: The cause must be just. All means of avoiding war or ending aggression must be seen to be "impractical and ineffective." There must be an adequate prospect for success in putting an end to the aggression or evil. The use of weaponry must be used with prudence. They must not "produce evils and disorders graver than the evil to be eliminated." Every act of self-defense or war that is aimed at the indiscriminate destruction of whole cities is prohibited. Non-combatants must never be targeted.

6. The sixth commandment is a command that demands fidelity. Any act which is contrary to the dignity of chastity, such as fornication, adultery, polygamy, divorce and remarriage (without an annulment), open or free marriages, same-sex marriages or unions, homosexual and bisexual acts, masturbation, contraceptive use, pornography, prostitution, incest and rape are forbidden. Artificial insemination and the use of a surrogate uterus are forbidden. The sixth commandment is a call to authentic sexual integration, authentic life and love.

7. The seventh commandment is a prohibition against stealing. Stealing is characteristic of a lack of charity and injustice. Often stealing is done in subtle ways: For example, on the part of employers in a business a violation of the seventh commandment is often exemplified by business fraud, ignorance of contracts, and the mistreatment of workers through unfair wages and lack of health and retirement benefits. On the part of the employee this injustice and lack of charity is often seen in acts of laziness and all forms of lack of effort in the work environment. The seventh commandment forbids social relationships based solely on economic factors, as opposed to the nature of the human person. It acknowledges that the goods of creation are for the entire human family. The "author, center, and goal of all economic and social life is the human person." The seventh commandment demands the tithing of one's talent and treasure to God.

8. The eighth commandment is a prohibition against bearing false witness against one's neighbor. Lying, duplicity, hypocrisy, boasting, dissimulation (hiding under a false appearance), rash judgment (assuming without reason the moral fault of another), detraction

(disclosing another's faults to someone who did not know them), betrayal of confidences, calumny (character assassination), and slander (a false statement that damages a person's reputation) are all acts contrary to the dignity of persons.

9. The ninth commandment is a prohibition against coveting one's neighbor's wife. It prohibits moral permissiveness, and seeks the purification of the social moral climate. This commandment calls one to live a life of decency, chastity and modesty. It is a call for purity of heart, intention, and vision.

10. The tenth commandment is a call to avoid coveting another's goods. It is a call to avoid greed, envy, and all immoderate desires. It is a call to desire a detachment from all that is contrary to the glory and honor of God. One is called to desire God above all.

Natural Law, Natural Order

The natural law is based on the laws of nature, the natural order of things, and the implications that follow. Catholic moral teaching is based on the natural law. The Ten Commandments are based on the natural law.

Nature has laws--that is why we have science. If these laws are followed, authentic living follows.

Our actions are immoral when--acting in sufficient freedom and according to the guide and dictation of sufficient right reason--our actions are at variance with the natural law, the natural order.

Actions are good and right when they are in conformity with the natural law, the natural order.

Think of a car. Each part of the car has its unique purpose which cannot be used in any other way, without diminishing, damaging or destroying the vehicle. The environment, like a car, is made up of parts that have unique purposes which cannot be used in any other way without it diminishing, damaging, or destroying the environment. Society, like a car, is made up of many parts that have unique purposes which cannot be used in any other way, without diminishing, damaging, or destroying it. We too, like a car, are made up of parts that have unique purposes which cannot be used in any other way, without diminishing, damaging, or destroying our humanness.

If things don't fit or work as they should, or were meant to, or were evolved to, then one must not do such things. If things fit or work as they should, or were meant to, or were evolved to, then one must do such things.

Being in harmony with oneself, others, and the world is the means of living life abundantly and authentically.

A Catholic seeks to be faithful to the natural law, the natural order of "things."

Reflections
How do you see the Commandments as a roadmap to happiness? How do the Commandments serve as an "owner's manual?"

Are the Commandments written in the hearts of every human person? Are they universal truths?

Homework
Catechism of the Catholic Church (CCC)
Numbers 2083-2557

Homework Prayer Exercise—Getting to Know Jesus
Step One
Read the Acts of the Apostles, chapter 1.

Step Two—Selecting a Section
Read the Acts of the Apostles, chapter 1:6-11. Read the footnotes. Collect the facts. What is being said? What is going on?

Step Three
Meditate on the passage. What is God saying to me in this passage from the Bible? Is there something in my life that God wants to talk to me about?

Step Four
Pray to God. Share your feelings and thoughts with him.

Step Five—Taking Action
What do I feel and think God wants me to do? What is he calling me to do?

24

CATHOLIC SPIRITUALITY
(Cf. CCC 2258-2619; 2700-2719; 2725-2745; 2777-2856)

Prayers in General
Prayer as gift

"Prayer is the raising of one's mind and heart to God or the requesting of good things from God" (CCC 2559). Prayer is founded upon humility and a contrite heart (Ps. 130:1; cf. Lk. 18:9-14). One must recognize that one needs help in the endeavor of prayer (Rm. 8:26) and one must recognize that whether we realize it or not, prayer is an encounter between God's longing for us and our longing for him (cf. Jn. 4:10). Prayer is the response of faith to the free promise of salvation and also a response of love for God, who is love itself (cf. Jn. 7:37-39; 19:28; Isa. 12:3; 51:1; Zech. 12:10; 13:1).

Prayer as covenant

When one prays, one prays from the heart, which is the dwelling place where one is, where one lives, where one withdraws to. The heart is the core of our being. The heart is

> our hidden center, beyond the grasp of our reason and of others; only the Spirit of God can fathom the human heart and know it fully. The heart is the place of decision, deeper than our psychic drives. It is the place of truth, where we choose life or death. It is the place of encounter, because as image of God we live in relation; it is the place of covenant.
>
> St. Augustine (cf. CCC 2563)

Prayer is a committed relationship of life and love. It is meant to be an inseparable relationship of encounter between the Creator and his creation.

Prayer as communion

Prayer is a communion between the individual, God, and his body the Church. While one may invoke each person of the Trinity and pray to each person of the Trinity, it is traditionally understood that prayer is directed toward the Father, through the Son, and in the Holy Spirit in a mystical community called the Church, the Church on earth, in purgatory, and in heaven. "In the Holy Spirit, Christian prayer is a communion of love with the Father, not only through Christ, but also *in him...*" (CCC 2615).

The Scriptures are clear on the necessity of interceding on behalf of others (cf. Lk. 16:9; 1 Cor. 12:12, 20f, 12:26; Heb. 12:22f; Rev. 5:8). The apostles often make reference to the need of praying for others and the need of the prayers of others. God intended this so that people of faith could be members of an authentic community where each member depended on the other, where each member cared for the other, where each member could live out the command of love of neighbor.

The Church is a communion of faithful on earth, in purgatory, and in heaven. At the heart of this communion is the reality that relationships built on the foundation of grace are relationships that never end. Whether from earth or from heaven, we pray as a community of faith, as the Church. Prayer is a communion between the individual, God, and his body the Church.

Jesus and prayer

Jesus teaches us to pray and reminds us that he prays for us, in us, and with us. As St. Augustine summarizes:

> He prays for us as our priest, prays in us as our Head, and is prayed to by us as our God. Therefore let us acknowledge our voice in him and his in us.
>
> St. Augustine (CCC 2616)

From the *Sermon on the Mount* one is taught that prayer to the Father requires a conversion of the heart. Reconciliation, love of enemies, prayers for persecutors, attentive prayer, purity of heart, and the seeking of the kingdom are all at the core of a conversion of the heart (cf. Mt. 5:23-24, 44-45; 6:7, 14-15, 21, 25, 33).

This conversion of heart leads to praying in faith, an adherence to God beyond what is limited to feelings and understanding. One in faith can therefore be assured of one's access to the Father and the assurance that if one *seeks* and *knocks* one will receive answers, for Christ is the *door* and the *way* (Mt. 7:7-11, 13-14). One can be confident that whatever is asked for in prayer and in faith will be received (Mk. 11:24). One is reminded that in Jesus "all things are possible to him who believes" (Mk. 9:23; cf. Mt. 21:22).

It is important to remember, however, that an authentic prayer of faith is always one that is embodied by a heart disposed to do the will of the Father. Simply crying out "Lord, Lord..." is of little benefit if the heart is far from the will of God (cf. Mt. 7:21). An authentic prayer of faith embodies the divine plan of God within it (cf. Mt. 9:38; Lk. 10:2; Jn. 4:34). It realizes the importance of struggle and of patience and perseverance (cf. Lk. 18:1-8). Therefore, prayer is inseparable from works.

Mary

Mary's intercessory prayers have a unique role in the plan of salvation. At the Annunciation her prayer opened the way for Christ's conception (cf. Lk. 1:38); at Pentecost her prayer helped form the Church (Acts 1:14). In her *fiat*, she was the perfect disciple, the perfect model of the Church; she was what all are called to be: "Behold I am the servant of the Lord; let it be [done] to me according to your word" (Lk. 1:38).

Mary teaches a person how to pray by her example of humility, love, obedience, faith, and trust. She teaches us "to be wholly God's, because he is wholly ours" (2617).

Expressions of Prayer
Vocal Prayer

Vocal prayer is a form of prayer that lays the groundwork and nourishes all other forms of prayer. As vocal prayer progresses it opens one's being for the higher forms of prayer. Vocal prayer is the initial form of contemplative prayer.

Vocal prayer is the incarnation of a heart's interaction with God. Words bring flesh to prayer. Human nature demands that one's whole body participate in the worship of God--body, soul, and spirit. Prayer is the worship of God with one's whole being (cf. Mt. 11:25-26; Mk. 14:36).

Meditation

For the Carthusian monk, Guigo II, "meditation is the busy application of the mind to seek with the help of one's own reason the knowledge of hidden truth." Meditation in a most profound way moves a person away from unhealthy, *worldly* things.

Meditation is the seeking of the life of God. The mind seeks to search out the mystery of life in meditation. Through Sacred Scripture, Sacred Tradition, spiritual books, sacred icons, liturgical texts and seasons as well as through history and creation one encounters many answers to the mystery of life. One also encounters the path that one must travel.

Meditation makes a person encounter his or her deepest self. The book of life is opened to be explored. In this exploration one asks: "Lord, what do you want me to do?" Meditation helps one to be well grounded in the life of Christ (cf. Mk. 4:4-7; 15-19).

Meditation eventually will transform itself into contemplation, the only means for complete union with God.

Contemplative Prayer

Contemplation is the quest for the one "whom my soul loves" (*Song of Songs* 1:7; cf. 3:1-4). One enters this form of prayer in quiet, poverty, and pureness of faith. One seeks to be offered up to God in this experience; one seeks to be purified and transformed into the image and likeness one was meant to be transformed into; that is, in the image and likeness of Jesus Christ. Contemplation is love welcoming love (cf. Lk. 7:36-50; 19:1-10). It is victory in the total surrendering. In contemplation the "Father strengthens our inner being with power through his Spirit so 'that Christ may dwell in [our] hearts through faith' and we may be 'grounded in love'" (Eph. 3:16-17) (CCC 2714).

Contemplation is the entrance into the sphere of the experience of God which transcends the limits of anything we hear, see, touch, smell, imagine, etc. It is beyond the limits of the internal and external senses. The God who transcends all speaks in silence to the heart of the person engaged in contemplation. He speaks with a presence of such intensity that the senses are incapable of grasping the fullness of this presence.

> The spirit helps us...for we do not know how to pray as we ought; but the Spirit himself makes intercession for us with groanings that cannot be expressed in speech (cf. Rom. 8:26).

Aspects of Prayer

Blessing

Blessing exemplifies the basic movement of prayer. When one prays, one is praying in an ascending order. One prays in the power of the Holy Spirit, through the Son, to the Father. In such a fashion one can be said to be blessing God [making God happy] who is the source of all blessings [happiness] (cf. Eph. 1:3-14; 2 Cor. 1:3-7; 1 Pet. 1:3-9). Because "God blesses, the human heart can in return bless the One who is the source of every blessing" (CCC 2626).

Adoration

Adoration is an act of humility, the doorway to holiness. In an act of adoration a person makes himself or herself aware that he or she is a created being in the presence of an almighty, omniscient Creator (cf. Ps. 95:1-6). Adoration is the realization that one has been saved by a Savior, by the King of all kings. It is the recognition that one has been set free from the slavery of sin to be a child of God (cf. Ps. 24:9-10).

Petition

Through one's petitions to God one is making present, in the most obvious of ways, the reality that one is in a relationship with God. In the act of asking, beseeching, pleading, invoking, entreating, and crying out to God one is showing one's need and love for God (cf. Rm. 15:30; Col. 4:12). A petition is an acknowledgement that one is a sinner in need of a savior. It is an act of turning toward God (cf. Rm. 8:22-24, 26). Prayers of petition require the awareness that one is in need of forgiveness (cf. Lk. 18:13) and that one is in need of the gifts of humility and trust (cf. 1 Jn. 1:7-2:2; 3:22).

Intercessions

An intercessory prayer is a unique form of a prayer of petition. It is closely modeled on Jesus' prayers. While it is true that Jesus is the one intercessor (cf. Rm. 8:34; 1 Jn. 2:1; 1 Tim. 2:5-8; Heb. 7:25), Jesus has granted the gift to all in grace to intercede in him, with him, and through him. A person of faith is a member of a community of love, the Church, the Body, the Bride of Christ (cf. Col. 1:24; 2 Cor. 11:2). As a consequence each member is to help and love the other members. But God demands even more; he calls one to love even those who are outside the boundaries of the mystical Body. One must also pray for persecutors and all enemies of the Gospel (cf. Lk. 6:35).

Thanksgiving

One gives thanks to God for being freed from sin and slavery. One gives thanks for the gift of grace, the gift of eternal life with God. One gives thanks for being made a *new creation* in Christ (cf. 2 Cor. 5:17). Because of the precious gift of immortality, because of all God's precious gifts, every event in one's life, even the most difficult, the most painful, are worthy of thanksgiving. As St. Paul states: "Give thanks in all circumstances; for this is the will of God in Christ Jesus for you" (1 Thess. 5:18). In the mystery that is life, even the most hideous of circumstances can be transformed into a gift. Within the mystery of suffering is the mystery of love, and within the mystery of love is the mystery of suffering.

Praise

When one praises God one is worshipping God for simply being God. One is not focused on God's gifts, his "goodies," but simply on God. One praises God because *HE IS*. It is the prayer of the pure of heart and consequently it is the prayer that embraces all other prayers.

The Battle of Prayer

Prayer is a gift that requires grace. Prayer is always brought about by an act of God. A person's part in the experience of prayer is to respond to this initiative. One must remember that even before one can cry out to God, God is already there initiating that cry.

Prayer is a battle because it is a struggle against the consequences of original sin, concupiscence, and the temptations of the devil. Time constraints, the inability to experience or understand the supernatural, a preoccupation with sensuality, the sense that prayer is an escape rather than an encounter, the sense of discouragement, dryness, wounded pride, sin, and so forth all have an impact on a person's ability to pray. What is required of the person is a response, in grace, to the battle with the armaments of humility, trust, and perseverance (CCC 2726-2728).

The battle in prayer is extremely important for a person's spiritual growth, for the wounds of the battle help one see where one is on this spiritual road. One is able to see if one is closer to victory or defeat by observing one's wounds. For example, distractions in prayer help one to see what one is attached to, which master one serves (cf. Mt. 6:21, 24). Is one vigilant in the battle or has one become lax (cf. Mt. 26:41)? Dryness in prayer can tell one whether one is being asked to walk by faith or if one is being asked to repent and turn back to God; in other words, is the dryness due to progress in holiness or is it due to sinfulness? Does distress help one to trust more or does it lead to despair (cf. Rm. 5:3-5)? Prayers that seem not to be answered can clarify one's motives in prayer: Does one love God as an instrument of selfishness or as a God who deserves love for simply being God?

In humility, trust and perseverance all prayers are heard, yet not all prayers are answered the way one wants them to be answered. The sense of unanswered prayers can often lead to the abandonment of the spiritual life for the self-seeking of heart. Thus, the love-driven gifts of humility and trust are so important for they empower the love-driven gift of perseverance that is essential for any battle (cf. 1 Thess. 5:17; Eph. 5:20; 6:8).

Prayer in General, In Conclusion

Prayer is not the manipulating of God to acquire something that God did not know we needed; quite the contrary, God knows all, including our needs. He knows what we will ask and all the free will decisions we will make in advance. He knows what we need and how it fits within his providence--that sphere of representativeness that is between two extremes, predestination and absolute, undeterred free will.

Why pray if God is all knowing? We pray to show our need, our love, and our dependence upon God, not because God

186

needs this love or dependence, but because we do. We pray because it teaches us about ourselves and our priorities. We pray because it develops our spiritual brain, and thus brings light, happiness, and peace into our life and world.

Atheists often argue against the belief in God because prayers are not provable objectively. The fact is that prayers are always answered, but not necessarily in the manner in which one expects the prayer to be answered. Prayers are answered in such a fashion that one's eternal destiny, one's salvation is always in the forefront. Prayer is always answered with the understanding that this earthly life is but a blink of the eye when compared to eternity. Prayer is always understood from the perspective of the present and future good of the world and with the understanding that all prayers are interconnected—at the level of the individual, the community, and the world.

When we look upon the history of our prayers and desires, we see that our prayers were in fact answered, but most often in ways we did not expect. This is beautifully illustrated in the words of an unknown civil war soldier:

> I asked for strength that I might achieve; I was made weak that I might learn humbly to obey. I asked for health that I might do greater things; I was given infirmity that I might do better things. I asked for riches that I might be happy; I was given poverty that I might be wise. I asked for power that I might have the praise of men; I was given weakness that I might feel the need of God. I asked for all things that I might enjoy life; I was given life that I might enjoy all things. I got nothing that I asked for, but everything that I had hoped for. Almost despite myself, my unspoken prayers were answered; I am, among all men, most richly blessed.

Reflections

How does prayer give you comfort?

What expressions of prayer do you find most appealing?

What aspects of prayer do you feel a need to work on?

Homework
Catechism of the Catholic Church (CCC)
Numbers 2559-2758

Homework Prayer Exercise—Getting to Know Jesus
Step One
Read the Acts of the Apostles, chapter 2.

Step Two—Selecting a Section
Read the Acts of the Apostles, chapter 2:1-13. Read the footnotes. Collect the facts. What is being said? What is going on?

Step Three
Meditate on the passage. What is God saying to me in this passage from the Bible? Is there something in my life that God wants to talk to me about?

Step Four
Pray to God. Share your feelings and thoughts with him.

Step Five—Taking Action
What do I feel and think God wants me to do? What is he calling me to do?

25

THE "OUR FATHER" AND "BEATITUDES"

Our Father, Who art in heaven, hallowed be Thy name; Thy kingdom come; Thy will be done on earth as it is in heaven. Give us this day our daily bread; and forgive us our trespasses as we forgive those who trespass against us; and lead us not into temptation, but deliver us from evil. Amen.

The *Our Father* is a summary of the virtues that Jesus taught us.

The *Our Father* teaches us the path to authentic, genuine humanness: In the *Our Father* Jesus teaches us how to pray, and therefore how to invigorate the spiritual dimension of our nature. Since he experienced all things we experience, except sin, he knows well our needs (cf. Heb. 4:15).

Jesus in the *Our Father* teaches us the summary of the whole Gospel, the summary of what new life in God is all about. In this prayer one is empowered by the Spirit to cry out "abba," "Father" (cf. Jn. 6:63; Gal. 4:6)! In the Lord's Prayer one is brought into the presence of God. In the *Our Father* one enters a prayer of "straightforward simplicity, filial trust, joyous assurance, humble boldness, and certainty of being loved" (cf. Eph. 3:12; Heb. 3:6; 4:16; 10:19; 1 Jn. 2:28; 3:21; 5:14). As a prayer the *Our Father* reveals the Father and reveals one's own innermost being: It enlightens one to the Father and to one's core self.

Our Father
By saying "Our Father" one is saying that one is entering a relationship. He is our God and we are his people (cf. Jn. 1:17; Hos. 2:21-22; 6:1-6). One accepts the reality that one has also

189

entered a relationship that implies not individualism but a sense of communion, of membership. One is a member of the community of faith (cf. Acts 4:32; Jn. 11:52).

Who art in heaven
The phrase "who art in heaven" is not primarily a reference to a *place* because heaven is not a *place* as commonly understood. Heaven is a place in the sense that it is a dimension beyond space and time: Heaven is another dimension of reality. Consequently the phrase, used in the context of this prayer, is primarily a reference to God's majesty and his presence in the hearts of the just. Heaven, "the Father's house, is the true homeland toward which we are heading and to which, already, we belong."

Hallowed be thy name
The phrase "Hallowed be thy name" is a phrase that conjures up the holiness, preciousness, and majesty of God (cf. Ps 8:5; Isa. 6:3). It reminds one that God is worthy of all praise and thanksgiving (cf. Ps 111:9; Lk. 1:49).

Thy Kingdom Come
God's kingdom became present in the first coming and will find its fulfillment in the second coming (cf. Tit. 2:13). As a follower of Christ one is called to help bring about the fulfillment of this kingdom. A person is called upon to help build the kingdom of God here on earth, a kingdom of love.

Thy will be done on earth as it is in heaven
This phrase is an affirmation that
1) all are called to be saved and come to the truth (cf. 1 Tim. 2:3-4; 2 Pet. 3:9; Mt. 18:14).
2) all must love one another (Jn. 13:34; cf. 1 Jn. 3; 4; Lk. 10: 25-37).
3) one must do all things according to God's will (Eph. 1:9-11).

4) all are called to imitate Christ in his obedience and surrendering to the Father's will (Heb. 10:7; Lk. 22:42; Jn. 4:34; 5:30; 6:38; 8:29; Gal. 1:4).

Give us this day our daily bread

This statement is an expression of God's goodness, a goodness that transcends all other goodness. The "Our" reminds one that one is a member of a community, a community built upon the foundation of solidarity. It is a call in trust and in a spirit of surrender to God; it is a call for God to meet the individual and the community's material and spiritual needs. It is a call to responsibility and justice (cf. Lk. 16:19-31; Mt. 25:31-46).

And forgive us our trespasses as we forgive those who trespass against us

Love of God and love of neighbor are one reality. Any true love of God implies the love of neighbor, and any real love of neighbor implies a true love of God. How can one love God if one does not love one's neighbor (cf. 1 Jn. 4:20; Mt. 5: 43-44; 6:14-15; 5:23-24; 18:23-35; Mk. 11:25)? How can an individual ask for God's forgiveness if that individual is unwilling to forgive those whom God loves?

And lead us not into temptation

This petition is a call to be set free from the snares of evil. The spirit of discernment and strength become intrinsic to this petition. The Spirit guides one to determine between temptations, trials and tribulations that are for one's personal growth in the life of God (cf. Lk. 8:13-15; Acts 14:22; Rm. 5:3-5; 2 Tim. 3:12) and those temptations, trials and tribulations that lead to sin and death (cf. Jas. 1:14-15). One discerns the difference between being tempted (which is not sinful and in fact can lead to great spiritual growth) and consenting to temptation. The Spirit helps discern and unmask the lies behind the temptations (cf. Gen. 3:6) and helps one to persevere through them to become strong in God (cf. 1 Cor. 10:13; Rev. 16:15).

But deliver us from evil

This is a petition that asks for protection from evil (cf. Jn. 17:15). Evil seeks to distort God's providential plan and seeks to destroy people in the process under the guise of doing good for them (cf. Jn. 8:44; Rev. 12:9). One finds confidence in this petition in that just as one has been delivered from evil in the past, one will be delivered from the evil in the present and in the future if one perseveres in the spiritual battle.

By praying the *Our Father* we become aware or knowledgeable of ourselves, others, creation, and most especially God.

Jesus taught us the *Our Father*. The *Our Father* brings about and expresses the nature of virtue, and the development of the whole person, body, soul, and spirit.

The Beatitudes (Mt. 5:3-12)

Blessed are the poor in spirit,
  for theirs is the kingdom of heaven.
Blessed are they who mourn,
  for they will be comforted.
Blessed are the meek,
  for they will inherit the land.
Blessed are they who hunger and thirst for righteousness,
  for they will be satisfied.
Blessed are the merciful,
  for they will be shown mercy.
Blessed are the clean of heart,
  for they will see God.
Blessed are the peacemakers,
  for they will be called children of God.
Blessed are they who are persecuted for the sake of righteousness,
    for theirs is the kingdom of heaven.
Blessed are you when they insult you and persecute you and utter every kind of
evil against you [falsely] because of me. Rejoice and be glad, for your
reward will be great in heaven. Thus they persecuted the prophets who were
before you.

Matthew 5: 3-12

192

The beatitudes flow from the gifts of the Spirit and dispose a person to obey these gifts. The beatitudes are reminders that a person cannot be fully human without acknowledging and exploring their spiritual side. Sadly, the spiritual is repressed by too many in this modern world.

The beatitude of being "poor in spirit" promotes confidence in God and complete dependence on God (cf. Is. 61:1; Zep. 2:3). It also engenders a humble predisposition. The beatitude of being "mournful" is that beatitude which fosters recognition of God's consolation and comfort. The beatitude of being "meek," engenders the recognition of one's place in the kingdom of God (cf. Ps. 37:11). The beatitude of "hungering and thirsting for righteousness" promotes conformity to God's will and a willing submission to God's plan of salvation for all. The beatitude of being "merciful" properly orders the virtue of justice in accordance to the *spirit* of the law as opposed to the *letter of the law*. The beatitude of being "pure of heart" is that assurance that God's presence will always be with the pure of heart (cf. Ps. 24:4; 42:3). The beatitude of being a "peacemaker" is one that promotes peace in one's heart and in the hearts of others. It promotes a docile, gentle spirit that is ordered to the providential plan of God. The beatitude that entails being unjustly "persecuted" is that beatitude which empowers one to seek justice at whatever cost, even at the cost to one's life.

The beatitudes express the human person's vocation as a physical and spiritual being. They shed light on a Christian's duties and attitudes. They sustain hope amidst a world of trials and tribulations. They "proclaim the blessings and rewards already secured, however dimly, for Christ's disciples."

The beatitudes express a person's innermost desire, that person's desire for happiness. This desire for happiness has been placed at the very core of the human person in order to draw him or her to God, the source of all happiness.

The beatitudes challenge and confront people. They force people to make virtuous choices regarding their eternal destiny.

Reflections
What is Jesus teaching us with the *Our Father*?

What part of the *Our Father* do you like best?

What are the beatitudes about?

What is your favorite beatitude?

How does living the *Our Father* and the *Beatitudes* make us better people?

Homework
Catechism of the Catholic Church (CCC)
Numbers 1716-1728; 2759-2865

Homework Prayer Exercise—Getting to Know Jesus
Step One
Read the Acts of the Apostles, chapter 9.

Step Two—Selecting a Section
Read the Acts of the Apostles, chapter 9:1-19. Read the footnotes. Collect the facts. What is being said? What is going on?

Step Three
Meditate on the passage. What is God saying to me in this passage from the Bible? Is there something in my life that God wants to talk to me about?

Step Four
Pray to God. Share your feelings and thoughts with him.

Step Five—Taking Action
What do I feel and think God wants me to do? What is he calling me to do?

26

CHRISTIAN HISTORY
(PART ONE)

In the Beginning: Jesus died and the world would never be the same.

The apostles hid in the "upper room" and feared what would happen. Would they be captured? Would they be forgotten? What were they to do? Perhaps they hoped that all would just go away!

Then something happened! In the middle of a crowded Jerusalem, Peter with the other apostles stood up and proclaimed Jesus Christ as Messiah, as Lord and Savior.

What happened between the time in the upper room and the time when the apostles fearlessly proclaimed Jesus Christ as Lord and Savior?

The answer to this mystery empowered the apostles to proclaim the Gospel of Jesus Christ to the world.

James the Great, the son of Zebedee, evangelized Palestine and perhaps Spain. He was decapitated in 43 AD in Jerusalem. Matthias evangelized Palestine, Scythia, and Armenia. On his return to Jerusalem in 51 AD he was stoned to death by a hostile mob. Nathaniel or Bartholomew evangelized Palestine, Asia Minor, Armenia, central India and Iran. He was flayed and crucified in Iran in 57 AD. James the Less, the son of Alphaeus, evangelized Palestine and was stoned to death by a mob in the year 60. Andrew is believed to have evangelized Palestine, Asia Minor, Scythia, and Greece. He was crucified in Patras, Greece in the year 65. Simon bar Jonah, who would forever be known as Peter, the Rock, is believed to have evangelized Palestine, Syria, Asia Minor and Rome. He was crucified upside down during the persecution of the emperor Nero on Vatican Hill in the year 67 AD. Thomas evangelized Palestine, Osroene, Armenia, Egypt, and India. His great efforts in India earned him the title of "apostle to the Indians." He was stabbed to death in the midst of a Hindu mob in Burma in 72 AD. Simon the Zealot evangelized Palestine, Egypt, North Africa, Britain, and Iran and Jude evangelized Palestine, Osroene, Armenia, and Iran. While Simon and Jude were in Iran, they were attacked by a mob led by pagan magi and were killed: Simon being mutilated and sawed to pieces, and Jude being impaled by a spear. Both died in 79 AD. Matthew evangelized Palestine, Egypt, Ethiopia, and Iran. Philip evangelized Palestine, North Africa, and Asia Minor. He was crucified upside down in 87. It is unknown how Matthew died: some accounts have him as martyred and others have him as dying of natural causes in 90 AD. The apostle John was the last to die after evangelizing Palestine and Asia Minor. He died in exile in the year 100. His death marked the end of the apostolic age.

Paul, the Apostle to the Gentiles: Paul is the Church's greatest evangelist and missionary apostle. Paul was a tent maker, but more importantly, an educated theologian. The majority of the New Testament is the work of this inspired author.

Paul was beheaded in Rome during the persecution of Nero in 64 AD on the Ostian Way.

The Ten Roman Persecutions
The First General Persecution (64): The emperor Nero persecuted Christians after the burning of Rome. He arrested, tortured, and killed many. The apostles Peter and Paul were put to death during his reign of terror.

The Second General Persecution (95-100): The emperor Domitian sought to purge the Empire of Christians. Pope Clement and the apostle John would die during this persecution.

The Third General Persecution (112-138): Christians were persecuted under the reigns of the emperors Trajan and Hadrian for refusing to worship the pagan gods. The edicts of Nero and Domitian were reinstituted and the persecution of Christians resumed. St. Ignatius of Antioch and St. Polycarp, both disciples of the apostle John, were martyred during this persecution.

The Fourth General Persecution (161): The persecution began under the emperor Marcus Aurelius who sought to blame a series of natural disasters on the Christians. St. Cecilia and St. Justin were martyred under this particularly vicious purge.

The Fifth General Persecution (202): An imperial edict by Emperor Septimius Severus sought to establish a single religion for the entire empire, the pagan religion. Among its victims are Sts. Perpetua, Felicity and Irenaeus.

The Sixth General Persecution (235): The Emperor Maximin of Thrace had a hatred of all religions and persecuted all, particularly Christians. Popes Pontian and Antherus died under his persecution.

The Seventh General Persecution (249-251): Emperor Decius sought to wipe out Christianity from the Empire. Many abandoned the faith under this persecution.

The Eighth General Persecution (257-260): The Emperor Valerian sought to repress Christianity by exiling and killing a large amount of Christians, including Sts. Cyprian, Lawrence, Agnes of Rome, and Pope Sixtus II.

The Ninth General Persecution (275): The Emperor Aurelian sought to establish the worship of one god, the sun god Mithra. With his assassination in 275, the persecutions ended.

The Tenth General Persecution (303): Emperor Diocletian was the last great persecutor of Christians. His reign of terror lasted ten years and would be known for its extreme violence.

Constantine, the Eastern Emperors, and Charlemagne
Constantine freed the Catholic Church from persecution with the Edict of Milan in 313 AD. Despite his kindness towards Catholics, Constantine would be baptized on his deathbed into a heretical sect of Christianity known as Arianism—baptized by the Arian bishop Eusebius of Nicomedia

The successors of Constantine, in Constantinople, would not be so kind to Catholics, particularly the eastern emperors, who often favored Arianism over Catholicism.

The eastern emperors, residing and ruling from Constantinople, modern day Turkey, would habitually oppose the popes doctrinally and politically for many centuries until the rise of the Frankish kings, particularly the Holy Roman Emperor Charlemagne (King of parts of modern day Italy, France, and Germany).

Charlemagne would become the great protector and promoter of the popes and the Roman rite of Catholicism. Charlemagne would free the Church and the popes from the yoke of Constantinople.

Church Councils
Jerusalem (ca. 50) affirmed the role of Gentiles in the Church.

Nicaea (325) condemned the heresy of Arianism and affirmed that the Son was consubstantial (one with) the Father. The heresy of Arianism argued that the Son was created and not co-eternal with the Father. Arianism therefore denied the reality of the Trinity.

Constantinople I (381) condemned the heresy of Macedonianism which argued for a hierarchy in the Trinity instead of an equality. The council declared that the Holy Spirit was consubstantial (one with) the Father and the Son.

Councils of Hippo (393), Carthage III (397), and Carthage IV (419): A list of books compiled by Pope Damasus I are accepted to become what we now call the Bible.

Ephesus (431) condemned Nestorianism and Pelagianism. The heresy of Nestorianism denied the title "Mother of God" thus separating Christ's human nature from his divine nature; thereby making Christ essentially two distinct Persons. Pelagianism held essentially five key heretical points: 1) Adam would have died whether he sinned or not; 2) The sin of Adam injured only himself and was not passed on to further generations; 3) Newborn children are not affected or wounded by *original sin.* 4) Christ's salvific event was not absolutely necessary for salvation, since sinless people existed prior to Christ; 5) One could work oneself into heaven by means of one's human efforts alone.

In response, the council affirmed the reality that the Son of God was the second Person of the Trinity and that he had two natures, one human, one divine—without change, confusion, separation or division between the natures. It thus affirmed the title of Mary as the "Theotokos" "God-bearer," the "Mother of God." Against Pelagianism the Church affirmed the necessity of Christ's life, death, and resurrection for our salvation and the wiping away of *original sin.* It affirmed that grace was necessary for salvation and that one could not earn or work oneself into heaven without the aid of grace. It affirmed that *original sin* is passed down to the entire human race and is cleansed in baptism.

Chalcedon (451) condemned Monophysitism. Monophysitism denied Christ's two natures (divine and human) and argued for a composite nature. The council reaffirmed the teaching that the Son of God was one Person with two natures, without change, confusion, separation or division between the natures. Jesus was fully human, fully divine. He was God and man.

Constantinople II (553) re-condemned the Nestorian heresy.

Constantinople III (680) condemned Monothelitism which argued that Christ had only one will. Constantinople affirmed that Jesus had two wills, a human will and a divine will. His human will was in perfect conformity with his divine will.

Nicaea II (787) condemned Iconoclasm which forbade the use of images as prayer aids. Nicaea affirmed the use of images for inspiring prayer. The incarnation, an icon of God, made images of the invisible God visible and thus representable.

Lateran I (1123) issued decrees banning simony (the buying and selling of something spiritual, such as religious offices) and lay investiture (the appointing of bishops by lay persons, as opposed to by the Church's clergy). It also affirmed the gift of celibacy in the priesthood.

Lateran II (1139) ended the papal schism between Innocent II and Anacletus II. Anacletus was declared an anti-pope. Clerical celibacy was also reaffirmed and usury—the taking of interest for a loan--was prohibited.

Lateran III (1179) condemned the Cathari who renounced baptism and marriage.

Lateran IV (1215) condemned the Albigenses/Cathars and Waldenses. Albigensianism rejected the sacraments and Church authority. The Waldenses rejected the sacraments, purgatory, the communion of saints and Church authority. The council reaffirmed its always held beliefs in these teachings.

Lyons I (1245) deposed Frederick II and planned a crusade to free the Holy Land.

Lyons II (1274) reunited the Church with the Orthodox churches and enacted reforms in discipline regarding the clergy.

Vienne (1311-1312) enacted reforms in the Church and abolished the Knights Templars.

Constance (1414-1418) ended the papal schism and condemned the theology of John Huss.

Basle, Ferrara, Florence (1431-1445) reunited the Church with the Orthodox churches and again enacted disciplinary reforms.

Lateran V (1512-1517) dealt with the neo-Aristotelian influences in the Church and also enacted disciplinary reforms for the clergy.

The Council of Trent (1545-1563) affirmed what Protestantism denied. It reminded the Protestants of the beliefs that were always held from the beginning of the Church. It affirmed that the deposit of faith was found in Sacred Scripture and Sacred Tradition—and needed the Magisterium for authentic interpretation. It affirmed the reality of the seven sacraments. The doctrine of Transubstantiation was reiterated; that is, that bread and wine, once consecrated, become the body, blood, soul, and divinity of Christ. It declared that justification is by faith, but not by faith alone: works are necessary. It rejected the negative view held by Protestants regarding human nature. Protestants believed that *original sin* "destroyed" human nature; The Catholic Church would reassert the faith and declare that *original sin* "wounded" but did not destroy human nature. The Catholic Church would reassert the reality of free will and the reality of providence--early Protestantism believed in absolute predestination and the lack of free will; that is, some people were predestined to heaven and some to hell.

Vatican I (1869-1870) clarified and reaffirmed the always held teaching of papal primacy in honor, jurisdiction, and infallibility.

Vatican II (1962-1965) was a pastoral council that sought "renewal, modernization, and ecumenism." Vatican II also reasserted the faith of 2000 years of Catholicism.

The Crusades (and what led up to them)

In the year 610 Mohammed, a wealthy merchant of Mecca in Arabia had what he argued was a vision of what he was to become--the great prophet foretold by Moses.

Thus arose the beginnings of Islam. Mohammed, in his attempt to convert his home, Mecca, would be driven out to Medina. He would conquer Medina and impose Islam upon the inhabitants. In 630 he would return to capture Mecca. By the time of his death in 632 much of Arabia had been conquered.

Under the Caliphs, his successors, Islam would conquer Syria, Armenia, Palestine, Cyprus, Egypt, and North Africa by the year 711.

In 732, an attempt to conquer Gaul (France) was thwarted by Charles Martel at the Battle of Poitiers. Eighth century France would experience Muslim incursions into Aquitaine, Burgundy, Bordeaux, Autun, and Toulouse. In 734 Avignon was captured, Lyons sacked in 743, and Marseilles plundered in 838. In 889 Tolon would fall to Islamic forces. In 1020 Narbonne was sacked.

By the year 800 Italy would come under attack. In 800 Ponza and Ischia were plundered. Civitavecchia, the port of Rome, was sacked in 813. In 827 Syracuse was invaded. In 831 Palermo was conquered. In 837 Naples was attacked. Messina was captured in 842. In 846 Taranto and Bari fell. In 846

Muslims sacked Rome and St. Peter's Basilica, forcing Pope Sergius II to flee the Vatican. In 849 Enna was conquered. Malta and Anzio fell in 871, Capua and Calabria in 872. In 879 Pope John VIII was forced to pay tribute or a tax of 25,000 *mancuses* a year to Aghlabid Muslims. In 900 Catania was captured. In 934 Genoa was attacked. By 965 all of Sicily was in Muslim control. In 1005 Pisa was sacked. In 1010 Cosenza was attacked. And in 1015 Sardinia fell.

Muslims made incursions into Spain and Portugal between 711 and 718. Spain, save for small areas in the Northwest, came under Islamic control. A Muslim presence would remain till 1492.

In Greece, Crete would be invaded in 820. In 902 Demetrias was sacked and destroyed. In 904 Thessalonica would fall.

In 1009 the Church of the Holy Sepulcher, the site where Jesus was crucified, was destroyed and pilgrims were massacred.

In 1067, a group of approximately 6000 German pilgrims were attacked, leaving two-thirds of their number dead.

The eleventh century saw the Seljuk Turks or Tartars establish the caliphate of Bagdad and conquer most of Asia Minor. In 1071, the Seljuk Turks made safe pilgrimages to Jerusalem impossible.

It is under these conditions that Pope Urban II called for the First Crusade in 1095 to free the Holy Land from the hands of Islamic forces. Englishmen, Frenchmen, Italians and Germans became the first crusaders. The Crusaders would take possession of Jerusalem in 1099.

The Second Crusade, headed by Conrad III of Germany and Louis VII of France, took place in 1147. Lack of discipline, and the lack of unity among the leaders, led to its failure. The Islamic threat to the West would be renewed after this failure.

The Third Crusade took place in 1190 and was led by Frederick Barbarossa of Germany, Philip Augustus of France and Richard the Lionhearted of England. The Crusade was plagued by difficulties and abuses. Frederick Barbarossa drowned; 100,000 disillusioned Germans returned home to Germany. Philip of France found it impossible to campaign with Richard the Lionhearted of England, and thus returned to France. Despite this, Richard was able to gain control of the city of Jaffa and to win entry into Jerusalem for Christian pilgrims.

The Fourth Crusade began in 1212 and ended in an ignoble and moral disaster. The original intention of protecting the Christians in Constantinople from Islamic conquest, resulted in the siege of Constantinople, its plundering, and the dividing of the spoils between the leaders of the Crusade and Venetian merchants.

The Fifth Crusade from 1217-1221 was led by King Andrew II of Hungary and John of Brienne. The crusaders captured Damietta at the mouth of the Nile, only to lose it again. The Crusade was a failure.

The Sixth Crusade in 1248 was led by St. Louis IX, the King of France. St. Louis captured Damietta but was himself taken captive. He was released for a ransom and the return of Damietta to the Muslims.

The Seventh Crusade was led by St. Louis IX, King Edward I and Charles of Anjou in 1270. Saint Louis died of fever at Tunis. Charles of Anjou negotiated a treaty, and Edward returned to England after a few minor victories.

And finally, at the Battle of Lepanto, the Ottoman Empire's attempt to conquer Europe and extinguish Christianity and Western Civilization was thwarted in 1571 by a Holy League of maritime nations of southern Europe led by Pope Pius V.

The word "crusade" would eventually be used for every Christian-Muslim conflict (i.e., Vienna, Hungary, the Balkans, etc.).

The Crusades were a response to unprovoked Muslim aggressions against Christian states.

The Crusades, as with any human endeavor, came with abuses. Competing commanders, different agendas, disorganization, and the desire for revenge caused many to lose sight of the purpose of the Crusades. Looting, the killing of innocent Jews and Muslims took place, but never under the sanction of the popes or the Catholic Church, and in no way to the extent that anti-Catholic extremists would like people to believe.

Modern scholarship is correcting many of the embellishments regarding the atrocities associated with the Crusades.

The Crusades were not colonialist or commercial endeavors, nor were they intended to force Christianity upon Muslims and Jews. The goal was the defense of Europe, the protection of Christians in the East, and the recovery of the Holy Land for Christendom. Did abuses take place? There has never been a war in the history of the world where abuses did not take place!

It is estimated that anywhere from 300,000 to 1 million people were killed during the approximately six centuries of Crusades, most of which were combatants. In the modern era, the six years of World War II (1939-1945) killed approximately 30 million civilians and 30 million combatants.

It can be argued that western civilization, despite all its problems, flaws, and over-secularization, would not exist as the shining light of the world if it were not for the Crusades.

The Inquisitions

The Inquisitions were instituted by the Church and civil authorities to protect the Church and the State from beliefs detrimental to the common good. They were law courts that sought to balance the good of the individual with the good of society in general. As with every human endeavor, abuses took place, but overall, the process was just—contrary to modern myths.

The Medieval Inquisition operated from 1184-1500 and executed 2000 individuals. The Spanish Inquisition operated from 1481-1834 and had 3,230 executions. The Portuguese

Inquisition operated from 1540-1794 and executed 1,175 criminals.

The total number of death sentences handed down by the inquisitions, over a 700 year period of time, is 6,405—this averages to 9 people a year being executed for crimes against the Church and the State. To put this statistic in perspective, the United States executed 25 criminals in 2014.

As with many things, people often seek to misrepresent the truth for an agenda, and sadly this becomes popularized in the culture. As with the Crusades, modern scholarship has brought and continues to bring a new perspective into our understanding of the Inquisitions.

Secularism's Threat to Christianity

The Church will always been persecuted for it will always be a source of contradiction in a world that is always tempted to abandon, deny, or manipulate God.

The French Revolution—with its atheist "cult of reason"-- forced 20,000 priests to resign under the threat of death or imprisonment. Thirty thousand priests were forced to leave France and those who refused were executed by guillotine or deportation to French Guiana. France's 40,000 churches were either closed, sold, destroyed, or converted for secular uses.

Under Germany's Secular-Atheist Liberal Movement of 1871-1878, half of the Prussian bishops were imprisoned or exiled, a quarter of the parishes lost their priests, half of the monks and nuns were exiled or fled persecution, a third of the monasteries and convents were closed, and 1800 parish priests were imprisoned or exiled.

Hitler, an admirer of the atheists Nietzsche and Schopenhauer, abolished religious services in schools, confiscated Church property, circulated anti-religious and anti-Christian material to his soldiers, and closed theological institutions. Church schools were closed, crucifixes and crosses were removed from schools, Christian presses were shut down, and Christian welfare organizations were banned. Thousands of Christian lay persons and clergymen and nuns were arrested and sent to Nazi concentration camps. Over 300 monasteries and institutions were confiscated by the SS. More than 2,600 priests were killed in Nazi concentration camps. The Dachau Concentration Camp had one barrack dedicated solely for priests.

The militant atheistic Soviet Union confiscated churches and persecuted Christians. Leon Trotsky's regime killed twenty-eight bishops and 1,200 priests. Lenin killed at least 40,000 priests. Between 1917 and 1969 the Soviets destroyed 41,000 of 48,000 churches. Before the communist revolution there were 66,140 priests. On the eve of WWII there were only 6,376.

Mao's atheist China equals in terms of carnage that of the Soviet Union.

The Spanish (atheist) Red Terror of 1936 killed 6,832 priests, 2,265 members of Catholic religious institutes, and 283 nuns. Between 1930 and 1936 the Jesuit religious order was dissolved, Church property was confiscated, religion was prohibited from being taught, and 58 churches were burned to the ground.

Mexico's atheist reign of terror led by the "Red Shirts" and the Radical Socialist Party led between 1926 and 1934 to the expulsion and assassination of over 4,000 priests. In 1926 there were approximately 4,500 priests in Mexico; in 1934 there were only 334.

From 1917 to 2007 approximately 148 million people were killed by atheist run countries. In fact, atheistic states have a 58 percent greater chance of mass murdering their populations than any other group.

The Nobel Prize winner Aleksandr Solzhenitsyn wrote of atheistic communism: *"If I were asked today to formulate as concisely as possible the main cause of the ruinous revolution that swallowed up some 60 million of our people, I could not put it more accurately than to repeat: 'Men have forgotten God; that's why all this has happened.'"*

When one examines the *Encyclopedia of Wars* by Charles Philips one sees that of all the wars in recorded history, only 123 of them can be attributed to religion. That is seven percent of all the wars in history. If we eliminated Islam from the mix, war in the name of religion would account for only three percent of all wars.

Reflections
How do you see God working in history?

How do you see the abuse of one's freedom causing problems in history?

27

CHRISTIAN HISTORY
(PART TWO)

Western civilization, as we know it, owes, it can be argued, its existence to the Catholic Church.

The Role of Monks

The monks and their monasteries were responsible for fostering a common language (Latin), for protecting, copying, and preserving ancient texts, for developing and elevating astronomy, art, music, arithmetic, geometry, logic, grammar, and rhetoric to heights never before achieved. They developed a common script with letters, punctuation, spaces, and paragraphs. Through Cathedral Schools they preserved and reproduced for all generations the works of Aristotle, Cicero, Seneca, Lucan, Pliny, Statius, Trogas, Pompeius, Virgil, Horace, Martial, Suetonius, Plato, Ovid, etc. Upon the request of Pope Damasus I, they compiled a book which would eventually be known as the Bible.

With over 37,000 monasteries, the monks, known as the *agriculturists of Europe*, saved and perfected the art of agriculture and laid the foundation for industry. They transformed much of Europe, such as modern day Germany, from a forest into a country, while at the same time planting and conserving trees in what we would now call *preserves*. The monks were the first environmentalists.

The monks introduced crops, developed new production methods (such as complicated irrigation systems), raised better producing bees, produced better fruits and vegetables, invented champagne, perfected the brewing of beer and the making of cheese. They reared cattle and horses, developed the corn trade, managed and perfected wine through the vineyards, and even developed salmon fisheries.

The monks became the great technical advisors to the west, and became rightly the fathers of what would eventually become the Industrial Revolution. They were the leading iron producers, and the leading miners of salt, lead, iron, and marble. They were masters of glasswork and master clock workers. They were among the first to use the byproducts of their iron production as fertilizer for crops.

The monks would become the educators of Europe by opening schools for all who desired an education, no matter what their economic or social status was. The world's first comprehensive school system for the populace was created by the monks. Individual monasteries became known for their specialties. St. Benignus of Dijon was known for its education in medicine, the monks of St. Gall were known for their painting and engraving. The German monasteries were known for their work in teaching Greek, Hebrew and Arabic. Others schools were known for astronomy, philosophy, law, rhetoric, mathematics, geometry, metallurgy, agriculture, navigation, food production, landscaping and preservation.

Some of the greatest artists in world history were Catholic.

Church and Science

When we look to one religious order, the Jesuits, whose existence is less than five hundred years old, we find the following: When examining the history of science between 900 BC and 1800 AD, we are amazed to find that five percent of history's greatest mathematicians are recognized as Jesuit priests—this is particularly impressive when you consider that the Jesuit order did not exist until the sixteenth century. Thirty-five craters on the moon are named after Jesuit scientists.

When we look at the great founders of disciplines in science we find the following: Roger Bacon, a Franciscan, and Bishop Grosseteste are often referred to as the forerunners of the modern scientific method. The priest Roger Boscovich is often referred to as the father and forerunner of atomic physics, the father of modern atomism. The priest Athanasius Kircher was a master chemist who debunked alchemy and astrology and laid the foundation of Egyptology. Kircher made the interpreting of the Rosetta stone possible. The priest Nicolas Zucchi invented the reflecting telescope. Jean Buridan, the Catholic professor at the Sorbonne, laid the foundation for much of Newton's work, particularly his first law. The priest Nicolaus Steno is acknowledged as a pioneer in modern geology and is considered the father of stratigraphy. The monk Gregor Mendel became the father of genetics and the laws of inheritance. The Abbot Richard of Wallingford is known for being among the greatest pioneers of Western trigonometry. The priest Giambattista Riccioli laid the foundation and principles that would be responsible for all of modern astronomy. The Belgian priest, astronomer, and professor of physics, Monsignor Georges Henri Joseph Édouard Lemaître was the first to derive what is now known as the Hubble constant. He is also the originator of what is now called the *big bang* theory for the origin of the universe. The paleontologist, geologist, philosopher and Jesuit priest Pierre Teilhard de Chardin was part of the team that discovered Peking Man.

Antoine Laurent Lavoisier is associated with the *revolution in chemistry*, Erwin Schrodinger with wave mechanics, Blaise Pascal for his theory of probability and the mechanical adding machine, Enrico Fermi with atomic physics, Marcello Malpighi with microscopic anatomy, and Alexander Fleming with penicillin.

The list of Catholic brilliance in the sciences is exhaustive! The Catholic Church is rightly acknowledged by historians of science as the *father of modern science*.

Church in General

The Catholic Church invented the university, and university system, for those who desired an education, whether wealthy or poor, whether high class or low class. All were offered an education, if they so desired one. Schools dedicated to preserving and cultivating knowledge were opened throughout Europe by the Church. The university system was made up of professors that taught classes from prepared texts, used the Socratic or dialectical method, and ultimately conferred degrees—Bachelor of Art's and Master's degrees.

Under the protection of the popes, the greatest promoters of education the world has ever seen, universities taught civil and canon law, art, philosophy, theology, ethics, geometry, logic, and many other subjects.

No institution or group has done more for the education of peoples than the popes and the Catholic Church. No institution that has ever existed has done more for the advancement, preservation, and cultivation of knowledge than the Catholic Church.

The Catholic Church would be responsible for the spread of knowledge by the creation and distribution of massive encyclopedias of knowledge. The Church would spread this scientific knowledge worldwide through its missionaries.

Western civilization owes its sense of international law and civil law to the Church's legacy. The priest Francisco de Vitoria is often referred to as the father of modern international law. In his work on the mistreatment of natives by the Spanish in the *new world* Francisco affirmed the belief that there are innate natural laws that make all people equally free—whether baptized or not—equally having the right to life and liberty, property and culture. Vitoria would be responsible for laying down what we now call the *law of nations*, laws among nations in peacetime and war.

The foundations of modern civil law are often attributed to the monk Gratian as a consequence of his work *Concordance of Discordant Canons* (ca. 1140). Scholars see in canon law the first systematic collection of law and its philosophical implications. The pagan principles of *blood duels*, *trial by battle*, and *trial by fire and water* were abolished.

Taking the best of the ancient world and reformulating it within the concept of the person as the image of God, the Church would elevate law to unheard of standards. Natural rights and universal moral laws and claims based on the natural order would become the norm for all nations under Catholic tutelage. A violation of the law was seen as a violation of the natural moral order, a violation to the intended harmony assumed between persons, and persons and creation.

The Church affirmed the right to property, self-defense, and equal protection under the law. Trials were to be rational, systematic procedures that not only meted out justice, but also took into account mitigating circumstances (such as insanity, duress)—a revolution for its time.

Way before Adam Smith, the foundations for modern economic systems or what has become known as *scientific economics* were laid down by the Catholic Church. Abbot Etienne Bonnot de Condillac, the abbot Robert Jacques Turgot, and Francois Quesnay are often referred to as the *founders of the economic sciences*. Nicolas Oresme is considered the founding father of monetary economics; he would lay the foundation for what would evolve into Gershan's law. Cardinal Cajetan would become known as the founder of the *expectation theory* in economics. Pierre de Jean Olivi, a Franciscan clergyman, would become known as the founder of the *value theory of economics*. The abbot Ferdinando Galiani would be instrumental in laying the foundations for the idea that utility and scarcity are determinants to price.

The Catholic Church revolutionized the world by bringing to it a charitable spirit. The Catholic Church is the world's largest systematic, gratuitous, empathetic, merciful, charitable organization that has ever existed. Basing itself on the sacredness of human life, the uniqueness of the individual, and a preferential option for the poor, the elderly, the widowed, and the ill, the Church would revolutionize the world. They would abolish the pagan and barbarian practices of infanticide, abortion, euthanasia, and gladiatorial games.

The early Church was known for providing shelter for travelers and the homeless, for providing clothing and food for the poor, and for establishing hospices for the dying. The Church provided for the first systematic, gratuitous, institutionalized care of widows and orphans. During times of plagues, Catholics were renowned for staying and risking their lives burying the dead and caring for the ill.

The Catholic Church invented hospitals. The modern system, where institutions of care are staffed by doctors and nurses, is a gift of Catholicism to the world. Doctors diagnosed illnesses and prescribed remedies. By the fourth century every major city in Europe had a hospital.

The Church would elevate the status of women to unheard of levels. No institution in the records of history has done more for women than the Catholic Church. It is the Church that gave women equal protection and status in marriage— holding men equally responsible and punishable for adultery and fornication. Women became the founders and abbesses of self-governing religious orders and communities. Pope Benedict XIV promoted the first two women professors in western history to professorships: the physicist Laura Bassi and the mathematician Maria Gaetana Agnesi. Women religious built and ran their own schools, convents, colleges, hospitals, hospices, and orphanages. The American Church, in all its dimensions, is the product of religious women! The Church has produced more famous women than any other institution. The list of canonized women saints alone—at least 5,000--is a mark of this truth.

Pope John Paul II is rightly acknowledged along with Ronald Reagan as being responsible for the fall of the Soviet Union. Pope Pius V saved Europe at the battle of Lepanto from Islamic conquest.

The Catholic Church is rightly acknowledged as the *father of modern science and the father of the best in the modern world.*

The Church is made up of humans, not walking gods. The Church has a long legacy of sin, but the fact remains: *No institution in world history, it can be argued, has done more for the advancement of human beings than the Catholic Church!*

For an in-depth study of Catholicism's influence on the west I highly recommend, Thomas Woods, *How the Catholic Church Built Western Civilization.* Washington: Regnery, 2005. I am greatly indebted to his magnificent research.

Reflections
How do you see God working in history?

How do you see the abuse of one's freedom causing problems in history?

APPENDIX 1
RITE OF CHRISTIAN INITIATION OF ADULTS

Rite of Christian Initiation of Adults
Process of Formation

Period of Evangelization and Pre-catechumenate
This is a time, of no fixed duration or structure, for inquiry and introduction to Gospel values, an opportunity for the beginnings of faith.

First Step: Acceptance into the Order of Catechumens
This is the liturgical rite, usually celebrated on some annual date or dates, marking the beginning of the Catechumenate proper, as the candidates express and the Church accepts their intention to respond to God's call to follow the way of Christ.

Period of the Catechumenate
This is the time, in duration corresponding to the progress of the individual, for the nurturing and growth of the catechumen's faith and conversion to God; celebrations of the word and prayers of... [protection] and blessing are meant to assist the process.

Second Step: Election or Enrollment of Names
This is the liturgical rite, usually celebrated on the First Sunday of Lent, by which the Church formally ratifies the catechumen's readiness for the sacraments of initiation and the catechumens, now the elect, express the will to receive these sacraments.

Period of Purification and Enlightenment
This is the time immediately preceding the elects' initiation, usually the Lenten season preceding the celebration of this initiation at the Easter Vigil; it is a time of reflection, intensely centered on conversion, marked by celebration of the scrutinies and presentations and of the presentation rites on Holy Saturday.

Third Step: Celebration of the Sacraments of Initiation
This is the liturgical rite, usually integrated into the Easter Vigil, by which the elect are initiated through baptism, confirmation, and the Eucharist.

Period of Postbaptismal Catechesis or Mystagogy
This is the time, usually the Easter season, following the celebration of initiation, during which the newly initiated experience being fully a part of the Christian community by means of pertinent catechesis and particularly by participation with all the faithful in the Sunday Eucharistic celebration.

Rite of Christian Initiation of Adults, USCCB

THOSE WHO MAY ALSO BE BROUGHT INTO FULL INITIATION DURING THE EASTER VIGIL

[Being initiated into the fullness of the Catholic faith also takes into account those who have already been baptized in another Christian community. They receive at the Easter Vigil the sacraments of Eucharist and Confirmation. And Catholics who have not completed their sacraments of Initiation, can do so at the Easter Vigil.]

The *Period of the Catechumenate* begins after the *Rite of Acceptance*. Catechumens and candidates are encouraged to attend Sunday Mass and reflect upon the Liturgy of the Word. Journaling one's insights from the Word and Homily is highly recommended. Sharing after Mass is also highly recommended.

During the *Period of the Catechumenate* prayers for protection from evil (RCIA, #94 A-K) are recited, as well as prayers of blessings (RCIA, #97, A-I). A priest or deacon can also choose to perform the *Rite of Anointing of the Catechumens* with the *oil of catechumens* (RCIA #98-102, A-B)

SCRUTINIES

First Scrutiny (Third Sunday of Lent)
Rite of Christian Initiation of Adults, #150f.

The Presentation of the Creed
Rite of Christian Initiation of Adults, #157f.

Second Scrutiny (Fourth Sunday of Lent)
Rite of Christian Initiation of Adults, #164f.

Presentation of the Lord's Prayer
Rite of Christian Initiation of Adults, #178f.

Third Scrutiny (Fifth Sunday of Lent)
Rite of Christian Initiation of Adults, #171f.

MYSTAGOGY

This is a time for sharing one's experience of the Easter Vigil.
The reviewing of parish ministries within your parish community is highly recommended.

A representative from each ministry, or a delegate to explain each ministry within your faith community, can be assigned to give a presentation during the period of mystagogy.

APPENDIX 2
FOUNDERS OF PROTESTANT DENOMINATIONS

Who's your founder?

> The blessed apostle Paul teaches us that the Church is one, for it has 'one body, one spirit, one hope, one faith, one baptism, and one God.' Furthermore, it is on Peter that Jesus built his Church, and to him he gives the command to feed the sheep; and although he assigns like power to all the apostles, yet he founded a single chair, and he established by his own authority a source and an intrinsic reason for that unity. Indeed, the others were that also which Peter was; but a primacy is given to Peter, whereby it is made clear that there is but one Church and one Chair—the Chair of Peter. So too, all are shepherds, and the flock is shown to be one, fed by all the apostles in single-minded accord. If someone does not hold fast to this unity of Peter, can he imagine that he still holds the faith? If he deserts the chair of Peter upon whom the Church was built, can he still be confident that he is in the Church?
>
> Cyprian of Carthage (ca. 251)
> De Catholicae Ecclesiae Unitate, 2-7

If we want to find the true Christian faith--in all its fullness-- we need to look at its foundation. Depending on what statistics we look at there are as much as 30,000 groups, cults, and denominations each claiming to have the authentic Christian faith.

Who is right? By looking at the founders of these groups we can come up with some key insights. For the purpose of this work, we will look at the founders of the main Christian and pseudo-Christian ecclesiastical communities in the United States and Europe.

All quality historians and all quality history books, whether Catholic or secular, recognize Jesus as founding the Catholic Church (ca. 33 AD).

Now let us look at some of the Protestant and pseudo-Christian ecclesiastical communities. Remember, there was no such thing as a Protestant Church until the sixteenth century;

Jesus can never be claimed as the founder of any Protestant denomination. Let us look at some of their founders:

Denomination	Founder
Lutherans	Martin Luther (ca. 1517)
Anabaptists	Nicholas Storch/ Thomas Munzer (ca. 1521)
Swiss Reformed	Ulrich Zwingli (ca. 1522)
Hutterites	Jacob Hutter (ca. 1528)
Anglicans	Henry VIII (ca. 1534)
Calvinists	John Calvin (ca. 1536)
Familists	Hendrik Niclaes (ca. 1540)
Unitarians	Michael Servetus (ca. 1553)/ Joseph Priestly (ca. 1785)
Presbyterians	Calvin/ John Knox (ca. 1560)
Arminianism	Jacobus Arminius (ca. 1560-1609
Puritans	T. Cartwright (ca. 1570)
Congregationalists	Robert Brown (ca. 1582)
Baptists	John Smyth (ca. 1609)
Dutch Reformed	Michaelis Jones (ca. 1628)
Quakers	George Fox (ca. 1650)
Mennonites	Menno Simons (ca. 1653)
Cameronians	Richard Cameron (ca. 1681)
Pietism	Philip Jacob Spener (1675)
Amish	Jakob Amman (ca. 1693)
Church of the Brethren	Alexander Mack (ca. 1708)
Moravians	Count Zinzendorf (ca. 1727)
Calvinistic Methodist	Howell Harris (ca. 1735)
American Dutch Reformed	Theodore Frelinghuysen (ca. 1737)
Seceders	Ebenezer Erskine (ca. 1740)
Shakers	Ann Lee (ca. 1741)
Methodists	John Wesley (ca. 1744)
Universalists	John Murray (ca. 1779)
Episcopalians	Samuel Seabury (ca. 1784)
African Methodist Episcopal Zion	Richard Allen (ca. 1787)
Unitarians	Joseph Priestley (ca. 1794)
Harmony Society Church	George Rapp (ca. 1803)
Mormons	Joseph Smith (ca. 1829)
Disciples of Christ	Barton W. Stone/ Alexander Campbell (ca. 1832)

Seventh Day Adventist	William Miller (ca. 1844)/ Ellen G. White
Christadelphians	John Thomas (ca. 1848)
Christian Reformed	Gysbert Haan (ca. 1857)
Salvation Army	William Booth (ca. 1865)
Christian Scientists	Mary Baker Eddy (ca. 1879)
Jehovah's Witnesses	Charles Taze Russell (ca. 1884)
Nazarenes	Phineas Bresee (ca. 1895)
Pentecostals	C.F. Parham/ William Seymour/ A.J.Tomlinson (ca.1903/1906)
Alliance	Albert Benjamin Simpson (ca. 1905)
Church of God in Christ	Charles Mason (ca. 1907)
Foursquare	Aimee Semple McPherson (ca. 1918)
Church of God	Joseph Marsh (ca. 1920)
Worldwide Church of God	Herbert W. Armstrong (ca. 1934)
Confessing Church	Martin Niemoller (ca. 1934)
Evangelical Free	E. A. Halleen (ca. 1950)
Moonies	Sun Myung Moon (ca. 1954)
Children of God	David Mo Berg (ca. 1969)
Universal Church of the Kingdom of God	Macedo de Bezarra (1977)

Offshoots of the Lutherans include the Lutheran Brethren, the Evangelical Covenant Church, the Evangelical Free Church, the Evangelical Lutheran Church in America, the Missouri Synod Lutherans, the Wisconsin Synod Lutherans, and the Moravian Church.

Offshoots of the Anabaptists include the North American Baptist, the Advent Christian Church, the Seventh Day Adventist, the Amish, the Conservative Mennonites, the General Conference of Mennonites, the Old Mennonite Church, the Brethren in Christ, the Hutterite Brethren, the Independent Brethren, and the Mennonite Brethren.

Offshoots of the Anglican Church include the United Church of Christ, the Free Will Baptist, the Conservative Baptist, the Progressive National Baptist, the American Baptist, the

Independent Bible Churches, the Friends United, the Friends General Conference, the United Methodist, the African Methodist, the Episcopal, the Free Methodist, and the many offshoots of the Pentecostal churches.

Offshoots of Calvinism include the Presbyterian Church in America, the Presbyterian Church in the USA, the Orthodox Presbyterian, the Reformed Presbyterian, the Reformed Church in America, the Christian Reformed, the Churches of Christ, the Disciples of Christ, and the "Christian Churches."

The Catholic Church has many rites, yet one faith that traces itself back to Jesus Christ, the apostles and their successors, the bishops. Their Catholic identity is found in their union to the successor of St. Peter, the pope, in proclaiming the one true faith—in diverse cultural expressions--of Jesus Christ. Whether one is a member of the Roman, the Mozarabic, the Ambrosian, the Byzantine, the Chaldean, the Syro-Malabarese, the Alexandrian, the Coptic, the Abyssinian, the Antiochene, the Malankarese, the Maronite, or the Armenian rite, one is a member of the one Catholic Church founded by Jesus Christ through his apostles.

APPENDIX 3
BOOKS OF THE BIBLE

OLD TESTAMENT (HEBREW SCRIPTURES)

Genesis emphasizes the goodness of creation, the gift of human freedom and the consequences of abusing this freedom. It teaches us that sin impacts our relationship with the self, others, creation, and God. It is a book of hope, reminding us that God can bring good even out of evil, and that he is always there for us: "I am your God, and you are my people."

Exodus reminds us that God liberates the enslaved. That he sustains his people and is faithful to his people, even when they are unfaithful to him.

Leviticus teaches us the way to holiness. Holiness is about being in harmony with the self, neighbor, creation and neighbor. Obedience to God's laws bring holiness and thus happiness.

Numbers reminds us that we have been gifted with free will. Free will enables us to make an act of faith. Faithfulness makes us participators in fulfilling God's will.

Deuteronomy teaches us that God wants all of us, not just a part of us. He desires our total commitment, our total love, our total faith.

Joshua tells us that good ultimately triumphs over evil. God's providential will cannot be thwarted.

Judges communicates to us that God works through his people, and that he always raises up people in times of need to protect and guide his followers.

Ruth explains to us that God works through ordinary people, and his works are directed toward the good of all people, Israelites and non-Israelites.

1 and 2 Samuel reminds God's people that perfect faith leads to harmonious living. Since the people of God did not have this perfect faith, they would need to be ruled by Kings—who would attempt to impose structure and harmony.

1 and 2 Kings is a follow up to 1 and 2 Samuel. It describes the history of Israel's and Judah's kings. It shows us the blessedness of kings but also the difficulties that kings can bring.

1 and 2 Chronicles communicates to us that our future as individuals and nations depends on our faithfulness to God.

Ezra and Nehemiah describes the return from exile and the rebuilding of Jerusalem and the Temple. Lack of faith led to exile, faithfulness led to the return to the holy land.

Tobit encourages faithfulness in times of suffering. Patience and faithfulness will overcome the pangs of suffering.

Judith teaches us that faith and courage are rewarded by God's saving power.

Esther is a testament to the power of faith, love and hope. God loves those who have an open, loving, faithful heart, and he is always there for those who call upon him with such a pure heart.

1 Maccabees is a witness to the power of faith. Faith leads to freedom from slavery. For the faithful, God raises up leaders and heroes of great faith to come to their rescue in times of need.

2 Maccabees depicts how people respond to persecutions, injustices, and suffering. For those of faith and perseverance, God ultimately brings vindication.

Job is an exploration of the mystery of suffering, and how many good people suffer. It is a call to persevere in faithfulness, for those who remain faithful will ultimately be vindicated.

Psalms are hymns and songs used in worship. Jesus prayed the psalms. The psalms express the heart's human longings and how they can only be satisfied in the fulfillment of all desires, God.

Proverbs is a collection of wisdom acquired through human experience. They are aids to living a wise, good, and godly life.

Ecclesiastes reminds us that life is a mystery: One may not always have the answers to life's problems. In these times, we must continue in faith, trust and perseverance.

Songs of Songs is a love song. It portrays the beauty of human love as a symbol of God's love for his people.

Wisdom teaches us that the righteous and seekers of wisdom will be rewarded by God.

Sirach reminds us that God's wisdom surpasses all human wisdom. Therefore obedience to God leads to the fullness of wisdom.

Isaiah is a reminder of the gifts that flow from faithfulness to God. In order to be a follower of God one must be just to the poor and the needy. And for those suffering and persevering in hope, the promise of a Messiah is given. This Messiah, this Savior, will come for the Jewish people and for the peoples of all nations.

Jeremiah is a call to repentance and renewal. It is a reminder that God is always there for his people, to love them, renew them, and save them.

Lamentations are poems of grief and hardship reminding us that following God is not always easy. On the other hand, it also reminds us that not following God is even more painful and heartbreaking.

Baruch attests to the fact that no matter where one may find oneself, faithfulness and hope to God's promises is the call of every human being.

Ezekiel demonstrates that sin ultimately leads to the disintegration of individuals and ultimately societies. Yet God is always there to renew his people.

Daniel is a call to always hope in God, particularly in times of oppression and persecution. Victory is always there for the faithful.

Hosea comforts us in reminding us that God loves us like a loving parent.

Joel explains to us that God allows for evil and disasters in life in order to help us refocus on the truly important, our love of God, neighbor, self, and creation. He reminds us of our call to be people of continual repentance, renewal and dependence on God.

Amos reaffirms our recognition that injustice and hypocrisy are often found in the wealthy and the ruling classes. Comfort and power can make one lose sight of the need for God—which in turn leads to inevitable catastrophes.

Obadiah is an affirmation that God protects righteous nations. Holiness fosters harmonious societies; evil fosters disintegration.

Jonah is a story of a God that desires the salvation of all. He calls the evil to return back to him.

Micah is a call to avoid injustice and the worship of anything that is not God. Micah foretells of a new future, a new future which will begin with the coming of the Messiah.

Nahum recalls to the faithful that God protects the just. Justice leads to healthy societies, injustice leads to catastrophes.

Habakkuk is a call for faith amidst times of doubt. It is a call to faith in times of injustice and suffering.

Zephaniah is a reminder that sinfulness has disastrous consequences.

Haggai describes the building of the Temple. It is a reaffirmation that God restores the faithful, even when they have been unfaithful to him in the past. Haggai is a call to worship God first and foremost.

Zechariah tells us that history is in God's hands. Those who remain faithful share in his divine providence and will be rewarded by his divine providence.

Malachi is a call to faithfulness to one's vocation, such as the gift of marriage.

NEW TESTAMENT

Matthew, Mark, Luke, and John

The four books of the Gospel of Jesus Christ is an account of the long-awaited noble, powerful, merciful, and compassionate Messiah. It is the account of the Son of God who existed from all eternity being incarnated. It is the account of Jesus the Christ, the Savior, the Messiah, the God-man who took upon the sins of the world to save the world. It is the story of the prophet of all prophets, the King of all kings, the Lord of all lords, who came to perfect, purify, and fulfill the law and to teach us by words and deeds the way to truth, life, and eternal salvation. It is an account of Jesus who came to heal us, redeem us, and teach us to live life authentically, abundantly, and everlastingly.

Acts is an account of the beginning of the fulfillment of Jesus' will to evangelize the world.

Romans reminds us that we are justified by faith, and this justification is expressed in authentic expressions of faith—holy works.

228

1 Corinthians is a call to repentance, conversion, and renewal in Christ. The Christian life is one of continual repentance, conversion, and renewal in Christ.

2 Corinthians is a call to witness the faith in good times and in bad, when it is popular and when it is not.

Galatians warns us against those who seek to preach a false gospel. It is a reminder to be faithful to the apostles and their successors.

Ephesians is a call to live a life in union with God and one another.

Philippians is a reminder to the faithful that whether we live or die, we belong to the Lord, and we will be with him forever.

Colossians tells us to remain focused on Christ and only Christ as our way, our truth, and our life. Let us not be swayed by false visions of reality.

1 Thessalonians teaches those who are united with Christ in faith, hope and love that they will live with him eternally. That in Christ, death has been conquered, no longer having its sting.

2 Thessalonians is a call to remain faithful in times of difficulty. Trust in God's providence. He is the Lord of history.

1 Timothy, 2 Timothy, and Titus (Pastoral Letters)
These letters are focused on the proper functioning of the Church. They give advice to lay leaders, bishops, priests and deacons.

Philemon is a call to treat all people as equals in Christ. It is a call to protect the good in society and to seek, in prudence, to overcome the evil.

Hebrews reiterates that Jesus is our Savior, our Messiah, our King, our Lord, our Priest, our Prophet, our salvation.

James is a letter guiding the faithful in living life in freedom. Freedom is lived when one is freed from sin, when one lives out one's faith through the fruits of that faith, through the holy works of God.

1 Peter is a call to persevere in times of persecution. It is a reminder that God is the great vindicator.

2 Peter teaches us that God rewards the faithful and virtuous with abundant life on earth and eternal life with him.

1 John, 2 John, 3 John are three letters/epistles calling us to avoid false gospels that seek to steal away our souls. It is a call to be faithful to the apostles and their successors, the true guardians of the incarnated Son of God.

Jude is a warning against false teachers and ungodly people.

Revelation is a call to persevere, to hang on, in times of great persecution. It is a testament that God is in control of history. It is a testament that God will always, ultimately, triumph over evil.

APPENDIX 4
POPES, FROM PETER TO FRANCIS

The term "pope" finds its origins in the Greek "pappas," "father." Priest continue to be referred to as "Father" to this day. The Latin version of "pappas," "papa," would eventually be rendered "pope" in the English speaking world. Today, "pope" is exclusively used for the bishop of Rome, the successor of St. Peter.

1. St. Peter (32-67)
2. St. Linus (67-76)
3. St. Anacletus (Cletus) (76-88)
4. St. Clement I (88-97)
5. St. Evaristus (97-105)
6. St. Alexander I (105-115)
7. St. Sixtus I (115-125)
8. St. Telesphorus (125-136)
9. St. Hyginus (136-140)
10. St. Pius I (140-155)
11. St. Anicetus (155-166)
12. St. Soter (166-175)
13. St. Eleutherius (175-189)
14. St. Victor I (189-199)
15. St. Zephyrinus (199-217)
16. St. Callistus I (217-22)
17. St. Urban I (222-30)
18. St. Pontain (230-35)
19. St. Anterus (235-36)
20. St. Fabian (236-50)
21. St. Cornelius (251-53)
22. St. Lucius I (253-54)
23. St. Stephen I (254-257)
24. St. Sixtus II (257-258)
25. St. Dionysius (260-268)
26. St. Felix I (269-274)
27. St. Eutychian (275-283)
28. St. Caius (283-296)
29. St. Marcellinus (296-304)
30. St. Marcellus I (308-309)
31. St. Eusebius (309 or 310)
32. St. Miltiades (311-14)
33. St. Sylvester I (314-35)
34. St. Marcus (336)
35. St. Julius I (337-52)
36. Liberius (352-66)
37. St. Damasus I (366-84)
38. St. Siricius (384-99)
39. St. Anastasius I (399-401)
40. St. Innocent I (401-17)
41. St. Zosimus (417-18)
42. St. Boniface I (418-22)
43. St. Celestine I (422-32)
44. St. Sixtus III (432-40)
45. St. Leo I (the Great) (440-61)
46. St. Hilarius (461-68)

47. St. Simplicius (468-83)
48. St. Felix III (II) (483-92)
49. St. Gelasius I (492-96)
50. Anastasius II (496-98)
51. St. Symmachus (498-514)
52. St. Hormisdas (514-23)
53. St. John I (523-26)
54. St. Felix IV (III) (526-30)
55. Boniface II (530-32)
56. John II (533-35)
57. St. Agapetus I (535-36)
58. St. Silverius (536-37)
59. Vigilius (537-55)
60. Pelagius I (556-61)
61. John III (561-74)
62. Benedict I (575-79)
63. Pelagius II (579-90)
64. St. Gregory I (the Great) (590-604)
65. Sabinian (604-606)
66. Boniface III (607)
67. St. Boniface IV (608-15)
68. St. Deusdedit (Adeodatus I) (615-18)
69. Boniface V (619-25)
70. Honorius I (625-38)
71. Severinus (640)
72. John IV (640-42)
73. Theodore I (642-49)
74. St. Martin I (649-55)
75. St. Eugene I (655-57)
76. St. Vitalian (657-72)
77. Adeodatus (II) (672-76)
78. Donus (676-78)
79. St. Agatho (678-81)
80. St. Leo II (682-83)
81. St. Benedict II (684-85)
82. John V (685-86)
83. Conon (686-87)
84. St. Sergius I (687-701)
85. John VI (701-05)
86. John VII (705-07)
87. Sisinnius (708)
88. Constantine (708-15)
89. St. Gregory II (715-31)
90. St. Gregory III (731-41)

231

91. St. Zachary (741-52)
92. Stephen II (III) (752-57)
93. St. Paul I (757-67)
94. Stephen III (IV) (767-72)
95. Adrian I (772-95)
96. St. Leo III (795-816)
97. Stephen IV (V) (816-17)
98. St. Paschal I (817-24)
99. Eugene II (824-27)
100. Valentine (827)
101. Gregory IV (827-44)
102. Sergius II (844-47)
103. St. Leo IV (847-55)
104. Benedict III (855-58)
105. St. Nicholas I (858-67)
106. Adrian II (867-72)
107. John VIII (872-82)
108. Marinus I (882-84)
109. St. Adrian III (884-85)
110. Stephen V (VI) (885-91)
111. Formosus (891-96)
112. Boniface VI (896)
113. Stephen VI (VII) (896-97)
114. Romanus (897)
115. Theodore II (897)
116. John IX (898-900)
117. Benedict IV (900-03)
118. Leo V (903)
119. Sergius III (904-11)
120. Anastasius III (911-13)
121. Lando (913-14)
122. John X (914-28)
123. Leo VI (928)
124. Stephen VIII (929-31)
125. John XI (931-35)
126. Leo VII (936-39)
127. Stephen IX (939-42)
128. Marinus II (942-46)
129. Agapetus II (946-55)
130. John XII (955-63)
131. Leo VIII (963-64)
132. Benedict V (964)
133. John XIII (965-72)
134. Benedict VI (973-74)
135. Benedict VII (974-83)
136. John XIV (983-84)
137. John XV (985-96)
138. Gregory V (996-99)
139. Sylvester II (999-1003)
140. John XVII (1003)
141. John XVIII (1003-09)
142. Sergius IV (1009-12)
143. Benedict VIII (1012-24)
144. John XIX (1024-32)
145. Benedict IX (1032-45)
146. Sylvester III (1045)
147. Benedict IX (1045)
148. Gregory VI (1045-46)

149. Clement II (1046-47)
150. Benedict IX (1047-48)
151. Damasus II (1048)
152. St. Leo IX (1049-54)
153. Victor II (1055-57)
154. Stephen X (1057-58)
155. Nicholas II (1058-61)
156. Alexander II (1061-73)
157. St. Gregory VII (1073-85)
158. Blessed Victor III (1086-87)
159. Blessed Urban II (1088-99)
160. Paschal II (1099-1118)
161. Gelasius II (1118-19)
162. Callistus II (1119-24)
163. Honorius II (1124-30)
164. Innocent II (1130-43)
165. Celestine II (1143-44)
166. Lucius II (1144-45)
167. Blessed Eugene III (1145-53)
168. Anastasius IV (1153-54)
169. Adrian IV (1154-59)
170. Alexander III (1159-81)
171. Lucius III (1181-85)
172. Urban III (1185-87)
173. Gregory VIII (1187)
174. Clement III (1187-91)
175. Celestine III (1191-98)
176. Innocent III (1198-1216)
177. Honorius III (1216-27)
178. Gregory IX (1227-41)
179. Celestine IV (1241)
180. Innocent IV (1243-54)
181. Alexander IV (1254-61)
182. Urban IV (1261-64)
183. Clement IV (1265-68)
184. Blessed Gregory X (1271-76)
185. Blessed Innocent V (1276)
186. Adrian V (1276)
187. John XXI (1276-77)
188. Nicholas III (1277-80)
189. Martin IV (1281-85)
190. Honorius IV (1285-87)
191. Nicholas IV (1288-92)
192. St. Celestine V (1294)
193. Boniface VIII (1294-1303)
194. Blessed Benedict XI (1303-04)
195. Clement V (1305-14)
196. John XXII (1316-34)
197. Benedict XII (1334-42)
198. Clement VI (1342-52)
199. Innocent VI (1352-62)
200. Blessed Urban V (1362-70)
201. Gregory XI (1370-78)
202. Urban VI (1378-89)
203. Boniface IX (1389-1404)
204. Innocent VII (1404-06)
205. Gregory XII (1406-15)
206. Martin V (1417-31)

207. Eugene IV (1431-47)
208. Nicholas V (1447-55)
209. Callistus III (1455-58)
210. Pius II (1458-64)
211. Paul II (1464-71)
212. Sixtus IV (1471-84)
213. Innocent VIII (1484-92)
214. Alexander VI (1492-1503)
215. Pius III (1503)
216. Julius II (1503-13)
217. Leo X (1513-21)
218. Adrian VI (1522-23)
219. Clement VII (1523-34)
220. Paul III (1534-49)
221. Julius III (1550-55)
222. Marcellus II (1555)
223. Paul IV (1555-59)
224. Pius IV (1559-65)
225. St. Pius V (1566-72)
226. Gregory XIII (1572-85)
227. Sixtus V (1585-90)
228. Urban VII (1590)
229. Gregory XIV (1590-91)
230. Innocent IX (1591)
231. Clement VIII (1592-1605)
232. Leo XI (1605)
233. Paul V (1605-21)
234. Gregory XV (1621-23)
235. Urban VIII (1623-44)
236. Innocent X (1644-55)

237. Alexander VII (1655-67)
238. Clement IX (1667-69)
239. Clement X (1670-76)
240. Blessed Innocent XI (1676-89)
241. Alexander VIII (1689-91)
242. Innocent XII (1691-1700)
243. Clement XI (1700-21)
244. Innocent XIII (1721-24)
245. Benedict XIII (1724-30)
246. Clement XII (1730-40)
247. Benedict XIV (1740-58)
248. Clement XIII (1758-69)
249. Clement XIV (1769-74)
250. Pius VI (1775-99)
251. Pius VII (1800-23)
252. Leo XII (1823-29)
253. Pius VIII (1829-30)
254. Gregory XVI (1831-46)
255. Blessed Pius IX (1846-78)
256. Leo XIII (1878-1903)
257. St. Pius X (1903-14)
258. Benedict XV (1914-22)
259. Pius XI (1922-39)
260. Pius XII (1939-58)
261. St. John XXIII (1958-63)
262. Paul VI (1963-78)
263. John Paul I (1978)
264. St. John Paul II (1978-2005)
265. Benedict XVI (2005-2013)
266. Francis (2013—)

PETER 67 (Pont.): Peter was the first pope chosen by Jesus to lead his Church. He would die during the persecution of the Church begun by the Roman Emperor Nero. He would be crucified upside down on Vatican Hill.

LINUS 67-76 (Pont.): The first successor of Peter, the second pope, Linus, was chosen by Peter, prior to his death, to lead the Church. As Tertullian writes in 193 AD in his work *Adversus Marcionem libri quinque*: *"From his chair in Rome, Peter commanded Linus to sit down [as his successor]."*

Linus is best known for encouraging the growth of the clergy in Rome.

He is often referred to as the Linus of 2 Timothy 4:21 in the Bible, prior to his ascending to the papacy.

ANACLETUS 76-88 (Pont.): [Ana]Cletus, the third pope, is best known for building an oratory for the burial of the martyrs and drawing up rules for the proper consecration or ordination of bishops.

CLEMENT 88-97 (Pont.): The fourth pope Clement of Rome, a friend of Peter and Paul (prior to their deaths), brought about reform in the Corinthian community and asserted the importance of papal authority and apostolic succession.

Our apostles knew through our Lord Jesus Christ that there would be strife for the title of bishop. For this cause, therefore, since they had received perfect foreknowledge, they appointed those who [were properly chosen], and afterwards added the codicil that if they should fall asleep [that is, die], other approved men should succeed to their ministry (Letter to the Corinthians, 44).

It is quite relevant to note that the apostle John was still alive at the time when Clement was demanding reform in the Corinthian community. John sensed no obligation to interfere with the Corinthians or with Clement. One may surmise from this reality that the Roman church--from its earliest foundation--enjoyed supremacy of honor and jurisdiction by virtue of being the church where the successor of Peter resided.

EVARISTUS 97-105 (Pont): The fifth pope, Evaristus, developed parishes and was responsible for the origin of what would become known in time as the "college of cardinals."
 The apostle John dies during his reign.

ALEXANDER I 105-115 (Pont.): The sixth pope, Alexander I, allowed for the use of holy water in churches and houses.
 He is also known for prescribing that the bread to be consecrated into the Body of Christ was to be unleavened. He is believed to have formalized the "institution narrative" within the Mass.

SIXTUS I 115-125 (Pont.): The seventh pope, Sixtus I, emphasized the importance of sacred vessels being handled by sacred ministers. Sixtus was responsible for continuing the standardization of the liturgy.

TELESPHORUS 125-136 (Pont.): The eighth pope, Telesphorus, composed the "Gloria" and instituted the period of fasting for seven weeks prior to Easter.
 He is also known for inserting new prayers into the liturgy of the Mass.

HYGINUS 136-140 (Pont.): The ninth pope, Hyginus, decreed that all churches should be consecrated. He instituted the use of godparents for infant baptisms and further organized the ecclesiastical hierarchy.
 He fought the false teachings of the Gnostics Valentinus and Cerdo. In general, Gnostics believed matter (such as the body and all of creation) was evil. Only the spirit was good. The goal in life was to free oneself from the body and all matter. Gnostics argued that one was not saved by God's grace, but by "enlightenment," or "secret knowledge."

234

Hyginus asserted the goodness of matter and spirit, body and soul. He affirmed that salvation was through the free gift of grace, offered to all.

PIUS I 140-155 (Pont.): The tenth pope, Pius I, opposed agnosticism and is believed to have established the date for Easter as the first Sunday after the March full moon.

Pius excommunicated and expelled Marcion from the Church for rejecting the Old Testament.

Pius was also known for reminding the faithful and the clergy of the primacy--in honor and jurisdiction--of the See of Rome, the See of Peter.

ANICETUS 155-166 (Pont.): The eleventh pope, Anicetus, emphasized the celebration of Easter as the central Christian feast.

He also warned the faithful regarding the evils of Gnosticism.

SOTER 166-175 (Pont.): The twelfth pope, Soter, affirmed that the Sacrament of Matrimony was only valid if witnessed and blessed by a priest.

He fought the heresy of Montanism which believed in an earthly thousand-year reign (Millenarianism) and believed that mortal sins could not be forgiven. Soter rejected Millenarianism and emphasized God's forgiveness of mortal sins through the Sacrament of Penance.

ELEUTHERIUS 175-189 (Pont.): The thirteenth pope, Eleutherius, sent Fugatius and Damian to convert the Britons.

He also condemned Montanism.

VICTOR 189-199 (Pont.): The fourteenth pope, Victor, emphasized the Roman celebration of Easter.

He excommunicated the Gnostic Florinus and the Adoptionist Theodotus. Adoptionism argued that Jesus was a human being who, at some point, perhaps at his baptism in the Jordan, received divine power from God.

Victor affirmed the Son of God's incarnation—the taking on of flesh from Mary--and the two inseparable natures of the Son of God, divine and human.

ZEPHYRINUS 199-217 (Pont.): The fifteenth pope, Zephyrinus, emphasized that all persons fourteen and over were to receive communion.

He condemned Montanism, Adoptionism, and Modalism—Modalism being the belief that the Father, Son, and Holy Spirit were successive modes of revelation of one divine Person (i.e., the Father became the Son and the Son became the Spirit). Modalism denied the distinction of three Persons in one God and the belief in the Trinity.

Zephyrinus was able to obtain the release of Christians from the mines of Sardinia, the "island of death," including the future pope Callistus.

CALLISTUS 217-222 (Pont.): The sixteenth pope, a former slave, Calixtus or Callistus, was a pope known for his exceptional compassion, especially toward those who had abandoned the faith and then desired reconciliation through the Sacrament of Reconciliation.

Callistus emphasized the Church as made up of saints and sinners.

Callistus excommunicated Sabellius for denying the distinction between the Father and the Son (a form of Modalism). Callistus affirmed that the Father eternally begets the Son and the Son is eternally begotten by the Father.

URBAN I 222-230 (Pont.): The seventeenth pope, Urban I, was known for acquiring property for Church use during a brief period of quiet in Church-State relations.

He instituted the collection of funds during Mass for the Christian community.

Urban affirmed his predecessor's policy of compassion toward repentant apostates.

PONTIAN 230-235 (Pont.): The eighteenth pope, Pontian, ordered the habitual use of the "Confiteor," the "Profession of Faith," and the salutation "*Dominus vobiscum*," the "Lord be with you."

After being condemned by the emperor Maximinus Thrax to the mines of Sardinia, the "island of death," he resigned as pope to allow his successor to lead the Church. He is the first pope to resign in history.

ANTERUS 236 (Pont.): The nineteenth pope, Anterus, ordered that the acts of the martyrs and their relics be gathered together for future generations.

FABIAN 236-250 (Pont.): The twentieth pope, Fabian, struggled against the persecutions of the emperor Decius.

Hermetical life flourished during his pontificate.

He reorganized the Church in Rome to deal with its growing numbers. He divided Rome into seven ecclesiastical districts, with a deacon and sub-deacon in charge of each.

CORNELIUS 251-253 (Pont.): The twenty-first pope, Cornelius, opposed the heresy of Novatianism which believed that serious sins such as apostasy could not be forgiven, and that the Church was solely made up of saints. Cornelius readmitted lapsed Catholics to the Church after the Sacrament of Reconciliation and long penances. He argued that the Church was made up of saints and sinners. He excommunicated Novatian.

LUCIUS I 253-254 (Pont.): The twenty-second pope, Lucius I, was preoccupied with the moral life of his sheep. He reiterated the ban on premarital sexual relationships and the living together before marriage.

He continued his predecessor's approach toward lapsed Catholics.

STEPHEN I 254-257 (Pont.): The twenty-third pope, Stephen I, continued to oppose the heresy of Novatianism. He also dealt with those who called for the re-baptism of lapsed, heretical, or schismatic Christians. Stephen readmitted, without re-baptism, those who sought communion through the Sacrament of Reconciliation and long penances.

SIXTUS II 257-258 (Pont.): The twenty-fourth pope, Sixtus II, put an end to the Novatian heresy by his strong leadership.

He forbade re-baptism for the lapsed. He asserted the validity of baptism as being dependent on the proper Trinitarian formula—not on the moral standing of the one performing the baptism.

DIONYSIUS 259-268 (Pont.): The twenty-fifth pope, Denis or Dionysius, reorganized the parishes in Rome after the destruction brought about by the emperor Valerian's persecutions.

He ransomed the release of the persecuted Catholics in Gallienus.

Dionysius warned the east regarding its philosophical watering down of the doctrine of the Trinity—which at times sounded more Tritheistic than Trinitarian.

FELIX I 269-274 (Pont.): The twenty-sixth pope, Felix I, reiterated the teaching of Christ as being God and man, as having two natures in one Person.

EUTYCHIAN 275-283 (Pont.): The twenty-seventh pope, Eutychian, emphasized the importance of relics for inspiring the faithful.

He also instituted the blessing of crops.

CAIUS 283-296 (Pont.): The twenty-eighth pope, Caius, upheld the long tradition that one should be made a bishop only after having been made a deacon and priest.

MARCELLINUS 296-304 (Pont.): The twenty-ninth pope, Marcellinus, served during the atrocities of the Emperor Diocletian's persecution. This was a time when many churches and sacred texts were destroyed.

MARCELLUS I 308-309 (Pont.): The thirtieth pope, Marcellus I, re-affirmed the long-standing tradition that no council could be held without the approval of the pope.

He divided the Roman Church into twenty-five parishes led by one priest per parish.

EUSEBIUS 309 (Pont.): The thirty-first pope, Eusebius, allowed those who had apostatized during Diocletion's persecution to return to communion after the Sacrament of Reconciliation and long penances.

MILTIADES 311-314 (Pont.): The thirty-second pope, Miltiades helped to persuade the emperor Constantine to issue the Decree of Tolerance, allowing Christians to worship freely. He was given Empress Fausta's palace, the Lateran, by Emperor Constantine.

Miltiades excommunicated Donatus who argued that grave sinners could not be readmitted into the Church, and that sacraments administered by those in mortal sin—deacons, priests, and bishops--were to be held as invalid. Miltiades allowed for grave sinners to return, after the Sacrament of Reconciliation and penances. He also declared that the validity of the sacraments were not dependent on the moral status of those who administered them.

Miltiades saw the rise and spread of the heresy of Arianism throughout the Christian world. Arius and more particularly his followers rejected the divinity of Christ and the doctrine of the Trinity.

SYLVESTER I 314-335 (Pont.): The thirty-third pope, Sylvester I, celebrated the first ecumenical council of Nicaea, convened by Emperor Constantine. Nicaea was called to deal with primarily the Arian heresy. Sylvester confirmed its teachings and the creed that came from it.

We believe in one God, the Father Almighty, maker of all things visible and invisible; and in one Lord Jesus Christ, the Son of God, the only-begotten of his Father, of the substance of the Father, God of God, Light of Light, very God of very God, begotten (γεννηθέντα), not made, being of one substance (ὁμοούσιον, consubstantialem) with the Father. By whom all things were made, both which be in heaven and in earth. Who for us men and for our salvation came down [from heaven] and was incarnate and was made man. He suffered and the third day he rose again, and ascended into heaven. And he shall come again to judge both the living and the dead. And [we believe] in the Holy Ghost. And whosoever shall say that there was a time when the Son of God was not (ἦν ποτε ὅτε οὐκ ἦν), or that before he was begotten he was not, or that he was made of things that were not, or that he is of a different substance or essence [from the Father] or that he is a creature, or subject to change or conversion — all that so say, the Catholic and Apostolic Church anathematizes them.

Sylvester also affirmed the importance of Sunday as a holyday of obligation—as the new Sabbath.

MARK 336 (Pont.): The thirty-fourth pope, Mark, put together the first firm calendar of feast days. He collected a list of anniversaries for the death of bishops (*Depositio episcoporum*) and martyrs (*Depositio martyrium*).

JULIUS I 337-352 (Pont.): The thirty-fifth pope, Julius I, founded the archives of the Holy See and decreed that Christmas should be celebrated on December 25.

He vigorously supported the teachings of Nicaea.

Julius I also insisted upon the primacy of Rome in honor and jurisdiction when he addressed the supporters of the continuing Arian heresy: "Can you be so ignorant of the custom...that it is from Rome that what is just is defined" (*Julii ep. Ad. Antiochenos, c. xxii*).

His pontificate would experience the sad loss of Emperor Constantine to the heresy of Arianism. Constantine would be baptized on his deathbed by the Arian bishop Eusebius of Nicomedia. This would be a portent of the long history of conflicts that would ensue between emperors and popes, Arianism and Catholicism.

LIBERIUS 352-366 (Pont.): The thirty-sixth pope, Liberius, continued the fight against the heresy of Arianism. The emperor Constantius exiled, threatened, and browbeat the pope and bishops in his attempt to foster Arianism. Upon Constantius' death, and freed from intimidation, Liberius condemned the Arian council of Rimini and affirmed his role as the "champion of Nicene orthodoxy."

He mandated that all future Christians would have to accept the Nicene Creed before being admitted into communion with the Catholic Church.

DAMASUS I 366-384 (Pont.): The thirty seventh pope, Damasus I, had the Hebrews scriptures translated into the vernacular by Jerome. He also compiled a list of books that would become the Bible.

He introduced into the liturgy the use of the Jewish praise "alleluia." He emphasized the singing and reciting of the psalms, especially for priests and religious.

In an age of multiplying heresies he condemned the following:

1. Arianism, which denied the divinity of Christ and the Trinity.
2. Donatism, which argued that grave sinners could not be readmitted into the Church, and that the sacraments administered by those in mortal sin were to be held as invalid.
3. Priscillianism, which denied the preexistence of the Son and denied the humanity of the incarnate Son.
4. Apollinarianism, which argued that the *Logos* took the place of the mind in Jesus.
5. Macedonianism, which denied the divinity of the Holy Spirit.

Damasus taught firmly that Rome was the "apostolic see"[the See of Peter].

His selecting of the books that would become the Bible and his brilliant opposition to the above mentioned heresies rightly makes him one of the greats among the popes: "Where Peter is, there is the Church."

During Damasus' pontificate the emperor Theodosius I declared Christianity the "state religion" on February 27, 380.

SIRICUS 384-399 (Pont.): The thirty-eighth pope, Siricus, emphasized leniency in the re-admittance of heretics, set standards in age and qualifications for ordinations, accentuated Easter and Pentecost as the preferred seasons for baptism, and re-stated the practice of celibacy for priests. He forbid the sentencing to death of heretics.

ANASTASIUS I 399-401 (Pont.): The thirty-ninth pope, Anastasius I upheld that God is the sustainer of all creation. He also ended the schism that developed between the church in Rome and the church in Antiochia.

He instituted the bowing of heads by deacons, priests and bishops during the reading of the Gospel during Mass.

He also banned certain aspects of Origen's writings, such as the preexistence of the soul and universalism—the belief that all would eventually be saved.

INNOCENT I 401-417 (Pont.): The fortieth pope, Innocent I, brought about the elimination of gladiatorial games. He also preserved the faithful during the sack of Rome by Alaric of the Goths.

He reminded all churches that in disciplinary and liturgical matters the "Roman custom" was to be the norm.

He affirmed Damasus' choice of books to be placed in the Bible, and also congealed the canon of the Mass.

He emphasized that the Sacrament of Confirmation was best conferred by bishops.

He re-asserted the condemnation of Pelagianism—which argued, in part, that you could be saved without the grace of God (i.e., by works alone).

ZOSIMAS 417-418 (Pont.): The forty-first pope, Zosimas fought for the rights of the Church against foreign and secular interference.

He anathematized Pelagius, his followers, and his teachings.

BONIFACE I 418-422 (Pont.): The forty-second pope, Boniface I, entrusted Augustine to write a treatise on the errors of Pelagianism.

He insisted on the importance of papal primacy: *"It has never been lawful for what has been decided by the apostolic see [the See of Peter] to be reconsidered."* Augustine would reiterate this stance against the heretical Pelagians.

CELESTINE I 422-432 (Pont.): The forty-third pope, Celestine I, called the council of Ephesus, which condemned Nestorianism and Pelagianism.

The Heresy of Nestorianism denied the title "Mother of God" thus separating Christ's human nature from his divine nature; thereby making Christ essentially two distinct Persons. In response, the council affirmed the reality that the Son of God was the second Person of the Trinity and that he had two natures, one human, one divine—without change, confusion, separation or division between the natures. The council thus affirmed the traditional titles for Mary: "Theotokos" "God-bearer," "Mother of God."

Against Pelagianism the Church affirmed the necessity of Christ's life, death, and resurrection for the wiping away of "original sin" and salvation. It affirmed that grace was necessary for salvation and that one could not earn or work oneself into heaven without the aid of grace. It affirmed that "original sin" was passed down to the entire human race and was cleansed in baptism.

SIXTUS III 432-440 (Pont.): The forty-forth pope, Sixtus, III, asserted the authority of the Church over any State authority. As Sixtus reminded the faithful: "Only God and his Church can save one's soul: one's country, no matter how great, cannot save one's soul."

Sixtus continued to promote the decisions of the Council of Ephesus.

LEO I 440-461 (Pont.): The forty-fifth pope, Leo I, called the fourth and fifth ecumenical councils.

The Council of Chalcedon (451) condemned Monophysitism which denied Christ's two natures and argued for a composite nature. The council reasserted the teaching that the Son of God is one Person with two natures, without change, separation, confusion, or division between the natures. Jesus is fully human, fully divine. He is God and man. This teaching came from Leo's Tome, to which the council Fathers cried out: "Peter has spoken through Leo."

Leo also condemned Manichaeism, a religious and ethical doctrine floating around since the third century which infiltrated much of Christian thought. It held that there were two equal, eternal principles, one good, one evil, one spirit, one matter, one light, one darkness. Leo confirmed that God had no equal.

Leo also gained legendary status for repelling Attila the Hun from sacking Rome.

HILARY 461-468 (Pont.): The forty-sixth pope, Hilary, emphasized the need for an intellectually and spiritually astute clergy. He affirmed the supremacy of the See of Rome.

241

He combatted the Macedonian heresy, an anti-Nicene group that denied the divinity of the Holy Spirit.

SIMPLICUS 468-483 (Pont.): The forty-seventh pope, Simplicus, stood protecting Christianity during the fall of the western empire. He encouraged his bishops to be familiar with the teachings of Nicaea, Ephesus, and Chalcedon. He continued to combat the lingering heresy of Arianism.

FELIX III 483-492 (Pont.): The forty-eighth pope, Felix III, worked on calming the disturbances in the Eastern Church. He continued to fight the lingering eastern heresy of Monophysitism.

GELASIUS I 492-496 (Pont.): The forty-ninth pope, Gelasius I, was known as the "father of the poor," and the "Good Shepherd."

He inserted the "Kyrie eleison" into the Mass.

He is the first pope of record to be referred to as the "Vicar of Christ" (Roman Synod, 495).

His pontificate was, with the fall of the western empire, troubled by intrusive barbarian kings, most of whom were Arian.

He tried to expunge the vestiges of Pelagianism in the Church.

ANASTASIUS II 496-498 (Pont.): The fiftieth pope, Anastasius II, was responsible for condemning Traducianism—the heresy that argued that the human soul was not created directly by God but created by parents in the same way as a body.

SYMMACHUS 498-514 (Pont.): The fifty-first pope, Symmachus, spent the Church's wealth on the poor, expelled the Manicheans from Rome, ransomed war prisoners from northern Italy, and liberated the slaves of Rome.

HORMISDAS 514-523 (Pont.): The fifty-second pope, Hormisdas, brought an end to the Acacian (Monophysitism) schism which began in 484. The east would abandon Monophysitism—that Christ only had one nature--and would accept the Catholic teaching on Christ's two natures. The thirty-five year schism between east and west was resolved. Unity was restored under Peter's successor.

JOHN I 523-526 (Pont.): the fifty-third pope, John I, opposed the attacks of Theodoric, the Arian king of Italy, on the Church. John was imprisoned by Theodoric and died in captivity. The death of Theodoric would bring about better relations between John's successor and Theodoric's grandson Athalaric.

FELIX IV 526-530 (Pont.): The fifty-fourth pope, Felix IV, fought Semi-Pelagianism. Semi-Pelagianism (unlike Pelagianism which argued that one could attain one's salvation through human effort solely) argued that the beginning of faith and perseverance in faith could be acquired by free will, but its increase was dependent solely on God. Felix IV responded to the heresy of Semi-Pelagianism by affirming Augustine's teachings on grace and free will; that is, grace cooperating with free will is necessary for the beginning of faith, the perseverance of faith, and the increase of faith.

BONIFACE II 530-532 (Pont.): The fifty-fifth pope, Boniface II, reiterated the teachings of Felix IV on the role of grace and free will.

He brought comfort to the people during times of scarcity.

JOHN II 533-535 (Pont.): The fifty-sixth pope, John II, approved of emperor Justinian I's request to have the *Theopaschite Formula*--which stated that "One of the Trinity suffered in the flesh"--accepted. Justinian pursued, in his own words, the approval of the "head of all the churches." John approved the formula: John's approval however reiterated his predecessor Hormisdas' concern—that the formula was unnecessary and could be easily misinterpreted.

AGAPITUS 535-536 (Pont.): The fifty-seventh pope, Agapitus, pronounced Arian converts ineligible for Holy Orders. Those already ordained as Arians were, upon conversion, to live as lay Catholics.

The Gothic Wars began during his pontificate. The eastern empire in Constantinople sought to absorb the Ostrogoth Kingdom of Italy—hoping to resurrect the old Roman Empire.

SILVERIUS 536-537 (Pont.): The fifty-eighth pope, Silverius, continued the struggle against the Monophysites. The Empress Theodora, a Monophysite, forced Silverius to resign and had him exiled. By popular demand he returned to Rome, but was exiled a second time and died shortly of starvation.

His reign was troubled by the turmoil ensuing from the Gothic Wars.

VIGILIUS 537-555 (Pont.): The fifty-ninth pope, Vigilius, continued to condemn the Monophysites.

He affirmed the Second Council of Constantinople, re-condemning Nestorianism—the belief that Jesus was two distinct persons as opposed to the second Person of the Trinity; thereby, denying Mary the ancient titles "Theotokos," "God-bearer," "Mother of God."

His reign was lived amidst the turmoil of the Gothic Wars.

PELAGIUS I 556-561 (Pont.): The sixtieth pope, Pelagius I, reorganized papal finances and reorganized papal properties.

He condemned simony—the buying and selling of ecclesiastical privileges.

He was responsible for restoring Rome and its environs after the ending of the Gothic Wars. Rome technically remained in the domain of the east, but the Byzantine (eastern) empire's influence on the west would never be the same.

JOHN III 561-574 (Pont.): The sixty-first pope, John III, would experience the decline of Italy under the control and influence of the Lombards--Germanic tribes who controlled Italy between 568 and 774.

BENEDICT I 575-579 (Pont.): The sixty-second pope, Benedict I, struggled to keep the people of Rome and France safe from Lombard invasions.

Benedict was active pastorally, ordaining twenty-one bishops. He confirmed the Fifth Ecumenical Council, Constantinople II, which affirmed that Jesus was the second Person of the Trinity, with two natures, a human nature and a divine nature—with no confusion, change, division, or separation between the natures.

Benedict died with Rome under siege and famine, and on the verge of being sacked.

PELAGIUS II 579-590 (Pont.): The sixty-third pope, Pelagius II, reaffirmed the praying of the divine office as mandatory for priests.

He continued his predecessor's attempts to fight off Lombard attacks.

He died helping the poor and ill in the plague that hit Italy.

The conversion of the Visigoths took place during his reign.

GREGORY I 590-604 (Pont.): The sixty-fourth pope, Gregory I, removed unworthy clergymen from office, particularly those who were not living a celibate life.

He improved the beauty of the Liturgy, saved persecuted Jews, and served as a temporal leader in the west during a time of turmoil.

He provided for the proper management of papal lands, and reorganized the central administration of the church in Rome.

He held off Lombard invasions into Rome. He even converted many Lombards.

His pontificate was marked with providing food for the poor and comfort in plague-stricken times.

He sent Augustine (the future Augustine of Canterbury) along with 40 monks, to convert the English.

SABINIAN 604-606 (Pont.): The sixty-fifth pope, Sabinian, stressed spiritual renewal and the importance of daily prayer in all its forms.

His papacy was marked by a renewal of hostilities with the Lombards.

He served as pope while Rome was under the constant threat of famine.

BONIFACE III 607 (Pont.): The sixty-sixth pope, Boniface III, reaffirmed that only the bishop of Rome, the pope, was a universal bishop—that only the See of St. Peter was the head of all the churches.

BONIFACE IV 608-615 (Pont.): The sixty-seventh pope, Boniface IV, helped to reform the morality of lax clergy.

He transformed the Roman Pantheon into a Christian church dedicated to all saints, and in particular to the Blessed Virgin Mary.

His papacy would be troubled by famine, plague and natural disasters.

DEUSDEDIT I 615-618 (Pont.): Deusdedit I, the sixty-eighth pope, spent his pontificate helping the poor, the lepers, and the plague-stricken.

He added an evening prayer into the Liturgy of the Hours.

BONIFACE V 619-625 (Pont.): Boniface V, the sixty-ninth pope, was faced with the new religion of Islam and the civil wars in Italy. He provided sanctuary for all in his churches.

HONORIUS I 625-638 (Pont.): Honorius I, the seventieth pope, sent missionaries throughout the world to expand the proclamation of the Gospel of Jesus Christ. He particularly focused his attention on the growing English church.

Honorius greatest failure was his inability to adequately deal with the rise of a new heresy, Monothelitism. Monothelitism denied Christ's two wills—a human will, and a divine will. In his attempt to placate the eastern, Byzantine emperor, Honorius failed to refute Monothelitism. Honorius' writings therefore were ambiguous: *"the Word acted through Christ's two natures as if there was only one will."*

Honorius would die before any official position could be agreed upon. Honorius was not opposed to "two wills" as much as to "two contrary wills." He was concerned, according to his successor Pope John IV, with pointing out that Christ's human will was not affected by original sin.

Honorius' position, whatever it may have been, was not presented as an infallible teaching but as a theological speculation.

SEVERINUS 640 (Pont.): The seventy-first pope, Severinus, struggled against the Byzantine emperor Heraclius over the Monotheletic heresy. He helped clarify Honorius' misplaced speculations and attempts to placate the emperor by teaching that Christ had two wills, a human will and a divine will, in perfect conformity with each other.

JOHN IV 640-642 (Pont.): The seventy-second pope, John IV, put an end to any ambiguity, at least for western Catholics--regarding the theology of

Monothelitism. John IV affirmed Severinus' philosophy on Christ's two wills--one divine, one human, in perfect conformity with each other—as the official teaching of the Church. He wrote to reprimand Emperor Constantine III for misrepresenting or misunderstanding Pope Honorius' theological speculations on the issue. Emperor Heracllius would disavow Monothelitism on his deathbed.

THEODORE I 642-649 (Pont.): Theodore I, the seventy-third pope, struggled against the abuses of the emperor Costans II who wanted to revive the heresy of Monothelitism.

Theodore assured ecclesiastical order in the clergy by excommunicating bishops who held to the Monotheletic heresy.

MARTIN I 649-655 (Pont.): The seventy-fourth pope, Martin I, condemned the eastern bishops' pattern of placing more obedience on emperors than on popes.

He called a synod in the Lateran, which once again condemned Monothelitism and the Emperor Constans' support for it. Infuriated, Constans, would eventually have Martin exiled. Martin would die from the effects of cold, harsh treatment, and starvation.

EUGENE I 654-657 (Pont.): The seventy-fifth pope, Eugene I, warned all the faithful to be aware of the intrigues of the Byzantine emperor.

He rejected the proposal by the emperor and his patriarch to formulate a compromise formula on Christ's wills: they argued that each of Christ's natures had a will, but because Christ was one Person, the second Person of the Trinity, there was only one will. Eugene rejected the compromise formula by arguing that while it was true that Jesus' human will and divine will were in perfect conformity with each other, they were still two wills—and never became one will.

The pope reaffirmed the necessity of clerical celibacy.

VITALIAN 657-672 (Pont.): The seventy-sixth pope, Vitalian, was responsible for converting the Lombards to Christianity.

He also strengthened the English Church ecclesiastically and pastorally during the English famine.

The assassination of Emperor Contans in Sicily put an end for a while at attempts to revive the heresy of Monothelitism.

ADEODATUS II 672-676 (Pont.): The seventy-seventy pope, Adeodatus II, was known for bringing monastic reform and for providing for the needs of pilgrims and the poor. His pontificate was primarily pastoral in nature.

DONUS 676-678 (Pont.): The seventy-eighth pope, Donus, brought an end to the schism in the Church in Ravenna, which had previously existed as an independent See from Rome.

He encouraged the bishops to support the schools in Germanic Gaul and in Cambridge, England.

He also dealt with Syrian monks in Rome that held to the heresy of Nestorianism. He dispersed the monks into monasteries throughout the Church in order to squash the heresy.

AGATHO 678-681 (Pont.): The seventy-ninth pope, Agatho, organized the sixth ecumenical council. A revival in the east of Monothelitism led to the council. Agatho sent a delegation to the emperor and to the sixth ecumenical council. The pope's letters were read, and the conclusion of the council ended with the words, "Peter has spoken through Agatho." The heresy of Monothelistism was finally put to death in the east.

LEO II 682-683 (Pont.): The eightieth pope, Leo II, improved the splendor of the liturgy to reflect the majesty of God. He emphasized the sprinkling of holy water as a sign of blessing and as a reminder of one's baptism.

Since Agatho died before the end of the sixth ecumenical council, Leo II ratified the council's findings. He explained Honorius' ambiguous and perhaps lapse into Monothelitism as caused by "negligence and laxity" in theological speculation.

BENEDICT II 684-685 (Pont.): Benedict II, the eighty-first pope, continued to disseminate the conclusions of the sixth ecumenical council. And for a while, the Church in Rome experienced some relief from the conflicts with the eastern emperors and the Eastern Church.

He made the Church a sanctuary for all who needed sanctuary, and was a great supporter of the poor.

JOHN V 685-686 (Pont.): John V, the eighty-second pope, restored order to the disobedient and turbulent dioceses of Sardinia and Corsica.

His papacy was marked with ill health.

CONON 686-687 (Pont.): The eighty-third pope, Conon, defended the Church against the emperor's desire to name himself as the "head of the Church."

Like his predecessor, Conon's reign was marked by ill health and little accomplishments.

SERGIUS 687-701 (Pont.): Sergius I, the eighty-fourth pope, did much to strengthen and grow the Church in England.

Sergius, like his predecessors, continued opposing the intrusions from the Byzantine, eastern emperors. When Emperor Justinian II called for a council, often referred to as the Quinisext Council, to promulgate disciplinary and ritual changes and adjustments, Sergius refused to approve the council, and thus made it invalid.

Liturgically, Sergius introduced the "Agnus Dei" into the Mass, established the feast of the Exaltation of the Cross, and enriched the solemnity of the four great Marian feasts (Annunciation, Dormition, Nativity, and Presentation).

JOHN VI 701-705 (Pont.): The eighty-fifth pope, John VI, defended the Church against invasions from emperors and Lombards.

He spent his pontificate protecting civilians, ransoming prisoners and slaves, and persuading invaders to withdraw.

JOHN VII 705-707 (Pont.): John VII, the eighty-sixth pope, enjoyed better relations with the Lombards.

Upon Justinian's restoration as emperor, John refused to acknowledge Justinian's renewed effort to have parts of the Quinisext Council approved.

SISINNIUS 708 (Pont.): The eighty-seventh pope, Sisinnius, reign was plagued with illness and frailty. He died shortly after his election. His only ecclesiastical legacy is the ordination of a bishop for Corsica.

His pontificate marks the beginnings of the Muslim threat to Europe.

CONSTANTINE 708-715 (Pont.): Constantine, the eighty-eighth pope, travelled to Constantinople to bring about a détente between west and east. He was successful. His success was due to Justinian's willingness to allow the pope to accept and reject whatever canons he favored or disfavored from the Quinisext Council. Papal primacy in honor and jurisdiction was affirmed.

GREGORY II 715-731 (Pont.): The eighty-ninth pope, Gregory II, fought against the emperor-led heresy of Iconoclasm. Iconoclasm argued that icons or pictures fostered idolatry. Gregory reasoned that as long as one did not worship an icon, the use of icons was fully acceptable as an aid to prayer and worship.

Gregory continued to grow the infant Church in Germany. He emphasized Roman liturgical practices amongst the German peoples.

He fostered the growth of monasteries and the restoration of monasteries destroyed by the barbarians.

GREGORY III 731-741 (Pont.): The ninetieth pope, Gregory III, condemned the heresy of Iconoclasm and excommunicated Emperor Leo III and the eastern patriarch Anastasias in 731.

He reinforced the growth of the Church in England, Germany, and northern Europe.

ZACHARY 741-752 (Pont.): The ninety-first pope, Zachary, defended Italy against Rachis, the Duke of Friuli. He made a truce with the Lombards that would last for thirty years.

He encouraged the emperor of the east to reject the Iconoclasm heresy.

STEPHEN II 752-757 (Pont.): Stephen II, the ninety-second pope, was known for his compassion and love for the poor, and for the establishment of pilgrim hospices.

He consecrated Pipin the Short as king of the Franks, of France, which would inaugurate the beginning of the Carolingian dynasty—a union that would protect the Church from the influences and attacks of the eastern emperors and Lombards.

This union would give rise to the Papal States, an independent papal country.

Pepin and his successors would spread the Roman Rite of the Liturgy throughout Europe.

PAUL I 757-767 (Pont.): The ninety-third pope, Paul I, freed prisoners who were incarcerated for debts.

He continued to fight the heresy of Iconoclasm and provided refuge for eastern Christians fleeing persecution from the emperor.

STEPHEN III 768-772 (Pont.): The ninety-fourth pope, Stephen III, highly influenced Pepin's son and successor Charlemagne's spirituality and encouraged the support of the Christians in Palestine.

He called the Lateran synod in 769. The synod would encourage an orderly process in regards to papal elections and would approve the traditional veneration of images.

ADRIAN I 772-795 (Pont.): Adrian I, the ninety-fifth pope, called the seventh ecumenical council into session, Nicaea II (787). The council condemned Iconoclasm. Nicaea affirmed the use of images for inspiring and aiding prayer. The incarnation, an icon of God, made images of the invisible God visible, and thus made all of God's creation worthy of being prayer aids to the artificer.

Under his reign, the Lombard kings would, like the emperors of the east, lose their power to harass the Holy See. Charlemagne, king of the Franks, defeated the Lombards and was crowned by the pope as "king of the Lombards," and "protector of St. Peter." Charlemagne gave "the successor of St. Peter," Adrian, three-fourths of Italy as a gift.

Adrian would also excommunicate those who were still holding to the heresy of Adoptionism—which held that Christ was only an "adopted son" of God.

Besides his liturgical and doctrinal work, Adrian established church-run farms dedicated solely for the feeding of the poor.

LEO III 795-816 (Pont.): The ninety-sixth pope, Leo III, crowned Charlemagne the emperor of the west.

He founded the University of Paris.

He condemned the lingering heresy of Adoptionism in Spain.

STEPHEN IV 816-817 (Pont.): The ninety-seventh pope, Stephen IV, stressed the importance of obedience to the Church by secular authorities. He crowned Ludovico king of France.

PASCHAL I 817-824 (Pont.): The ninety-eighth pope, Paschal I, saw the revival of the heresy of Iconoclasm in the east by Emperor Leo V. Paschal reprimanded Leo V and provided refuge for the fleeing Greek clergy.

EUGENE II 824-827 (Pont): The ninety-ninth pope, Eugene II, was a reforming pope, publishing a collection of disciplinary canons dealing with simony, the qualifications and duties of clerics, clerical education, monastic arrangements, marriage, Sunday observance, etc. He reaffirmed the Council of Nicaea II against the eastern emperor Leo V. He also sent missionaries to bring about the conversion of the peoples of Denmark.

VALENTINE 827 (Pont.): Valentine, the one hundredth pope, was known for his goodness and charity during his short reign. He died within forty days after his election.

GREGORY IV 827-844 (Pont.): The one hundredth and first pope, Gregory IV, organized an army under the leadership of the Duke of Tuscany and defeated the Saracen Muslims—thus protecting Christendom.

His pontificate was preoccupied by the many military conflicts taking place throughout Europe.

SERGIUS II 844-847 (Pont.): The one hundredth and second pope, Sergius II, was present when Rome was sacked and placed under siege by the Saracen Muslims. St. Peter's and St. Paul's churches were vandalized, plundered and stripped bare. The Duke of Spoleto led an army that defeated the Saracen Muslims and freed Rome. The surviving Muslim fleet sank on the way home.

LEO IV 847-855 (Pont.): The one hundredth and third pope, Leo IV, was known for rebuilding St. Peter's and the city of Rome after the sack of Rome by Muslim Saracens. His administrative gifts made the renewal and restoration of Rome possible. In 849 he organized the fleets of Naples, Amalfi, and Gaeta and defeated the Muslims at Ostia.

He denounced weak prelates, and reinstated improperly deposed ones. He was a great enforcer of discipline and reform.

BENEDICT III 855-858 (Pont.): The one hundredth and fourth pope, Benedict III, was primarily devoted to repairing the extensive damages due to the repeated flooding from the Tiber.

He was dedicated to continuing reform and discipline in the Church.

NICHOLAS I 858-867 (Pont.):   The one hundredth and fifth pope, Nicholas I, united forces with Emperor Louis II to combat Saracen Muslim advances.

He was a great advocate, protector, and provider for the poor and homeless. He affirmed the Church's authority over secular powers.

In his assertions of papal power he often conflicted with the kings and emperors. He deposed all bishops unwilling to be obedient to Rome, and corrected secular leaders who wanted too much influence and control over the Church.

He was a great teacher and defender of the Sacrament of Matrimony.

ADRIAN II 867-872 (Pont.): The one hundredth and sixth pope, Adrian II, was elected as Muslim attacks were taking place in southern Italy.

While Louis II was preoccupied with the Muslims, the Duke of Spoleto pillaged Rome—for reasons lost to history.

Adrian's papacy was marked with many disappointments and few accomplishments, except for the approval of the eighth ecumenical council, Constantinople IV, re-affirming the use of Icons and holy images as aids to prayer and liturgy.

JOHN VIII 872-882 (Pont.):   John VIII, the one hundredth and seventh pope, was preoccupied by the continual Muslim incursions into Italy.

He sustained Cyril and Methodius as the Catholic "apostles to the Slavs."

MARINUS I 882-884 (Pont.): The one hundredth and eighth pope, Marinus I, fostered great relations with the English Church.

He also rehabilitated the former excommunicated Formosus and restored him to his See. Formosus would become a future pope.

ADRIAN III 884-885 (Pont.): The one hundredth and ninth pope, Adrian III, was preoccupied with Muslim incursions.

His reign was short and mostly uneventful, dying during his journey to settle a dispute regarding the successor to the Holy Roman Emperor in Germany.

STEPHEN V 885-891 (Pont.): The hundredth and tenth pope, Stephen V's reign, was troubled by "pagans and evil Christians."

His pontificate would experience the fall of Charlemagne's dynasty.

While his reign was primarily preoccupied with political issues, he was able to strengthen ties with the German and French churches, and the eastern emperor.

Stephen assisted in the mutual support required between east and west in curbing Muslim incursions into Europe.

FORMOSUS 891-896 (Pont.): The one hundredth and eleventh pope, Formosus, sent out missionaries and succeeded through his zeal in converting the Bulgarians to Christianity and spreading Christianity throughout England and northern Germany.

BONIFACE VI 896 (Pont.): The hundredth and twelfth pope, Boniface VI, died fifteen days after his election.

STEPHEN VI 896-897 (Pont.): The hundredth and thirteenth pope, Stephen VI, was a man dominated by politics. His pontificate was essentially an uneventful and short reign, yet, due to circumstances, an unforgettable one. He presided over the "cadaver synod" where the corpse of Pope Formosus was pronounced guilty of sins against the papacy and thrown into the Tiber River.

ROMANUS 897 (Pont.): The hundredth and fourteenth pope, Romanus, rehabilitated the memory of Pope Formosus.

He resigned from the papacy after four months to live the remainder of his life as a monk in a monastery.

THEODORE II 897 (Pont.): The hundredth and fifteenth pope, Theodore II, recovered the body of Formosus from the Tiber River and had him buried in the Vatican.

Little else is known of him, for his pontificate lasted only twenty days.

JOHN IX 898-900 (Pont.): The hundredth and sixteenth pope, John IX, emphasized during his pontificate the importance of the state in protecting the rights of the Church.

John sanctioned the consecration of a metropolitan and three bishops for the Church of the Moravians.

He forbade the re-ordination of any validly ordained cleric.

BENEDICT IV 900-903 (Pont.): The hundredth and seventeenth pope, Benedict IV, was able to maintain the integrity of the Holy See amid great trials and tribulations. Upon the defeat of Louis II by Berendgar I of Friuli, Rome was without a protector and thus fell into anarchy.

During the chaos Benedict exercised his pastoral power by his generosity to the destitute, and his work to restore order in the streets and politics of Rome. He would die amidst this anarchy.

LEO V 903 (Pont.): The hundredth and eighteenth pope, Leo V, was overthrown in a palace coup by the priest Christopher after only thirty days as pope. He was imprisoned by Christopher and later murdered as he languished in captivity.

SERGIUS III 904-911 (Pont.): The hundredth and nineteenth pope Sergius III, aided by Duke Alberic I of Spoleto, would restore order to Rome. His ties to Alberic and the Roman nobility would assure the much needed stability of Rome.

His only doctrinal decision was in reaffirming the double procession of the Holy Spirit against the Eastern Church's discomfort. The pope preferred the expression that "the Holy Spirit proceeded from the Father and the Son," as opposed to "from the Father through the Son." Given the theology of the Trinity, both expressions are valid. This controversy—often referred to as the *Filioque* [and the Son] question--was primarily due to misunderstandings and emphasis. This controversy, however, would be a partial reason, along with political distrust, for the split between the Eastern and Western Church.

ANASTASIUS III 911-913 (Pont.): The hundredth and twentieth pope, Anastasius III, accomplished very little during his pontificate due to hostile internal politics within and without the Church.

LANDO 913-914 (Pont.): Lando, the hundredth and twenty-first pope, reigned for six months. His reign's only recorded accomplishment was the restoration of S. Salvatore of Fornovo after its destruction by the Muslims.

JOHN X 914-928 (Pont.): The hundredth and twenty-second pope, John X, put together a coalition of Italian leaders and put an end to sixty-years of Muslim incursions into southern Italy by routing the Saracen Muslims at Garigliano.

He presided over the synod of Hohenaltheim in Swabia, which was dedicated to the strengthening of Church discipline.

He wanted to reconvert the Normans who had relapsed into paganism.

LEO VI 928 (Pont.): The one hundredth and twenty-third pope, Leo VI, tried to heal the competing factions in the Church. He also sought to enforce Church discipline among the hierarchy in Dalmatia and Croatia.

STEPHEN VII 928-931 (Pont.): Stephen VII, the one hundredth and twenty-forth pope, was known for encouraging a spiritual renewal in the Church.

JOHN XI 931-935 (Pont.): The one hundredth and twenty-fifth pope, John XI, tried to curb the moral decay of Rome.

He encouraged the work of the reforming abbey of Cluny—naming it a model for all monastic reform.

He became known in his later years as a pastoral pope, focusing on the administration of the sacraments.

LEO VII 936-939 (Pont.): The one hundredth and twenty-sixth pope, Leo VII, helped to reform, renew, and reorganize monastic life. He also brought reform to religious houses in Rome.

STEPHEN VIII 939-942 (Pont.): The one hundredth and twenty-seventh pope, Stephen VIII, sought reform within the monasteries of Rome and southern Italy.

MARINUS II 942-946 (Pont.): The one hundredth and twenty-eighth pope, Marinus II, was a reforming pope, seeking to reform all aspects of Church life. He shunned war, devoted himself to reforming the secular clergy and monks, and cared for the poor. He approved of synods in Germany to root out abuses by the clergy and monks.

AGAPITUS II 946-955 (Pont.): Agapitus II, the one hundredth and twenty-ninth pope, worked on reforming and improving the morality of the priests and religious. Like most of the popes of the tenth century, his work was significantly restricted by the hostile political forces at work in Rome and Italy. In many ways, the popes were hostages of Rome.

JOHN XII 955-964 (Pont.): John XII, the one hundredth and thirtieth pope, insisted that it was the Church's responsibility—as opposed to the State's—to oversee religious and secular issues.

He continued monastic reforms.

He sought to support the Spanish church in its struggle with a Muslim dominated Spain.

He was deposed by the hostile western emperor, Otto I of Germany.

LEO VIII 963 (Pont.): Leo VIII, the one hundredth and thirty-first pope, had a short reign and accomplished little. His papacy was hindered by the manipulations and paralyzing control of Emperor Otto I of Germany.

BENEDICT V 964-966 (Pont.): The one hundredth and thirty-second pope, Benedict V, was exiled to Hamburg by Otto I. The Romans sought to protect him from Otto, but when Otto laid siege to Rome and attempted to starve it out, the people turned Benedict over. Benedict died in exile.

JOHN XIII 965-972 (Pont.): John XIII, the one hundredth and thirty-third pope, was imprisoned for ten months by his opponents. He was released by Otto I, the emperor of the west.

John XIII helped bring about the conversion of Poland and Bohemia. He reaffirmed the practice of celibacy for the clergy. He brought reform to English monasteries.

BENEDICT VI 973-974 (Pont.): The one hundredth and thirty-fourth pope, Benedict VI, was responsible for the growth of the Hungarian church.

He continued monastic reforms, and banned the practice of charging fees for ordinations and consecrations.

BENEDICT VII 974-983 (Pont.): The one hundredth and thirty-fifth pope, Benedict VII, was a reforming pope. Through a synod held in 981 in St. Peter's Benedict prohibited simony, the buying and selling of ecclesiastical privileges. This ban was communicated to the entire Church, worldwide.

Ad limina visits became common under his pontificate—the obligation of a bishop to come before the pope, at stated times, to give an account of the condition and morale of his diocese.

JOHN XIV 983-984 (Pont.): The one hundredth and thirty-sixth pope, John XIV, accomplished little during his short pontificate. He is best known for receiving the malaria stricken emperor Otto, who died in the pope's arms after having received absolution for his sins.

JOHN XV 985-996 (Pont.): The one hundredth and thirty-seventh pope, John XV, began the first modern canonization process—a detailed study and documentation of a person's earthly heroic virtues and heavenly intercessory powers.

He was able to broker peaceful settlements among the many quarrelsome European powers.

His papacy saw the conversion of the Russian Prince Vladimir of Kiev.

John's pontificate would see the rise of the heresy of Gallicanism—the belief that the French church could be independent of the pope.

GREGORY V 996-999 (Pont.): Gregory V, the one hundredth and thirty-eighth pope, condemned simony and continued reforms in the Church, including excommunicating King Robert II of France for ignoring the Church's teaching on the Sacrament of Matrimony.

His papacy, like those throughout the tenth century, was hindered by secular intrusions and threats—deposition or death. It was a century where popes were poisoned, suffocated, starved, mutilated, and deposed on the slightest whim of the powers of the time, whether emperor or king. It was also a time when the Muslim threat was ever present.

SYLVESTER II 999-1003 (Pont.): The one hundredth and thirty-ninth pope, Sylvester II, desired reform and the repressing of debauchery in the west. He condemned simony and nepotism. He reasserted the importance of the vow of celibacy for the clergy. He organized and brought growth to the church in Poland and Hungary.

He was renowned for his brilliance, having a pioneering force on science, music, mathematics, and literature.

JOHN XVII 1003 (Pont.): The one hundredth and fortieth pope, John XVII, accomplished little during his short pontificate. He is known for his continued evangelization of the Slavs.

JOHN XVIII 1004-1009 (Pont.): The one hundredth and forty-first pope, John XVIII, fought abuses in the German and French churches. He condemned the French king, Robert II, for persecuting Jews.

His pontificate also marked an easing of tensions between the Church in the west and the Church in the east.

SERGIUS IV 1009-1012 (Pont.): The one hundredth and forty-second pope, Sergius IV, began his pontificate as the destruction of the Holy Sepulcher in Jerusalem by Caliph al-Hakim occurred. His pontificate was preoccupied with the Muslim control of Sicily, and the Muslim threat to Europe.

He died amidst the political upheaval in Rome. Rome's instability would eventually precipitate the papacy's move to Avignon, France.

BENEDICT VIII 1012-1024 (Pont.): The one hundredth and forty-third pope, Benedict VIII, made laws prohibiting simony and the minimum age for holy orders. At the synod of Pavia in 1022 Benedict reiterated the call for clergy celibacy. He condemned the abuse of concubinage among some clergy.

Forming an alliance with the Italian domains of Pisa and Genoa, he defeated—personally engaging in the battle--the Muslim invaders of northern Italy and Sardinia in 1016.

JOHN XIX 1024-1032 (Pont.): The one hundredth and forty-fourth pope, John XIX, reasserted papal supremacy and universal jurisdiction against the Eastern Church in its pursuance of independence and separation from Rome. The distrust between east and west would eventually give birth to the Eastern Orthodox Church.

BENEDICT IX 1032-1045 (Pont.): Benedict IX, the one hundredth and forty-fifth pope, followed the policies of his predecessor. However, due to the instability of Rome, Benedict spent most of his time seeking refuge from his opponents. He retired to the monastery of Grottaferrata.

SYLVESTER III 1045 (Pont.): Sylvester III, the one hundredth and forty-sixth pope, was elected pope in Benedict's absence. He resigned his pontificate

256

when Benedict returned to Rome from the monastery of Grottaferrata. Sylvester returned to his former See in Sabina. Benedict would be reelected as pope.

BENEDICT IX 1045 (Pont.): Benedict IX, elected a second time, now became the one hundredth and forty-seventh pope. After twenty days in office, and with the continued upheaval in Rome, Benedict retired once again and withdrew to his family property in Tusculum.

GREGORY VI 1045-1046 (Pont.): Gregory VI, the one hundredth and forty-eighth pope, was forced to abdicate under the political pressure and threat of King Henry III of Germany. He was taken by Henry to Germany to live out his life in exile, dying in Cologne.

CLEMENT II 1046-1047 (Pont.): The one hundredth and forty-ninth pope, Clement II, re-condemned the practice of simony. He died before he could bring about more reform.

BENEDICT IX 1047-1048 (Pont.): Benedict IX, upon the encouragement of the Roman populace and clergy, would come out of retirement to be elected pope for the third time. He becomes the one hundredth and fiftieth pope.

He grew in holiness and would end his last years as a monk in the Monastery of St. Basil in Grottaferrata.

Despite being pope on three different occasions, little can be attributed to his pontificate due to the disorderly nature of his era.

DAMASUS II 1048 (Pont.): Damasus II, the one hundredth and fifty-first pope, dies twenty-three days after his election of malaria in Palestrina.

LEO IX 1049-1054 (Pont.): The one hundredth and fifty-second pope, Leo IX, was known for bringing holiness and humility to the Church, especially elevating holiness in the monks and priests. He reiterated the ban on simony and clerical un-chastity. He would reform the Roman Curia by placing Cardinals in crucial positions of authority. He condemned Berengar of Tours for denying the real presence of Christ in the Eucharist.

He was, much like John Paul II, a travelling pope, encouraging reform everywhere he went.

Politically he was unable to stop Norman conquests in southern Italy—being captured and held prisoner for nine months.

Leo's period in office would mark the break between east and west. The patriarch of the east, Michael Cerularius, a fervently anti-Latin and anti-west patriarch, viewed Leo's appointment of a bishop in Sicily and the holding of a synod in Siponto as a personal affront to Byzantium and its sphere of influence. Cerularius immediately cut off relations with the west. Leo in turn excommunicated Michael Cerularius. Thus began, for political reasons, a schism that would last till this very day.

VICTOR II 1055-1057 (Pont.): The one hundredth and fifty-third pope, Victor II, emphasized the necessity of increasing the treasury of the Church to meet the needs of the poor and the disenfranchised of society.

He held a synod, attended by 120 bishops, which condemned simony, clerical un-chastity, and the alienation of Church property—that is, the stealing of Church property by emperors and kings.

As pope he was an extraordinary diplomat, healing many rifts among the European royal families.

STEPHEN IX 1057-1058 (Pont.): The one hundredth and fifty-fourth pope, Stephen IX, desired to raise the intellectual and moral standards of the clergy. He prevented marriage between blood relatives and denounced clerical marriages.

NICHOLAS II 1059-1061 (Pont.): The one hundredth and fifty-fifth pope, Nicholas II, renewed the prohibition against the investiture of bishops without the approval of the pope. Only the popes or his appointed bishops were permitted to choose bishops—no lay authority, whether king or emperor!

He held a synod that re-condemned clerical marriage and concubinage. Berengar of Tours, having once denied the real presence in the Eucharist, now signed a document affirming his belief in the real presence.

ALEXANDER II 1061-1073 (Pont.): Alexander II, the one hundredth and fifty-sixth pope, was a champion in Church reform and in the reacquiring of lands conquered by Muslims.

He condemned simony, forbade attendance at Mass celebrated by married priests, and condemned lay investiture without ecclesiastical approval.

He sent a representative to Byzantium to repair the break of 1054 with the Eastern Church, now recognized as the Orthodox Church. Eastern distrust still remained and no progress was made.

GREGORY VII 1073-1085 (Pont.): The one hundredth and fifty-seventh pope, Gregory VII, affirmed the pope's universal power over spiritual and secular powers. He reprimanded and reformed hesitant France and Germany in regards to simony and married priests. He sought to free the Church from centuries of lay and royal political control—freedom from the threats of kings and emperors. This would lead to the excommunication of Henry IV over the issue of lay investiture—i.e., kings and emperors appointing their favorite bishops.

Gregory's legacy would be profound, impacting the Church from Norway and Denmark in the north to Spain in the west.

He would die before calling a Crusade to free the holy land from the Muslims.

VICTOR III 1086-1087 (Pont.): The one hundredth and fifty-eighth pope, Victor III, was plagued by the anti-pope Guibert (Clement) and his army. Victor's pontificate was one spent partially in Rome—when it was safe--and partially in the monastery of Monte Cassino.

During his short pontificate the Pisan and Genoese navies defeated the Muslims at Mahdia, eastern Tunisia.

URBAN II 1088-1099 (Pont.): The one hundredth and fifty-ninth pope, Urban II, was an astute politician and reformer.

During his pontificate Guibert's (Clement's) army was defeated by Henry IV. Henry would be embroiled in combat with his son, Conrad of Germany. Rome was left to Urban.

As pope he would renew legislation against simony, clerical marriage, and lay investiture. Given the turmoil of his time, he brought diplomatic and prudent reform to all spheres of society.

He took a cautious approach to dealing with France and England, and expanded the Church's power in Spain and Sicily by his successful conquests of Muslim forces.

In response to the Eastern Church's concern for survival against Muslim incursions, he called the First Crusade to free the Holy Land, protect the west from Muslim incursions, and to help the east.

His pontificate saw the Eastern Church accept the *Filioque* as a variation on their own teaching regarding the procession of the Holy Spirit. While unification was not obtained, understanding for the future was laid.

Urban died two weeks after the capture of Jerusalem.

PASCAL II 1099-1118 (Pont.): Pascal II, the one hundredth and sixtieth pope, struggled against Henry V over the issue of lay investiture. With the death of Henry IV and Conrad's rise to power (now Henry V), the issue of lay investiture was still unresolved. Henry V, formerly Conrad, entered into Rome with his army, imprisoned the pope, retained the power to appoint bishops, and forced Pascal to crown him emperor with the promise of never excommunicating him.

England and France would accept the prohibition against lay investiture as long as an oath of allegiance or homage was paid to them as kings.

Attempts at reunion with the Eastern Church continued under Paschal—the stumbling block being papal jurisdiction. While the east acknowledged the successor of Peter as having primacy of honor, they were not willing to accept his primacy in jurisdiction.

GELASIUS II 1118-1119 (Pont.): The one hundredth and sixty-first pope, Gelasius II, was under constant attack by politicians and manipulators.

Immediately after his election, Cencio Frangipane imprisoned him. The pope was freed by Genoese sailors. Henry V, upon hearing of his freedom, started to make his way to Rome from Lombardy. Once again, Gelasius was forced to flee. Gelasius anathematized Henry V and Henry left Rome. Gelasius returned to Rome only to be attacked by Frangipane once again. He would make his escape to France and die in exile.

CALLISTUS II 1119-1124 (Pont.): Callixtus II or Callistus II, the one hundredth and sixty-second pope, made an agreement with Henry V assuring the pope the right to appoint bishops. This agreement finally ended the issue of lay investiture with Henry V. Henry satisfied himself with France's and England's approach to lay investiture.

Callixtus called the ninth ecumenical council (Lateran I). It issued decrees banning simony (the buying and selling of something spiritual, such as religious offices) and lay investiture (the appointing of bishops by lay persons, as opposed to by the Church). It also affirmed the gift of celibacy in the priesthood.

HONORIUS II 1124-1130 (Pont.): The one hundredth and sixty-third pope, Honorius II, struggled against the Muslim Saracens. He sanctioned the founding of the Premonstratensian canons and the Knights Templar.

He continued reforms in the Church.

INNOCENT II 1130-1143 (Pont.): The one hundredth and sixty-fourth pope, Innocent II, called the eleventh ecumenical council—Lateran II. Clerical celibacy was reaffirmed and usury—the taking of interest for a loan--was prohibited.

CELESTINE II 1143-1144 (Pont.): The one hundredth and sixty-fifth pope, Celestine II, helped to settle, with the help of St. Bernard, the internal problems within the Church.

He tried to bring peace in the war between Scotland and England.

LUCIUS II 1144-1145 (Pont.): The one hundredth sixty-sixth pope, Lucius II, reigned during the end of the Middle Ages. His reign was short and was brought to an abrupt end when, in his attempts to calm rioting in Rome, he was struck in the head by a stone and killed.

EUGENE III 1145-1153 (Pont.): The one hundredth and sixty-seventh pope, Eugene III, was an ardent reformer seeking to raise clerical and monastic standards. He spent much of his time dealing with his predecessor's problem in Rome, the "commune," a Roman run government independent of ecclesiastical control and influence.

Eugene would reject the notion of the separation of Church and State. Under God, all temporal and spiritual affairs are entrusted to the Church.

Eugene promoted the Second Crusade: The Second Crusade, headed by Conrad III of Germany and Louis VII of France, took place in 1147. Lack of discipline, and the lack of unity among the leaders, led to its failure. The Islamic threat to the West would be renewed after this failure.

ANASTASIUS IV 1153-1154 (Pont.): The one hundredth and sixty-eighth pope, Anastasius IV, was able to bring harmony, for a time, between the religious and political leaders in Rome.

ADRIAN IV 1154-1159 (Pont.): The one hundredth and sixty-ninth pope, Adrian IV, was a strong defender of papal supremacy against the emperor of the west, Frederick.

ALEXANDER III 1159-1181 (Pont.): Alexander III, the one hundredth and seventieth pope, excommunicated the emperor Barbarossa for his attempts to control the papacy. When Barbarossa attempted to kill or imprison Alexander, the pope defeated him at Legnano with the aid of the Lombard League.

Alexander called the eleventh ecumenical council, Lateran III, which condemned the Cathari. The Cathari heresy renounced baptism and marriage arguing that the body and matter were evil. The Church affirmed the gift of marriage and the beauty of the body. The council also required that future popes were to be elected by a two-thirds majority.

Alexander was forced to leave Rome after renewed civil chaos and anti-papal, anti-Church sentiments.

LUCIUS III 1181-1185 (Pont.): The one hundredth and seventy-first pope, Lucius III, encouraged all in authority to suppress heresies within their territories. He produced *Ad abolendium*, often referred to as the charter of the Inquisition.

Church inquisitions took place during three periods of history:

1) The Medieval Inquisition (1184-1500)
2) The Spanish Inquisition (1481-1834)
3) The Portuguese Inquisition (1540-1794).

Contrary to popular secular belief, the Inquisitions sought, in the spirit of their era, to bring about justice and peace amongst peoples. The Church could only excommunicate heretics, the role of punishment was reserved to the State. (The number of people sentenced to death during the six hundred and ten years of Inquisitions averages to ten persons a year—for perspective,

261

thirty-five people were executed by receiving the death penalty in the United States in 2014.).

Lucius was forced to take refuge in Verona due to hostilities in Rome. His pontificate was also troubled by the continued tension with the eastern emperor, Frederick.

URBAN III 1185-1187 (Pont.): The one hundredth and seventy-second pope, Urban III, struggled against Emperor Frederick I Barbarossa over the proper relationship between the empire and the Church.

Under his pontificate, Jerusalem fell to the Muslims.

GREGORY VIII 1187 (Pont.): Gregory VIII, the one hundredth and seventy-third pope, wanted to aid the struggling and persecuted Christians in the Holy Land.

In his short fifty-seven day pontificate he was able to acquire a period of détente between the emperor and the papacy.

CLEMENT III 1187-1191 (Pont.): The one hundredth and seventy-fourth pope, Clement III, brought peace and the papacy back to Rome after six years of Roman mayhem.

He encouraged a Third Crusade to free Christians in the Holy Land. The Third Crusade took place in 1190 and was led by Frederick Barbarossa of Germany, Philip Augustus of France and Richard the Lionhearted of England. The Crusade was plagued by difficulties and abuses. Frederick Barbarossa drowned, 100,000 disillusioned Germans returned home to Germany. Philip of France found it impossible to campaign with Richard the Lionhearted of England, and thus returned to France. Despite this, Richard was able to gain control of the city of Jaffa and to win entry into Jerusalem for Christian pilgrims.

With the death of Frederick, Henry, the son, was crowned Emperor Henry VI by the pope. Henry returned the Papal States to the papacy.

CELESTINE III 1191-1198 (Pont.): The one hundredth and seventy-fifth pope, Celestine III, reminded the faithful that marriage was indissoluble.

He approved the Order of the Teutonic Knights whose role was to defend pilgrims on their visits to the Holy Land.

Henry VI, the new emperor of the west, would after a short period of détente with Clement retake his father's hostile approach to the Church. Henry ignored the pope and the Church regarding appointments to ecclesiastical offices.

Celestine was able to recover lost lands in Spain from the Muslims.

INNOCENT III 1198-1216 (Pont.): The one hundredth and seventy-sixth pope, Innocent III, promoted the Fourth Crusade and other smaller European Crusades and called for the twelfth ecumenical council.

The Fourth Crusade began in 1212 and ended in an ignoble and moral disaster. The original intention of protecting the Christians in the Holy Land was diverted, against the pope's wishes, into Constantinople. This resulted in the siege of Constantinople, its plundering, and the dividing of the spoils between the leaders of the Crusade and Venetian merchants.

Innocent supported the growth of the Franciscans and the Dominicans, and guided them to preach against the Albigenses (Cathars), and the Waldenses. Minor Crusades were also led against the Albigenses.

He called the twelfth ecumenical council, Lateran IV, which condemned the Albigenses and Waldenses. The Albigenses (Cathars) rejected the sacraments such as baptism and marriage and Church authority. The Waldenses rejected the sacraments, purgatory, the communion of saints and Church authority.

The council approved the term "transubstantiation" to explain the Church's teaching on the Eucharist.

His only successful Crusade was at the battle of Las Navas de Tolosa which thwarted the Muslim attempt to invade Spain.

HONORIUS III 1216-1227 (Pont.): The one hundredth and seventy-seventh pope, Honorius III, organized the Fifth Crusade and helped Christianity spread into Estonia.

The Fifth Crusade from 1217-1221 was led by King Andrew II of Hungary and John of Brienne. The Crusaders captured Damietta at the mouth of the Nile, only to lose it again. The Crusade was a failure.

Honorius put together the *Compilatio quinta*, often regarded as the first book of canon law.

He approved the rule of St. Francis and the work of the Dominicans. He continued the suppression of the heretical Albigenses and Waldenses.

GREGORY IX 1227-1241 (Pont.): Gregory IX, the one hundredth and seventy-eighth pope, was a great supporter of St. Francis of Assisi, whose rule he influenced, and a great guide to St. Clare and her "Poor Clares," whose rule he composed.

Gregory's relationship with the emperor Frederick II was stormy. At first he excommunicated him for his constant and habitual delays in joining the Crusade to free Jerusalem. Finally joining the Crusade and negotiating the surrender of Jerusalem, Frederick returned to Italy, not seeking revenge, but reconciliation. At Ceprano, peace between pope and emperor was obtained. Papal territories would be maintained, and the excommunication would be lifted.

Gregory instituted an inquisition to be led by the Dominicans to deal with the Albigenses and Waldenses. He encouraged the Franciscans, Dominicans, and Teutonic Knights to convert the pagan peoples of the northernmost parts of Europe.

He re-established the University of Paris, founded the University of Toulouse, and lifted the ban on Aristotle's writings, which would ultimately serve the Church's theology, alongside Plato.

The year 1238 manifested the resumption of conflict between the pope and the emperor. As the emperor sought to expand his empire, the pope sought to protect his churches, particularly in Sicily. Conditions got so serious that the pope excommunicated Frederick and Frederick tried to overthrow Gregory. Gregory marched on Rome, capturing all territory. Just before entering into Rome the pope died. Frederick left, without invading Rome, and awaited the future from Sicily.

CELESTINE IV 1241 (Pont.): The one hundredth and seventy-ninth pope, Celestine IV, died approximately fifteen days after his election.

INNOCENT IV 1243-1254 (Pont.): The one hundredth and eightieth pope, Innocent IV, was elected after eighteen months as the Cardinals attempted to obtain the release of two Cardinals imprisoned by Emperor Frederick II. Unable to settle issues, and fearing the threats of Frederick, Innocent escaped from Rome and travelled to Lyons, France. From Lyons he called the thirteenth ecumenical council. The council deposed the emperor and planned a Crusade.

The Sixth Crusade in 1248 was led by St. Louis IX, the King of France. St. Louis captured Damietta but was himself taken captive. He was released for a ransom and the return of Damietta to the Muslims. Emperor Frederick II died in December of 1250. His son Conrad IV would die in 1254, to be succeeded by Frederick's son Manfred. Manfred would move toward Rome, routing the papal troops at Foggia. Near death, Innocent, upon hearing the bad news, died.

Innocent IV granted Oxford University its charter—officially recognizing Oxford as a University.

ALEXANDER IV 1254-1261 (Pont.): The one hundredth and eighty-first pope, Alexander IV, lost most of the Papal Lands and Italy to Frederick II's son, Manfred. He was a complete political failure.

In terms of the papacy's spiritual domain, he had great success. He reformed abuses, brought better relations with the Eastern Church, and promoted the mendicant orders.

URBAN IV 1261-1264 (Pont.): The one hundredth and eighty-second pope, Urban IV, never was able to reside in Rome due to the city's turmoil and warring factions. He however was still able to strengthen the Church by appointing Cardinals and recovering most of the Papal States, which had been lost by Alexander IV.

On the verge of an agreement with the Eastern Church, now willing to acknowledge the pope as having primacy in honor and jurisdiction—jurisdiction being the stumbling block—died before an agreement could be made.

CLEMENT IV 1265-1268 (Pont.): The one hundredth and eighty-third pope, Clement IV, would be freed from the antagonistic Hohenstaufen royal family with the death of the last Hohenstaufen, Conrad-- defeated and beheaded by Charles, the count of Anjou.

Clement's attempts to re-unite with the Eastern Church, the Orthodox, failed.

Clement would produce the document *Licet ecclesiarum* which declared that all appointments to benefices were to be made by the pope. All bishops today are appointed by the pope.

GREGORY X 1272-1276 (Pont.): The one hundredth and eighty-fourth pope, Gregory X, was elected after three years of debate between the Cardinals. Gregory's pontificate was guided by his desire for a Crusade, reunion with the Eastern Orthodox, and clerical reform.

The fourteenth ecumenical council, Lyons II, provided a temporary union with the Eastern Church. The Eastern Church accepted the Roman creed, the "double procession of the Holy Spirit," and the primacy of the See of Peter. The Catholic Church, west and east, was reunited, at least momentarily. No Crusade was undertaken.

INNOCENT V 1276 (Pont.): Innocent V, the one hundredth and eighty-fifth pope, attempted to solidify the union between the western and eastern Church. He sent delegates to the eastern or Byzantine emperor, Michael Palaeologus, along with the decisions of Lyons, but died before the emperor could solidly incorporate the Orthodox into the Catholic Church.

ADRIAN V 1276 (Pont.): The one hundredth and eighty-sixth pope, Adrian V, died 39 days after his election. There are no accomplishments attributed to him.

JOHN XXI 1276-1277 (Pont.): The one hundredth and eighty-seventh pope, John XXI, sought to lead a Crusade to recapture the Holy Land, to continue the process of reunion between the Orthodox and Catholic communions, and to maintain peace among competing royal families.

He wanted to convert the Tatars, but died before a mission could be launched.

NICHOLAS III 1277-1280 (Pont.): Nicholas III, the one hundredth and eighty-eighth pope, sent missionaries to convert the Tartar kings.

He dealt with the continually feuding and maneuvering European royal families.

He was able to steady the Papal States, stabilizing its boundaries till their complete loss in 1860.

MARTIN IV 1281-1285 (Pont.): The one hundredth and eighty-ninth pope, Martin IV, sought better cooperation between the kings and lords of Europe, to no avail.

His pontificate would see the breakup of the fragile union obtained at Lyons II with the Eastern Church. The eastern emperor Andronicus II Palaeologus rejected the results of the council of Lyons. The reunion obtained by Pope Gregory X was lost.

Locally, Martin extended the power of the mendicant orders in their missionary endeavors.

HONORIUS IV 1285-1287 (Pont.): The one hundredth and ninetieth pope, Honorius IV, brought order to the Papal States and to the city of Rome.

He encouraged the growth of the University of Paris.

He sought peace with Islam with no success.

He condemned a heretical sect called the "apostolics," a group that held to an extreme view of evangelical poverty tainted by Gnosticism. They rejected anything of the "flesh" such as money, property, marriage, and the eating of meat.

NICHOLAS IV 1288-1292 (Pont.): The one hundredth and ninety-first pope, Nicholas IV, established the University of Montpellier.

He struggled against the Muslim Saracens and brought peace to the court of Portugal.

He also emphasized the Church's missionary efforts, bringing Catholicism to China.

He wanted a Crusade to free the Holy Land but could not raise enough support for the endeavor.

CELESTINE V 1294 (Pont.): The one hundredth and ninety-second pope, Celestine V, struggled against the kings and lords of his time who attempted to manipulate the Church. Being unable to struggle further, he resigned from the papacy and left it into the hands of a stronger pope. While often referred to as the "angel pope" he was poorly equipped for the political dimensions associated with the papacy of his time.

BONIFACE VIII 1294-1303 (Pont.): The one hundredth and ninety-third pope, Boniface VIII, founded the University of Rome.

He continued work on the development of canon law.

He published *Unam Sanctum* which declared that there is only "One, Holy, Catholic and Apostolic Church," that it is necessary for salvation, and that it is headed by Jesus Christ and his representative--the successor of Peter. *Unam Sanctum* declared that the Church had two powers, one spiritual, one temporal, with the secular power subject to the spiritual—for salvation is in the sphere of the spiritual.

BENEDICT XI 1303-1304 (Pont.): The one hundredth and ninety-fourth pope, Benedict XI, brought peace between the papacy and the kingdom of France.

He extended the rights of the Dominicans and Franciscans to preach and hear confessions in their missionary works.

CLEMENT V 1305-1314 (Pont.): The one hundredth and ninety-fifth pope, Clement V, was forced into captivity in Avignon, France due to the instability in Rome. It would be seventy years before the papacy would return to Rome.

With no future Crusade likely, Clement suppressed the Knights Templar.

He founded universities in Orleans and Perugia, and decreed the establishment of chairs of Oriental languages in Paris, Oxford, Bologna, and Salamanca.

JOHN XXII 1316-1334 (Pont.): The one hundredth and ninety-sixth pope, John XXII, was elected after two years of debate by the Cardinals.

He instituted the "Sacra Rota," a tribunal or court intended to deal with religious matters.

Against the renegade *Spiritual Franciscans*, called the *Spirituals*, who denied the right to private property, John asserted that the right to own private property and even wealth was not contrary to the spirit of the Gospel or the spirit of Francis.

John expanded the Church into Anatolia, Armenia, India and Iran.

He founded the University of Cahors.

He declared, in opposition to some speculation, that the souls of the just see God "face to face" upon death, prior to the final judgment.

BENEDICT XII 1335-1342 (Pont.): The one hundredth and ninety-seventh pope, Benedict XII, required bishops to live in their dioceses.

He brought renewal and reform to the Benedictine, Franciscan, and Dominican orders. He also fostered reform in local churches and within the inner workings of the papal offices.

He would write *Beneditus deus* stating that the "souls of the just have an intuitive, face-to-face vision of the divine essence" upon death—after the first judgment.

Politically, his attempt to prevent what would become the Hundred Years War between France and England was unsuccessful.

As with every pope before him, the independence and freedom of the papacy was always being undermined by secular powers: Benedict condemned the German manifesto *Fidem Catholicam* which proclaimed that kings and emperors derived their authority from God alone, and not from the Catholic Church.

CLEMENT VI 1342-1352 (Pont.): The one hundredth and ninety-eighth pope, Clement VI, was unable to end the Hundred Years War. He was successful however in stopping Muslim incursions into Smyrna—albeit temporarily—and Imbros.

He sought to rekindle discussions for reunion with the Church in the east, but had no success.

In his document *Unigenitus*, he described the importance of the "treasury of merits" that the saints had built up for the good of the Church. This was a confirmation of the ancient theology regarding the practice of the granting of indulgences.

When the Black Death—plague—struck Avignon in 1348, he defended and protected the Jews of Avignon, who had been blamed for the plague by the French populace.

INNOCENT VI 1352-1362 (Pont.): Innocent VI, the one hundredth and ninety-ninth pope, worked at correcting the abuses within the Church. He required bishops to live and work in their dioceses. He fostered a spirit of reform among the Dominicans and the Knights of St. John. He worked to curb the radicalness of the *Spiritual* Franciscans.

He was able to restore the Papal States, previously being run by tyrants, to the papacy with the aid of the Spaniard Gil de Albornoz. He would modernize the administration of the Papal States.

His papacy saw the incursion of hostile mercenaries into Avignon. The popes, having escaped Roman turmoil, were now being faced with upheaval in Avignon.

URBAN V 1362-1370 (Pont.): The two hundredth pope, Urban V, brought back the papacy to Rome, but after the renewal of turmoil and disturbances in Rome, he was forced to return to Avignon.

He was a reforming pope like his predecessor.

He founded universities in Orange, Krakow and Vienna. He embraced the Orthodox Byzantine Emperor John Palaeologus' reunion with the Catholic faith. The eastern people and clergy, however, still mistrusting the west, were not ready for reconciliation. The schism would continue.

GREGORY XI 1371-1378 (Pont.): The two hundredth and first pope, Gregory XI, through the intervention of St. Catherine of Siena, brought the papacy in 1277 back to its home in Rome, to the See of Peter.

From Rome he would begin reforms amongst the religious orders by combatting laxity and restoring discipline. He was a strong suppressor of heresy in France, Germany and Spain.

He would condemn the thoughts of John Wycliffe. Wycliffe would be the harbinger of Protestantism that would come to the fore in the sixteenth century. John Wycliffe argued for a "Bible alone," "Sola Scriptura," approach to Christianity. He denied the full presence of Christ in the Eucharist, taking a position somewhat similar to the future Martin Luther (impanation-consubstantiation rather than transubstantiation). Wycliffe also promoted the preaching of the Gospel by non-ordained, lay preachers. He argued for the superiority of the State over the Church. Unlike his Protestant descendants of the sixteenth century, however, he rejected the notion of "justification by faith alone," or "once saved always saved." He also rejected the idea that the clergy could own property.

URBAN VI 1378-1389 (Pont.): The two hundredth and second pope, Urban VI, was the victim of what would become known as the Great Western Schism. Antipopes sought to overthrow him and take his role as the head of the Church.

Urban's pontificate began with reform in mind, simplifying the lifestyles of Cardinals, and the freeing of the Church from its dependence on foreign States.

His attempts at bringing reform were tainted by truculence and paranoia on his part, so much so that the Cardinals thought his election and elevation to the papacy had impacted his sanity. Using the excuse that Urban's election had taken place under the fear of mob violence—mobs broke into the papal palace and even into the conclave--the Cardinals asked him to abdicate. When he refused, they claimed his election invalid. The Cardinals rushed to the city of Fondi and elected Cardinal Robert of Geneva as pope, who took the name Clement VII.

The Cardinals, hoping to have solved the problem, made things worse. France adhered to Clement, England and Germany and most of Italy stood by Urban. Spain remained neutral. Urban remained in Rome, Clement went to Avignon.

Urban, despite becoming mentally unstable, had still been properly elected. Clement had no valid claim to the papacy.

Urban died in 1389 of suspicious causes. In his mental instability he had alienated the Roman population, the royal houses of Europe, and brought anarchy to the Papal States, leaving the treasury of the Church empty.

BONIFACE IX 1389-1404 (Pont.): Boniface IX, the two hundredth and third pope, was elected while the antipope Clement was still alive. The Western Schism, therefore, continued: Clement refused to resign.

When antipope Clement died in 1394, the supporters of Clement elected a new antipope, Benedict XIII.

Boniface was not daunted by contenders to the papacy. Boniface, as the authentically and properly elected pope, restored stability to Italy and to the Papal States.

Boniface died in 1404 as the rightful successor of Urban, the successor of Peter.

INNOCENT VII 1404-1406 (Pont.): The two hundredth and fourth pope, Innocent VII, was elected the successor of Boniface, the successor of Peter. He was unable to end the Schism. The antipope Benedict refused to resign.

Despite the turmoil of the age, Innocent was able to bring reform to the Franciscans, and was able to improve the University of Rome by adding faculties of medicine, philosophy, logic, rhetoric and Greek. He is considered the father of humanism.

GREGORY XII 1406-1417 (Pont.): The two hundredth and fifth pope, Gregory XII, was the successor of Innocent, the successor of Peter. Upon his election he called for a meeting with the antipope Benedict. Negotiations, politics, and distrust prevented a meeting.

Cardinals on both sides, Avignon and Rome, were tired of the schism and sought to depose both men at a council in Pisa in 1409 and elect Alexander V as pope. This attempt at a solution was a disaster. Having no authority while a living pope reigned, the council was invalid: Alexander V was now another antipope. Christendom now had one pope, Gregory XII, and two antipopes, Benedict XIII and Alexander V.

The antipope Alexander V would die and be succeeded by another antipope John XXIII in 1410.

A council was called by the antipope John XXIII at the behest of King Sigismund of Germany—to put an end to the schism. John XXIII was deposed. The council then turned to Gregory. Being pope he refused to accept any decisions from a council not in accord with apostolic tradition. Gregory therefore called the sixteenth ecumenical council upholding the deposing of the antipopes Benedict XIII and John XXIII; Gregory then abdicated as pope for the good of the "chair of Peter." The Western Schism was over.

As the schism roared throughout Europe, a man by the name of John Huss was churning out an innovative vision of Christianity. The council, after dealing with the schism, would have to deal with John Huss and his innovations.

John Huss, the second precursor, after John Wycliffe, to the Protestant Reformation would be dealt with in the same council that ended the schism.

John Huss, a spiritual disciple of Wycliffe, planted the seeds of Protestantism that would come to fruition in the sixteenth century. Instead of the Catholic belief in free will, he argued for the predestination of the elect— some predestined to heaven, some to hell; Instead of the Catholic teaching that the Church is made up of saints and sinners, Hus argued for a Church made up of only saints; Instead of the Catholic understanding that God's Word is known

270

through Sacred Scripture and Sacred Tradition, as interpreted by the successors of the apostles, the bishops, Hus argued for the "Bible alone" approach to the Word; Instead of the need for priests and bishops to administer sacraments, Hus argued that sacraments were unnecessary—i.e. Hus rejected the need to confess mortal sins to a priest.

The council rejected *Hus' innovations* as contrary to the Church's always held beliefs.

The end of the Western Schism and the council would bring about the birth of the Renaissance.

MARTIN V 1417-1431 (Pont.): The two hundredth and sixth pope, Martin V, succeeded Gregory with universal approval—albeit the antipope Benedict XIII would remain unrepentant and alive till 1420.

Martin reorganized the Roman curia after years of division, rescued the Papal States from anarchy, sought to bring peace between England and France, and sought reunion with Constantinople ecclesiastically and politically.

Acting contrary to his era, and European history in general, Martin denounced ant-Jewish preaching, the baptism of Jewish children under twelve, and forced conversions.

He promoted art and education and can rightly be seen as the first Renaissance pope and patron.

EUGENE IV 1431-1447 (Pont.): The two hundredth and seventh pope, Eugene IV, called the seventeenth ecumenical council, often referred to as the Basle-Ferrara-Florence Council. The council reunited the Eastern (Orthodox) Church to Rome. The Orthodox accepted papal primacy, the *Filioque*, purgatory, and transubstantiation. This union would eventually fall apart again, as politics overcame theology.

Eugene would refute the idea that a council was superior to a pope. The Church would uphold that a council's validity was dependent upon papal approval.

NICHOLAS V 1447-1455 (Pont.): The two hundredth and eighth pope, Nicholas V, restored peace in the Papal States, Rome, and all of Italy.

He founded the Vatican library.

He would make the Church the preeminent leader of Renaissance culture by being a patron of scholars and humanists. He preserved Greek and Roman classics, patristic writings, and fostered Renaissance art and architecture.

His reign would be dimmed, however, by the capture and sacking of Constantinople by the Muslim Turks.

CALLISTUS III 1455-1458 (Pont.): Calixtus III (or Callistus III), the two hundredth and ninth pope, sought to organize a Crusade to recapture Constantinople from the Muslim Turks. The European powers by this time had lost interest in

Constantinople and Eastern (Orthodox) Christianity. They were too preoccupied with their own territorial aims. In spite of this lack of interest, a Crusade was mounted with limited success: Muslims were routed at Belgrade (1456), Lesbos (1457), and on several Christian islands in the Aegean Sea.

Callistus would reopen the case of Joan of Arc and in 1456 the original charges by the English of heresy and witchcraft were proven false and her innocence was declared. This would open the way for her future canonization.

PIUS II 1458-1464 (Pont.): The two hundredth and tenth pope, Pius II, wanted to start a Crusade against Muslims to recapture ancient Constantinople, the Holy Land and ultimately protect Europe. Once again the European royal families were more preoccupied with their own power and own territorial gains. Crusades and Christian reform, and in some cases Christianity in general, were no longer concerns. Christianity was on the decline, and secularism was beginning it ascendance. One's earthly destiny was beginning to overcome one's eternal destiny. With the exception of a few crusaders from Venice and Hungary, the Crusade, with so few volunteers, could not proceed. Pius died of a broken heart upon seeing the lack of faith.

PAUL II 1464-1471 (Pont.): The two hundredth and eleventh pope, Paul II, pursued a Crusade, like his predecessors, against the Muslim Turks. And like Pius before him, he was unable to raise the necessary amount of crusaders. Even with the conquest of Negroponte in Greece by the Muslims, Paul's cries for a Crusade went unheeded.

In an increasingly faithless generation, Paul gave red hats to Cardinals, reminding them of their willingness—if need be--to shed their blood for the faith.

SIXTUS IV 1471-1481 (Pont.): The two hundredth and twelfth pope, Sixtus IV, was an accomplished theologian and mediator of disputes.

With European forces unwilling to sacrifice for a Crusade, Sixtus raised his own forces and defeated the Muslims in Otranto, Southern Italy. He also had minor successes in the Aegean, such as at Smyrna.

At the request of the Spanish government, he permitted the setting up of an Office of the Inquisition—for the protection of Catholicism and society.

He attempted to expand the Papal States without success.

He was, nevertheless, able to transform Rome from a medieval city into a Renaissance city. He was a patron of letters and arts, and a founder of Renaissance institutions. To Rome came the greatest painters, sculptors, and artists of the age.

The western world as we know it would flow from the breath of Rome and its popes.

INNOCENT VIII 1484-1492 (Pont.): Innocent VIII, the two hundredth and thirteenth pope, unable to mount a Crusade entered into negotiations with the Ottoman Empire, the Muslim Empire now in control of Constantinople, the future Turkey. A costly peace agreement from the pope's point of view was made with the Muslim sultan Bayezid II in 1489, which included the yearly payment of 40,000 ducats to the sultan.

Near his death, the Muslims were expelled from Granada, Spain.

Innocent died with the Papal States in disarray.

ALEXANDER VI 1492-1503 (Pont.): The two hundredth and fourteenth pope, Alexander VI, restored order to Rome, promised Church reform, and sought a united effort to protect Europe from Muslim conquest.

He was pope when Columbus discovered the New World.

His pontificate was marred with European power struggles, and melees within Rome. While he was able to overcome the control of the powerful families of Rome, he was not able to control Europe's fracases, which he often found himself in the middle of.

In terms of the New World which had recently been discovered he gave monarchs freedom in regards to their territorial conquests.

While his pontificate was primarily absorbed in politics, he did confront Girolamo Savonarola in 1498 for his lack of prudence and compromise in terms of Church and societal reform. The Dominican priest Savonarola's fanaticism, obstinacy, disobedience, and outright hatred for the Renaissance Church and epoch led to his excommunication, and ultimately to his sad execution. While good intentioned, his lack of prudence and willingness to compromise, led to his sad but avoidable ending.

While Alexander protected the faith infallibly, he was subject to many human weaknesses, particularly nepotism, simony, un-chastity, and immoral political machinations. His pontificate would not be forgotten by the future Protestant Reformers.

He is considered a patron of the Renaissance.

PIUS III 1503 (Pont.): The two hundred and fifteenth pope, Pius III, died within ten days. His death was a sad moment for the reformers of the Church, who saw in Pius holiness and integrity. Lack of reform would give rise to the birth of the Protestant Revolt or Reformation.

JULIUS II 1503-1513 (Pont.): The two hundredth and sixteenth pope, Julius II, sought to restore the Papal States and to free the papacy from political and foreign domination. He would become known as the "warrior pope" in his efforts to secure independence for the papacy. His diligent labors would gain him another title, the "re-founder of the Papal States."

Julius summoned the Fifth Lateran Council: The council dealt with the neo-Aristotelian influences in the Church and also enacted disciplinary reforms for the clergy. Sadly, the reforms called for at the council were ignored.

Julius granted a dispensation to Henry VIII to marry Catherine of Aragon.

He founded the first dioceses in South America.

He was the great patron of artists, notably Michelangelo, Raphael, and Bramante. Michelangelo would complete the Sistine Chapel's ceiling during Julius' pontificate. He would also commission Bramante to prepare plans to build the new St. Peter's, to be financed in part by the selling of indulgences — which would be illicitly and inappropriately granted. The Protestant Revolt would clutch to this abuse!

In the end, Julius would be considered and saluted by future Italians as the man who envisioned a unified, single Italy.

LEO X 1513-1521 (Pont.): The two hundredth and seventeenth pope, Leo X, was an astute politician and Renaissance man.

Like all popes his papacy took care of the poor and needy.

Leo's great weakness was his inability to sense the signs of the times—the much desired and needed reforms within the Church and society. While he was able to complete the sessions of the Lateran Council, with its calls for reform, no major reform took place. Nepotism and the traditional ecclesiastical abuses continued.

The grumblings of an Augustinian, reform minded monk, Martin Luther, would not be taken seriously by Leo. This grumbling monk would become the founder of Protestantism!

When the bishop of Magdeburg and Mainze arranged for the Dominican John Tetzel in 1517 to promote indulgences in his dioceses, Martin Luther posted his famous *Ninety-Five Theses* on the door of the Church in Wittenberg condemning the practice.

After debates between the theologian John Eck and Luther at Leipzig in 1519, Leo condemned Luther's teachings in *Exsurge Domine* in 1520. Luther burned the document. Leo excommunicated Luther in the document *Decet Romanum ponificem*. Protestantism was born. "Bible alone" Christianity was born.

Lutheranism would argue for a new type of Christianity which held to

1) a Bible only approach to the Word of God.
2) the predestination of the elect and a rejection of free will.
3) a faith without works approach to salvation and a denial of purgatory.
4) a fusing of sanctification, justification, and salvation.
5) a *destroyed* human nature rather than a *wounded* human nature after the Fall.
6) a rejection of the Sacraments as understood by Catholics—including the rejection of the doctrine of Transubstantiation.

7) the rejection of papal infallibility, councils, apostolic succession, and the infallibility of the Church in general.

Leo's pontificate would also see the birth of the Anabaptist Protestants— who denied infant baptism--founded by Nicholas Storch and Thomas Munzer in 1521.

ADRIAN VI 1522-1523 (Pont.): The two hundredth and eighteenth pope, Adrian VI, struggled with both Protestantism and Islam.

He wanted to bring reform to the Church and battled Muslim incursions and threats to Belgrade, Hungary, Rhodes, and ultimately Europe and Christianity in general. Inner reform became difficult as he found himself clashing with the predominance of secular minded Cardinals opposed to change. Adrian became increasingly isolated.

While not taking Luther or the Protestant Revolt seriously, he blamed the rise of the *protesting Christians*, at the diet of Nuremberg in 1522, on the curia of Cardinals who failed to live what they preached.

While recognizing the cause of the Lutheran Revolt, human weakness and evil, he could not accept Luther's doctrinal changes, which he condemned as heresy.

Adrian's pontificate would see the birth of the Swiss Reformed Protestant Church founded by Ulrich Zwingli in 1522.

Adrian died with many good intentions, but no time to carry them out.

CLEMENT VII 1523-1534 (Pont.): The two hundredth and nineteenth pope, Clement VII, desired peace and reunion with the east.

His vacillating and indecisive policies, however, led to the sack of Rome in 1527 by the western emperor Charles V. He would be captured, and then released by Charles in return for parts of the Papal States.

The poor relationship between Clement and Charles would allow for the spread of Lutheranism in Germany, Denmark and Sweden, and the spread of Zwinglianism in Switzerland.

Clement reigned during Henry VIII's split with the papacy--Henry making himself the head of the English Church. Henry VIII would confiscate all Catholic property, destroy monasteries, kill Catholic clergy, and essentially exterminate Catholicism from England. Ironically, despite destroying the Catholic Church in England, Henry VIII died with a Catholic Rosary in his hands.

Clement's pontificate saw the rise of Hutterite Protestants--believers in complete pacifism and communal living--founded by John Hutter in 1528.

While Europe was in turmoil, new dioceses were being formed in Mexico and South America.

Clement was a patron of the Renaissance, supporting theorist like Machiavelli, artists like Cellini, Raphael, and Michelangelo. The Last Judgement scene in the Sistine Chapel was painted during his rule.

Like his predecessors, Clement was blind to the threat of Protestantism—particularly its appeal to the royal houses of Europe who found in Protestantism a way to have complete control of their dominions.

PAUL III 1534-1549 (Pont.): The two hundredth and twentieth pope, Paul III, after close to twenty-years of Protestantism, realized that Protestantism was a threat to the Catholic and Orthodox world and could no longer be ignored. With the development of peace between France and the western empire, Protestantism could now be addressed.

During his pontificate Paul appointed seventy-one new Cardinals known for integrity, brilliance, and admirability. He would foster renewal within the Church by approving new congregations such as the Theatines, Barnabites, Somaschi, and Ursulines. He would approve of the "society of Jesus," the Jesuits. The Jesuits, founded by the mystic Ignatius of Loyola, would eventually recapture much of what was lost by evangelizing and teaching.

Paul III called the Council of Trent, the nineteenth ecumenical council, to deal with the issue of Protestantism. Sadly, with renewed threats by the emperor Charles, Paul III was forced to suspend the council, after the seventh session, for a future date.

During his pontificate new branches of Protestantism developed. John Calvin would found what would become known as the Calvinists, better known as Presbyterians in the United States, in 1536, and Henry Niclaes would be the founder of the Familists in 1540. The Huguenots, inspired by John Calvin's theology, would flourish in the southern and central parts of France, making up to—at the height of its popularity--one-eighth of the French population.

Regardless of a Europe being torn apart by Protestantism, Paul was still a Renaissance pope at heart, promoting artists, writers and scholars. He restored the University of Rome, enriched the Vatican library, and supervised the work on the new St. Peter's.

During Paul's pontificate, Martin Luther, the founder and father of Protestantism would die. Unlike his successors, Luther would doubt what he had begun. In a moment of discouragement, he would write: *"Who called upon you to do things such as no man ever before? Are you infallible? See how much evil arises from your doctrine…. Are you alone wise and are all others mistaken? Is it likely that so many centuries were all wrong? It will not be well with you when you die. Go back, go back; submit, submit"* (Grisar, II, 79, V. 319f).

JULIUS III 1550-1555 (Pont.): The two hundredth and twenty-first pope, Julius III, reopened the Council of Trent in 1551, whose work had remained unfinished due to the turmoil of the time. The council, after its fifteenth session, was forced to recess due to the outbreak of the Habsburg-Valois War.

Even with the war Julius was able to make reforms regarding pluralism, monastic discipline, and the Roman curia.

276

He established the Collegium Germanicum for the training of German priests in apologetics—to combat the Lutheran Revolt.

He promoted the faith in the Indies, the Far East, and the Americas.

England returned to the Catholic fold, albeit for a very short period, with the reign of the Catholic Queen Mary I.

In the course of Julius' pontificate Pseudo-Protestant Unitarianism—which denied the Trinity--was founded by Michael Sevetus in 1553.

MARCELLUS II 1555 (Pont.): Marcellus II, the two hundredth and twenty-second pope, focused on strengthening the faith in Russia and in spreading the faith to the Mongolian people.

He was a great supporter of the Servites and the Augustinian hermits.

He is considered the first Counter-Reformation reform pope, fully dedicated to completing the Council of Trent and implementing the reforms associated with the council.

Unfortunately for Christendom, he died twenty-two days into his reign.

PAUL IV 1555-1559 (Pont.): Paul IV, the two hundredth and twenty-third pope, continued to bring reform and to clarify Catholic teaching against Protestant belief.

His attempts at reform were often distracted by his preoccupation with the politics of his time. His pontificate saw the death of Mary I of England and the return of England to Protestantism.

Paul IV appointed reform minded bishops and Cardinals. He created an *Index of Forbidden Books*—books detrimental to the Catholic mindset. He appointed a commission to reform the missal and Roman breviary. He sought to repress public immorality and violence in Rome.

While reform minded, he lacked the qualities to bring about any profound reform.

PIUS IV 1559-1565 (Pont.): The two hundredth and twenty-fourth pope, Pius IV, completed the Council of Trent's work and became a leading force in the Counter-Reformation, the bringing back of Protestants to the Catholic faith.

He was the perfect pope for this time of disorder. The legendary Cardinal Charles Borromeo would be entrusted in helping Pius foster the reform.

The summary of the Council of Trent is a follows:

1. It declared that the deposit of faith was found in Sacred Scripture and Sacred Tradition as interpreted by the Magisterium—the successors of the apostles in union with the successor of Peter.
2. It affirmed the reality of the seven sacraments.
3. The doctrine of Transubstantiation was reiterated: that bread and wine, once consecrated, become the body, blood, soul, and divinity of

the Resurrected, Glorified Christ under the species, appearances, of bread and wine.

4. It declared that justification is by faith, but not by faith alone: works are necessary.

5. It rejected the negative view held by Protestants regarding human nature. Protestants believed that "original sin" destroyed human nature; The Catholic Church would reassert that "original sin" "wounded" but did not destroy human nature.

6. The Catholic Church, thus, would reassert the reality of free will and the reality of providence against early Protestantism's belief in absolute predestination and the lack of free will--that is, the belief that some people are predestined to heaven and some to hell.

7. It affirmed the reality of purgatory and the communion of saints as being biblical and part of the deposit of the faith.

With the help of Cardinal Charles Borromeo Pius reformed the Rota, the sacred penitentiary, and the papal chancery. He initiated the forming of a catechism based on the Council of Trent, and funded the Roman Seminary for the training of priests.

Pius continued the Renaissance tradition of supporting artists and scholars, and founding universities.

In spite of the reforms, Protestantism would continue to spread in Germany under Lutheranism and France under the influence of Calvinism. In England John Knox, a Calvinist, would become the founder of Protestant Presbyterianism in 1560. Protestant Puritanism would be founded around 1564 and brought to it fulfilment by its foremost theologian Thomas Cartwright.

PIUS V 1566-1572 (Pont.): The two hundredth and twenty-fifth pope, Pius V, intended to enact all the decrees of the Council of Trent. He continued the Catholic Counter-Reformation.

Pius brought reform to religious and secular life. He made a review of religious orders, even abolishing some like the *Humiliati* for their complete collapse into immorality. He continued appointing competent bishops and cardinals. He published the Roman Catechism, a revised Roman breviary, a revised Roman missal, and revised the Vulgate. He returned the use of indulgences to their proper theological intent—eliminating abuses.

Politically and militarily, he won a miraculous victory, against all odds, against the Muslims at Lepanto in 1571. The Battle of Lepanto thwarted the Ottoman Empire's attempt to conquer Europe and extinguish Christianity and Western Civilization. A Holy League of maritime nations of southern Europe led by Pius V secured the miraculous victory. The feast of Our Lady of Victory was established upon this triumph.

GREGORY XIII 1572-1585 (Pont.): The two hundredth and twenty-sixth pope, Gregory XIII, opened many seminaries for the spiritual and intellectual training of priests, which had prior to the Protestant Revolt been lacking.

He restructured the Roman College (later named the Gregorian University). He established the English College, German College, Greek College, Maronite College, Armenian College, and Hungarian College. He used the nunciatures—papal embassies—to overview the progress of reform.

He fostered additions to canon law, supported Church reformers such as St. Teresa of Avila, St. John of the Cross, and St. Philip Neri.

He was able to send missionaries to strengthen and establish churches in India, China, Japan, Brazil, and the Philippines, establishing the Diocese of Manila.

He created the Gregorian universal calendar by correcting the flaws in the Julian calendar. Gregory dropped eleven days from the calendar, converting October 4, 1582 into October 15, 1582—thereby giving us the modern calendar.

During his reign the Protestant Brownists or Congregationalists—believers in autonomous self-governing, individual churches--were founded by Robert Browne in 1582.

SIXTUS V 1585-1590 (Pont.): The two hundredth twenty-seventh pope, Sixtus V, was a reform minded pope.

Within two years after his election, he brought improvement and stability to the Papal States. He brought financial independence to the Vatican and elevated the standard of living within the Papal States.

Sixtus fixed the number of Cardinals at seventy, and chose suitable bishops and cardinals. He developed the inner administration of the Vatican by forming fifteen congregations dedicated to secular and spiritual reform—a structure that would not change till Vatican II.

His post-Trent reforms dealt with simony and pluralism—the possession by a bishop of more than one diocese at a time. He made the *ad limina* visit by bishops mandatory—making the condition of each diocese answerable to the pope.

He became a patron of building and scholarship. He made Rome into a Baroque city.

He is often referred to as the "iron pope" for his energetic and astute leadership qualities.

URBAN VII 1590 (Pont.): The two hundredth and twenty-eighth pope, Urban VII, died thirteen days after his election of malaria. His sudden death brought great sorrow to the reforming bishops.

GREGORY XIV 1590-1591 (Pont.): The two hundredth and twenty-ninth pope, Gregory XIV, despite being hindered by Spanish manipulations, was able to continue the reform.

He was influential in mitigating the effects of the plague, food shortages, and lawless anarchy in Rome.

He enforced the requirement that bishops had to reside in their dioceses, and defined the qualifications and qualities necessary in the choosing of bishops.

INNOCENT IX 1591 (Pont.): The two hundredth and thirtieth pope, Innocent IX, helped limit the effects of the plague hitting Europe. He curbed the lawlessness of Rome. In response to the plague, he improved the sanitary conditions of the Papal States.

In terms of Church reform, his works were limited by his short pontificate and the belligerence between Spain and France.

CLEMENT VIII 1592-1605 (Pont.): The two hundredth and thirty-first pope, Clement VIII, brought peace to France and Spain, and thereby freed the papacy from Spain's domination.

As pope he accepted the Edict of Nantes, giving Protestant Huguenots religious freedom and equal rights. He continued reforming religious houses and published the Clementine edition of the Vulgate. He also issued revised editions of the pontifical, breviary and missal.

Clement's pontificate saw the fruits of the Catholic Counter-Reformation. Europe was returning to its Catholic roots. Some countries, however, such as England and Sweden, remained firmly in Protestant hands.

LEO XI 1605 (Pont.): The two hundredth and thirty-second pope, Leo XI, died seventeen days after his election. Within his short pontificate he was able to put in motion guidelines for reforming papal elections.

PAUL V 1605-1621 (Pont.): The two hundredth and thirty-third pope, Paul V, continued putting into effect Trent's reform agenda for Europe.

His reign marked the declining influence of the papacy in secular affairs. Kings, princes, emperors, and leaders of countries found in Protestantism a way to free themselves from Catholicism.

Notwithstanding the papacy's diminished powers, Paul was able to condemn the rise of Gallicanism in France—the belief that a local church was autonomous and not answerable to the pope.

To aid in the missions of China, he allowed the use of the vernacular in China.

The Baptist Protestant denomination would be founded by John Smyth during his pontificate.

His pontificate encouraged the science of astronomy (thirty-five craters on the moon are named after Jesuit astronomer priests).

GREGORY XV 1621-1623 (Pont.): The two hundredth and thirty-fourth pope, Gregory XV, assisted in the re-conversion of many parts of Europe, particularly France.

He instituted the Congregation for the Propagation of the Faith dedicated to the concerns of the missions overall and missions in formerly Catholic territories.

He sought to mitigate the ill treatment of Catholics in Protestant England.

He finalized the process for the election of all future popes: elections were to take place in a closed conclave and by a secret ballot. This procedure remains in effect to this day.

URBAN VIII 1623-1644 (Pont.): The two hundredth and thirty-fifth pope, Urban VIII, worked on sacred texts such as the pontifical and the breviary.

He instituted a more formalized approach to the canonization of saints (i.e., two miracles, heroic virtues).

He fostered missions to foreign lands. He established new orders such as the Lazarists.

He had Berniini complete the building of St. Peter's and consecrated the Church in 1626.

He sought to remain neutral in the Thirty Years War.

His sad legacy is that—under Protestant pressure--he condemned his friend Galileo. Galileo sought to confirm Nicholas Copernicus' work, a work dedicated to Pope Paul III. With the Protestant Revolt in full bloom, conditions were changing. The early Protestants—taking a strict, literal interpretation of the Scriptures--saw in the papacy's approval of Copernicus and Galileo a rejection of the Bible's vision of the Earth as the center of all reality. In order to assuage the situation Urban sought to have Galileo publish his work as a theory rather than a fact. Galileo refused. Given the spirit of the time, the pope sent Galileo into house arrest (Ironically, history would affirm Urban's position: Galileo argued for circular orbits, yet Kepler and Cassini would prove that the orbits were in fact elliptical).

Urban's reign would close with the devastation of the Papal States and papal finances after an ill-advised war against the French supported league of Venice, Tuscany and Modena.

His papacy would also see the birth of the Protestant Dutch Reformed Church under the leadership of Michaelis Jones in 1628.

INNOCENT X 1644-1655 (Pont.): The two hundredth and thirty-sixth pope, Innocent X, advised the Tzar of Russia, Alexis I, to emancipate the servants of Glebe.

He condemned, like his predecessors Pius V and Gregory XIII, Jansenism, which argued that

1) the human person is devoid of free will in regards to the acceptance or denial of grace—one was either predestined to heaven or hell.
2) Christ did not die for all, only for those he gave grace to.
3) only the holy are worthy of communion.
4) one should not focus on Christ's humanity, only his divinity.

Innocent affirmed free will; that Christ's died for all—desiring all to be saved; and that Christ's humanity was worthy of worship.

During his pontificate, the Protestant Quakers were founded by George Fox in 1650 and the Protestant Mennonites by Menno Simons in 1653.

ALEXANDER VII 1655-1667 (Pont.): The two hundredth and thirty-seventh pope, Alexander VII, was able to readmit the Jesuits into Venice. He approved the Jesuit process of enculturating Chinese practices into Catholic liturgy.

He accepted the conversion of Queen Christina of Sweden, following her abdication.

He had no interest in politics and therefore delegated the Papal States to the care of the Congregation of State.

He had Bernini enclose the piazza of St. Peter's within two semicircle colonnades.

The Jesuit theory of probabilism—on how to resolve doubts of conscience regarding law--arose during his pontificate: Probabilism is often summarized by the motto, "A doubtful law does not oblige." Probabilism came into conflict with probabiliorism which holds that when in doubt one should follow the option more probably true. This issue remained unresolved by Alexander. Alexander did denounce, nevertheless, laxism--always taking the most permissive option--and rigorism--always taking the strictest option.

He, like his predecessor, condemned Jansenism.

CLEMENT IX 1667-1669 (Pont.): The two hundredth and thirty-eighth pope, Clement IX, acted as an intermediary in bringing peace between France, Spain, England, and the Netherlands.

He continued his denouncing of Jansenism in the French Church.

CLEMENT X 1670-1676 (Pont.): The two hundredth and thirty-ninth Pope, Clement X, helped prevent Poland from falling into Muslim hands. After being refused by the Protestant king of Sweden, Charles XI, Clement turned to the Ukrainian nobleman John Sobieski and defeated the Muslim Turks at Dniester in 1673.

With the throne of Poland left vacant, Clement helped elect John Sobieski as king of Poland; thus, assuring Poland's Catholic future.

In terms of France, the French king Louis XIV continued French hostilities. He interfered with Church appointments, confiscated Church property, and stole income from religious communities to further his military aspirations. Clement's successor would inherit this problem.

Clement's pontificate would see the birth of Protestant Pietism under Philip Jacob Spener in 1675.

INNOCENT XI 1676-1689 (Pont.): The two hundredth and fortieth pope, Innocent XI, eliminated nepotism and strengthened and supported the king of Poland against the onslaught of Islam.

He called for a new evangelization of Europe through preaching and teaching—catechizing—a strict observance of monastic vows, and a rigorous selection process for bishops and priests.

Regarding the issue of probabilism, Innocent favored probabiliorism which held that when in doubt one should follow the option more probably true.

In terms of France's infringements upon the Church, Innocent did not remain silent. France responded with the renewal of the heresy of Gallicanism—the view that a council was superior to a pope, and that a pope had no say in temporal affairs. Innocent responded by refusing to approve the appointment of bishops, leaving thirty-five dioceses without a bishop. Feeling outmaneuvered, Louis XIV unleashed a violent persecution on the Protestant Huguenots hoping to induce the good favor of the pope. While no fan of the Huguenots, Innocent deplored the excessively violent treatment of them. Innocent continued his opposition to Louis. He refused the French ambassador to Rome, refused to approve the king's choice for archbishop of Cologne, and in 1688 excommunicated Louis and his ministers.

Innocent greatest desire and perhaps greatest accomplishment was the protection of Europe from Muslim conquest. With the help of Emperor Leopold I and John III Sobieski of Poland, and the formation of the Holy League of the empire, Poland, Venice, and Russia, Innocent was able to save Vienna, liberate Hungary, and recover Belgrade.

His reign would see the rise of a Catholic English King, James II, and his fall by the Protestant William of Orange.

ALEXANDER VIII 1689-1691 (Pont.): The two hundredth and forty-first pope, Alexander VIII, was politically inexperienced. At first he improved relations with Louis XIV, but in so doing alienated Emperor Leopold I. And when relations with Louis soured once again, Alexander found himself neither favored by Louis or Leopold.

He was an active protector of the faith. He continued to condemn Jansenism and Spanish Quietism.

INNOCENT XII 1691-1700 (Pont.): The two hundredth and forty-second pope, Innocent XII, continued reforms in the Papal States and the Church. He fostered impartial justice and the economical administration of the Papal States. He was a great founder of charitable intuitions such as hospitals, orphanages, and places of refuge for the homeless, disabled, poor and needy in general.

To elevate the quality of the clergy he founded the Congregation for the Discipline and Reform of Regulars. And in his legendary decree, *Romanum decet pontificem*, he gutted the heart out of nepotism by forbidding popes from granting estates, offices, or revenues to relatives. Only one relative, and only if worthy, could hold the office of bishop or cardinal.

Innocent was able to break a fifty-year political-religious deadlock between France and the papacy. In 1693 Innocent restored the French hierarchy. Despite a restored hierarchy, the heresy of Gallicanism would remain in France till the French Revolution and the rise of Napoleon.

On his deathbed Innocent approved Philip V as king of Spain.

Innocent's reign would see the rise of the Protestant Amish faith founded by Jakob Amman in 1693.

CLEMENT XI 1700-1721 (Pont.): The two hundredth and forty-third pope, Clement XI, was politically naïve. Caught between the political intrigues of Philip V of Spain and Emperor Leopold, he could satisfy neither.

Under Leopold's successor Joseph I, the Papal States were invaded. Under the threat of the destruction of Rome, the pope was forced to renounce support for Philip V and support the emperor's choice of the Habsburg duke, Charles, as king of Spain. This led to a rupture with Spain.

When the world seemed to be collapsing around Clement, the Muslim threat came to the fore. The entire Peloponnese fell into the hands of the Muslims. The pope allied England, France, Germany, and eventually Spain to combat the Muslim incursion into southern Greece.

Doctrinally, he placed the penalty of excommunication on those who continued to profess Jansenism.

Clement is known for enriching the resources of the Vatican library, making it one of the greatest in the world.

He extended missionary activity into China, India, and the Philippines.

His pontificate witnessed the birth of the Protestant Church of the Brethren under the influence of Alexander Mack in 1708.

INNOCENT XIII 1721-1724 (Pont.): The two hundredth and forty-fourth pope, Innocent XIII, asserted the need for reform and obedience from those within the French and Spanish clergy.

He helped the Knights of Malta in their struggles against Islam.

He reign was troubled by constant illness.

BENEDICT XIII 1724-1730 (Pont.): Benedict XIII, the two hundredth and forty-fifth pope, was a pastoral priest by nature, delighting in visiting the sick, administrating the sacraments, and giving religious instruction.

Benedict was not an effective administrator or politician, being easily manipulated by the secular powers. He left the Papal States in financial distress.

CLEMENT XII 1730-1740 (Pont.): The two hundredth and forty-sixth pope, Clement XII, reigned during the decline of the papacy's political influence.

He condemned the Masonic movement for its secret oaths, religious indifference, and threats to the Church by States.

He founded a college for the Uniat Maronite Catholics in Rome.

He build the first museum of antiquity in Europe.

His papacy saw the birth of the Protestant American Dutch Reform Church under the influence of Theodore Frelinghuysen in 1727, the Protestant Calvinist Methodist Church under the influence of Howell Harris in 1735, and the Protestant Seceder Church under Ebenezer Erskine in 1740.

BENEDICT XIV 1740-1758 (Pont.): Benedict XIV, the two hundredth and forty-seventh pope, saw the invasion of the Papal States and was preoccupied with the turbulent politics of his time.

Outside of the political sphere, he impressed on his bishops the need to be accessible to their people in their dioceses. He improved the training and selection of clergy. He started a reform, or renewal, of the Jesuit order that was beginning to lose the spirit of its founder, Ignatius of Loyola.

In a letter to the Portuguese bishops he called for the more humane treatment of Indians in South America.

His papacy saw the birth of the Protestant Shakers under the direction of Ann Lee in 1741 and the Protestant Methodist Church under John Wesley in 1744.

His scholarly interests guided him in establishing schools of higher mathematics, chemistry, and surgery. In spite of being wary of the Enlightenment movement, he received great respect for his modernity from the French *philosophes*—Voltaire dedicating his work Mahomet to him in 1745.

CLEMENT XIII 1758-1769 (Pont.): Clement XIII, the two hundredth and forty-eighth pope, was uncompromising in upholding the rights of the Holy See.

Clement defended the Jesuits against the political families of Portugal, Spain, France, and parts of Italy. Being the founders of schools, universities, and being among the brightest of scholars and reformers, the Jesuits were feared by Protestants and royal families. They were expelled in many countries and many anti-Jesuit governments sought to dissolve the order.

Clement had to fight the German Heresy of Febronianism. Febronianism argued that the state, guided by the Scriptures and subject to an ecumenical council, was to determine Church affairs. The pope was not to interfere in the affairs of the State.

His pontificate would see the rise of secularism, anti-religious sentiments, and the growth of materialism. The negative dimensions of the Enlightenment were starting to corrupt its initial spirit.

CLEMENT XIV 1769-1774 (Pont.): The two hundredth and forty-ninth pope, Clement XIV, sought to promote peace throughout Europe. Pressured by political powers, the long discussed issue of the status of the Jesuits, with their fourth vow of obedience to the pope, was now reaching a breaking point: the Bourbon states vowed a complete break with Rome if the Jesuits were not suppressed. Under such pressure, and with reluctance, Clement dissolved the Jesuit order. The Catholic school system in Europe would never fully recover, much to the joy of the Enlightenment leaders.

With Clement XIV, the world seemed to have gotten an upper hand on the papacy.

PIUS VI 1775-1799 (Pont.): The two hundredth and fiftieth pope, Pius VI, sought to restore the administration and finances of the Papal States.

His pontificate was marked by the rise of secular atheism, an anti-Christian spirit, and State controlled churches.

Pius fought the heresy of Josephinism, named after the Habsburg emperor Joseph II of Austria. Josephinism argued for State supremacy over the Church. Emperor Joseph II confiscated all Church property, much like Henry VIII, and suppressed all monasteries and certain religious orders in his empire.

The French Revolution began during Pius' pontificate. Pius VI remained cautious during its initial developments. But when an oath of loyalty to the Revolution's ideals was required of the clergy, Pius forbade the taking of such an oath and suspended priests and prelates who took the oath.

The French Revolution and its subsequent Reign of Terror led to the persecution of the Church. Twenty-thousand priest were forced to resign under the threat of death or imprisonment. Thirty-thousand were forced to leave France and those who refused were executed by guillotine or deportation to French Guiana. France's 40,000 churches were either closed, sold, destroyed, or converted for secular uses. With a complete break with France, Napoleon invaded the Papal States, forcing the pope to flee from Rome. He died in exile. Napoleon's promise that he would wipe out the Church seemed on the verge of being accomplished. What he did not know was that Pius had made provisional plans for the election of a pontiff during a Church crisis.

PIUS VII 1800-1823 (Pont.): The two hundredth and fifty-first pope, Pius VII, was elected under Austrian protection.

He would be the first pope to reason that Christianity and democracy were compatible.

He would reinstate the Jesuit order.

Open to Napoleon's overtures, he was able to make an agreement, a Concordat, with Napoleon in 1801 restoring Catholicism in France as the religion of the people, but *not of the State*. Hoping to mitigate Napoleon's antagonism toward the Church, Pius crowned him Emperor. As Napoleon embarked on his wars, Pius tried to remain neutral. An infuriated Napoleon went south and annexed what was left of the Papal States. Pius excommunicated Napoleon. Napoleon in turn arrested Pius and placed him in exile in Savona and then in Fontainebleau. With the defeat of Napoleon, Pius began picking up the pieces, restoring the Papal States, and restoring the Church and its institutions in France.

In non-Catholic countries where State churches existed, he pled for tolerance and religious freedom.

LEO XII 1823-1829 (Pont.): The two hundredth and fifty-second pope, Leo XII, re-instituted the work of the Jesuits.

He was able to emancipate from the Muslim Turks the Catholic Armenians.

He sought to raise the religious spirit amongst the masses of people in an age of rising secularism.

PIUS VIII 1829-1830 (Pont.): The two hundredth and fifty-third pope, Pius VIII, strengthened the Church in Armenia and promoted increased missionary efforts in the poorest of the poor countries.

He opposed indifferentism in religious matters, and attacks on the sacredness of marriage. In regards to mixed marriages, the Catholic party had to promise to raise his or her children in the Catholic faith—a policy that holds to this very day.

The United States witnessed its first Provincial Council in Baltimore in 1829—assuring a close tie to the papacy.

Against past practices, he allowed for the charging of interest on loans.

GREGORY XVI 1831-1846 (Pont.): The two hundredth and fifty-fourth pope, Gregory XVI, founded the Egyptian and Etruscan museums.

He relied on Austria to govern the Papal States.

He rejected the philosophy of separation of Church and State.

He warned of the dangers of a secular dominated press.

He condemned two extremes, atheistic rationalism and fundamentalistic fideism.

Revolutions throughout Europe were a constant threat during his papacy.

He was a great missionary pope, founding seventy New World dioceses and appointing 200 missionary bishops. He denounced the slave trade, and encouraged the formation of a native clergy in the mission territories. His missionary scope extended from South America to Canada and the United States, creating four dioceses in Canada and ten dioceses in the United States.

During his pontificate the Protestant Disciples of Christ Church was founded by Barton Stone and Alexander Campbell in 1832, and the Seventh Day Adventists Church was founded by William Miller and Ellen White in 1844.

PIUS IX 1846-1878 (Pont.): Pius IX, the two hundredth and fifty-fifth pope, experienced the loss of political influence but the gain of spiritual power.

Under his pontificate Italian nationalism was reaching its apex. Despite his efforts to maintain the Papal States against the rising fervor of Italian nationalism, the Papal States in 1861 were annexed, with the exception of Rome and its immediate environs, into the new "Kingdom of Italy." By 1870 Rome and its environs were incorporated into the Italian State.

Under Germany's Secular-Atheist Liberal Movement of 1871-1878, half of the Prussian bishops were imprisoned or exiled, a quarter of the parishes lost their priests, half of the monks and nuns were exiled or fled persecution, a third of the monasteries and convents were closed, and 1800 parish priests were imprisoned or exiled.

Notwithstanding political setbacks and persecutions, his pontificate enjoyed many achievements. In terms of the Old and New World, he founded over 200 new dioceses in mostly the United States and British Colonies. He restored hierarchies to England and the Netherlands. He restored the Latin Patriarch in Jerusalem. The last vestiges of Gallicanism and Josephinism disappeared.

He wrote the *Syllabus of Errors* condemning those dimensions of modern thought that were dangerous for the common good. The *Syllabus of Errors* warned against pantheism, naturalism, atheistic rationalism, indifferentism, latitudinarianism, socialism, communism, liberalism, and secret societies. He warned against an atheistic approach to the study of the Scriptures. He defended the rights of the Church against the State. He reaffirmed the traditional meaning of marriage, and reaffirmed natural law Christian ethics.

Vatican I was held during his pontificate. Vatican I reaffirmed the always held teaching regarding the infallibility of the pope when he speaks *ex-cathedra:*

We teach and define that it is a dogma Divinely revealed that the Roman pontiff when he speaks ex cathedra, that is when in discharge of the office of pastor and doctor of all Christians, by virtue of his supreme Apostolic authority, he defines a doctrine regarding faith or morals to be held by the universal Church, by the Divine assistance promised to him in Blessed Peter, is possessed of that infallibility with which the Divine Redeemer willed that his Church should be endowed in defining doctrine regarding faith or morals, and that therefore such definitions of the Roman pontiff are of themselves and not from the consent of the Church irreformable.

288

The council also condemned pantheism, materialism, and atheism.

In 1854, Pius declared as infallible teaching the doctrine of the Immaculate Conception of the Blessed Virgin Mary.

His death marked the beginning of the modern papacy, freed from temporal concerns and vastly enhanced in its spiritual authority. Being freed from temporal concerns, the Church experienced a spiritual regeneration that would flow into the pontificates of successive generations.

His pontificate would see the founding of the Christadelphians under John Thomas in 1848, the Protestant Christian Reformed under Bysbert Haan in 1857, and the Salvation Army by William Booth in 1865.

LEO XIII 1878-1903 (Pont.): The two hundredth and fifty-sixth pope, Leo XIII, warned against the evils of socialism, communism, nihilism, and freemasonry.

He promoted the study of astronomy and the natural sciences.

He set down guidelines for biblical research.

He wrote the famous document *Rerum Novarum*, which gained him the title "worker's pope." *Rerum Novarum* promoted just wages, workers' rights, and the goodness of trade unions. It also upheld the right to own private property. Governments were only valid as long as they assured the common welfare of their people.

Leo censored the heresy of Americanism—the belief that American ideals and practices should guide the Church.

Outside of Europe he established 248 Sees, regular hierarchies in North Africa, India and Japan, as well as 38 new dioceses in the United States.

He is the first pope to explicitly call Protestants back to the Catholic Church.

After a study of the Anglican hierarchy, he pronounced their orders invalid.

During his pontificate the Protestant Christian Scientists Church was founded by Mary Baker Eddy in 1879, the Pseudo-Christian Jehovah's Witnesses Church was founded in 1884 by Charles Taze Russell, and the Protestant Nazarenes Church was founded by Phineas Bresee in 1895.

PIUS X 1903-1914 (Pont.): The two hundredth and fifty-seventh pope, Pius X, sought to free the papacy from political interventions and persecutions. Recognizing that the Papal States were lost for good, he encouraged Catholics to vote in Italian elections and to build up the Italian nation.

He condemned the heresy of Modernism—a secular, atheist movement. Modernism was an attempt to take Christ out of the family, the school, and the community in general.

Pius reorganized the curia, adjusted the curricula of seminaries, revised the breviary, and prepared for a new catechism and a new edition of canon law. He encouraged lay involvement in the Church, frequent communion (even by children as young as seven), and revived Gregorian chant. He is often referred to as the father of the modern liturgical movement.

Protestant Pentecostalism was founded during Pius' pontificate under the influence of C.F. Parham, William Seymour, and A.J. Tomlinson between 1903 and 1906. The Protestant Alliance Church was founded by Albert Benjamin Simpson in 1905, and the Protestant Church of God in Christ was founded by Charles Mason in 1907.

BENEDICT XV 1914-1922 (Pont.): Benedict XV, the two hundredth and fifty-eighth pope, was chosen for his diplomatic experience at the outbreak of WWI. Despite his protests against merciless methods of warfare, such as the use of poisonous gas, and attempts to prevent other countries, such as Italy, from entering the war, his words went unheeded.

Benedict opened a Vatican office dedicated to reuniting prisoners-of-war with their families, and persuaded Switzerland to accept for treatment any soldier, no matter the side, suffering from tuberculosis.

With the loss of many fathers during the war, Benedict was a strong supporter of the Save the Children Fund.

When peace was achieved in 1919, the Vatican was left out of the peace settlement. It would also be left out of the newly formed League of Nations. Benedict's warnings about the harshness and anti-Christian nature of the Treaty of Versailles went unheeded. The exclusion of the Vatican from the newly formed League of Nations would likewise prove costly.

The Treaty of Versailles ensued, a treaty that inevitably led to WWII. The League of Nations would be useless in preventing WWII.

His pontificate saw the rise of the Protestant Foursquare Church founded by Aimee Semple McPherson in 1918, and the Church of God by Joseph Marsh in 1920.

PIUS XI 1922-1939 (Pont.): Pius XI, the two hundredth and fifty-ninth pope, wanted to make the papacy relevant in the modern world. He encouraged the laity to combat the rise of secularism. He promoted Christian education and social teaching, lamenting the arms race, economic injustice and unemployment.

He reiterated, under secular attacks, the unitive, procreative, and indissoluble nature of marriage, and lamented the evil of contraception.

He made a concordat between the Church and Benito Mussolini so as to protect Christianity in Italy. The concordat made the Vatican an independent country.

He opposed the rise of totalitarian and atheist regimes, at an expense. In 1936 the Spanish (atheist) Red Terror killed 6,832 priests, 2,265 members of Catholic religious institutes, and 283 nuns. Church property was confiscated, religion was prohibited from being taught, and 58 churches were burned. In Mexico the Radical Socialist Party led by the "Red Shirts" between 1926 and

1934 led to the expulsion and execution of 4000 priests. By 1934 Mexico had only 334 priests.

Pius pontificate also witnessed the destruction of the Eastern Church. Before the communist revolution there were 66,140 priests in Russia; on the eve of WWII there were only 6,376.

In 1933 he signed a concordat with Adolf Hitler, but rescinded it when Hitler ignored its provisions. Pius would declare Nazism as "fundamentally anti-Christian."

Prior to his death he would write, *Uni humani generis*, denouncing anti-Semitism. In a Europe that had always had anti-Jewish feelings and actions, from Church to State, this was a refreshing appeal.

In terms of the missions, they doubled under his pontificate.

Pius ordained the first six Chinese bishops and the first native Japanese bishop.

He founded the Pontifical Institute of Archaeology, improved the Vatican observatory, and founded the Pontifical Academy of Sciences.

His pontificate would see the birth of the Protestant Worldwide Church of God founded by Herbert W. Armstrong in 1934, and the founding of the Protestant Confessing Church by Martin Niemoller in 1934.

PIUS XII 1939-1958 (Pont.): The two hundredth and sixtieth pope, Pius XII, was elected with WWII looming. Not able to avert the War he sought to bring it to an end.

As pope he provided relief for prisoners of war and refugees, particularly Jews. He denounced the persecution and genocide of Jews. It is estimated that Pius saved 860, 000 Jews.

Under Hitler, religious services were cancelled, theological institutions were closed, and anti-Catholic materials were given to soldiers. Catholic publications were shut down, Catholic youth leagues abolished, and thousands of priests, nuns, and lay Catholics were imprisoned or murdered. Over 300 monasteries were confiscated by the Nazis and 2,600 priests were killed in Nazi concentration camps. The Dauchau concentration camp had a barrack dedicated for priests alone.

Pius XII's reputation was damaged after the war by communists seeking to keep Catholicism out of Communist Europe. The KGB sponsored Rolf Hochhuth authored a play called, *The Deputy*, which portrayed Pius in the most negative of ways. This play would mar Pius reputation till the opening of the Vatican archives. History is rehabilitating the communist smear of Pius. He is currently being considered for canonization.

After WWII, the world powers did not want to repeat the mistakes of post-WWI. Instead of ignoring the Church, the rise in the number of ambassadors to the Holy See increased, recognizing that the universal, Catholic Church had an eye on the world. The Universal Declaration of Human Rights would be steered in its formation by the Catholic philosopher and Vatican advisor Jacques Maritain.

Pius defined the Assumption of the Blessed Mary into Heaven as a teaching always held by the Church.

He described the Church as the "mystical body of Christ."

He favored the historical-critical method for biblical study.

Foreseeing the dangers of the media, he set up guidelines for the holy use of audio-visual media.

In terms of his missionary efforts he built up the hierarchies of China, Burma, and several African countries.

The Protestant Evangelical Free Church was founded in 1950 by E.A. Halleen.

JOHN XXIII 1959-1963 (Pont.): The two hundredth and sixty-first pope, John XXIII, called the second Vatican Council to complete the work of Vatican I.

He hoped to encourage Protestant ecclesiastical communities and the Orthodox churches to return back to the Catholic Church. He also wanted to renew the Church and prepare it for the future.

He followed his predecessor's argument that the basis for peace is based on the dignity of the human person and the natural human rights due to all.

He called for a solidarity of nations, with the rich helping the poor.

He also helped broker a resolution during the Cuban missile crisis.

PAUL VI 1963-1978 (Pont.): Paul VI, the two hundredth and sixty-second pope, promoted justice in civil, social and international life.

He concluded Vatican II. The following documents were produced by the council:

1) *Sacrosanctum concilium*, Constitution on the Sacred Liturgy
2) *Inter Mirifica*, Decree On the Means of Social Communication
3) *Lumen Gentium*, Dogmatic Constitution On the Church
4) *Orientalium Ecclesiarum*, Decree On the Catholic Churches of the Eastern Rite
5) *Unitatis Redintegratio*, Decree on Ecumenism
6) *Christus Dominus*, Decree Concerning the Pastoral Office of Bishops In the Church
7) *Perfectae Caritatis*, Decree On Renewal of Religious Life
8) *Optatam Totius*, Decree On Priestly Training
9) *Gravissimum Educationis*, Declaration On Christian Education
10) *Nostra Aetate*, Declaration On the Relation Of the Church to Non-Christian Religions
11) *Dei Verbum*, Dogmatic Constitution On Divine Revelation
12) *Apostolicam Actuositatem*, Decree On the Apostolate of the Laity
13) *Dignitatis Humanae*, Declaration On Religious Freedom

14) *Ad Gentes*, Decree On the Mission Activity of the Church
15) *Presbyterorum Ordinis*, Decree On the Ministry and Life of Priests
16) *Gaudium et Spes*, Pastoral Constitution On the Church In the Modern World.

He was a pope during troubled times—a time of political and sociological upheaval.

Paul's pontificate would produce the prophetic document *Humanae Vitae*. The encyclical emphasized the Church's always held teaching on marriage as being a bond of life and love, a state of life and love which is unitive and procreative. The encyclical warned and prohibited acts contrary to the dignity of marriage and the family, such as artificial contraception, abortion, and sterilization.

In response to the teachings of Vatican II, Bishop Marcel Lefebvre broke with Rome, founding the Catholic Traditionalist Church. He was excommunicated in 1988.

Some Traditionalist, under John Paul II, would return back to Rome under the rite of the Society of Peter. Others would remain in schism.

Under Paul's pontificate, the Protestant Children of God Church was founded by David Mo Berg in 1969, and the Universal Church of the Kingdom of God was founded by Macedo de Bezarra in 1977.

JOHN PAUL I 1978 (Pont.): John Paul I, the two hundredth and sixty-third pope, died thirty-three days after his election. He is known as the "smiling pope." He had hoped to continue the implementation of Vatican II and correct the ambiguous interpretations of the council's teachings.

JOHN PAUL II 1978-2005 (Pont.): The two hundredth and sixty-fourth pope, John Paul II, was known as the great missionary pope, proclaiming the faith and visiting 129 countries. He was often referred to as the pope who saw the world as his parish.

Under his pontificate the Catholic Church grew to a population of over one billion people. Vocations to the priesthood increased—his priests being referred to as "John Paul II priests."

John Paul II is known for his summary of Catholic teaching on the dignity of the human person—often referred to as the *theology of the body*.

John Paul II emphasized the dignity of the human person, social justice, and freedom of conscience and worship. He argued for a new economic order, one based on the rights of workers and human dignity.

He would reemphasize Paul VI's prophetic *Humanae Vitae*.

He affirmed that the theistic evolution of species was not contrary to Catholic understanding.

He would assert that the ordination of women to the priesthood was not within the *deposit of the faith*.

293

Under his pontificate, the *Catechism of the Catholic Church* was produced.

He is the first pope to recognize the existence of the state of Israel.

He helped bring about the demise of communism.

He withdrew the teaching license of several schismatic theologians.

BENEDICT XVI 2005-2013 (Pont.): The two-hundredth and sixty-fifth pope, Benedict XVI, was renowned for fighting secularism, atheism, and relativism.

He was a scholar at heart, with a compellingly beautiful writing style. He continued the work of his predecessor, John Paul II.

He revived the Tridentine Mass and a love for the traditions of the Church.

He forbade persons with homosexual orientations from applying for the priesthood.

He, like his predecessor, dealt with the clergy scandal of pedophilia, hebephilia and ephebophilia, bringing about much reform.

After bringing much renewal in the clergy and the hierarchy, he resigned.

He would retire to a monastery, Mater Ecclesiae, within the Vatican grounds.

FRANCIS 2013 (Pont. Reigning): The two-hundredth and sixty-sixth pope, Francis, became the first New World pope in history, being from Argentina.

He was a reforming pope, dedicated to breathing new life into all dimensions of the Catholic Church.

He inherited a world and a Church troubled by secularism and the rebirth of moral paganism.

Francis would oppose the rise of Christian persecutions throughout the world by secularists and Muslims.

He would play an important role in bringing about better relations between Cuba and the United States.

As with every pope, history will have to await his legacy.

Francis is the inheritor of a Church where one-fourth of the world's healthcare is provided by its institutions, where the largest charitable organization in the world, Catholic Charities, provides for the poorest of the poor and the neediest of the needy, and where 1,358 universities provide for the education of future generations.

APPENDIX 5
BIBLE APOLOGETICS

Sacred Scripture

Jer. 30:1-3: inspired by God....
2 Tim. 3: 16-17: useful for teaching, correction...

Sacred Tradition

2 Jn. 1:12: do not intend...paper and ink
Jn. 16:12-13: I have much more to tell you, but you cannot bear it now
1 Cor. 11:2: hold fast to traditions I handed on to you
1 Cor. 15:1-3: being saved if you hold fast to the word I preached
2 Thess. 2:15: hold fast to traditions, whether oral or by letter
2 Thess. 3:6: shun those not acting according to tradition
Jn. 21:25: whole world could not contain the books of Jesus' words
2 Tim. 1:13: take as your norm the sound words that you heard from me
2 Tim. 2:2: what you heard from me entrust and teach to others
1 Pet. 1:25: God's eternal word=preached to you
Rom. 10:17: faith comes from what is heard
Mk. 16:15: go to the whole world and proclaim gospel

Magisterium
Magisterium—apostles and their successors, the bishops

2 Pet. 1:20: no prophecy is a matter of private interpretation
2 Pet. 3:15-16: Paul's letters can be difficult to grasp and interpret
Acts 15:1-21: apostles meet in a council to interpret and set the doctrine of belief for the Gentiles
Acts 8:26-40: the deacon Philip is needed to authentically interpret the Scriptures to the Ethiopian eunuch

Nature of the Church

1 Cor. 3:11: Church founded by Christ
1 Cor. 6:15; 12:12-27; 1 Col. 1:18; Rom. 12:5; Eph. 1:22f; 5:30: body of Christ
1 Cor. 3:9-10, 16: God's building and Temple
2 Cor. 11:2; Eph. 5:25, 27, 29; Rev. 19:7: bride of Christ
Lk. 12:32; Jn. 10:3-5, 11: flock of Christ
Mt. 16:18f; 28:19-20: Church will last forever
Eph. 4:11-16: possesses the means of salvation

One true Church

Jn. 10:16: there shall be one fold and one shepherd
Jn. 17:17-23: I pray that they may be one, as we are one
Eph. 4:3-6: there is one Lord, one faith, one baptism, one God and Father
1 Cor. 12:13: in one spirit we were baptized into one body
Col. 3:15: the peace into which you were called in one body

Infallible in faith and morals

Mt. 16:18-19: upon this rock (kepa) I will build my Church
Mt. 18:17-18: if he refuses to listen even to the church/ power to legislate and discipline
Mt. 28:18-20; Jn. 20:23; 1 Cor. 11:24: power delegated to apostles and successors/ I am with you always
Lk. 10:16: whoever hears you, hears me; rejects you, rejects me/ speaking with Christ's voice and authority
Jn. 14:26: Holy Spirit to teach and remind them of everything
Jn. 16:12-13: Spirit of truth will guide you to all truth
1 Tim. 3:15: Church is the pillar and foundation of truth
Acts 15:28: apostles speak with voice of Holy Spirit

Infallibility tied to apostolic succession

Jn. 20:21: Jesus gave the apostles his own mission
1 Tim. 3:1, 8; 5:17: identifies roles of bishops, presbyters (priests) and deacons to govern his Church
1 Tim. 4:14: gift of ordination conferred by the laying on of the hands
1 Tim. 5:22: do not lay hands for ordination too readily
Acts 1:15-26: Matthias is chosen to succeed Judas—apostolic succession
Acts 14:23: they appointed presbyters in each community
Tit. 1:5: commission for bishops to ordain priests—succession of authority

Infallibility tied to primacy of Peter

Mt. 16:18-19f: upon this rock/Peter/kepa I will build my Church with power to bind and loose
Lk. 9:32; Mk. 16:7: "Peter and his companions"
Mt. 18:21; Mk. 8:29; Lk. 8:46; 12:41; Jn. 6:68-69: spoke for apostles
Lk. 22:32: Peter's faith will strengthen his brethren
Jn. 21:17: given Christ's flock as chief shepherd
Acts 1:13-26: headed meeting which elected Matthias
Acts 2:14: led apostles in preaching on Pentecost
Acts 2:41: received first converts
Acts 3:6-7: performed first miracle after Pentecost
Acts 5:1-11: inflicted first punishment: Ananias and Saphira

Acts 8:21: excommunicated first heretic, Simon Magnus
Acts 10:44-46: received revelation to admit Gentiles into Church
Acts 15: led first Church counsel
Acts 15:7-11: pronounces first dogmatic decision
Gal. 1:18: after conversion, Paul visits Peter
Mt. 10:1-4; Mk. 3:16-19; Lk. 6:14-16; Acts 1:13: Peter's name always heads list of apostles

The Trinity, Father, Son, and Holy Spirit

Trinity
Gen. 1:26: "Let *us* make man in *our* image, after *our* likeness"
Gen. 3:22: "the man has become like one of *us*"

Elohim—plural noun for God, a oneness and a plurality

Mt. 3:16f: voice, Jesus, image of dove—at Jesus' baptism
Mt. 17:5: Transfiguration—voice, beloved one, cloud/shadow
Mt. 28:19: baptize in the name of the Father, the Son, ...
2 Cor. 13:13: "grace of the Lord Jesus Christ and the love of God and the fellowship of the Holy Spirit be with you"

OT—Father NT—Son ACTS—Holy Spirit
211 AD—Tertullian/ sign of the cross

Gen./ Heb. 5:5: Father eternally generates
Jn. 1:1-4f: Son is eternally begotten
Jn. 15:26: Holy Spirit eternally proceeds

Analogy: water as liquid, gas, solid/ sun, ray, light

Christ
Mt. 1:23: "Emmanuel...God is with us."
Ex. 3:14; Jn. 8:58; Jn. 18:4-8: "I AM": 11 times in John's Gospel alone
Col. 2:9: "In Christ the fullness of deity resides in bodily form"
Jn. 10:30; 14:9-11; 17:11; 17:21: the Father and I are one
Jn. 20:28: "my Lord (Yahweh) and my God (Elohim)"
Jn. 20:16: Rabbuni—used usually to address God
2 Tim. 4:18; 2 Pet. 3:18; Rev. 1:6; Heb. 13:20-21: phrase "to him be glory for ever" usually reserved for God
Mt. 5:1-12: Sermon on the Mount. Jesus is the New Moses, but greater. Whereas Moses received the commandments and then brought them to the people, Jesus gives the law to the people from the mount directly. Jesus is God as the lawgiver from the mount as God was the lawgiver to Moses from Sinai. Jesus is God and the New Moses!

Mt. 19:28; 25:31; Jn. 5:22; Acts 10:42: judging living and dead, a divine prerogative

Mt. 9:6: forgiveness of sin, a divine prerogative

Jn. 1:3; Col. 1:16f; Heb. 1:2: creator of all things, a divine prerogative

Mk. 1:1; Lk. 1:32; Jn. 1:34: Son of God

1 Cor. 2:8: Lord of Glory

Rev. 17:14; 19:16: King of Kings

Rev. 1:8f: Alpha and Omega

Mt. 1:21; Jn. 3:14-15: Savior

Jn. 1:1-5, 14; Mt. 1:23; Lk. 2:52: assumed a human nature

Jn. 4:34; Mk. 14:36: divine and human will

Jn. 14:28: "the Father is greater than I"—in Jesus' human nature the Father is greater; in Jesus' divine nature, he is equal to the Father. Why is this? See next quote from Philippians 2:7f. Emptied himself of all except what was necessary for our salvation.

Phil. 2:7f: assumed a human, rational soul

1 Pet. 2:22; Jn. 8:46; 2 Cor. 5:21; Heb. 4:15: immune from sin

Holy Spirit

Acts 5:3-4: lie to Holy Spirit is a lie to God

Jn. 15:26: proceeds from the Father

Lk. 1:35: makes us aware of the Incarnation

Jn. 20:22-23: the forgiveness of sins

1 Cor. 6:11 Rom. 15:16: justification and sanctification

Rom. 5:5: charity of God

Jn. 14:16-17; 15:26: spirit of truth

Acts 6:5: strengthens our faith

Rom. 8:9-11; 1 Cor. 3:16; 6:19: dwells within us

Acts 8:29: guides our works

1 Cor. 12:11; 1 Cor. 12:4-11: supernatural gifts and supernatural life

Cf. Jn. 14:16-18; Acts 5:3f; 1 Cor. 2:10f; 3:16; 6:11, 19f; 1 Pet. 1:1-3; Eph. 4:4-6: attests to his divinity and consubstantiality or oneness with the Father and the Son

Is. 11:1-2: gifts of spirit—wisdom, understanding, counsel, fortitude, knowledge, piety, fear of the Lord

Gal. 5:22-23: fruits of the spirit—love, joy, peace, patience, kindness, generosity, faithfulness, gentleness, and self-control

Seven Sacraments
Baptism

Original sin

Gen. 2:16-17: the day you eat of that tree, you shall die

Gen. 3:11-19: God's punishment for eating of the tree

Rom. 5:12-19: many became sinners through one man's sin

1 Cor. 15:21-23: by a man came death; in Adam all die

Eph. 2:1-3: we all once lived in the passions of our flesh

Baptism
Mt. 28:19; Mk. 16:16; Jn. 3:5: commanded by Christ
Acts 2:38, 41; 8:12, 38; 9:18; 10:48: taught and administered by the apostles
Mk. 1:4, 8; Jn. 1:33; 3:5; Tit. 3:5: laver of regeneration
Mk. 16:16; Acts 2:38; 8:12f; 16:33; Rom. 6:3-6; Gal. 3:27; 1 Cor. 6:11; Eph.
5:26; Col. 2:12-14; Heb. 10:22: takes away all sin
Acts 2:38; 19:5f: receive the Holy Spirit
Gal. 3:27; Mk. 10:38; Lk. 12:50; Rom. 6:3: put on Christ, and are baptized into
his death and resurrection
1 Cor. 12:13, 27: enter into the Church

Of Infants
Rom. 5:18-19: all are born of Adam's sin and need baptism
Jn. 3:5/ Mk. 16:16: baptism necessary for salvation
Mk. 10:14: let the children come; to such belongs the kingdom
Lk. 18:15: people were bringing even infants to him
Acts 16:15: she was baptized, with all her household
Acts 16:33: he and all his family were baptized at once
1 Cor. 1:16: I (Paul) baptized the household of Stephanas
Col. 2:11-12: baptism replaces circumcision (which was done on the eighth
day) for being part of the people of God, of the new covenant. Old Testament
infants did not make a choice regarding their circumcision, their being part of
the people of God; their parents did--likewise in baptism

Mt. 8:5ff/ Mt. 15:21f
Faith of parents speaks for infants/children (i.e., Servant was healed
through centurion's faith/ daughter was healed through mother's faith

Confirmation
Completes baptism

Acts 19:5-6: Paul imposed hands on baptized & they received Holy Spirit
Acts 8:14-17: laid hands upon them; they received the Holy Spirit
2 Cor. 1:21-22: put seal on us/ given Spirit in our hearts
Eph. 1:13: you were sealed with the promised Holy Spirit
Heb. 6:2: instruction about baptism and laying on of hands

Holy Eucharist

Mal. 1:11: prophesied—"Gentiles" offering sacrifice!!
Ex. 16:15: prefigured/ *man hu* which has its origins in the Hebrew word *"man"*
but often rendered *"manna."* The "unknown" food from heaven!
Mt. 26:26-28; Mk. 14:22-24; Lk. 22:19f: "Do this in remembrance of me"
1 Cor. 10:16: Eucharist—participation in Christ's body and blood

1 Cor. 11:23-29: receiving unworthily=guilty of his body and blood
~Ex. 12:8, 46: Paschal Lamb had to be eaten
~Jn. 1:29: Jesus is Lamb of God—therefore to be eaten
~1 Cor. 5:7: Jesus is "paschal lamb who has been sacrificed"
Jn. 6:35-71: Real Presence
    Gen. 9:3-4; Lev. 17:14: eating food and drinking blood forbidden/
    explains why they abandoned Jesus
    Jn. 6:63: requires gift of God to understand (cf. Jn. 3:6)
    There are several dimensions to the Eucharist, one is symbolic (to do
    the will of Father/ the gift of faith), the other is "real presence" and
    "real sacrifice" (Jn. 4:31-34; Mt. 16:5-12)

Penance

James 5:16: confess your sins to one another—*not simply to God*
James 5:13-15: prayer of presbyters forgives sins
Mt. 18:18; 16:19: whatever you bind and loose on earth…in heaven
Jn. 20:22-23: "Jesus breathed on them and said to them, 'Receive the Holy
Spirit.' Whose sins you forgive are forgiven them, and whose sins you retain
are retained."
    **"Receive the Holy Spirit" is a reference to Genesis 2:7 where God
    breathed life into man. In the forgiveness of sins, we have new life!**

Mortal and Venial Sins
1 Jn. 5:16-17: some sins are deadly, some sins are not deadly

Anointing of the Sick

James 5:14f: presbyters pray over sick, anoint and bring forgiveness of sins
Mk. 6:12-13: anointed the sick, many cured

Holy Orders

Lk. 22:19; Jn. 20:22f: *Instituted by Christ*
"Do this in memory of me." "As the Father sent me, I send you…receive the
Holy Spirit."
Acts 6:1: ministry of ordained an deacon
1 Tim. 3:1-16: bishops and deacons/ qualifications
Rom: 16:1: Deaconess: name given historically to the wife of a deacon. (found
only in RSV, NJB).). "deaconoi" also commonly used for ministers that are not
ordained as well.
Acts 20:17-28: Presbyters summoned and told them that they have been
appointed by the Holy Spirit as overseers of the Church
Acts 13:3: they laid hands on them and sent them off
Acts 14:23: they appointed presbyters in each church
Tit. 1:5: appoint presbyters in every town, as I directed you

give grace/ ordained by those ordained

1 Tim. 4:14: gift received through the laying on of hands by presbyters

2 Tim. 1:6: gift of God you have through imposition of hands

Father Quote

Mt. 23:9: Call no man your father?

Acts 7:2: Stephen calls Jewish leaders "fathers"

Acts 22:1: Paul calls Jerusalem Jews "fathers"

Rom. 4:16-17: Abraham called "the father of us all"

1 Cor. 4:14-15: I became your father in Christ

1 Tim. 1:2: my true child in the faith

Tit. 1:4: my true child in our common faith

Heb. 12:7-9: we have earthly fathers to discipline us

Philemon 1:10: whose father I became in my imprisonment

1 Jn. 2:13,14: I write to you fathers…

Celibacy

Mt. 19:12: celibacy praised by Jesus who was celibate

1 Cor. 7:8; Saint Paul was celibate

1 Cor. 7:32-35: celibacy is recommended for full-time ministers

1 Tim. 5:9-12: pledge of celibacy taken by older widow
Order of Religious and virgins

Matrimony

Mt. 19:5: leave father and mother, join wife, and two shall become one flesh

Mk. 10:7-12: what God has joined together, no man must separate

Eph. 5:22-32: union of man and wife as image of the inseparable nature between Christ and his Church

1 Thess. 4:4: acquire a wife for yourself in holiness and honor

Divorce and remarriage (without an annulment—declaration of nullity), contrary to God's will

Mal. 2:14-16: for I hate divorce, says the Lord

Mk. 10:11-12: if either divorces and remarries=adultery

1 Cor. 7:10-11: if wife separates, stay single or reconcile

Rom. 7:2-3: death frees one to remarry
as does annulments—see below

Annulment/ Declaration of Nullity—based on following:

Mt. 5:32-33; Acts 15:20; 15:29; Mt. 19:5-9: reference to "unlawful marriages"

Lev. 18: examples of some "unlawful marriages"

Mt. 14:3-12: King Herod's marriage to Heordias, Herod's brother Philip's wife,

301

viewed as "unlawful."

Mary

Mary's unique dignity
Lk. 1:42: "most blessed among women"
Lk. 1:48: "all generations will call me blessed"
Lk. 1:28, 30: "full of grace," found favor with God

Mother of God
Mt. 1:21-23: Emmanuel which means 'God is with us'
Lk. 1:43: Mother of my Lord

Mary without sin--Immaculate
Lk. 1:28, 30: "full of grace" the Lord is with you (*kecharitomene*) / Jesus is "full of grace" (Jn. 1:14).
Lk. 1:35: "to overshadow" Mary "to overshadow" the Ark of the Covenant (Ex. 40: 34-35)
Ex. 40: ark made perfect in every detail to allow God's presence to fill it

Without sin because of the Savior
Lk. 1:47: "my spirit rejoices in God my Savior"

What about Rom. 3:23? "All have sinned and are deprived of the glory of God" This is a generalization for the mass of humanity since Jesus never sinned and infants do not sin until they reach the age of childhood, the age of reason.

In Genesis 1:2f we are reminded that from the immaculately created cosmos God created Adam. In Romans 5:14 and 1 Corinthians 15:22 we are reminded that Jesus is the second Adam. If the first Adam was created from pristine organic materials, what would the second Adam be created from? Obviously an immaculate, pristine Mother!

Perpetual Virginity
Zech. 12:10: "as one mourns an only son"
Mary's children never mentioned

"brothers and sisters?"
What about Mt. 12:46, John 7:5; Acts 1:14; Gal. 1:19; Mark. 3:31-35; 6:3? In the Hebrew and Aramaic there was no word for cousin, uncle, nephew, niece, half-brother or sister, or close relative. The NT alone uses the word brother for all kinds of relationships 325 times. In acts 1:15f Peter addresses the 120 brothers! James and Joseph are referred to as "the brothers of Jesus" and yet are "sons of another [the other] Mary, a disciple of Christ" (cf. Mt. 13:55; 28:1; cf. Mt. 27:56: Jn. 19:25 "Mary of Clopas")). Jesus himself refers to all of us as being "all brothers" (Mt. 23:8). Other examples of "brothers" used in a non-

302

familial sense are Rom. 14:10, 21; 1 Cor. 5:11; 2 Cor. 8:18; 1 Thess. 4:6; 1 Jn. 3:17; 4:20.

In Gen. 14:14 Lot is described as Abraham's brother, yet Lot is the son of Aran. Lot was Abraham's nephew. Jacob is called the brother of Laban, yet Laban is his uncle (Gen. 29:15). When we look to Dt. 23:7-8 and Jeremiah 34:9 we notice the appellation brothers is used in terms of a person who shares the same culture or national background. In 2 Samuel 1:26 and 1 Kings 9:13 we notice that brother is used in terms of a friend. In Amos 1:9 brother is used as an ally.

"*firstborn*" (Lk. 2:7)

Ex: 11:5: "every first-born child shall die"—no implication of further births guaranteed

Gen. 27; Ex. 13:2; Nm. 3:12-13; Dt. 21:15-17: firstborn referred to rights and privileges

Ex. 13:2; Nb. 3:12: firstborn referred to the opening of the womb of a woman

Ex.13: 1-16: 34:20: firstborn to be consecrated to God; firstborn referred to being sanctified

Zech. 12:10: "only son" and "first born"

Gen. 49:3: firstborn as preeminent in pride and power

Gen. 12:15-17: birthright as a double share of the father's property which cannot be denied

Ps. 89:28: divine protection and promise

Ex. 4:22: Nation of Israel as "firstborn"

Rom: 8:29: Jesus, firstborn among many (future Christians)

Col. 1:15: Firstborn of all creation

Col. 1:18: Firstborn of new creation

Rev. 1:5: firstborn of the dead, and the ruler of the kings on earth.

"*until*" (Mt. 1:25)

heos-hou: this compound word makes no further implications

Lk. 1:80: John in desert until day of his manifestation (John remained in the desert after Jesus' manifestation)

Mt. 28:20: I am with you until the end of the age (Jesus will not cease to be with us after the end of the age)

1 Tim. 4:13: until I arrive, attend to reading, teaching… (they obviously will not stop reading or teaching after Paul's arrival")

1 Cor. 15:25: he must reign until he has put his enemies under his foot (Will he cease to reign after this? Obviously not!)

Jn. 19:26-27: unheard of in Jewish culture to give your mother into the care of a non-family member

Assumption

Psalm 16:10: the beloved will not know decay

Lk. 1:28: since Mary was full of grace, she bore no original sin and therefore could not experience decay

303

Gn. 5:24; Hb. 11:5: If Enoch was taken up to heaven, why not Mary?
2 Kg. 2:11: If Elijah was taken up to heaven, why not Mary?
Mt. 27:52: If many saints who had fallen asleep were resurrected "caught up" (in some translations) to meet the Lord in the air, why not Mary?
Rev; 12:1f: Mary clothed with the sun

Saints

Communion of saints
Rom. 8:35-39: death cannot separate us from Christ. Therefore, death cannot separate us from his body, the Church. Christ is the head, his body is the Church. The head and body are inseparable in this world and in heaven (cf. Eph. 1:22-23; 5:21-32; Col. 1:18, 24; Rom. 12:5)
Col. 1:24: Make up what is lacking in the sufferings of Christ…
Mk. 9:4: example of communion of saints

Intercessory power of saints
Tob. 12:12: angel presents Tobit and Sarah's prayer to God
Rev. 5:8: elders offer prayers of the holy ones to God
Mk. 9:4: Jesus conversing with Moses and Elijah
Rev. 6:9-11: martyrs under altar seek earthly vindication
Sir. 48:14: in death he did marvelous deeds

Veneration of saints
1 Thess. 1:5-8: you became an example to all believers
Heb. 13:7: imitate the faith and life of leaders
Jos. 5:14: Joshua fell prostrate in veneration before angel
Dan. 8:17: Daniel fell prostrate in terror before Gabriel
Tob. 12:16: Tobiah and Tobit fall to ground before Raphael
Mk. 9:4: build three tents

Relics of saints
2 Kgs. 13:20-21: contact with Elisha's bones restored life
Acts 5:15-16: cures performed through Peter's shadow
Acts 19:11-12: cures through face cloths that touched Paul

Statues (Ex. 20:4-5 prohibition)
Ex. 25:18-19: make two cherubim of beaten gold
Nb. 21:8-9: bronze serpent on pole
1 Kgs. 6:23-29: temple had engraved cherubim, trees, flowers
1 Kgs. 7:25-45: temple had bronze oxen, lions, pomegranates

The Last Things

Purgatory
Wis. 3:1-8: gold in a furnace

Rev. 21:27: nothing unclean enters into heaven
1 Cor. 3:15: he will be saved but only as through fire
Mt. 12:36: account for every word on judgment day
Mt. 5:26: will not be released until the last penny is paid
1 Cor. 15:29-30: people being baptized for the dead
2 Tim. 1:16-18: Paul prays for dead friend Onesiphorus
1 Pet. 3:18-20; 4:6: Jesus preached to spirits in prison
Mt. 12:32: sin against Holy Spirit unforgiven in this age or in the age to come
2 Macc. 12:44-46: atoned for dead to free them from sin

Temporal punishment
2 Sam. 12:13-14: David, though forgiven, still punished for sin
Nb. 20:12: Moses would not enter the promised land

Indulgences:
Rom. 12:4-8: Body of Christ
Col. 1:24: make up what is lacking in sufferings

Being saved
I have been saved (if in a state of grace I am currently saved at this moment in time)
Eph. 2:5-8: by grace you have been saved through faith
2 Tim. 1:9: he saved us, called us, according to his grace
Tit. 3:5: he saved us through a bath of rebirth

No assurance of salvation
Mt. 7:21: not everyone who says "Lord, Lord," will inherit
Mt. 24:13: those who persevere to the end will be saved
Phil. 2:12: work out your salvation in fear and trembling
1 Cor. 9:27: drive body for fear of being disqualified
1 Cor. 10:11-12: those thinking they are secure, may fall
Gal. 5:4: separated from grace, you have fallen from grace
2 Tim. 2:11-13: must hold out to the end to reign with Christ
Heb. 6:4-6: describes those who have fallen
Heb. 10:26-27: if sin after receiving truth, judgment remains
1 Pet. 1:9: as you attain the goal of your faith, salvation
Mt. 10:22: he who endures to the end will be saved
Rom. 13:11: salvation is nearer now than when you first believed
1 Cor. 3:15: he will be saved but only as through fire

Faith and works (inseparable)
Jam. 2:24: a man is justified by works and not by faith alone
Jam. 2:26: faith without works is dead
Gal. 5:6: only thing that counts is faith working in love
1 Cor. 13:2: faith without love is nothing
Jn. 14:15: if you love me, keep my commandments

Mt. 19:16-17: if you wish to enter into life, keep my commandments
Phil. 2:12: work out your salvation with fear and trembling.
Mt. 7:21: not everyone who says "Lord, Lord," will inherit
Rom. 2:2-8: eternal life by perseverance in good works
Eph. 2:8-10: we are created in Christ for good works
Rom. 2:5-8: God will repay each one according to his works
2 Cor. 11:15: their end corresponds to deeds
1 Pet. 1:17: God judges according to one's works
Rev. 20:12-13: dead judged according to their deeds
Col 3:24-25: will receive due payment for whatever you do

Hell
Mt. 13:49-50; 25:33-46: those who go to hell
Mt. 25:41; 2 Thess. 1:6-9: eternal punishment

Heaven
Mt. 5:3-12; 22:32; 25:33-40; Rom. 8:17: reality

Particular Judgment
Lk. 23:43; 2 Cor. 5:8; Phil. 1:23-24; Heb. 9:27: soul judged immediately upon death

Parousia: Time of second coming unknown
Mt. 24:44: be prepared, Jesus coming at unexpected hour
Mt. 25:13: stay awake, you know neither the day nor hour
Lk. 12:46: master will come at unexpected day and hour
1 Thess. 5:2-3: day of the Lord will come like a thief in the night
2 Pet. 3:9-10: day of the Lord will come like a thief
Rev. 3:3: if not watchful, will come like a thief
Mt. 24:36: no one but Father alone knows day and hour

Last Judgment
Acts 24:15; Jn. 5:28-29: body reunited in a glorified form with our souls—rapture is for those still living when Christ returns. They will be judged and go eternally with God, **raptured** into heaven, or sent to hell.
Phil. 3:20-21: glorified resurrected body

New Heaven and a New Earth
2 Pet. 3:13; Rev. 21:1-4

APPENDIX 6
CATHOLIC SPIRITUALITY

I
The Awakening

People are hungry for God. People are hungry for love. Are you aware of that? Do you know that? Do you see that? Do you have eyes to see? Quite often we look but we don't see. We are all passing through this world. We need to open our eyes and see.[1]

Mother Teresa

When one's eyes are open to the reality of God, then one can be said to be awakened. There is a point in life where one is faced with the reality that there is something which is beyond the self and the here and now, something which transcends the limits of one's being. This moment is a moment of choice. Does one seek to explore and enter into this mystery of that which is not limited to the self or does one repress the experience? The choice made is the choice that will help govern one's life.

What attracts you to God?

One is awakened and moved to follow the ways of grace by being enlightened to the presence of God. Traditionally, people have been attracted to God in the following ways:

Meaning and Purpose

People are often awakened or attracted to God because God gives them a sense of meaning and purpose in life (cf. Dt. 6:24-25). One recognizes that one must be more than some complex organism that is born, lives, struggles, and dies in emptiness. Life in many ways would be a farce if that were so. Life would be inevitably on the edge of disintegration. There must be more to life than mere existence, than mere survival.

Life needs purpose and meaning, a purpose and meaning that transcends the here and now.

God provides this purpose and meaning, for he is the source and summit of all meaning and purpose.

Truth

Many are attracted to God because he is Truth (1 Jn. 4:6). Such people seek truth in life, no matter where they may find it. Such people find great comfort in God because he is the goal of their quest, truth itself. Hence, life

---

[1] *Mother Teresa, One Heart Full of Love* (Ann Arbor: Servant Publications, 1984), 11.

becomes for such individuals a delving into the mysteries of God, which consumes the entirety of their lives and gives them their ultimate joy.

Good

Some people find God by seeing the good around them. Malcolm Muggeridge, a world-renowned reporter for the BBC, was such a person in many respects. It was in seeing the good that was in the heart of Mother Teresa of Calcutta that he was able to find Christ. In Mother Teresa he saw Jesus Christ, and his life would never be the same again. God is good, and those who have found authentic goodness have found God (cf. Rm. 12:2).

Beautiful

Many are attracted to God because they see in the beauty of creation the handprint of God. For them all of creation echoes the beauty and providence of God. To find authentic beauty is to find the source of all beauty, God (cf. Wis. 13:3).

The Four Ways

While it is true that most people will find an affinity for one of the above ways in which we are attracted to God, all the above ways should be a part of one's attraction to God.

The spiritual journey is a chase after the heart of God, and this entails continual growth and maturity into the ways of God.

A Hardened Heart

I felt at the time that religion would impede my work. I wanted to have nothing to do with the religion of those I saw all around me. I felt that I must turn from it as from a drug. I felt it indeed to be an opiate of the people and not a very attractive one, so I hardened my heart. It was a conscious and deliberate process.[2]

Dorothy Day

Dorothy Day would eventually respond to God and soften her heart and become a world leader in the Church's work for the poor and the disenfranchised.

A hardened heart is one of the most problematic dilemmas that one can experience along one's journey in life (cf. Jn. 12:40). It is so problematic because it is so difficult to overcome and to heal. There is perhaps nothing more obtrusive to the gift of grace than a heart that is unwilling to open itself up to the possibility of an all-engulfing God.

---

[2] Dorothy Day, *The Long Loneliness* (New York: Curtis Books, 1972), 10.

A hardened heart is a frightened heart, a heart unwilling to take a chance at experiencing anything beyond its comfort level. There is a fear that what one may find if one opens one's heart will be too overwhelming to deal with.

A hardened heart is most often the consequence of some unresolved issue or deep psychological scar that has never been dealt with properly. One cannot conquer what one does not recognize.

When one examines the lives of atheists, it is astonishingly common to find these people lacking in good fatherly figures. It is difficult to pray "Our Father who art in heaven" when the only experience of a father has been one that has been experienced as evil, mean-spirited, or non-existent. When looking at the lives of the world's major atheists, such as men like Nietzsche, one is struck by this lack of fatherly guidance. For people such as this, often a miracle is necessary to soften the heart.

It is here where the communion of saints becomes so significant (cf. Jn. 2:1-14; Rev. 5:8). The communion of the faithful here on earth and in heaven has a profound effect on the softening of hearts throughout the world, for by themselves people with hardened hearts are much too weak to respond to the grace that is being showered upon them. A tragic event or the power of the prayers of the saints is often the only way these people soften their hearts. In many ways, they are very much like addicts. They often need to hit rock bottom before they can acknowledge the need of another. It is through the prayers of others, known and unknown, that the world's hearts are softened.

One must, thus, never underestimate the power of praying for others. St. Monica prayed for thirty years for the conversion of her son, Augustine. Her prayers were successful in softening his heart and he became the great St. Augustine.

II
Foundational Points

The Dignity of the Human Person

Christ ...in the very revelation of the mystery of the Father and of his love, makes man fully manifest to himself and brings to light his exalted vocation.[3]

The human person has been created in the "image and likeness of God" (cf. Gen. 1:27). This image and likeness to God is seen in a person's expression of his or her powers of the intellect, will, and freedom.[4] However, it is in Christ,

---

[3] GS 22.
[4] Ibid., 17.

the Savior and Redeemer, that the divine image is ennobled and most perfectly manifested.[5]

The human person is gifted with an immortal and spiritual nature. The human person is the only act of creation that God willed for its own unique sake.[6] From the very moment of conception, the human person is born to eternal life.[7]

The human person has been endowed with the gift of freely seeking, perceiving and loving the good and the true. This is a gift that is found at the very core of the person. It is a natural law that has been embedded into the core of a person's conscience.[8]

At the beginning of time humanity had a choice to live with God or live without him (cf. Gen. 3:1-24). The choice to live without God caused a wound, a wound that would forever affect human nature. This wound would come to be known as original sin, a sin of such a great nature that it destroyed the possibility of eternal life and happiness.

God would not allow humanity to remain separated from eternal life with him. He sent his only begotten Son to restore us to new life in God (2 Cor. 5:17). Sin was forgiven by the merits of Christ.

Yet even though the deep, penetrating cut of original sin was cleansed by the blood of Christ on the cross, a scar persisted, a scar called concupiscence. Thus, scarred, but not destroyed, human nature is forever tempted and inclined, on this earthly journey, toward evil and error.

Thus, human nature is involved in a spiritual battle, a battle between good and evil, light and darkness (cf. Jn. 1:5; 8:12; 12:35).[9] It is a spiritual battle, however, that is fought with the gift of God's grace that was restored to us in Christ Jesus.

The gift of grace is that gift that enables one to become a child of God (cf. 1 Jn. 5:1). A person, through the merits of Christ and the gift of grace, is able to grow in the spiritual and moral life.[10]

Grace[11]

Grace is...rooted in us, and worked into us like leaven, from our earliest years, until the thing thus present becomes fixed in a man like a natural endowment, as if it were one substance with him. But,

---

[5] Ibid., 22.
[6] Ibid., 24.
[7] CCC 1703.
[8] GS 15-17; CCC 1704-1707.
[9] GS 13; CCC 1706.
[10] CCC 1709.
[11] Cf. CCC 1996-2005. See Henri de Lubac, *A Brief Catechesis on Nature and Grace*, trans. Brother Richard Arnandez (San Francisco: Ignatius Press, 1984) for a historical survey of the relationship between nature and grace.

for the man's own good, it manages him in many different ways, after its own pleasure. Sometimes the fire flames out and kindles more vehemently; at other times more gently and mildly. The light that it gives kindles up at times and shines with unusual brightness; at others it abates and burns low. The lamp is always burning and shining, but when it is specially trimmed, it kindles up with intoxication with the love of God....[12]

Pseudo-Marcarius

The Christian is one who responds to live life in love, the love of God, neighbor, and self (cf. Lk. 10:27). The Christian is one who is moving toward total authenticity, toward total and full *human-ness*. The Christian is radically oriented to respond to one's ultimate destiny of union with the self-communicating God of love. The spiritual journey is a call to be awakened, purified, and illuminated to one's true nature. The spiritual life is a call to reality, to see reality as it truly is and to see one's own self as one truly is.

Grace is the fundamental reality of the spiritual journey. Grace is a participation in the life of God, which justifies, sanctifies, deifies, and makes one a co-heir with God (cf. Jn. 1:12-18; 17:3; Rom. 8:14-17; 2 Cor. 5:17-18; 2 Pet. 1:3-4). Grace is the gift of God himself—the giver is the gift.[13] Grace is a supernatural, gratuitous, and perfecting gift and favor that is always present—existentially present—at the very core of the person waiting to be accepted or rejected in freedom.[14] When a person truly seeks to understand his or her very core, he or she is bound to end up finding grace, finding God.

Habitual Grace

Habitual grace or sanctifying grace is that gift of the Holy Spirit that gives an individual the capacity to act in accordance with the demands of faith, hope and love. It is with the person, unless eliminated by mortal sin.[15]

Actual Graces

Flares of grace, divine touches, wounds of love, darts of love are often what are referred to as actual graces.[16] An actual grace is a gift, a special flare or moment of God's self-communicating, that enables a person to act in a

---

[12] *Fifty Spiritual Homilies of St. Macarius the Great*, trans. A.J. Mason (Willits: Eastern Orthodox Books, 1974), Homily VIII, n. 2.

[13] Karl Rahner, *Foundations of the Christian Faith: An Introduction to the Idea of Christianity*, trans. by William V. Dych (New York: Crossroad Publishing, Co., 1984), 120.

[14] Cf. Rahner, *Foundations*, 128.

[15] Cf. Ia, q. 105, a.4; Ia IIae, q. 9, a.6; q. 10, a.4; q. 109, a.2, 3, 4, 10. All quotations and citations regarding St. Thomas Aquinas' *Summa* will always be cited in full in this text in order to alleviate confusion.

[16] Cf. *Spiritual Canticle*, st. 1, nos. 17-22; *Living Flame*, St. 1, no. 27. All quotations and citations from St. John of the Cross and St. Teresa of Avila are taken from the Institute of Carmelite Studies' editions.

salutary, beneficial, curative, and holy manner. Often this flare of grace is experienced as an interior impulse, attraction, inspiration, illumination, or interior light. At times it is experienced as a special moment of strength, courage or endurance. At other times it arouses good thoughts and feelings that seem to come from nowhere.[17]

The life of grace is a taste of heaven, for it is a taste of God.[18]

St. Thomas Aquinas

Grace and Nature[19]

We are body and soul (cf. 1 Thess. 5:13; Mt. 10:28). This reality has a profound impact on the spiritual life. If a person's body is healthy, psychologically and physically, grace has a much more profound impact on the spiritual life of the person, depending on the person's free-will response to God's self-communication. If, however, the body is ill, psychologically or physically, then the spiritual life is subject to difficulties in its progress. Likewise, if the person's spiritual life is weak, then a person's soul will be unhealthy, and so too will the body. The body will be subject to all kinds of psychological and related physical ailments. Hence, one is called to foster a healthy physical and spiritual life. If one's bodily existence is ailing, one should seek all the medical attention within one's capacity (i.e., medication, counseling, etc.) (cf. 1 Tim. 5:23). If one's spiritual life is unhealthy, one must seek a deeper conversion so as to promote a healthy bodily existence.

What about the cross? It is true that at times, despite all the medical attention one may have access to, the body bears incurable wounds. This is the mystery of the cross and the mystery of grace. Despite it all, Christ, the *Great Physician*, takes the weaknesses and wounds of a person and elevates them into strengths: Who better to understand a person's weakness than one who is weak?

Grace not only builds upon nature, but it also heals and elevates it to new heights (cf. 2 Cor. 12:10). Thus, grace is often the source of the healing of many ailments, whether physical, psychological, or spiritual.

Grace and Merit

[Faith] apart from works is dead (cf. Jms. 2:14-26).

Grace and good works are inseparable realities in the life of a person. Authentic faith always points to authentic holy works and authentically holy works are always marked by authentic faith. It is this reality between grace and

---

[17] Cf. Ia, q. 105, a.4; Ia IIae, q. 9, a.6, q. 10, a.4; q. 109, a.2, 3, 4, 10.
[18] Cf. IIa IIae, q. 24, a.3 ad 2um; Ia IIae, q. 69, a.2.
[19] See De Lubac, *Nature and Grace*.

merit that exemplifies the reality of the spiritual journey, since all are called to perfection (cf. Rom. 8:28-30) and the spiritual battle (cf. 2 Tim. 4).

Justification[20]

Justification flows from grace. Grace provides the person with the possibility of entering into the Paschal Mystery--Jesus' life, death, resurrection and ascension. Consequently, grace justifies a person. It makes one a "new creation" in God (cf. Rom. 3:22; 6:3-4, 8-11; 1 Cor. 12; Jn. 15:1-4).

There are essentially six key aspects in regard to justification:

1) "Justification is not only the remission of sins, but also the sanctification and renewal of the interior man," conversion (cf. Mt. 4:17).[21]

2) Justification detaches a person from sin, from enslavement, through the continual offer of forgiveness. It reconciles and heals the person's innermost being.

3) Justification is the acceptance of God's righteousness. It is the acceptance of the life of faith, hope, and love—a life in obedience to God's will.

4) Justification has been merited by Christ's Passion (cf. Rom. 3:21-26). Justification implies a blood atonement for sins and the gift of eternal life through the gift of baptism into Christ's life, death, and resurrection (either by a baptism of desire, blood, or water).

5) Justification establishes the cooperation between grace and freedom. On God's part there is the continual offer of grace. On the person's part there is the demand for continual conversion (cf. Mt. 4:17) and the continual assent to faith. It demands response to the Spirit and cooperation in divine love.

6) Justification entails the sanctification of the whole being (cf. Rom. 6:19, 22).

The Moral Law[22]

The moral law is that which guides a person on the spiritual journey. There are three kinds of moral laws, all of which are interrelated, and all of which find their source of being at the core of the person (cf. Phil. 2:12-13).

Natural Law

Natural law finds its impetus in God's wisdom and the immutable gift of reason.[23] The goal of the moral law is life in Christ (cf. Rom. 10:4).

---

[20] Cf. CCC 1987-1995.
[21] Council of Trent (1547): DS 1528.
[22] Cf. CCC 1950-1974; 2031-2046.
[23] Cf. GS 10.

The natural law is written and engraved in the soul of each and every man, because it is human reason ordaining him to do good and forbidding him to sin.... But this command of human reason would not have the force of law if it were not the voice and interpreter of a higher reason to which our spirit and our freedom must be submitted.[24]

Where then are these rules written, if not in the book of that light we call the truth? In it is written every just law; from it the law passes into the heart of the man who does justice, not that it migrates into it, but that it places its imprint on it, like a seal on a ring that passes unto wax, without leaving the ring.[25]

Leo XIII/ St. Augustine

The natural law is nothing other than the light of understanding in us by God; through it we know what we must do and what we must avoid. God has given this light or law at creation.[26]

St. Thomas Aquinas

Through the natural law one practices that which is good and attends to one's eternal destiny, one's salvation.[27] The natural law promotes the dignity and the rights and duties of the person.

Revealed Law

Divine revelation, which is found in the Sacred Scriptures and Sacred Tradition, reveals that which is in the heart.[28] It aids, enlightens, and clarifies the natural moral law, which sin can often cloud.[29] The moral law finds its fulfillment in the law of love.

Ecclesiastical Law

The laws or precepts of the Church nourish and strengthen a person's ability to perceive and follow the innate natural law. The emphasis on these laws is on attending Mass on a regular basis, receiving communion, seeking reconciliation, fasting and abstaining from meat on appointed days, joining in the missionary efforts of the Church, and so on.

---

[24] Leo XIII, *Li bertas praestantissimum*, 597, quoted in CCC 1954.
[25] St. Augustine, *De Trin.* 14, 15, 21: PL 42, 1052.
[26] St. Thomas Aquinas, *Dec. praec.* I.
[27] Cf. GS 89.
[28] St. Augustine, *En. In Ps.* 57, 1: PL 36, 673.
[29] Pius XII, *Humani generis*: DS 3876; cf. *Dei Filius* 2: DS 3005.

To live well is nothing other than to love God with all one's heart, with all one's soul and with all one's efforts; from this it comes about that love is kept whole and uncorrupted (through temperance). No misfortune can disturb it (and this is fortitude). It obeys only [God] (and this is justice), and is careful in discerning things, so as not to be surprised by deceit or trickery (and this is prudence).[30]

St. Augustine

A holy person is a virtuous person (cf. Wis. 8:7; Phil. 4:8). A holy person is a virtuous person who seeks "to be like God"[31]; that is, to be in the image and likeness to which he or she was originally created in (cf. Gen. 1:27). Therefore, in order for one to comprehend the path that grace draws one toward, one needs to comprehend the virtues. There are two types of virtues, the acquired moral virtues and the infused moral virtues.

Acquired Moral Virtues

The acquired moral virtues are acquired by the repetition of acts under the direction of the light of *natural right reason*. Grace is not required to acquire these natural virtues.

For example, by the natural light of human reason and discipline one can learn to be just, temperate, courageous, and prudent.

Infused Moral Virtues

Infused moral virtues require a person's response to grace. Through a person's response to grace, the acquired virtues, which are guided by right reason, are elevated to a level that surpasses the limits of right reason alone. Only God can empower a person with infused moral virtues, for they are by nature supernatural acts of grace. These virtues are directed toward a person's supernatural last end and consequently are essential for eternal life.[32]

The Relationship Between Acquired and Infused Moral Virtues

Holiness at whatever level requires the proper interaction of the acquired and infused moral virtues.[33] The proper interaction of the acquired moral virtues and the infused moral virtues make for the perfect spiritual person. In such a case, all of a person's life, in all its aspects, is in perfect harmony, like five fingers on a hand.[34]

---

[30] St. Augustine, *De moribus eccl.* 1, 25, 46: PL 32, 1330-1331.
[31] St. Gregory of Nyssa, *De beatitudinibus*, 1: PG 44, 1200D.
[32] Cf. Ia IIae, q. 63, a.3, 4; q. 109, a.3.
[33] Cf. IIa IIae, q. 24, a.9.
[34] Cf. Ia IIae, q. 66, a.2.

The Theological Virtues (cf. 1 Cor. 13:13)

The theological virtues of faith, hope, and love empty a person of all that is not for the honor and glory of God and fills such a person with God's self-communicating, cleansing presence. A person is empty to be filled.

The human virtues are grounded in the theological virtues (cf. 2 Pet. 1:4), which enable a person to be animated, informed, and enlivened in Christ. Faith frees the intellect to soar into realms of knowing it had never before experienced (Is. 55:8-9). It penetrates the deep mysteries of God that are beyond the natural and rational boundaries.[35] Hope empties the memory of the unhealthy, worldly passing allurements that seek to compete with the bliss that comes from God. Love unburdens the will and the heart of all that is false and fleeting and helps one to cling to that which is of God.[36] In faith, hope, and love one moves toward union with God, toward peace, happiness, and light.[37]

Gifts of the Spirit

The gifts of the Holy Spirit are essential to the spiritual growth of the person and are essential for salvation.[38] The gifts of the Spirit are what transform a hardened heart into a docile heart, a heart ready for God's engulfing presence.[39]

Knowledge, understanding, wisdom, counsel, piety, fortitude, and fear of the Lord are the traditional gifts of the Spirit (Is. 11:2f). The gift of knowledge helps one to understand God's creation; the gift of understanding helps one to delve into the sphere of truth; the gift of wisdom, the highest of the gifts, aids one to perceive the divine; the gift of counsel helps one to direct one's actions according to God's will; the gift of piety aids one in proper worship; the gift of fortitude, helps one fight off the fears that confront one in the works of God, and the gift of fear of the Lord protects one from falling into disorderly temptations.

The Evangelical Counsels

The evangelical counsels are poverty, chastity, and obedience. They lead to spiritual perfection and the healing of moral wounds. *Poverty* is empowered by the theological virtue of hope, *chastity* by the theological virtue of love, and *obedience* by the theological virtue of faith. The counsels, thus, render to God what is due to him.[40]

The evangelical counsels take on a special meaning for those in religious life and holy orders. They, in a unique manner, point to life in heaven. *Poverty*

---

[35] Cf. *Ascent*, BK II, Ch. 1, no. 1.
[36] Cf. Ibid., BK II, Ch. 6, nos. 1-4.
[37] Cf. Ibid., BK II, Ch. 4, nos. 2-3.
[38] Cf. Ia IIae, q. 68, a.2.
[39] Cf. Ia IIae, q. 68, a.3.
[40] Cf. Ia IIae, q. 108, a.4; IIa IIae, q. 186, a.3, 4, 5, 7.

points to the reality that in heaven we will have no need, *celibacy* points to the fact that in heaven there will be no marrying, and *obedience* points to the fact that our eternal destiny will be consumed with being in perfect harmony with our Creator.

The Beatitudes (Mt. 5:3-12)

Blessed are the poor in spirit,
for theirs is the kingdom of heaven.
Blessed are they who mourn,
for they will be comforted.
Blessed are the meek,
for they will inherit the land.
Blessed are they who hunger and thirst for righteousness,
for they will be satisfied.
Blessed are the merciful,
for they will be shown mercy.
Blessed are the clean of heart,
for they will see God.
Blessed are the peacemakers,
for they will be called children of God.
Blessed are they who are persecuted for the sake of righteousness,
for theirs is the kingdom of heaven.
Blessed are you when they insult you and persecute you and utter every kind of evil against you [falsely] because of me. Rejoice and be glad, for your reward will be great in heaven. Thus they persecuted the prophets who were before you.[41]

The beatitudes flow from the gifts of the Spirit and dispose a person to obey these gifts.[42] The beatitude of being "poor in spirit" promotes confidence in God and complete dependence on God (cf. Is. 61:1; Zep. 2:3). It also engenders a humble predisposition. The beatitude of being "mournful" is that beatitude which fosters recognition of God's consolation and comfort. The beatitude of being "meek," engenders the recognition of one's place in the kingdom of God (cf. Ps. 37:11). The beatitude of "hungering and thirsting for righteousness" promotes conformity to God's will and a willing submission to God's plan of salvation for all. The beatitude of being "merciful" properly orders the virtue of justice in accordance to the "spirit" of the law as opposed to the "letter of the law." The beatitude of being "pure of heart" is that assurance that God's presence will always be with the pure of heart (cf. Ps. 24:4; 42:3). The beatitude of being a "peacemaker" is one that promotes peace in one's heart and in the hearts of others. It promotes a docile, gentle

---

[41] NABRE
[42] Cf. Ia IIae, q. 70, a.2.

317

spirit that is ordered to the providential plan of God. The beatitude that entails being unjustly "persecuted" is that beatitude which empowers one to seek justice at whatever cost, even at the cost to one's life. To live the life of the beatitudes is to live the life that brings one to experience the ultimate in happiness in a world filled with trials and tribulations.

The beatitudes express the human person's vocation as a spiritual being. They shed light on a Christian's duties and attitudes. They sustain hope amidst a world of trials and tribulations.[43] They "proclaim the blessings and rewards already secured, however dimly, for Christ's disciples."[44]

The beatitudes express a person's innermost desire, that person's desire for happiness. This desire for happiness has been placed at the very core of the human person in order to draw him or her to God, the source of all happiness.[45]

> We all want to live happily; in the whole human race there is no one who does not assent to this proposition, even before it is fully articulated.[46]

> How is it, then, I seek you, Lord? Since in seeking you, my God, I seek a happy life, let me seek you so that my soul may live, for my body draws life from my soul and my soul draws life from you.[47]

> God alone satisfies.[48]
>
> *St. Augustine/ St. Thomas Aquinas*

St. Thomas Aquinas says that another word for God is "happiness." The sad reality of life is that many people today, as in all generations, have failed to recognize that God alone is happiness and that God alone satisfies. Such people, sadly, end up chasing after things that appear at first sight to bring about happiness but in the end only bring about disappointment. Some people seek to fill this innate desire for happiness with fame, power, human achievement, drugs, illicit sex, and so forth, yet they never find peace and contentment.

> All bow down before wealth. Wealth is that to which the multitude of men pay an instinctive homage. They measure happiness by wealth; and by wealth they measure respectability.... It is a homage resulting from a profound faith...that with wealth he may do all

---

[43] CCC 1717.
[44] Ibid.
[45] Ibid., 1718.
[46] St. Augustine, *De moribus eccl.* 1, 3, 4: PL 32, 1312.
[47] Ibid., *Confessions*, 10, 20: PL 32, 791.
[48] St. Thomas Aquinas, *Expos. In symb. Apost.* I.

things. Wealth is one idol of the day and notoriety is a second.... Notoriety, or the making of a noise in the world—it may be called "newspaper fame"—has come to be considered a great good in itself, and a ground of veneration.[49]

John Henry Newman

If only people could recognize what the great saints have always recognized: That our soul will only rest in God (cf. Ps. 62:1).

The beatitudes challenge and confront people. They force people to make choices regarding their eternal destiny.

Freedom, Responsibility, and Personal Becoming

Man is rational and therefore like God; he is created with free will and is master over his acts.[50]

At the core of a person's nature or essence, intrinsic to him or her, is that person's freedom. Freedom is the means by which a person primarily becomes something. A person is so free that he or she has within his or her being the capacity to take control of his or her basic nature. A person is able to determine what he or she is and what he or she is to be. Therefore, at the heart of the definition of the person is the reality that the person is one who is open to becoming.[51]

Freedom is an openness to that which is beyond—a movement toward fulfillment. Because freedom is open and a movement toward fulfillment it allows for self-causation, that is, the power to become. Freedom entails a possibility for self-achievement, self-becoming. In freedom we can realize our potential. In the words of Karl Rahner,

...[Freedom] is a permanent constituent of man's nature. The true nature of freedom appears precisely in this, that in the Christian revelation it is the cause of both absolute salvation and absolute rejection by the final judgment of God.... In the Christian view...man is, through his freedom, capable of determining.... Through his free decision he is rather truly good or evil in the very ground of his being, and thus, in the Christian view, his final salvation or loss is already present, even though perhaps still hidden.[52]

---

[49] John Henry Newman, "Saintliness the Standard of Christian Principle," in *Discourses to Mixed Congregations* (London: Longmans, Green and Co., 1906), V, 89-90.
[50] St. Irenaeus, *Adv. Haeres.* 4, 4, 3: PG 7/1, 983.
[51] Cf. Karl Rahner, *Hearers of the Word*, trans. Michael Richards (New York: Herder and Herder, 1969), 3-179.
[52] Karl Rahner, *Grace in Freedom*, trans. Hilda Graef (New York: Herder and Herder, 1969), 210-211.

The person endowed with grace is on a journey—whether he is aware of it or not—toward the perfection of Christ, the God-man, the fully divine, fully human being. By seeking the God that dwells within, one can find one's true human potential, and by seeking to find one's full humanity, one can find the divine within whether in an explicit way or an implicit way.[53]

Christians are called into the *Mystery of God*. By making the choice to enter into this mystery one is making a choice to enter into the spiritual life, the beginning of the mystical life.[54]

The Limitations of Human Freedom

Human freedom is not absolute. It is limited and subject to errors. It is limited in that it demands obedience to the natural law that resides at the core of every person, and it is subject to error in that it is subject to the slavery and blindness that is associated with sin. As the *Catechism* states, "By deviating from the moral law man violates his own freedom, becomes imprisoned within himself, disrupts neighborly fellowship, and rebels against divine truth."[55] Human history attests to the sad consequences that result from the sinful abuse of freedom.

The Christian is called to live a life in imitation of Christ. The Savior who saved us from the slavery of sin is the one that all are called to imitate, for in this imitation is found the ultimate in liberation and freedom (cf. Gal. 5:1; Jn. 8:32; 2 Cor. 17; Rom. 8:21). In the grace of Christ one is educated and nourished in the ways of authentic freedom.[56]

In the early stages of the spiritual journey, the imitation of Christ is quite difficult, and therefore one's sense of freedom and liberation is curtailed.

Moral Conscience

Deep within his conscience man discovers a law which he has not laid upon himself but which he must obey. Its voice, ever calling him to love and to do what is good and to avoid evil, sounds in his heart at the right moment.... For man has in his heart a law inscribed by God.... His conscience is man's most secret core and his sanctuary. There he is alone with God whose voice echoes in his depths.[57]

Gadium et Spes

---

[53] Cf. Rahner, *Foundations*, 1-459.
[54] Cf. Karl Rahner, *Theology of Renewal*, trans. Cecily Hastings (New York: Sheed and Ward, 1964), 73.
[55] CCC 1740
[56] Ibid., 1741-1742.
[57] GS 16; Cf. Rom. 1:32; 2:14-16. All quotes and references from Scripture are from the RSV.

A person entrusted with this innate moral law, this conscience, is obliged to be faithful to this moral law in choosing what is right and just. In so doing one recognizes the ultimate in truth, truth itself, God himself, Christ himself.

Conscience is a messenger of him, who, both in nature and in grace, speaks to us behind a veil, and teaches and rules us by his representatives. Conscience is the aboriginal Vicar of Christ.[58]

John Henry Newman

Conscience directs a person to conversion and to hope. It enables one to recognize the evil one has done and to consequently ask for God's forgiveness. Conscience also helps one recognize the good and the power of hope. It directs one away from evil, unhappiness, despair, and moves one toward happiness, peace, and light.

The Formation of Conscience

One has a moral obligation to form one's conscience in accordance to right reason and the will of God. It is a life-long task. In the purgative stage of spirituality, the conscience is often poorly formed, while in the succeeding stages the conscience becomes more enlightened. The following are some general guidelines for the proper formation of one's conscience:

- Reflection, self-examination, and introspection make up the ground level of an informed conscience.
- Absorption in the Word of God (Ps. 119:105) and Sacred Tradition (the life of the Holy Spirit within the Church) serve as the blood of life for the conscience.
- The authoritative teachings of the Church that flow from Sacred Scripture and Sacred Tradition are essential (cf. 2 Thess. 2: 15).
- Reading the spiritual masters and the advice of good spiritual directors are extremely helpful in putting all the above into a concise vision of reality that corresponds to the innate reality at the core of one's being.

A well-formed conscience engenders freedom and peace of heart.

Determining a Well-Informed Conscience

There are essentially two key guides that help to determine if one has a well-informed conscience:

3) A good end does not justify an evil means.
4) Do unto others as you would like done unto you (cf. Mt. 7:12; Lk. 6:31; Rom. 14:21; 1 Cor. 8:12; Tob. 4:15).

---

[58] John Henry Newman, "Letter to the Duke of Norfolk," V, in *Certain Difficulties felt by Anglicans in Catholic Teaching* II (London: Longmans Green, 1885), 248.

An Uninformed Conscience[59]

Like all things human, even [the] conscience can fail to...[perceive] illusions and errors. It is a delicate voice that can be overpowered by a noisy, distracted way of life, or almost suffocated by a long-lasting and serious habit of sin.[60]

Pope John Paul II

There are two main reasons for an uninformed conscience:
3) The propensity toward laziness is at the heart of those who fail to seek a well-informed conscience.
4) A sinful life often blinds one to recognize the truth and often deadens a person's conscience.

The more correct conscience prevails, the more do persons and groups turn aside from blind choice and try to be guided by objective standards of moral conduct.[61]

Gadium et Spes

An Examination of Conscience

An examination of conscience is a powerful way of keeping one's conscience informed and open to the working of grace.

The following is a general method of examining one's conscience: One must first begin by praying to God for enlightenment. One must then ask oneself the following key questions: "Who am I as God sees me? What is happening in my life at this moment? How is God working in me? How is evil working in me? What is God asking of me? What would Jesus do in my situation?" From these key questions flows a profound examination of conscience.

Original and Personal Sin
Original Sin

There is nothing upon earth which does not demonstrate either the misery of man or the mercy of God; either the powerlessness of man without God—or his power in union with God.... Man does not know where he belongs. He has obviously gone astray and has fallen from his proper place. He cannot find his way back to it, though he seeks

---

[59] GS 16.
[60] John Paul II, *Celebrate 2000* (Ann Arbor: Servant Publications, 1996), 151.
[61] GS 16.

it everywhere in great anxiety but without success, moving about in impenetrable darkness....[62]

Blaise Pascal

At the beginning of time humanity had a choice to live with God or live without him (cf. Gen. 3:1-24). The choice to live without God caused a wound, a wound that would forever affect human nature. This wound would come to be known as the *original sin*, a sin of such great nature that it destroyed the possibility of eternal life with God and happiness.

God, in his love, would not allow humanity to remain separated from eternal life with him. He sent his only begotten Son to restore us to new life (2 Cor. 5:17). Sin was forgiven by the merits of Christ.

Concupiscence

Original sin distorted the harmony of creation and damaged the relationship between God and humanity. The second Person of the Trinity, the Son of God, came into the world and cleansed it of this damage, this original sin. While the sin was forgiven in Christ, the wound remained.

Human beings, in Christ, are capable of an intimate, personal, saving relationship with God, and are capable of experiencing eternal life with God in heaven. Yet despite this, because of the wound of original sin, a human being is still inclined and tempted toward that original rebellion; that is, human beings are inclined toward the temptations of evil.

The spiritual journey is a battle against concupiscence.

Personal Sin

Sin is a personal act in which reason, truth, and right conscience are offended. It is a failure to live up to the command of love of God and neighbor caused by a perverse attachment to that which is not for the honor and glory of God. It is an act of self-infatuation, disobedience (Gen. 3:5) and hatred toward God (Ps. 51:4).[63] It wounds the nature of the human person, the nature of solidarity, and the nature of the eternal law.[64]

Kinds of Sin[65]

Sin comes from the heart, from the very core of a person's being (cf. Mt. 15:19-20). The two main kinds of sins are sins of commission and sins of omission. Sins of commission are sins in which a person takes an active part in—such as in acts of fornication, impurity, licentiousness, idolatry, sorcery,

---

[62] *The Essential Pascal*, sel. and ed. Robert W. Gleason, S.J., and trans. G.F. Pullen (New York: New American Library, 1966), 69f.
[63] St. Augustine, *De civ. Dei* 14, 28: PL 41, 436.
[64] Ibid., *Contra Faustum* 22: PL 42, 418.
[65] Cf. CCC 1849-1850.

enmity, strife, jealousy, anger, selfishness, dissension, envy, drunkenness, carousing, etc. (cf. Gal 5:19-21; Rom. 1:28-32; 1 Cor. 9-10; Eph. 5:3-5; Col. 3:5-8; 1 Tim. 9-10; 2 Tim. 2-5). Sins of omission are sins that involve actions that are omitted in fostering the glory and honor of God. These are sins committed by people who keep quiet when evil is being done. People who do nothing to put an end to abortion or euthanasia, for example, commit serious sins of omission. Failing to stop gossip, vulgarity, and so forth, are other forms of sins of omission.

Gravity of Sin[66]

> If any one sees his brother committing what is not a mortal sin, he will ask, and God will give him life for those whose sin is not mortal. There is sin which is mortal…. All wrongdoing is sin, but there is sin which is not mortal (2 Jn. 5:16-17).

There are mortal/deadly sins and there are venial/non-deadly sins. Mortal sins involve the loss of sanctifying grace and love. It is a radical rejection of God, a radical turning away from God. Dying in mortal sin leads to hell. On the other hand, venial or non-deadly sins do not deprive one of heaven. In venial sin love remains, though it is offended and damaged.

In order to commit a mortal sin one needs to take into account the following conditions:

4) The sin must be one that involves a *grave matter*. Traditionally grave matter has been associated with the gross violation of the Ten Commandments.

5) Full knowledge and sufficiently deliberate consent is needed in the committing of a sin.

6) Unintentional ignorance (not feigned ignorance or hardness of heart) diminishes or removes the seriousness of the sin (i.e., pathological disorders, inordinate feelings and passions).

Venial sin is sin that does not meet the above requirements. Venial sin weakens love, disorders affections for created things, hinders virtuous progress, and disposes one toward mortal sin by damaging the conscience. Yet venial sin does not break a person's covenant or friendship with God. It does not deprive one of sanctifying grace nor of heaven.

> While he is in the flesh, man cannot help but have at least some light sins. Despise these sins which we call "light": if you take them for light when you weigh them, tremble when you count them. A number of light objects make a great mass; a number of drops fill a

---

[66] Cf. Ibid., 1854-1864.

river; a number of grains make a heap. What then is our hope? Above all, confession....[67]

St. Augustine

Communal Nature to Spirituality[68]

An error, "today abundantly widespread, is disregard for the law of human solidarity and charity, dictated and imposed both by our common origin and by the equality in the rational nature of all men, whatever nation they belong to. This law is sealed by the sacrifice of redemption offered by Jesus Christ on the altar on the Cross to his heavenly Father, on behalf of sinful humanity."[69]

Pius XII

The love of God and the love of neighbor are inseparable realities. To authentically love God one must authentically love one's neighbor, and to authentically love one's neighbor one needs to authentically love God.

The communal nature of spirituality promotes the common good of society, which promotes the defense of the fundamental rights of persons, the development of spirituality, and peace and security. Any form of sinful inequality is condemned.

Sin and Mercy[70]

All people fall short of the perfection of Christ and therefore sin is a cancer that engulfs this world (cf. 1 Jn. 8-9). Yet despite this sad reality, God's mercy never leaves a person. Even a mortal sin does not withdraw from the core of the person God's divine mercy,[71] for if it did, there would be no possibility of repentance, forgiveness, and conversion.

The Seven Capital Sins and Their Vices

The capital sins are commonly found in the early stages of the spiritual journey. They are often mortal, but not at all times.[72] A person, as a consequence of original sin, is susceptible to capital sins and their vices. A capital sin leads one to separation from God and all kinds of sins. They also lead from lesser sins to more serious sins.

The following is a brief description of the seven capital sins and what is often born of them: The capital sin of envy gives birth to hatred, slander, calumny, detraction, and joy at the misfortune of others. Anger leads to

---

[67] St. Augustine, *In ep. Jo.* 1, 6: PL 35, 1982.
[68] Cf. CCC 1878-1880; 1928-1942.
[69] Pius XII, *Summi pontificatus*, October 20, 1939; AAS 31 (1939) 423ff.
[70] Cf. 1846-1848; Cf. Lk. 15.
[71] Ia IIae, q. 88, a.2.
[72] *Dark Night*, BK I, Chs. 2-8.

disputes, fits of passion, insults, blasphemy, rudeness, haughtiness and contempt. Vanity leads to disobedience, boasting, hypocrisy, unholy rivalry, discord, and stubbornness. Sloth (or acedia) gives rise to malice, rancor, discouragement, cowardliness, spiritual apathy or stagnation, forgetfulness of spiritual obligations, and the seeking after forbidden things. Avarice gives rise to disloyalty, treachery, fraud, deceit, perjury, harshness, hardness of heart, and an excessive desire for acquiring and maintaining things. Gluttony leads one to engage in improper jokes, coarse, loutish behavior, impurity, foolish conversation, and stupidity. Lust gives rise to spiritual blindness, poor judgment, impetuous or rash decisions, fickleness, instability, capriciousness, self-infatuation, and an inordinate attachment to this present life.[73]

Prayer in General

Prayer is the fruit of joy and thanksgiving and the ascent of the person's very being to God.[74]

Evagrius Ponticus

For me prayer is a surge of the heart; it is a simple look turned toward heaven, it is a cry of recognition and of love, embracing both trials and joy.[75]

St. Therese of Lisieux

Prayer as gift

"Prayer is the raising of one's mind and heart to God or the requesting of good things from God."[76] Prayer is founded upon humility and a contrite heart (Ps. 130:1; cf. Lk. 18:9-14). One must recognize that one needs help in the endeavor of prayer (Rm. 8:26) and one must recognize that "whether we realize it or not, prayer is an encounter of God's thirst with ours. God thirsts that we may thirst for him" (cf. Jn. 4:10).[77] "Prayer is the response of faith to the free promise of salvation and also a response of love to the thirst of the only Son of God" (cf. Jn. 7:37-39; 19:28; Isa. 12:3; 51:1; Zech. 12:10; 13:1).[78]

Prayer as covenant

When one prays, one prays from the heart, which is the dwelling place where one is, where one lives, where one withdraws to.

---

[73] Cf. Ia IIae, q. 77, a.4f; q. 84, a.4.
[74] Evagrius Ponticus, *The 153 Chapters on Prayer*, 15, 35.
[75] St. Therese of Lisieux, *Manuscrits autobiographiques*, C 25r.
[76] St. John Damascene, *De fide orth.* 3, 24: PG 94, 1098C; CCC 2559.
[77] Cf. St. Augustine, *De diversis quaestionibu octoginta tribus* 64, 4: PL 40, 56; CCC 2560.
[78] CCC 2561.

The heart is our hidden center, beyond the grasp of our reason and of others; only the Spirit of God can fathom the human heart and know it fully. The heart is the place of decision, deeper than our psychic drives. It is the place of truth, where we choose life or death. It is the place of encounter, because as image of God we live in relation; it is the place of covenant.[79]

Prayer is a committed relationship of life and love. It is meant to be an inseparable relationship of encounter between the Creator and his creation.

Prayer as communion

Prayer is a communion between the individual, God, and his Body the Church. While one may invoke each person of the Trinity and pray to each person of the Trinity, it is traditionally understood that prayer is directed toward the Father, through the Son, and in the Holy Spirit in a mystical community called the Church, the Church on earth, in purgatory, and in heaven. "In the Holy Spirit, Christian prayer is a communion of love with the Father, not only through Christ, but also *in him*..."[80]

Jesus and prayer

Jesus teaches us to pray and reminds us that he prays for us, in us, and with us. As St. Augustine summarizes:

He prays for us as our priest, prays in us as our Head, and is prayed to by us as our God. Therefore let us acknowledge our voice in him and his in us.[81]

From the *Sermon on the Mount* one is taught that prayer to the Father requires a conversion of the heart. Reconciliation, love of enemies, prayers for persecutors, attentive prayer, purity of heart, and the seeking of the kingdom are all at the core of a conversion of the heart (cf. Mt. 5:23-24, 44-45; 6:7, 14-15, 21, 25, 33).

This conversion of heart leads to praying in faith, an adherence to God beyond what is limited to feelings and understanding. One in faith can therefore be assured of one's access to the Father and the assurance that if one *seeks* and *knocks* one will receive answers, for Christ is the *door* and the *way* (Mt. 7:7-11, 13-14). One can be confident that whatever is asked for in prayer and in faith will be received (Mk. 11:24). One is reminded that in Jesus "all things are possible to him who believes" (Mk. 9:23; cf. Mt. 21:22).

---

[79] Ibid., 2563.
[80] Ibid., 2615.
[81] St. Augustine, *En. In Ps.* 85, 1: PL 37, 1081; cf. GILH 7: CCC 2616.

It is important to remember, however, that an authentic prayer of faith is always one that is embodied by a heart disposed to do the will of the Father. Simply crying out "Lord, Lord…" is of little benefit if the heart is far from the will of God (cf. Mt. 7:21). An authentic prayer of faith embodies the divine plan of God within it (cf. Mt. 9:38; Lk. 10:2; Jn. 4:34). It realizes the importance of struggle and of patience and perseverance (cf. Lk. 18:1-8). Therefore, prayer is inseparable from works. In the words of Thomas Merton, prayer

> is inseparable from life and from the dynamism of life—which includes work, creation, production, fruitfulness, and above all love…. It is the very fullness of a fully integrated life. It is the crown of life and of all life's activities.[82]

Mary

> Mary, Mother of Jesus and of those who participate in his priestly ministry, we come to you with the same attitude of children who come to their mother. We are no longer children, but adults who desire with all our hearts to be God's children. Our human condition is weak; that is why we come to ask for your motherly aid so we are able to overcome our weakness. Pray for us so that we can, in turn, become people of prayer. We invoke your protection so that we may remain free from all sin. We invoke your love so that it may reign and we will be able to be compassionate and forgiving. We ask for your blessing so we can be like the image of your beloved Son, our Lord and Savior, Jesus Christ. Amen.[83]

> May the Virgin make our hearts humble and submissive like her son's heart. In her the heart of Jesus was formed. Let us learn to be humble, accepting humiliations with joy. We have been created for great things—why then should we stoop to things that would blur the beauty of our heart? How many things we can learn from the Virgin! Ask the Virgin to tell Jesus, "They have no more wine"—the wine of humility and submission, of goodness, of sweetness…. Ask Jesus to help you personalize your love for Mary—in order to be sources of joy, as he is; in order to be closer to her, as he is; in order to share with her everything, even the cross. Every one of us must

---

[82] *A Thomas Merton Reader*, Revised Edition. Edited by Thomas O. McDonnell (New York: Image Books, 1974), 400.
[83] Mother Teresa, *In My Own Words: Special Memorial Edition* (Liguori: Liguori Publications, 1996), 61.

carry his or her own cross; it is our sign of belonging to Christ. We need Mary to help us share it.[84]

Mother Teresa

Mary's intercessory prayers have a unique role in the plan of salvation. At the Annunciation her prayer opened the way for Christ's conception (cf. Lk. 1:38); at Pentecost her prayer helped form the Church (Acts 1:14). In her *fiat*, she was the perfect disciple, the perfect model of the Church; she was what all are called to be: "Behold I am the handmaid of the Lord; let it be [done] to me according to your word" (Lk. 1:38). This is at the heart of Christian prayer: "to be wholly God's, because he is wholly ours."[85]

Mary teaches a person how to pray by her example of humility, love, obedience, faith, and trust.

Mary's intercessory power is unique for she is the Mother of God, the spouse of the Holy Spirit. At the wedding feast of Cana (Jn. 2-12) the wine ran out. Jesus was not prepared to begin his public ministry. Yet when Mary, his mother, asked her Son to help the wedding couple—when Mary interceded—Jesus listened to the intercession of his mother and performed the miracle of turning water into wine. Mary's intercessory power is in her nature as the Mother of the Lord, for what good son can refuse the request of a good mother?

Jesus himself reminds all to have recourse to Mary at the foot of the cross when he turns over to John and the whole world Mary as our Mother, as the New Eve, as the Daughter of Zion, as the Mother of the Church.

When Jesus saw his mother, and the disciple whom he loved standing near, he said to his mother, "Woman, behold, your son! Then he said to the disciple, "Behold, your mother" (Jn. 19:26)!

Mary is our Mother. Christ gave the world a powerful intercessor for the needs of his people. Christ came into the world through Mary, and one is blessed to go to Jesus through Mary. Because we pray in the power of the Holy Spirit and the Mother of God is the spouse of the Holy Spirit, Mary becomes an essential part in Catholic spirituality.

It is important to recognize that Jesus could have entered the scene of history by simply walking out from the desert without any known origin, yet he chose a mother to enter the world, a mother from whom he took his flesh, a mother whom he listened to and loved. He never ceases to listen to her and to love her.

Mary never ceases to pray for us, now, and at the hour of our death!

---

[84] Mother Teresa, *Heart of Joy: The Transforming of Self-Giving* (Ann Arbor: Servant Books, 1987), 80-81; 139.
[85] CCC 2617.

The Church—A Communion

The Scriptures are clear on the necessity of interceding on behalf of others (cf. Lk. 16:9; 1 Cor. 12:12, 20f, 12:26; Heb. 12:22f; Rev. 5:8). The apostles often make reference to the need of praying for others and the need of the prayers of others. God intended this so that people of faith could be members of an authentic community where each member depended on the other, where each member cared for the other, where each member could live out the command of love of neighbor. What a precious act of love it is to pray for one another.

At the heart of this communion is the reality that relationships built on the foundation of grace are relationships that never end. Even death is not the end, nor is it a separation. Quite the contrary, death is simply the beginning of a new phase in eternal life, and in many ways a person who has died is closer to his or her loved ones than ever before. Just as a man or woman loved, cared for, and prayed for his or her loved ones on this earthly journey, they do the same in heaven, but in a much more powerful way. For the person who is in heaven is a person who dwells in the sphere of perfection and thus is a person who has been cleansed and purified of all his or her imperfections and sins (2 Macc. 12:46f). The powerful prayers of the pure of heart cannot be denied.

Whether from earth or from heaven, we pray as a community of faith, as the Church.

Expressions of Prayer

Vocal Prayer

Vocal prayer is a form of prayer that lays the groundwork and nourishes all other forms of prayer. As vocal prayer progresses it opens one's being for the higher forms of prayer.[86] Vocal prayer is the initial form of contemplative prayer.[87]

Vocal prayer is the incarnation of a person's heart's interaction with God. Words bring flesh to prayer. Human nature demands that one's whole body participate in the worship of God--body, soul, and spirit. Prayer is the worship of God with one's whole being (cf. Mt. 11:25-26; Mk. 14:36).

Meditation

What is meditating on Christ? It is simply this, thinking habitually and constantly of Him and of His deeds and sufferings. It is to have Him before our minds as One whom we may [reflect upon], worship, and address when we rise up, when we lie down, when we eat and drink, when we are at home and abroad, when we are working, or walking, or at rest, when we are alone, and again when we are in

---

[86] *Way*, Ch. 25.
[87] CCC 2702.

company; this is meditating. And by this, and nothing short of this, will our hearts come to feel as they ought.[88]

John Henry Newman

For the Carthusian monk, Guigo II, "meditation is the busy application of the mind to seek with the help of one's own reason the knowledge of hidden truth."[89] Meditation in a most profound way moves a person away from unhealthy, "worldly" things.[90]

Meditation is the seeking of the life of God. The mind seeks to search out the mystery of life in meditation. Through Sacred Scripture, Sacred Tradition, spiritual books, sacred icons, liturgical texts and seasons as well as through history and creation one encounters many answers to the mystery of life. One also encounters the path that one must travel.

Meditation makes a person encounter his or her deepest self. The book of life is opened to be explored. In this exploration one asks: "Lord, what do you want me to do?" Meditation helps one to be well grounded in the life of Christ (cf. Mk. 4:4-7; 15-19).

Meditation eventually will transform itself into contemplation, the only means for complete union with God.[91] As the *Catechism* states:

> Meditation engages thought, imagination, emotion, and desire. This mobilization of faculties is necessary in order to deepen our convictions of faith, prompt the conversion of our heart, and strengthen our will to follow Christ. Christian prayer tries above all to meditate on the mysteries of Christ, as in the *lectio divina* or the rosary. This form of prayerful reflection is of a great value, but Christian prayer should go further: to the knowledge of the love of the Lord Jesus, to union with him.[92]

Contemplative Prayer

Contemplative prayer in my opinion is nothing else than a close sharing between friends; it means taking time frequently to be alone with him who we know loves us.[93]

St. Teresa of Avila

---

[88] John Henry Newman, *Parochial and Plain Sermons* (London: Longman, Green, and Co., 1910) VI, 41.
[89] *Guigo II: The Ladder of Monks: A Letter on the Contemplative Life and Twelve Meditations*, trans. Edmund College, OSB, and James Walsh, S.J. (Kalamazoo: Cistercian Publications, 1981), 68.
[90] *Living Flame*, St. 3, no. 32; *Ascent*, BK III, Ch. 15, no. 2.
[91] *Ascent*, BK II, Ch. 16, no. 7.
[92] CCC 2708.
[93] *The Book of Her Life*, 8, 5.

Contemplation is the quest for the one "whom my soul loves" (Song of Songs 1:7; cf. 3:1-4). One enters this form of prayer in quiet, poverty, and pureness of faith. One seeks to be offered up to God in this experience; one seeks to be purified and transformed into the image and likeness one was meant to be transformed into; that is, in the image and likeness of Jesus Christ. Contemplation is love welcoming love (cf. Lk. 7:36-50; 19:1-10). It is victory in the total surrendering. In contemplation the "Father strengthens our inner being with power through his Spirit so 'that Christ may dwell in [our] hearts through faith' and we may be 'grounded in love'" (Eph. 3:16-17).[94]

Contemplation is the entrance into the sphere of the experience of God which transcends the limits of anything we hear, see, touch, smell, imagine, etc. It is beyond the limits of the internal and external senses. The God who transcends all speaks in silence to the heart of the person engaged in contemplation. He speaks with a presence of such intensity that the senses are incapable of grasping the fullness of this presence.

The spirit helps us...for we do not know how to pray as we ought; but the Spirit himself makes intercession for us with groanings that cannot be expressed in speech (cf. Rom. 8:26).

Aspects of Prayer

Blessing

Blessing exemplifies the basic movement of prayer. When one prays, one is praying in an ascending order. One prays in the power of the Holy Spirit, through the Son, to the Father. In such a fashion one can be said to be blessing God who is the source of all blessings (cf. Eph. 1:3-14; 2 Cor. 1:3-7; 1 Pet. 1:3-9). Through the grace of the Holy Spirit that descends through the Son and from the Father one is in turn blessed from the source of all blessings (cf. 2 Cor. 13:14; Rm. 15:5-6; Eph. 6:23-24). Because "God blesses, the human heart can in return bless the One who is the source of every blessing."[95] To bless is to make another happy!

Adoration

Adoration is an act of humility, the doorway to holiness. In an act of adoration a person makes himself or herself aware that he or she is a created being in the presence of an almighty, omniscient Creator (cf. Ps. 95:1-6). Adoration is the realization that one has been saved by a Savior, by the King of all kings. It is the recognition that one has been set free from the slavery of sin to be a child of God (cf. Ps. 24:9-10).

---

94 CCC 2714.
95 Ibid., 2626.

Petition

Through one's petitions to God one is making present, in the most obvious of ways, the reality that one is in a relationship with God. In the act of asking, beseeching, pleading, invoking, entreating, and crying out to God one is showing one's need and love for God (cf. Rm. 15:30; Col. 4:12). A petition is an acknowledgement that one is a sinner in need of a savior. It is an act of turning toward God (cf. Rm. 8:22-24, 26). Prayers of petition require the awareness that one is in need of forgiveness (cf. Lk. 18:13) and that one is in need of the gifts of humility and trust (cf. 1 Jn. 1:7-2:2; 3:22).

Intercessions

An intercessory prayer is a unique form of a prayer of petition. It is closely modeled on Jesus' prayers. While it is true that Jesus is the one intercessor (cf. Rm. 8:34; 1 Jn. 2:1; 1 Tim. 2:5-8; Heb. 7:25), Jesus has granted the gift to all in grace to intercede in him, with him, and through him (cf. Lk. 23:28, 34; Rm. 8:26-27; 10:1; 12:14; Acts 7:60; 12:5; 20:36; 21:5; Eph. 6:18-20; 2 Cor. 9:14; Phil. 1:3-4; 2:4; 1 Thess. 5:25; 2 Thess. 1:11; Col. 1:3; 4:3-4; 1 Tim. 2:1). A person of faith is a member of a community of love, the Church, the Body, the Bride of Christ (cf. Col. 1:24; 2 Cor. 11:2). As a consequence each member is to help the other members. Each member is called to love the other members. But God demands even more; he calls one to love even those who are outside the boundaries of the mystical Body. One must also pray for persecutors and all enemies of the Gospel (cf. Lk. 6:35).

Thanksgiving

One gives thanks to God for being freed from sin and slavery. One gives thanks for the gift of grace, the gift of eternal life with God. One gives thanks for being made a *new creation* in Christ (cf. 2 Cor. 5:17). Because of the precious gift of immortality, because of all God's precious gifts, every event in one's life, even the most difficult, the most painful, are worthy of thanksgiving. As St. Paul states: "Give thanks in all circumstances; for this is the will of God in Christ Jesus for you" (1 Thess. 5:18). In the mystery that is life, even the most hideous of circumstances can be transformed into a gift. Within the mystery of suffering is the mystery of love, and within the mystery of love is the mystery of suffering.

Praise

When one praises God one is worshipping God for simply being God. One is not focused on God's gifts, his "goodies," but simply on God. One praises God because *HE IS*. It is the prayer of the pure of heart and consequently it is the prayer that embraces all other prayers (cf. Rm. 8:16; 16:25-27; 1 Cor. 8:6; Acts 2:47; 3:9; 4:21; 13:48; Eph. 1:3-14, 20-21; 5:14, 19; Col. 1:15-20; 3:16; Phil. 2:6-11; 1 Tim. 3:16; 6:15-16; 2 Tim. 2:11-13; Jude 24-25; Jas. 1:17; Rev. 4:8-11; 5:9-14; 6:10; 7:10-12).

The Battle of Prayer

Prayer is a gift that requires grace. Prayer is always brought about by an act of God. A person's part in the experience of prayer is to respond to this initiative. One must remember that even before one can cry out to God, God is already there initiating that cry.

Prayer is a battle because it is a struggle against the consequences of original sin, concupiscence, and the temptations of the devil. Time constraints, the inability to experience or understand the supernatural, a preoccupation with sensuality, the sense that prayer is an escape rather than an encounter, the sense of discouragement, dryness, wounded pride, sin, and so forth all have an impact on a person's ability to pray. What is required of the person is a response, in grace, to the battle with the armaments of humility, trust, and perseverance.[96]

The battle in prayer is extremely important for a person's spiritual growth, for the wounds of the battle help one see where one is on this spiritual road. One is able to see if one is closer to victory or defeat by observing one's wounds. For example, distractions in prayer help one to see what one is attached to, which master one serves (cf. Mt. 6:21, 24). Is one vigilant in the battle or has one become lax (cf. Mt. 26:41)? Dryness in prayer can tell one whether one is being asked to walk by faith or if one is being asked to repent and turn back to God; in other words, is the dryness due to progress in holiness or is it due to sinfulness? Does distress help one to trust more or does it lead to despair (cf. Rm. 5:3-5)? Prayers that seem not to be answered can clarify one's motives in prayer: Does one love God as an instrument of selfishness or as a God who deserves love for simply being God?

In Summary

Prayer is not the manipulating of God to acquire something that God did not know we needed; quite the contrary, God knows all, including our needs. He knows what we will ask and all the free will decisions we will make in advance. He knows what we need and how it fits within his providence--that sphere of representativeness that is between two extremes, predestination and absolute, undeterred free will.

Why pray if God is all knowing? We pray to show our need, our love, and our dependence upon God, not because God needs this love or dependence, but because we do. We pray because it teaches us about ourselves and our priorities? We pray because it develops our spiritual brain, and thus brings light, happiness, and peace into our life and world.

Atheists often argue against the belief in God because answered prayers are not provable objectively. Prayer, unfortunately for the atheist, is not so simplistic a concept.

---

[96] Ibid., 2726-2728.

For the believer prayers are answered, but not necessarily in the manner in which one expects the prayer to be answered. Prayers are answered in such a fashion that one's eternal destiny is always in the forefront. Prayer is always answered with the understanding that this earthly life is but a blink of the eye when compared to eternity. Prayer is always understood from the perspective of the present and future good of the world and with the understanding that all prayers are interconnected—at the level of the individual, the community, and the world.

When we look upon the history of our prayers and desires, we see that our prayers were in fact answered, but most often in ways we did not expect. This is beautifully illustrated in the words of an unknown civil war soldier:

> I asked for strength that I might achieve; I was made weak that I might learn humbly to obey. I asked for health that I might do greater things; I was given infirmity that I might do better things. I asked for riches that I might be happy; I was given poverty that I might be wise. I asked for power that I might have the praise of men; I was given weakness that I might feel the need of God. I asked for all things that I might enjoy life; I was given life that I might enjoy all things. I got nothing that I asked for, but everything that I had hoped for. Almost despite myself, my unspoken prayers were answered; I am, among all men, most richly blessed.

In humility, trust and perseverance all prayers are heard.

The sense of unanswered prayers can often lead to the abandonment of the spiritual life. Thus, the love-driven gifts of humility and trust are so important for they empower the love-driven gift of perseverance that is essential for any battle (cf. 1 Thess. 5:17; Eph. 5:20; 6:8).

Victory leads to enlightenment, peace and happiness. Defeat leads to slavery (cf. Gal. 5:16-25).

Sacraments

For the Catholic sacraments are efficacious and therefore essential for growth in holiness. Sacraments produce what they signify. A sacrament imparts grace to the individual (Acts 2:38; 8:17; 19:4-7; 1 Pet. 3:19-22).[97] Thus, a person's disposition on receiving the sacraments has a great impact on his or her holiness.[98]

---

[97] Cf. Ibid., 1076-1130; 1210-1211.
[98] Cf. IIIa, q. 89, a.2.

Baptism[99]

> Baptism regenerates us in the life of the Son of God; unites us to Christ and to His Body, the Church; it anoints us in the Holy Spirit, making us spiritual temples.[100]
>
> *Pope John Paul II*

Baptism is a sacrament with real power and it is a sacrament that is necessary for salvation, for it is by baptism that we are "born again" of *water* and the *Spirit* (Jn. 3:5; Mk. 16:16). In baptism one enters into Christ's death and resurrection (cf. Rom. 6:3-4). One has put on Christ in baptism (Gal. 3:27). Baptism cleanses one from original sin, personal sin, and the punishment for sin (Mk. 16:16; Jn. 3:5; Acts 2:38f; 22:16; Rom. 6:3-6; Gal. 3:7; 1 Cor. 6:11; Eph. 5:26; Col. 2:12-14; Heb. 10:22). One becomes a new creation in Christ and a partaker in the divine nature (2 Pet. 1:4). One becomes a member of the Church as an adopted child of God (cf. 1 Cor. 12-13; 27). One becomes a Temple of the Holy Spirit (Acts 2:38; 19:5f) with an indelible mark or character on the soul which enables one to share in the priesthood of Christ and in his passion (Mk. 10:38f; Lk. 12:50).

Confirmation[101]

Confirmation perfects baptismal grace. Once confirmed one is strengthened by the Holy Spirit to be a powerful witness of Christ's self-communicating love to the world. One becomes a strengthened member in the mission of the Church, the proclamation of the Gospel. Like baptism, a sacred mark or seal is imprinted on the soul, forever changing it. In receiving this sacrament by a bishop or a delegated priest, one is making a commitment to profess the faith and to serve the world in word and deed as a disciple of Christ (Acts 19:5-6; 8:16-17; Heb. 6:1-2; 2 Cor. 1:21-22; Eph. 1:13).

The Eucharist[102]

St. Justin Martyr, in the year 150 AD, some fifty years after the death of the last apostle John, wrote to the Emperor Antoninus Pius regarding the long-standing practice of early Christian worship:

> On the day we call the day of the sun, all who dwell in the city or country gather in the same place.

---

[99] Cf. CCC 1213-1274.
[100] John Paul II, *Celebrate 2000: Reflections on Jesus, the Holy Spirit, and the Father* (Ann Arbor: Servant Publications, 1996), 40.
[101] Cf. CCC 1285-1314.
[102] Cf. Ibid., 1322-1405.

The memoirs of the apostles and the writings of the prophets are read, as much as time permits.

When the reader has finished, he who presides over those gathered admonishes and challenges them to imitate these beautiful things.

Then we all rise together and offer prayers* for ourselves...and for all others, wherever they may be, so that we may be found righteous by our life and actions, and faithful to the commandments, so as to obtain eternal salvation.

When the prayers are concluded we exchange the kiss. Then someone brings bread and a cup of water and wine mixed together to him who presides over the brethren.

He takes them and offers praise and glory to the Father of the universe, through the name of the Son and of the Holy Spirit and for a considerable time he gives thanks (in Greek: *eucharistian*) that we have been judged worthy of these gifts.

When he has concluded the prayers and thanksgiving, all present give voice by an acclamation by saying: 'Amen.'

When he who presides has given thanks and the people have responded, those whom we call deacons give to those present the "eucharisted" bread, wine, and water and take them to those who are absent.[103]

In explaining the mystery indicated by the word "eucharisted," Justin states in his *First Apology*:

We call this food Eucharist...since Jesus Christ our Savior was made incarnate by the word of God and had both flesh and blood for our salvation, so too, as we have been taught, the food which has been made into the Eucharist by the Eucharistic prayer set down by Him, and by the change of which our blood and flesh is nourished, is both the flesh and the blood of that incarnated Jesus.[104]

The Eucharist is the real presence of Christ--his real glorified, resurrected body and blood (Mt. 26:26-28; Mk. 14:22-24; Lk. 22:19f; Jn. 6:51f; 1 Cor. 10:16; 11:24f).

The Eucharist is the "source and summit of our faith." All things flow from the Eucharist and return back to it.

The Mass is the *re-presenting*, or making present of what took place once and for all at Calvary (Heb. 7:27; 9:12, 25-28; 10:10-14). Just as the Passover meal made present to those who participated in it the Exodus events, the Mass

---

[103] *Apol.* 65-67; PG 6, 428-429.

[104] St. Justin Martyr, *First Apology*, 66, quoted in William Jurgens, *The Faith of the Early Fathers*, vol. 1 (Collegeville: The Liturgical Press, 1970), 55.

in a fuller way makes present what happened at Calvary. At every Mass, Calvary is made present to all. Mass is a participation in that one and only sacrifice on the cross at Calvary (cf. Heb. 7:27).

The Eucharist is the "medicine of immortality, the antidote that we should not die, but live in Jesus forever."[105] The Eucharist increases a person's union with the Lord, forgives venial sins, and preserves that person from grave sin. By the fact that it strengthens the individual, it consequently strengthens the unity of the Church as Christ's mystical Body.

> ...and having received the Food that gives life immediately after the procession, I thought only of God and myself; and I beheld my soul, under the similitude of wax softened by the fire, impressed like a seal upon the bosom of the Lord....[106]
>
> St Gertrude the Great

Reconciliation/Penance[107]

The forgiveness of serious sin, or what we call mortal/deadly sin (1 Jn. 5:17) requires the authority of the priest as an authoritative, power-filled representative of God and of the community. When one looks at the Scriptures (Mt. 16:19; 18:18; Jn. 20:21-23) it becomes obvious that God entrusted his apostles with the gift of forgiving sins.

Jesus has an important reason for giving the world the Sacrament of Penance. When one sins one harms one's relationship with God, with the community, and one does damage to one's own being. That is because through sin one breaks the two commandments that God placed side by side, the love of God and the love of neighbor as oneself (Mt. 22:37-40).

The spiritual effects of the Sacrament of Penance are beautifully summarized in the *Catechism of the Catholic Church* (1496):

--reconciliation with God by which the penitent recovers grace;
--reconciliation with the Church;
--remission of eternal punishment incurred by mortal sins;
--remission, at least in part, of temporal punishments resulting from sin;
--peace and serenity of conscience, and spiritual consolation;
--an increase of spiritual strength for the Christian battle.

---

[105] Ignatius of Antioch, trans. Lake (Cambridge: Harvard University Press, 1998), *Ephesians*, 20.
[106] *The Life and Revelations of Saint Gertrude, Virgin and Abbess of the Order of St. Benedict*, trans. M.F.C. Cusak (Westminster: Christian Classics, 1983), 87f.
[107] Cf. CCC 1422-1470.

Anointing of the Sick[108]

> Are any among you sick? Let him call for the [priests] of the church, and let them pray over him, anointing him with oil in the name of the Lord; and the prayer of faith will save the sick man, and the Lord will raise him up; and if he has committed sins, he will be forgiven (Jas. 5:14-15).

This sacrament confers special grace on those suffering from illness or old age. It is a sacrament that can only be administered by a bishop or a priest. Its power is in the unifying of a person's sufferings with the Passion of Christ. It brings God's healing and loving presence upon the person. At times the healing is spiritual, and at times it is emotional or physical. God brings about what is best for a person's eternal destiny, his or her salvation. If a person is unable to receive the Sacrament of Penance it forgives the sins of the person (Mk. 6:12-13; Jas. 5:13-15).

Matrimony[109]

> How can I ever express the happiness of a marriage joined by the Church, strengthened by an offering, sealed by a blessing, announced by angels, and ratified by the Father? How wonderful the bond between two believers, now one in hope, one in desire, one in discipline, one in the same service! They are both children of one Father and servants of the same Master, undivided in spirit and flesh, truly two in one flesh. Where the flesh is one, one also is the spirit.[110]
> *Tertullian*

Christ elevated marriage to the level of a sacrament by the gift of grace. The reality of a man who gives himself completely, without doubt, without reservation, fully to his wife, and a wife who gives herself completely, without doubt, fully to her husband can only come about by the supernatural gift of grace. It is only in this way that two can really become one (Mt. 19:3-6; Mk. 10:6-9). Because of this unity to which God calls a couple, marriage must be holy, indissoluble, and open to life (1 Thess. 4:4; 1 Tim. 2:15). Marriage must mirror Christ's love for his own Bride, the Church (Eph. 5:25, 32-32). It mirrors God's covenant with his people. Marriage is, therefore, that which must be blessed by the Church.

---

[108] Cf. CCC 1499-1525.
[109] Cf. Ibid., 1601-1658.
[110] *Ad uxorem*, 2, 8, 6-7: PL 1, 1412-1413.

Holy Orders[111]

The Sacrament of Holy Orders is an indispensable part of the Church. Without it the Church would not be able to trace itself back to apostolic times, and therefore back to Christ.

The Church makes a distinction between the common priesthood of all the faithful (1 Pet. 2:9) and the ordained priesthood. All Christians are called to be a priestly people, a healing, loving, forgiving people, but some of the faithful are specifically set aside by Jesus for unique ministerial roles. The priesthood conferred by the Sacrament of Holy Orders is one that is specifically designated for teaching, leading worship, and meeting the pastoral needs of the people. Holy Orders are directed toward the holiness of the people of God.

The most important of the Holy Orders is that of the bishop because he serves as the visible head of the local or particular Church. Every bishop in the world can trace himself back in time to an apostle. Bishops have the fullness of the priesthood and are crucial in protecting the true faith. The preeminent of the bishops is of course the Pope, since he is the successor of the leader of the apostles, Peter.

The next order is the presbyter or what we commonly call the priest. He is a "prudent-coworker" and extension of the bishop. He receives his authority from the bishop, and teaches in power because of his tie to the tree of apostolic succession.

The final order is that of the deacon who likewise is attached to the bishop, but who is entrusted primarily with works of charity.

Holy Orders were instituted by Christ (Lk. 22:19; Jn. 20:22f), conferred by the imposition of hands by an apostle or his successor (Acts 6:6; 13:3; 14:23) and give grace (1 Tim. 4:14; 2 Tim. 1:6-7).

Holy Orders are at the service of the people of God, bringing Christ's gift of grace to the journeying faithful.

In Conclusion

In order to grasp the nature of the spiritual journey, one needs to grasp the foundational aspects that propel this journey. As we proceed to the traditional stages of the spiritual journey it will be essential to keep in mind what has been discussed in this foundational chapter.

III

The Purgative Stage
The Age of the Superficial

May the Lord Jesus touch our eyes, as he did those of the blind. Then we shall begin to see in visible things those which are invisible. May he open our eyes to gaze, not on present realities, but on the

---

[111] Cf. CCC 1536-1600.

blessings to come. May he open the eyes of our heart to contemplate God in Spirit, through Jesus Christ the Lord, to whom belong power and glory through all eternity.

Origen

The Pillars of Holiness
Humility

Humility is the first entry into religion, as it was Christ's first step into the world…. Humility has always been the cornerstone to sanctity….[112]

Francisco de Osuna

Humility is the doorway to holiness, for it is the doorway to true self-knowledge. It is important to realize that humility is not low self-esteem, rather it is the recognition that all of one's gifts are from God. Humility is just another name for self-knowledge—that ability to know ourselves the way God truly knows us. Humility avoids unnecessary and unworthy praise, self-seeking, the impressing of others or boasting, and the pursuit of worldly "things" such as fame. Humility promotes the awareness of the need for growth through the recognition of one's weaknesses and sins. It acknowledges the need for compassion, assistance and strength. It promotes a clear conscience and the strength to bear the cross. It rejoices in being corrected and sees reproaches as kisses from God. Humility helps one to be a person for others and recognizes that all things and activities are to be for the glory and honor of God, and that all of life is part of God's providential plan.[113]

Love[114]

God is love and whoever does not know love does not know God (cf. 1 Jn. 4:7). The guiding force of grace is love, for one always moves toward what one loves. Without love, outward deeds are of little significance. On the other hand, to love much is to authentically do much. Love makes one pure of heart: it makes what one appears outwardly the reality of what one is inwardly. In love all is done for the honor and glory of God. Love makes a person seek to turn all things to good. Love never seeks to justify or rationalize the evil one has done. Love makes one never long for special attention or affection to the exclusion of others. In love one recognizes the inseparable nature of the love of God and the love of neighbor. Any authentic love of God requires an authentic

---

[112] *Francisco de Osuna: The Third Spiritual Alphabet*, trans. and intro. Mary E. Giles (Mahwah: Paulist Press, 1981), 494f.
[113] Thomas a Kempis, *Imitation of Christ*, BK I, 2, 3, 7; BK II, 2, 4, 5, 12; BK III, 17, 20, 22, 24, 29, 35-36, 46, 50, 54.
[114] Ibid., BK I, 15, 19, 24; BK II, 3, 5, 8; BK III, 35.

love of neighbor and any authentic love of neighbor requires an authentic love of God. Love makes one acknowledge that if one seeks forgiveness one must be forgiving. Love makes a person look at the best in others. It is not suspicious of anyone.

Love is patient and kind; love is not jealous or boastful; it is not arrogant or rude. Love does not insist on its own way; it is not irritable or resentful; it does not rejoice at wrong, but rejoices in the right. Love bears all things, believes all things, hopes all things, endures all things. Love never ends (1 Cor. 13:4-8).

Silence

The spiritual journey requires an openness to silence, to calm (cf. Ps. 62:1). Silence allows a person to be open to God's will and therefore is a must in a person's spiritual journey. Silence allows one to read, reflect, meditate, and pray in an authentic manner. It allows one to spend time with God and learn from him. A person who talks too much is a person who knows too little. Silence permits growth in intimacy with God, for God speaks in the silence. Silence affords the opportunity for one to be prepared for work, for proclaiming the Gospel to the ends of the world. Silence helps one act prudently in one's work. It promotes sincere repentance and contrition. It promotes the recognition of one's sinfulness and allows one to search the depths of one's conscience. Silence promotes humility, love, mortification, and the seeking of truth. It recognizes the emptiness of "worldly" things. It allows one to experience peace of mind and to rest in the Lord. It keeps one focused on death, on one's eternal destiny, on one's purpose and meaning in life.[115]

Hunger for Truth

God is truth, and since he is truth, the spiritual path must be a quest for truth (cf. Jn. 4:24). Truth helps one seek to follow right reason and an informed conscience. It aids one to affirm the imperfections of human knowledge and thus the need for the correcting power of divine revelation. The hunger for truth helps one seek the advice of holy and learned people, and the advice of the saints and the Fathers of the Church. Truth grants one the gift of thinking about what is being said and not in who is saying it. One becomes cautious in what is being portrayed as truth. One sifts and distinguishes the good from the evil. The hunger for truth helps one experience life in authentic freedom. Often the devil makes what is evil seem very appealing in order to enslave a person. The hunger for truth helps one to seek beyond what one experiences through the senses. Truth opens the heart and guides one to discover the God who is within and helps one to seek all that is necessary for salvation.[116]

---

[115] Ibid., BK I, 24-25.
[116] Ibid., BK I, 2, 5; BK II, 45; BK III 4, 50.

> Love is a good disposition of the soul by which one prefers no being to the [experience] of God. It is impossible to reach the habit of this love if one has any attachments to earthly things.[117]
>
> St. Maximus Confessor

> Jesus has many lovers of his heavenly kingdom, but few cross-bearers.[118]
>
> Thomas a Kempis

> If God in His love for the human race had not given us tears, those being saved would be few indeed and hard to find....[119] Tears come from nature, from God, from suffering good and bad, from vainglory, from licentiousness, from love, from the remembrance of death, and from numerous other causes.... Tears can wash away sins as water washes away something written. And as some, lacking water, use other means to wipe off what is written, souls lacking tears beat and scour away their sins with grief, groans, and deep sorrow....[120]
>
> St. John Climacus

A person's passions, his or her affections or feelings, can help a person in seeking the good and avoiding the evil. Among the primary passions that affect a person are love, hatred, fear, joy, sadness, and anger. In and of themselves, feelings, affections, or emotions are neither good nor evil. They are neutral. It is what one does with these passions that can cause spiritual harm. In other words, if the feeling of love is picked up by the virtue of justice, one is likely to be merciful in the carrying out of justice. If, however, the feeling of love is picked up by a vice, such as lust, then authentic love becomes perverted. If the passions are in order with right reason and good will, then they are beneficial in the spiritual life, particularly in the early purgative stages. If these passions, however, are contrary to right reason and the proper use of the will, then they are the source of self-destruction and slavery (cf. Jn. 8:34).[121]

Detachment involves a healthy indifference to worldly concerns. By being detached of all one can love all authentically, the way God intended all to be loved. One seeks to be detached of all that is not for the glory and honor of God; on the other hand, *one is called to be attached to all that is for the glory*

---

[117] *Maximus Confessor: Selected Writings*, trans. George C. Berthold (Mahwah: Paulist Press, 1985), n. 1.

[118] Thomas a Kempis, *The Imitation of Christ*, BK II, Ch. 11.

[119] *John Climacus: The Ladder of Divine Ascent*, trans. Colm Luibheid and Norman V. Russell (Mahwah: Paulist Press, 1982), 137.

[120] Ibid., 139-140, 259.

[121] St. Augustine, *De civ. Dei*, 14, 7, 2: PL 41, 410; Ia IIae, q. 24, a.1, 3.

and honor of God. Mortification involves the denial of the passions and appetites in order to purify them and in order to purify one's direction toward God. Detachment and mortification are both essential aspects of the spiritual life for they help one to empty the self of all that is not of God.   They are lessons in self-mastery, which is at the heart of holiness and happiness.

One is called through detachment and mortification to lead a life of obedience, self-discipline and simplicity. One is called to avoid vanity and pride and the propensity for lying and gossiping, which are signs of self-infatuation. A person must be aware of deceptive and inordinate pleasures which are momentary, but that in the long run lead to sadness and remorse.   An individual must seek the best in people and fight off the innate inclination to see the worst in them. One must seek to uncover in others the image of Christ to love, and one must seek to model one's life after Christ's. A person must avoid trying to see his or her self as always better than others. One must be able to realize that others are often better in many ways. A person must avoid criticizing and judging others, for people are so often mistaken in their assessments of others and therefore offend God. People often judge according to their emotions and their self-will and stubbornness. They often judge with poorly formed, self-seeking opinions. Bearing the defects of others in patience and praying for their holiness is precious. It is so easy to fall into the trap of seeking perfection in others but refusing to see the imperfections in our very nature.

One must seek the submission of one's will to God's by being faithful to Scripture, Sacred Tradition, and the teachings of the Church and its authoritative leadership. One must seek to conform one's will to God's and not the other way around. A person must do, at times, what he or she doesn't want to do and to leave undone what he or she would like to do. An individual is called to rejoice in adversity, in not having his or her way. Not having one's way purifies one in order to put one's hope in God and not in "worldly" things.

A person must seek devout conversations and delve into all aspects of the spiritual life. One must, consequently, avoid "worldly" people for they lead one into dangerous waters.

A person must resist temptation by turning to God immediately. By doing so the person becomes humble, clean, and learned. However, given the reality of unavoidable temptations, one must take the opportunity to grow through times of temptation. A person's response to temptation shows that person who he or she truly is.

A person must continually seek to repent and experience sorrow for sin. A person must keep his or her eye continually on death by acts of meditation. A person is called to embrace suffering as a precious gift that purifies that person of all that is not of God.   One must pray that one does not find too much consolation, for too much consolation can lead to sins of presumption and pride.   One must unite one's sufferings to Christ's patiently, willingly, and without complaint. One must not seek so much rest as patience and endurance on this earthly journey.

All things and all works must be directed toward God for happiness. Anything not directed toward God is earthbound and ultimately a disappointment. One must find comfort in the reality that from all eternity God knew the path one would take and that God would always be there to meet one's deepest needs. A person must remember that all "things" are part of God's providential plan. Nothing happens by chance.[122]

Surrender and Trust

> Total abandonment consists of giving oneself fully to God because God has given himself to us. If God, who owes us nothing, is willing to give us nothing less than himself, can we respond by giving him only a part of ourselves?
>
> ...Jesus wants us to put all our trust in him. We have to renounce our desires in order to work for our own perfection. Even if we feel like a boat without a compass on the high seas, we are to commit ourselves fully to him, without trying to control his actions.
>
> I cannot long for a clear perception of my progress along the route, nor long to know precisely where I am on the path of holiness. I ask Jesus to make me a saint. I leave it to him to choose the means that can lead me in that direction.[123]
>
> *Mother Teresa*

Life is an adventure in which God is in control. God's providential will cannot be thwarted. Any attempt at thwarting God's will always leads to disappointments, anxieties, and every other kind of unhappiness one can imagine. Only in God's will is there rest (Ps. 62:2). Only in God's will is there peace and happiness.

The key to life is surrendering to God's will and trusting that he will take one to that place which is best for one's soul. Life must be experienced as an adventure: Every morning one must wake up and say: "Lord, what adventure do you have planned for me today? Will it be a joyous one or will it be a hard and difficult one? In any case, I'm ready for the adventure and I joyously take it on, for I know you are in control and that you will never abandon me! I surrender and I trust, for in surrendering and trusting I find the victory of my life."

---

[122] *Imitation of Christ*, BK I, 3-14; 16; 20-23; BK II, 2, 10; BK III, 9, 13, 15, 19, 20, 22, 24, 31, 35, 37-39, 46-50, 54.

[123] Mother Teresa, *Heart of Joy*, 125-126.

Surrendering and trusting in God is a life-long process, but it is the only process that can lead one to peace and contentment as well as purpose and meaning.

Predominant Inclinations and Faults

People are often unreasonable and self-centered. Forgive them anyway. If you are kind, people may accuse you of ulterior motives. Be kind anyway. If you are honest, people may cheat you. Be honest anyway. If you find happiness, people may be jealous. Be happy anyway. The good you do today may be forgotten tomorrow. Do good anyway. Give the world the best you have and it may never be enough. Give your best anyway. For you see, in the end, it is between you and God. It was never between you and them anyway.

Mother Teresa

All persons have a predominant fault or faults (cf. 2 Cor. 12:7). A predominant fault is a weakness that one bears as a consequence of one's natural temperament (or as a consequence of the development of a pathological disorder). Predominant faults tend to be troubling to the spiritual journey. Predominant faults have a powerful effect on one's feelings, judging, willing, acting, and so forth. They can at times be hidden and at times disguised as a virtue (i.e., poor self-esteem as humility). They can at times be sinless or at times be the source of a great many sins.

In the *purgative stage* of spirituality there is the beginning of a process of enlightenment: the old self is coming into conflict with the new self. The old way of life is now being replaced with a new way of life, a way that is happier and more productive. This *new self* becomes more and more new and healthy as it discards all that is negative in the old self and keeps all that is positive of the old self. Christ, the *Great Physician* (cf. Mk. 2:17), is beginning to open the eyes of the individual in ways that were never open before. One's life is beginning to be enlightened in ways never before and God is now challenging the person to change for the better. This revolutionary process, which begins the purgative stage, will grow to its ultimate fruition through the illuminative stage and into the unitive stage.[124]

It is important that in discussing the above predominate inclinations and faults, that one remember that in the spiritual person all of the theological virtues, the cardinal and capital virtues, and all the gifts of the Spirit are active. It is simply that some are more obviously active than others. Furthermore, as one progresses in the spiritual journey, the gifts and virtues become less and less hampered by the taint of sin and thus the fruits of the life of grace, such as

---

[124] Part of the enlightenment process may be the awareness that one is in need of psychological or psychiatric help.

346

charity, joy, peace, patience, benignity, goodness, longanimity, mildness, faith, modesty, continency, and chastity, flow more profusely and significantly.

The Blind Side

All people have a blind side; that is, a side to their personality that most people are able to spot, except for the person experiencing this blind spot. People can be egotistical, gossipers, compulsive manipulators and liars, vengeful, lacking self-esteem, etc., and not be in the least bit aware of these realities. Everyone around them, for the most part recognize the blindness, but they themselves are completely oblivious.

All people have various blind spots. The key to the spiritual life is being open to discovering these blind spots.

Blind spots are brought to light through all the gifts and virtues, but particularly the gifts of wisdom, understanding, and knowledge, and the capital virtue of humility. Through these gifts and in particular the infused gift of humility in combination with the gifts of the Spirit, one is able to see oneself the way one truly is. Let us again remember that humility is just another word for self-knowledge. Hence, guided by these gifts a person is able to reflect upon his or her actions and is able to make powerful examinations of conscience which enable that person to see what he or she could not see before.

The gifts and virtues also enable a person to reach out to others, particularly spiritual friends, who will in authentic love tell that person what that person may not want to hear regarding his or her character. True love can be hurtful at first, but in the end, it is most precious. True love tells one what one needs to hear, not what one wants to hear!

Prayer in the Purgative Stage

Prayer in this initial stage of spirituality is primarily focused on prayers of petition. A person is still very much self-absorbed and thus such a person is primarily concerned with getting "goodies" from God, as opposed to loving God for simply being God.

When praying for others there is often a secondary motive for the prayer which has an intended beneficial benefit for the petitioner. For example, a brother may pray for another brother going through a difficult time, with the intention that God will bring relief; however, mixed within this petition will often be the hope that God will take care of this brother during this difficult time because one is tired of having to be concerned for the brother and one is tired of having to support the brother. One can see that the prayer is not completely pure. It has a secondary motive.

Charismatic prayer is a very popular form of prayer in this early stage of spiritual development. Charismatic prayer, as emphasized in today's society, is that form of prayer that is marked with the charisms of the Holy Spirit—in particular the ability to speak in tongues, to interpret tongues, to prophecy, and to experience being "slain in the Spirit" (cf. 1 Cor. 12:8-10). Charismatic prayer is most often associated with those in the purgative stage of spirituality since those in this stage tend to be intensely sense-oriented in their experiences of God. Hence, by its very nature, charismatic prayer is bound to give way to higher forms of prayer along the spiritual path. As one progresses in the spiritual life, God does more of the communicating, and individuals do more of the listening. As one progresses there is less noise and more silence. Charismatic prayer, as one progresses, becomes more insight and discernment-oriented.

Prayer in the purgative stage--in the early stages of development--is quite simplistic and filled with many distractions. John Cassian, who would eventually progress to be a saint, described this early stage of spirituality in his life:

> In my soul are countless and varied distractions. I am in a fever as my heart moves this way and that. I have no strength to hold in check the scatterings of my thoughts. I cannot utter my prayer without interruption, without being visited by empty images and by the memory of words and doings....[125]

Prayer is often filled with distractions and dryness at this stage because there is a battle going on. There is a battle going on between the anxieties of the world and the peace of Christ. There is a battle going on between self-will and God's will. The *Dark Nights* will be the purifying fires that will cleanse these aspects of the spiritual person (The *dark nights* will be discussed in the upcoming chapters). In many ways, a person in this stage is divided: He or she is a self-infatuated person while at the same time a struggling Christ-centered person. The battle between these two aspects of the person's life is painful and purging.

Dryness and Distractions

Dryness in prayer is something that needs to be particularly addressed at this stage as well as distractions. I will first deal with the dryness.

One of the most tragic circumstances in the spiritual life is that people of prayer stop praying when dryness enters into their prayer life. Dryness in prayer is associated with the loss of a sense of consolation, peace, happiness, comfort, and good feelings. Where once a person was enthusiastic in his or her prayer life, now the person loses this sense and begins to find prayer burdensome. Such people often remark: "I'm just too tired to pray tonight. I'll pray another time." In more tragic cases, people that experience dryness for the first time often abandon the spiritual life altogether—this is particularly true of neophytes who are unaware of what is going on in their souls.

---

[125] *John Cassian: Conferences*, trans. Colm Luibheid (Mahwah: Paulist Press, 1985), Conference 10.

Dryness is God's way of purifying prayer. It is easy to pray when one gets "goodies" from God, but God in the dryness of prayer is saying: "I now want you to pray to me out of pure faith. I want you to pray to me for simply being me, not for the "goodies" you get from me." If one perseveres in prayer during this dryness, one will exit the dryness as a person of much more profound spiritual insight. One will experience a newness of life that is associated with progress in the spiritual life. One comes out of the dryness a better, more powerful, spiritual person. However, the sad reality is that too many people fail to persevere through the dryness. They give up so easily.

Hence, so many people who fail to persevere end up regressing. They stop praying until life becomes very empty. They restart their prayer life and find consolation and all the "goodies" associated with it. But then dryness again begins, and they again abandon prayer, until they feel a need for it. Life for such people is a continual cycle of progress and regression in the spiritual life. They move a little and then fall back again. They live their lives in this unending cycle, this unending cycle which hinders any great sense of fulfillment, peace, contentment, or happiness.

Life is filled with anxieties for such people for they fail to progress. That is why most Christians live and die in the purgative stage, for they fail to persevere in the battle of prayer. They are too willing to fall back on what they perceive as more safe. They fail to trust God enough. They fail to surrender to his will. They fail to realize that God knows what is best for our salvation and for our happiness. They fail to realize that he is the way, the truth, and the life (cf. Jn. 14:6).

Distraction is another factor that hinders most Christians in the spiritual life. Distractions are brought about by a failure to surrender and trust completely in God. Consequently, life's problems and anxieties enter into the prayer life of the person. Distractions will slowly be calmed as one progresses in perseverance in the spiritual life of prayer.

One little technique that can often be used in moments of distractions is to have at hand a favorite word that reminds one of God (i.e., love, peace, hope, and so forth). Whenever the distractions enter into one's prayers, then one can call upon this word to help refocus one's prayer back on God.

Prayer is a spiritual battle. Let us fight the good fight (cf. 1 Tim. 6:12; 2 Tim. 4:7).

Beginning to See Christ in Others

While the purgative stage is primarily a self-centered stage, the grace of God is moving the person to see in others aspects of Christ, albeit at this stage the person only sees at a very superficial level. A person at this stage is able to see the Christ in the great saints, but has a great deal of trouble seeing the Christ in the neighbor. This stage is still a very self-absorbed stage in the spiritual journey.

Backsliding

A person in the purgative stage of the spiritual journey is always in danger of backsliding. This is particularly true when one enters the first *dark night*, which will be discussed in the next chapter. Thus, a person at this stage must hold unto the gift of faith as his or her guide.[126] One must hold unto the words of Jesus that remind the world that he came that all "may have life and have it abundantly" (Jn. 10:10), and one must hold unto the words of St. Paul that remind us that in Christ all "may be filled with the fullness of God" (Eph. 3:19).

The purgative stage of the spiritual journey is a painful one, yet it is not a stage that is without hope or direction. For the faithful one knows that by holding on, by fighting the good fight, by being courageous, by living one day at a time, and by surrendering more and more to God's will, victory and happiness are at hand. Serenity and peace are close by. One must find comfort in a prayer similar to that of Reinhold Niebuhr:

> God grant me the serenity to accept the things I cannot change, courage to change the things I can, and the wisdom to know the difference. Living one day at a time; enjoying one moment at a time; accepting hardships as the pathway to peace. Taking as Jesus did this sinful world as it is, not as I would have it; trusting that He will make all things right if I surrender to His will; that I may be reasonably happy in this life and supremely happy with Him forever in the next.

A person that fails to persevere will find himself or herself permanently trapped in the superficial purgative stage of spirituality, where no lasting authentic peace and contentment can be found, for by its nature this early stage is a painful, purging stage. Most Christians live and die in this purgative stage. That is why most Christians live and die as superficial Christians.

Failing to move forward is easy for the uncommitted, for it is always easier to go back to where one has been than to go forward into the unknown. The unknown can be frightening, and requires surrendering and trusting in God. Most people are afraid to surrender and to move into the sphere of the unknown, for God may ask them more than they are willing to give!

New vs. Old Self

In Christ one becomes a new creation (cf. 2 Cor. 5:17). The purgative stage is the beginning of this new creative, revolutionary process that is taking place in a person.

If one so chooses to move beyond this point and enter more profoundly into the unknown, into the mystery of God, then one will experience an ever more profound experience of life.

---

[126] Cf. *Ascent*, BK II, Ch. 4, nos. 2-3.

IV

The First Dark Night
The Active Purification of the Senses

The greatest suffering of the souls in purgatory...is their awareness that something in them displeases God, that they have deliberately gone against His great goodness....[127]

St. Catherine of Genoa

Purgatory will have to be done here on earth or in the afterlife, for heaven is a place of perfection. Let us seek to do our purgatory here on earth, for what greater gift of love can we give the Father?

The active purification of the senses is a time of purification of the senses that gives liberty to the Spirit. It is a time when a person "pommels [his or her] body and subdues it" (1 Cor. 9:27). It is a time when the person's inner being is being prepared for a state of existence where nature and grace complement each other, where the body does not cause any hindrance for the soul. It is a time when a re-directing of one's energies is taking place to fight off occasions of sins. It is a time when sensuality and irritability, which are the hallmarks of this stage of the spiritual journey, are curbed by a burning fire.[128] It is a time, as St. Maximus Confessor explains, when a person's "affective drive is wholly directed to God."[129]

This stage is called a *Dark Night* for it is a time when the senses are deprived of the consolations that are usually associated with a relationship with God. To the person who first enters this stage, the person may feel he or she is falling away from God, but in reality, he or she is closer to God than ever before in his or her spiritual journey. God is now asking the person to follow him in faith and not out of an infatuation or desire for consolations or "goodies" from God.

The active purification of the senses is a time when a person actively seeks to purify his or her being of those things that hinder the spiritual life and ultimately happiness. While grace is clearly present in the process most of the work being done in the purification process is being done by the individual who actively struggles to purify that which is contrary to the glory and honor of God. In this active purification, the imagination, memory, intellect, and will begin to be purified of things that hinder a full experience of God. As William of St. Thierry states:

---

[127] *Catherine of Genoa: Purgation and Purgatory*, trans. Serge Hughs (Mahwah: Paulist Press, 1979), 77f.

[128] Cf. IIa IIae, q. 35, a.1, ad 4um.

[129] *Maximus Confessor: Selected Writings*, trans. George C. Berthold (Mahwah: Paulist Press, 1985), Third Century, n. 98.

Man's part is continually to prepare his heart by ridding his will of foreign attachments, his reason or intellect of anxieties, his memory of idle or absorbing, sometimes even of necessary business, so that in the Lord's good time and when he sees fit, at the sound of the Holy Spirit's breathing, the elements which constitute thought may be free at once to come together and do their work, each contributing its share to the outcome of joy for the soul. The will displays pure affection for the joy which the Lord gives, the memory yields faithful material, the intellect affords the sweetness of experience....[130]

Imagination

A person cannot think without images in this early stage. An image always accompanies an idea. In the active purification of the imagination, the imagination is directed by reason illumined by faith. When the imagination is filled with impurities, the intellect is disrupted and damaged from functioning properly. If the imagination is cleansed from impurities, the imagination compliments the intellect in its proper functioning.[131] The imagination is a faculty of great power in the spiritual journey. It is in need of constant purifying, even in the highly advanced in the spiritual life.[132]

Memory[133]

Concupiscence and personal sin cause us to retain dangerous memories, memories that hinder and stunt growth. As St. Maximus Confessor states, "the battle against memories is more difficult than the battle against deeds, as sinning in thought is easier than sinning in deed."[134] An ordered, healthy memory remembers the things of God, and a disordered memory forgets the good that God has done. For example, an individual who remembers the wrongs that another person or persons has done to him or her, can at times have trouble forgiving that person or persons. The pain of the memory can preoccupy one with hatred and miserable feelings, and therefore hinder one's focus on God.

Such people are often prone to forgetting God (Cf. Jer. 2:32; Ps. 105:13, 21). Such a person is prone to being focused on the here and now as opposed to eternity. One needs to heal and order the memory to its proper functioning. The theological virtue of hope helps to heal the memory by helping the person

---

[130] *William of St. Thierry: The Golden Epistle*, trans. Theodore Berkeley, OCSO (Kalamazoo: Cistercian Publications, Inc., 1971), n. 251.

[131] Cf. Ia, q. 78, a.4; q. 84, a.7.

[132] *Interior Castle*, 5th mansion, Ch. 4; 6th mansion, Ch. 1.

[133] *Ascent*, BK III, Chs. 1-15.

[134] *Maximus Confessor: Selected Writings*, trans. George C. Berthold (Mahwah: Paulist Press, 1985), First Century, n. 63.

avoid focusing on useless and dangerous memories. One's mind, directed by hope, turns to God.[135]

Intellect

The intellect can be wounded by concupiscence and personal sin. The wounded intellect leads to ignorance. It is wounded from perceiving truth and from grasping higher realities. One becomes absorbed in earthly considerations. One whose intellect is wounded is subject to neglect things of God and of salvation. One is prone to intellectual and spiritual pride and sloth, indifference, rash judgments, and spiritual and intellectual blindness. A person whose intellect is wounded is a person not willing to consult others, and not willing to listen to opposing opinions. Such a person thinks he or she knows it all (Mt. 23:16; 23f).[136]

The infused virtue of faith is the cure for a wounded intellect.[137] Faith is superior to reason and the senses. It enlightens reason, makes one adhere to truths and helps us judge according to these truths. Faith seeks understanding and the understanding that flows from this faith in turn nourishes the fruitfulness of faith.[138]

Will

The will is the faculty that tends toward the good known through the intellect. It has for its object the universal good that permits it to rise to the love of God. The will makes use of the other faculties, especially the intellect and the imagination, in guiding the person to the good.[139]

Concupiscence and personal sin cause defects in the will. Self-centeredness and egoism are the greatest wounds to the will. They lead one to forget the love of God and neighbor. They lead to thoughtlessness, agitation, discouragement, dissension, trouble, and anxiety. They lead to a battle where one tries to control God. They make one flee from all that requires sacrifice.

The cure for these wounds is found in the infused virtue of love.[140] Love moves one from being self-centered and ego-centered to other-centered. One becomes, through authentic love, a person for others.

---

[135] *Ascent*, BK II, Chs. 10, 11, 16, 22; BK III, Chs. 6f and 14.
[136] Ia IIae, q. 85, a.3; IIa IIae, q. 15; q. 35, a.4, ad 3um; q. 138; q. 167, a.1.
[137] IIae IIae, q. 7, a.2; *Ascent*, BK III, 6f.
[138] *Ascent*, BK II, Ch. 3, 9, 11.
[139] Cf. Ia, q. 80, a.1f
[140] *Ascent*, BK II, 6f.

Take, Lord, and receive all my liberty, my memory, my understanding, and my entire will, all that I have and possess. You have given all to me; to you, O Lord, now I return it; all is yours, dispose of me wholly according to your Will. Give me only your love and your grace, for this is enough for me.

St. Ignatius of Loyola

V

The Second Part of the First Dark Night
The Passive Purification of the Senses

Lead, Kindly Light, amid the encircling gloom
Lead Thou me on!
The Night is dark, and I am far from home—
Lead Thou me on!
Keep Thou my feet; I do not ask to see
The distant scene—one step enough for me.

I was not ever thus, nor pray'd that Thou
Shouldst lead me on.
I loved to choose and see my path, but now
Lead Thou me on.
I loved the garish day, and, spite of fears,
Pride ruled my will: remember not past years.

So long Thy power hath blest me, sure it still
Will lead me on,
O'er moor and fen, o'er crag and torrent, till
The night is gone;
And with the morn those angel faces smile
Which I have loved long since, and lost awhile.[141]

John Henry Newman

In the active purification of the senses, the person did most of the work in response to grace in purifying the senses of all that was not for the honor and glory of God. Now in the passive purification, God is doing most of the work.[142]

In the passive purification of the senses, one moves from an imperfect stage in one's relationship with God, one where self-interest and self-satisfaction are the main emphasis, to a more perfect stage, where one's main

---

[141] John Henry Newman, *Verses on Various Occasions* (London: Longmans, Green, and Co., 1910), 156-157.
[142] *Dark Night*, BK 1, Ch. 3.

emphasis is starting to be God-centered. One's emphasis is on, "What can I do for God?" as opposed to "What can God do for me?"[143]

The signs of this stage are well described by St. John of the Cross:[144]

1) One finds no comfort in the things of God or in the things of the world. One's focus is no longer on the desires of the senses for their own sake. It is a time when one must will his or her being through this period of dryness.

2) Anxiety is symptomatic of this period of purification. One feels a sense that one is not serving God. In fact, one even senses that one is going backwards in the spiritual journey. One can become sluggish, weak, and even depressed in one's journey. Yet the desire, the will, continues to move one forward in serving God.

3) An inability to meditate, to reflect, and to excite the imagination are the hallmarks of this stage. God is beginning to be primarily experienced by means of the spirit as opposed to that of the senses.

It is crucially important to recognize that *all three* conditions must exist in the person at the *same time*; otherwise, what one is dealing with most likely is the result of a sinful life or a life wounded by a medical or psychological problem.

Initial Infused Contemplation

When the mind receives the representations of things, it of course patterns itself after each representation. In contemplating them spiritually it is variously conformed to each object contemplated. But when it comes to be in God, it becomes wholly without form and pattern, for in contemplating the one who is simple it becomes simple and entirely patterned in light.[145]

God at this stage is transforming meditation into a higher form of prayer, initial infused contemplation. Contemplation transfers to the core of the person in a more profound manner the goods and energies which once were solely attained through the senses. Furthermore, it transfers to the core of the person spiritual gifts and strengths that transcend the ability of the internal and external senses to experience, because by its very nature contemplation is beyond the limits of the imagination and the gift of natural reason. It is because the gift of contemplation transcends the limits of the imagination and the gift of reason that the senses experience a sense of dryness, a sense of void. The reality is, however, that God is closest to the person at this stage for

---

[143] Cf. St. Catherine of Siena, *Dialogue*, Chs. 75, 144, 149.
[144] *Dark Night*, BK 1, Ch. 9; *Ascent*, BK II, Chs. 13f.
[145] *Maximus Confessor: Selected Writings*, Third Century, n. 97.

he is asking the person to love him in pure faith as opposed to loving him for the good things he gives.

In this initial stage of contemplation, a person is not yet completely aware of what is going on. All that one is aware of is that there is an inner desire for solitude and quiet.

While one has begun to enter into the initial sphere of contemplation at this stage of the spiritual life, one has not completely become removed from the ability of discursive meditation. In fact, at this stage, it is not unusual for a person to move back and forth between meditation and contemplation. When meditation is fruitful, then one should remain at this stage of prayer until God moves one forward. If meditation becomes dry, then one is being moved in grace to contemplation.[146]

Contemplation is fruitful when it becomes less and less distracted by concepts or thoughts. When one becomes overly burdened by these distractions, God is calling one back to the state of meditation. When one feels an inability to meditate, to use concepts and thoughts in prayer, then one is being called to contemplation.[147]

The Jesus Prayer

The *Jesus prayer* is often helpful during this transition from meditation to initial infused contemplation. The *Jesus prayer* is the unceasing repetition of the phrase "Lord Jesus Christ, Son of God, have mercy on me a sinner." One seeks during this repetition to find a state where one gazes at the heart of God without images or idle thoughts.[148]

Centering Prayer/Technique

Centering prayer is a powerful gift at this stage of the spiritual life. St. Teresa of Avila alludes to this reality in chapter 31,7 of her book *The Way of Perfection*. Centering prayer is a technique whereby a person chooses a favorite word, "a gentle word" (or even an image) that reminds him or her of God and then uses this word or image to chase away distractions to contemplative prayer. At this initial stage of infused contemplation, distractions are normal; hence, a centering word or image can help--in grace--move a person into a deeper experience of contemplation.

Gifts of the Spirit

The gifts of the Spirit are flowering at this point, particularly the gifts of knowledge, understanding, fortitude, and the fear of the Lord.

---

[146] Cf. *Dark Night*, BK 1, Ch. 10; *Ascent*, BK II, Ch. 13; *Life*, Ch. 14.
[147] Cf. Evargrius Ponticus, *The 153 Chapters on Prayer*, 9, 44, 69-70, 120.
[148] See John Climacus: *The Ladder of Divine Ascent*, trans. Colm Luibheid (Mahwah: Paulist Press, 1982), 103, 239, 262, 266, 274-276, 278-279, 286, 290.

Knowledge

One begins to know the fact that the things of the world are empty unless they are directed to the glory and honor of God.[149]

Understanding

One begins to penetrate the deeper aspects of the faith. One is cleansing one's experience of the faith of all phantasms, misrepresentations, and errors. One is moving beyond simple adherence to formulas and the simple recitation of prayers, to a more penetrating experience of those formulas and recited prayers.[150]

Fortitude

The desire to serve God at all cost is beginning to take effect. One is willing to follow in Christ's footsteps and carry the cross. The virtues of patience and longanimity are enhanced by this gift as one manages the trials and tribulations of life with Christ-like courage.[151]

Fear of the Lord

This gift of the Spirit makes one fear sin. "My flesh trembles for fear of thee, and I am afraid of thy judgments" (Ps. 118:120). This gift profoundly strengthens the person to live a virtuous, patient and chaste life out of fear of being condemned to hell.[152] Sins against chastity and patience are the hallmark of this level of the spiritual life.[153] When one enters into the deeper stages of the spiritual life, the fear of hell will be replaced by the fear of not loving enough.

How to get out of the Dark Night

St. John of the Cross teaches his disciples how one is to progress through the *dark night*:[154]

1) One must have an enlightened spiritual director.
2) One must persevere in patience, trust, and humility through this difficult time.
3) One must keep one's being focused on Jesus and his cross.
4) One must foster a docile spirit where one is open to God's providence.
5) One must will oneself through this period of purification in faith.

---

[149] IIa IIae, q. 9, a.4.
[150] IIa IIae, q. 8, a.7; q. 61, a.5.
[151] Cf. IIa IIae, q. 139, a.2.
[152] Cf. IIa IIae, q. 19, a. 9, a. 19.
[153] *Dark Night*, BK 1, Ch. 14.
[154] Ibid., Ch. 10.

The Effects of the Passive Purification of the Senses

The passive purification of the senses has subjected the senses to the Spirit. Our senses have been spiritualized. One is moved more by an attraction to God for being God as opposed to God for being a giver of things. One begins to have a profound knowledge of God and self. One becomes aware of a new sense of power in fighting sin and in penetrating the mysteries of God. The person is beginning to see the world and one's being as never before. One is entering the sphere of enlightenment. [155] One is entering the sphere of dependence on God and a joyful surrendering to God's will.

An Aside

The Dark Night and Psychological Considerations

The *dark night* of the senses and the *dark night* of the soul (which will be discussed just before the unitive stage) can be very confusing to people who are experiencing them and who are observing them. This is a very delicate and crucial time in the spiritual journey. Great harm can be done by spiritual directors, psychologists, and psychiatrists if they are not aware of what is going on. The sad reality of today is that most priests are inadequately trained in the field of spirituality and in the field of psychology or psychiatry, and the same can be said of psychologists and psychiatrists: most lack an understanding of spiritual theology. Hence, great harm can be caused to the person's spiritual journey, either by retarding their progress or leaving them in a stupor of uncertainty and confusion, when improper advice is given. It is of great relief that the Roman schools of theology have greatly emphasized this interaction between the psychological and the spiritual. It is my hope that this will filter down to all seminaries in the training of priests.

Given what has been said, it is unrealistic for a priest to have adequate training in the field of psychology or psychiatry, given that the most basic training of priests takes nine to ten years. Likewise, it is unrealistic for psychologist and psychiatrists to have an adequate training in spiritual theology, given their own extensive years of studies. The solution is to seek out a cooperative interaction in the counseling of persons. As the cliché goes: Two minds are better than one. A person can rightly claim, therefore, that two or three fields of study are better than one.

What is the harm that can be done by the misdiagnosis of a person? The danger for the uninformed spiritual director is that what may very well be a pathological condition in need of either psychological counseling or psychiatric help in the form of medication, or both, can be left untreated. The person in such a case may in fact not be experiencing a *dark night* at all. They may indeed simply be experiencing a psychological breakdown or the development of a "chemical imbalance." Failure to bring this to the attention of a psychologist or psychiatrist can be extremely harmful to the person. On the

---

[155] Cf. Ibid., Chs. 12 and 13; Siena, *Dialogue*, Ch. 4; *Life*, Ch. 31.

other hand, if a person is experiencing an authentic *dark night* then the use of medication can be extremely harmful to the progress of the person, for the medication could very well eliminate the very function of the *dark night*, the purification of the person's being.

Purification is by its very nature a painful experience--to medicate the painful experience so that one experiences bliss will only retard the very purpose of the *dark night*. It will definitely stifle the purgative process and can in fact lead one to regress back to a lower form of the spiritual life.

A final point to be made is that at times, one may find a person authentically experiencing a *dark night* and also experiencing a pathological disorder. This is a case where the close interaction of the spiritual director and the psychologist or psychiatrist is essential. Having said all this, the following is a brief guideline in helping one understand what is authentically a part of the *dark night* and what is more of a psychological or pathological problem.

Faith, hope, and love are the distinguishing marks between the *dark nights* and patently pathological conditions.

In the *dark nights*, no matter how bad things get, even to the edge of despair, there is always a sense of faith and hope, a sense that one will be able to will one's very self through the situation in grace. There is a sense of trust that God is in control and that even though a person may not be clear as to where God is taking him or her, there is the clear understanding that God will not leave the person abandoned. The will and trust—empowered by grace--to move on is never extinguished no matter how bad things get. Furthermore, and more importantly, one never loses a sense of the love of God or of neighbor in the *dark nights*. No matter how wrenching the pain of the purgation, the love of God remains and the love of neighbor remains. The striving for being a person for others always remains. Humility, patience, and calm grow during these *dark nights*—particularly when the individual is in the hands of a competent spiritual director.

In a pathological situation, the faith of a person is deeply damaged and can be lost at an explicit level. The ability to will one's being through the situation is often impossible. Trust is often lost. The future looks bleak. There is seemingly no hope, without a drastic change. Love of neighbor is often replaced by a dislike or hate for others. One becomes excessively or obsessively introspective or self-absorbed to the point of losing sight of concerns for others. Love of God is often turned into a sense of indifference or even bitter anger toward him. The sense that one is being purged is often replaced with the sense that one is cursed. One can begin to lose a grip on reality.

These key factors, when explored by competent individuals in the fields of spirituality, psychology, and psychiatry, are of great importance in determining whether one is experiencing a *dark night* or whether one is experiencing a pathological disturbance

The ultimate sign that one has gone through the *dark night* is that one comes out of it renewed and prepared for a deeper prayer and spiritual life. The ultimate sign that one has not gone through a *dark night* is that one becomes increasingly ill, with no cure in sight, until one turns to professional help.

VI
The Illuminative Stage
A Time of Enlightenment

Again Jesus spoke to them, saying, "I am the light of the world; he who follows me will not walk in darkness, but will have the light of life" (Jn. 8:12).

In the purgative stage the individual grows to love God with his or her whole heart primarily by means of the faculties of the senses. In the illuminative stage one begins to love God not only with one's whole heart, but also with one's whole soul. This love transcends the limits of the senses. In the final stage, the unitive stage of the spiritual journey, love becomes complete. One at this stage loves God with one's whole heart, soul, strength, and mind.

In the illuminative stage, the ease of prayer returns after the darkness. A greater capacity for work, service, teaching, directing, and organizing takes place at this stage. The illuminative stage is exemplified by "good works." It is the beginning of the mystical life. It is the time when everyday mysticism is experienced. As Karl Rahner states, it is a stage in life

--where one dares to pray into silent darkness and knows that one is heard, although no answer seems to come back about which one might argue and rationalize,
--where one lets oneself go unconditionally and experiences this capitulation as true victory,
--where falling becomes true uprightness,
--where desperation is accepted and is still secretly accepted as trustworthy without cheap trust,
--where a man entrusts all his knowledge and all his questions to the silent and all-inclusive mystery which is loved more than all our individual knowledge which makes us such small people,
--where we rehearse our death in everyday life and try to live in such a way as we would like to die, peaceful and composed....[156]

---

[156] Karl Rahner, *The Spirit in the Church*, trans. John Griffiths (New York: The Seabury Press, 1979), 21-22.

This is the mystical walk with and in God. This is the "mysticism of everyday life."

In the illuminative stage, the acquired virtues that were primarily predominant in the purgative stage are now brought to the service of the infused virtues. The acquired virtues and the infused virtues, therefore, work hand in hand for the good of the person's growth in the life of God.[157]

The virtues come together like never before in the illuminative stage. The acquired virtue of prudence and the infused virtue of prudence work hand and hand and are aided by the Spirit's gift of counsel. The fruits of this interaction are foresight, circumspection, and constancy. The acquired virtue of fortitude and the infused virtue of fortitude work hand and hand and are aided by the Spirit's gift of fortitude. The fruits of this interaction are patience, magnanimity, and longanimity. The acquired virtue of justice and the infused virtue of justice work hand and hand and are aided by the Spirit's gift of piety. The fruits of this interaction are obedience and a call for penance and religion. The acquired virtue of temperance and the infused virtue of temperance work hand and hand and are aided by the Spirit's gift of fear. The fruits of this interaction are chastity, meekness, and poverty.[158]

Acquired Prudence (cf. Prov. 14:15; 1 Pet. 4:7)

> The mind that has succeeded in the active life advances in prudence....[159]

Acquired prudence is that moral virtue that directs through right reason acts of justice, courage, temperance, and their related virtues. It preserves an individual from impulsiveness in temperament, imagination, and sensible appetites. It moves one to seek advice, obey what is reasonable, and gives the strength to deal with differences in the temperament of different characters. At this stage of the spiritual journey, the acquired virtue of prudence is well developed and prepares one for the powerful response to the infused gift of prudence—that moral virtue that is grace-elevated.[160]

Infused Prudence

Infused prudence is that moral virtue that transcends the limits of the natural gift of right reason. It is in a sense the consequence of taking an acquired moral virtue and infusing it with grace. Grace elevates that which was natural into the realm of that which is supernatural. The infused moral virtue

---

[157] Cf. Ia IIae, q. 63, a.4.
[158] Cf. Ia IIae, q. 63, a.4.
[159] *Maximus Confessor: Selected Writings*, Second Century, n. 26.
[160] Cf. Ia IIae, q. 58, a.5; q. 64, a.1.

of prudence is given in response to grace. It is marked by a profound love and zeal for God and for the burning desire for the salvation and good of all people. It directs all the virtues to that which can be considered their last end, which is God's eternal destiny for all. All acts are judged according to a pilgrim's eternal destiny. The focus is on eternity, and not simply on the temporal aspects of life, which the acquired virtues tend to be primarily focused on.[161]

The gift of counsel accompanies the infused moral virtue of prudence. Wise decisions are made which are based on the knowledge of self and God. This leads to mercy, the beatitude of mercy, for a person with the infused moral virtue of prudence is able to find a comfortable milieu between rigor and justice. It also leads to the preferential option for mercy.[162]

Foresight, circumspection, and constancy are the quintessential marks of a person with prudence in the illuminative stage of the spiritual journey. One is blessed with an elevated sense of foresight and circumspection; that is, that grace-empowered ability to consider all circumstances and their possible consequences, particularly as they pertain to one's eternal destiny. One is also blessed with the gift of constancy, that ability to remain--as a consequence of the insights brought about through foresight and circumspection--steadfast in faith in whatever life may bring.[163]

Prudence and Simplicity

Prudence moves a person to live life simply. Prudence enables an individual to do the most little of things in the most holy of manners.[164] St. Therese of Lesieux's *little way* exemplifies this reality.

Acquired and Infused Fortitude

The acquired moral virtue of courage or fortitude is elevated by grace into the realm of infused courage or fortitude. Aided by the Spirit's gift of fortitude, the moral virtue of fortitude raises an individual to new heights in the spiritual life, to new heights in patience, magnanimity, and longanimity or forbearance.

A person experiencing the grace of fortitude is a person whose patience in times of difficulty does not allow him or her to depart from right reason illumined by faith. Such a person has the patience and forbearance to endure and fight off any temptations that might cause him or her to yield to difficulties. One at this stage is able to bear, often beyond the natural abilities of the body, adversity, sadness, and injuries of all sorts for whatever length of time.

Such a person is able to see and bear the cross. This seeing and bearing of the cross is done with magnanimity, with a sense of calm and sacrifice. The

---

[161] Cf. Ia, q. 79, a.9.
[162] Cf. IIa IIae, q. 52, a.4.
[163] Cf. Ia IIa, q. 63, a.4.
[164] Cf. IIa IIae, q. 109, a.2 ad 4um.

end of the difficulty is seen, the victory of the cross is clearly perceived in such a person. Because of this reality, such an individual experiences a loftiness of spirit enabling him or her to disdain any hint of meanness or revenge as a consequence of the adversity encountered.[165]

Acquired and Infused Justice

Justice is a movement away from self-infatuation and a movement toward the good of others (cf. Lev. 19:15; Col. 4:1). Again, as with all the moral virtues, the acquired moral virtue of justice is at the service of the infused, grace-filled, moral virtue of justice. Aided by the Spirit's gift of piety, a person exemplifies a life of authentic faith and works.[166]

When discussing the moral virtue of justice, one must take into account the three expressions of justice that a person at this stage of the spiritual journey is radically aware of.

1. *Commutative Justice*: Commutative justice is aimed at the dignity of equality. Because of this reality, it is a form of justice that fights against any occurrences of theft, fraud, usury, false accusations, insults, unjust blame, defamation, slander, gossip, insinuation, and so on.[167]
2. *Distributive Justice*: Distributive justice is aimed at how public goods are used. It fights against any hint of favoritism, oppression, unrelieved poverty, and corruption of all kinds.[168]
3. *Social Justice*: Social justice or legal justice is preoccupied with the common good of society. It demands personal sacrifice,[169] and is inseparable from prayer:

Action and contemplation now grow together into one life and one unity. They become two aspects of the same thing. Action is charity looking outward to other men, and contemplation is charity drawn inward to its own divine source. Action is the stream, and contemplation is the spring. The spring remains more important than the stream, for the only thing that really matters is for love to spring up inexhaustibly from the infinite abyss of Christ and of God.[170]

---

[165] Cf. IIa IIae, q. 136, a.1.
[166] Cf. Ia IIae, q. 56, a.6, c and ad 3um.
[167] Cf. IIa IIae, q. 73-75.
[168] Cf. IIa IIae, q. 63, a.1f.
[169] Cf. IIa IIae, q. 58, a.6f.
[170] Merton, *No Man is an Island* (New York: Image Books, 1967), 65.

Guiding all three of these expressions of justice is that gift of *epikeia*, that gift that preserves the dignity of the human person at all cost, that gift that recognizes the spirit as well as the letter of the law.[171]

Justice and Veracity

Justice and veracity are intertwined with prudence and simplicity. Justice and veracity however are predominantly concerned with moral integrity, with telling the truth and acting according to it. In the illuminative stage sins of duplicity, hypocrisy, boasting, and mockery are extinguished.[172] There are no two-faced saints!

Acquired and Infused Temperance

Temperance elevated by grace to what is referred to as infused temperance--and aided by the Spirit's gift of fear--is that moral virtue that is exemplified by a sense of moderation in thought, action and feeling (cf. Sir. 5:2; 18:30; 37:27-31; Titus 2:12). Temperance finds its most precious expression in the evangelical counsels[173] of poverty, chastity, and obedience. Meekness (that ability to endure persecutions or injustices with patience and without resentment) is also a significant expression at this stage of the spiritual journey.

The Evangelical Counsels

Poverty is that gift that purifies a person of all attachments. It is that gift that unites the person to Christ Jesus. For St. Thomas Aquinas, Christ chose a life of poverty for four reasons, four reasons that all disciples are all called to imitate.[174]

1. Poverty frees one from the cares that are associated with earthly goods.
2. Poverty frees one to be concerned with the salvation of souls.
3. Poverty frees one for the desire of eternal goods.
4. Poverty frees one, in the absence and contradiction of earthly helps, to express the divine power that saves souls.

Poverty is true freedom. It moves the clouds of worldly attachments away from the spiritual life and detaches one of all that is not for the glory and honor of God. Love of God, love of neighbor and love of heaven are the all-consuming hungers of the poor in spirit.[175]

---

[171] Cf. IIa IIae, q. 120, a.1f
[172] Cf. IIa IIae, q. 109, a.2 ad 4um.
[173] The evangelical counsels are responsible for the majority of the grace-filled work of detachment that is necessary for holiness and thus happiness.
[174] III a, q. 40, a.3; q. 35, a.7.
[175] Cf. IIa, q. 23, a.1, ad 3um.

Chastity of heart and body are exemplified in the infused moral virtue of temperance. Whether one is a virgin, a religious, or a single, unmarried person, all are called to a chaste life, a life free of lewdness or salaciousness, a life which is pure in thought and action. It is empowered by the grace that accompanies the love of neighbor and the love of God.[176]

Obedience is a joyful submissiveness to that which is best for one's eternal salvation. Obedience delivers a person away from the slavery that is attached to self-will and self-infatuation. The fruits of obedience, thus, are rectitude, or righteousness in judgment, which is accompanied by a liberty of spirit: "Now the Lord is the Spirit, and where the Spirit of the Lord is, there is freedom" (2 Cor. 3:17).

Theological Virtues of Faith Hope and Love
Faith

Faith is a gift (Eph. 2:8) aided by the gift of understanding which is in conformity with reason, yet transcends the limits of reason.[177] Faith in the illuminative stage is freed to a great extent of all aspects of egoism, passions, jealousies, whims, etc., of all that can damage a person's response to the inner call of grace. For some at this stage, faith is greater in the faculty of the intellect, thereby producing the fruits of certitude and firmness in actions. In others, faith is greater in the will, thereby producing the fruits of devotion and confidence.[178] In either case, all aspects of one's life are being guided by the light of faith, which guides the individual to his or her eternal destiny of loving God for being God (Rom. 8:28).

Hope

Hope is that confidence in the help of God. Hope helps one to persevere (Mt. 10:22) and overcome trials and tribulations (Rom. 5:2-5). Hope, because of these trials and tribulations, purifies the person for the love of God (Cf. Wis. 3: 4-6). Hope is a walk into the mystery of the unknown. Yet it is a walk with a certain sense of certitude of direction. Hope makes a person advance more generously toward God by giving the person a greater desire for him. God becomes a person's end; God becomes all that is hoped for.

In the illuminative stage two lingering defects from the purgative stage are being polished off: *presumption and discouragement*. Presumption is that defect that fails to recognize the necessity of responding to grace in the spiritual journey. It is that defect that overemphasizes God's mercy and underemphasizes God's justice. Hence, people often feel they can be pardoned without repentance or in the worst case they can even feel assured of salvation. In the case of the defect of discouragement at this stage, a person

---

[176]Cf. IIa IIae, q. 151, a. 1-3.
[177]Cf. IIa IIae, q. 15.
[178] IIa IIae, q. 5, a.4.

can often feel that the spiritual journey is too difficult and thus hopeless. One often turns away from grace and goes back to a former way of life because one senses that grace is too inaccessible. In the illuminative stage these two defects against hope, against properly ordered confidence in God, are being completely finished off, completely extinguished.

Love
For John Climacus, "Love, by its nature, is a resemblance to God."[179] Love is the conformity of a person's will to God's, for all the other virtues follow the virtue of love (cf. 1 Cor. 13:4). In the illuminative stage, certain signs can be seen according to St. Thomas Aquinas:[180]

1. Mortal sins are a thing of the past, since love has conquered that inclination.
2. Because of love, earthly things such as pleasures, honors, wealth, etc., are no longer of great interest.
3. Because of love, one seeks to be engulfed in the presence of God, to love him, to think of him, to adore him, to pray to him, to thank him, to ask his pardon, to aspire to him.
4. One desires, out of the grace of love, to please God more than anything and anyone in the entire created realm of reality.
5. One seeks to love and know God in one's neighbor, in spite of the neighbor's defects. One loves one's neighbor for simply being a child of God, a child of God who is beloved by God. One loves in the illuminative stage God in one's neighbor and one's neighbor in God. Love of God and love of neighbor merge into one reality.

In the words of Dorothy Day, "we cannot love God unless we love each other, and to love we must know each other."[181] Love of neighbor is the most distinguishing characteristic of the illuminative stage (Cf. Mt. 5:44, 47, 48).

Zeal

Dearest Lord, teach me to be generous. Teach me to serve You as you deserve; to give and not to count the cost; to fight and not to heed the wounds; to toil and not to seek for rest; to labor and not to ask for reward, save that of knowing that I am doing Your will. Amen.

The illuminative stage of the spiritual journey is marked with tremendous zeal. It is a holy zeal that is directed toward the glory and honor of God and in particular the salvation of persons. Unlike the zeal that is predominant in the

---

[179] *John Climacus: The Ladder of Divine Ascent*, Step. 30, 286.
[180] Ia IIae, q. 112, a.5.
[181] Day, *The Long Loneliness*, 317.

purgative stage, this zeal is not lost during times of trials and tribulations, nor is it susceptible to bitterness.

Motives for Zeal

Zeal is nourished by a deep grace-filled thirst to love God and neighbor above all. It is signified by the following marks:

1. An intense desire to imitate Christ in all things.
2. An intense desire to bring all people into the kingdom of God.
3. An intense desire to overcome the enemies of the Church.
4. An intense desire to overcome indifference, inertia, lack of comprehension, ill will, and spiteful opposition.

Qualities of Holy Zeal

Holy zeal is enlightened by the light of faith. It is the fruit of the acquired and infused moral virtues, particularly the virtue of prudence and the gifts of the Holy Spirit, particularly the gifts of wisdom and counsel. Unlike bitter zeal, which is not of God, and which is self-seeking, proud, insensitive, impatient, rude and hate-filled, holy zeal, which is of God, is calm, humble, meek, patient, sensitive, and always other-centered. This type of zeal is expressed in the traditional spiritual and corporal works of mercy:

Corporal Works of Mercy
- Feeding the hungry
- Giving drink to the thirsty
- Clothing the naked
- Sheltering the homeless
- Visiting the sick
- Visiting the imprisoned

Spiritual Works of Mercy
- Instructing the ignorant
- Correcting sinners
- Advising the doubtful
- Showing patience to sinners and those in error
- Forgiving others
- Confronting the afflicted
- Praying for the living and the dead

In her fight against the injustices of the world, Dorothy Day could say with great ease: "It is natural for me to stand my ground...using...weapons as the works of mercy to show love and alleviate suffering."[182]

---

[182] Day, *The Long Loneliness*, 206.

The Holy Spirit in the Illuminative Stage

Wisdom, the highest of the gifts of the Spirit, at this stage of the spiritual life is very active in directing all the other gifts in the grace-filled, zeal-driven, saint of God.[183]

Fear

The gift of fear supplies strength to overcome the imperfections that are often intertwined with the virtues. In the purgative stage, the gift of fear tends to be one that is more servile in nature; that is, a person grows in the spiritual life out of a fear of eternal damnation. In the illuminative stage, the gift of fear is transformed into what has been traditionally called filial fear; that is, a fear that empowers the spiritual life not so much out of a fear of hell as much as a fear of not loving enough. For the people at this stage, the big fear consists in having to face Jesus after their earthly journey without having loved enough.

Love for the poor becomes very powerful at this stage, and thus the gift of fear in the illuminative stage is tied to the beatitude of the love for the poor.[184] St. Vincent de Paul would say: "it is better to feed the poor than to raise the dead."

Piety

The gift of piety is the gift of rendering to God what is rightly due to God. Human reason becomes illumined by faith at this stage like never before. Suffering takes on meaning and a sense of sweetness.[185] As John Henry Newman explains, "I am, I can never be thrown away. If I am in sickness, my sickness may serve Him; in perplexity, my perplexity may serve Him; if I am in sorrow, my sorrow may serve Him."[186] At this stage one finds in the mystery of suffering the mystery of love, and one finds in the mystery of love the mystery of suffering.

Prayer becomes more fervent and persistent as new insights into the mystery of life become illumined. Any hint of hardness of heart is replaced with an open heart. This predisposes a person to being open to interior silence, recollection, and detachment. The gift of piety corresponds, as a consequence, to the beatitude that emphasizes the power and preciousness of the meek.[187]

Knowledge

The gift of knowledge is a gift that elevates human knowledge to new heights. At this stage there is a radical knowledge of those things that are of God and those things that are not of God. The knowledge of good and evil is

---

[183] Ia IIae, q. 68, a.7.
[184] Cf. IIa IIae, q. 19.
[185] Cf. IIa IIae, q. 121.
[186] John Henry Newman, *Meditations and Devotions* (Westminster, MD: Christian Classics, 1975), 301.
[187] Cf. IIa IIae, q. 121.

powerfully perceived and felt with great sorrow at this stage. In the illuminative stage, the gift of knowledge is powerfully tied to the beatitude of the sorrowful.[188]

Fortitude

In the illuminative stage there is a heightened desire to fight the temptations of the flesh, the world, and the devil. There is also a heightened degree of patience and perseverance in the quest for justice. This stage is often associated with the beatitude regarding those who hunger and thirst for justice.[189]

Counsel

This gift overcomes the imperfections that hinder the virtue of prudence. It corresponds to the beatitude of the merciful, in that all actions are decided in favor of authentic mercy, a mercy that is properly balanced with justice. The gift of counsel at this stage also helps avoid the dangers of temerity, of recklessness and rashness, which often lead to unhealthy and even evil fanaticism. On the other hand, the gift of counsel helps to fight the danger of pusillanimity--that is, cowardliness and timidity in the face of danger or opposition.[190]

Understanding

Understanding in the illuminative stage is enlightened by the interior light of grace. Its primary impact in this stage of a person's journey is in helping to eliminate the imperfections that hinder the deep penetrations into the truths of faith. The gift of understanding is primarily directed to the purification of one's intentions; thus, it is often viewed to correspond to the beatitude of the pure of heart.[191] This purity of heart and deep penetration into the faith can be seen in St. Hildegard of Bingen's reflection on the nature of the Trinity:

[As] the flame of a fire has three qualities, so there is one God in three Persons. How? A flame is made up of a brilliant light and red power and fiery heat. It has brilliant light that it may shine, and red power that it may endure, and fiery heat that it may burn. Therefore, by the brilliant light understand the Father, Who with paternal love opens His brightness to His faithful; and by the red power, which is in the flame that it may be strong, understand the Son, Who took on a body born from a Virgin, in which His divine wonders are shown; and by the fiery heat understand the Holy Spirit,

---

[188] Cf. IIa IIae, q. 9.
[189] Cf. IIa IIae, q. 139, a.1, 2.
[190] Cf. IIa IIae, q. 139, a.1, 2.
[191] Cf. IIa IIae, q. 8, a.1, 4, 6, 7.

Who burns ardently in the minds of the faithful. But there is no flame seen where there is neither brilliant light nor red power nor fiery heat; and thus also where neither the Father nor the Son nor the Holy Spirit is known God is not properly worshipped.[192]

Wisdom

Eternal Wisdom shall be my bride, and I will be her Servitor. Oh God, if I could catch one glimpse of her, speak to her for a few moments.[193]

The highest of the gifts of the Spirit, wisdom, helps one judge all things in relation to God. Since all is seen in terms of God's providence and his will, then one in this stage of the spiritual journey experiences a sense of peace.[194] In the words of Dorothy Day,

I should know by this time that just because I feel that everything is useless and going to pieces and badly done and futile, it is not really that way at all. Everything is all right. It is in the hands of God. Let us abandon everything to Divine Providence.[195]

Wisdom brings about peace. One is in peace and one seeks to bring this peace to others. This gift corresponds, therefore, to the beatitude of the peacemakers.[196]

The Ten Commandments (Ex. 20:2-17; Dt. 5:26)[197]

Through the working of the commandments the mind puts off the passions.[198]

St. Maximus Confessor

1. I am the Lord your God: you shall not have strange gods before me.
2. You shall not take the name of the Lord your God in vain.
3. Remember to keep holy the Lord's Day.
4. Honor your father and your mother.

---

[192] *Hildegard of Bingen: Scivias*, trans. Mother Columba Hart and Jane Bishop (Mahwah: Paulist Press, 1990), BK II, Vision II, n. 6.
[193] *Henry Suso's Life*, in *Exemplar: Life and Writings of Blessed Henry Suso* (Dubuque: Priory Press, 1962), vol. I, 3.
[194] Cf. IIa IIae, q. 45, a.1, 2, 5, 6.
[195] Dorothy Day, *House of Hospitality* (New York: Sheed and Ward, 1939), 101.
[196] Cf. IIa IIae, q. 45, a.1, 2, 5, 6.
[197] CCC 2084-2550.
[198] *Maximus Confessor: Selected Writings*, First Century, n. 94.

5. You shall not kill.
6. You shall not commit adultery.
7. You shall not steal.
8. You shall not bear false witness against your neighbor.
9. You shall not covet your neighbor's wife.
10. You shall not covet your neighbor's goods.

The first commandment forbids acts of voluntary doubt (the disregarding or refusing to believe as true what God has revealed), incredulity (the refusal to assent to truth), heresy (the denial of truth), apostasy (the rejection of the Christian faith), schism (refusal to submit to the Catholic Church), despair (ceasing to hope in salvation), presumption (the counting on one's own capacities for salvation), indifference (the failure to appreciate or care in God's goodness), ingratitude (the refusal to return love for love), lukewarmness (a hesitation in responding to God's love), spiritual sloth (refusing the joy that comes from God), hatred of God (denying God's goodness), idolatry (divinizing worldly "things" such as power, pleasure, race, country, etc.), sacrilege (profaning things and persons of God), atheism (denial of God's existence), and agnosticism (a refusal to affirm or deny the existence of God). Occult beliefs and practices such as superstition, divination, magic and sorcery are also forbidden.

The second commandment demands a respect for the sacredness of the Lord's name. Acts of blasphemy (asserting words or thoughts of hatred, reproach, or defiance against God), the taking of oaths (the superficial misuse or lack of respect for God's name), false oaths (swearing to take God as a witness to something that is not true), and perjury (making a promise under oath with no intention of keeping it) are sinful.

The third commandment is a summons to keep the Lord's Day a holy day. It demands the faithful attendance of Sunday Mass, and an attitude of profound worship. It is a time to spend with God and to abstain from any work that distracts from authentically consecrating Sunday as a precious day of love of God and love of neighbor. One seeks comfort, but one also seeks to be challenged to grow.

The fourth commandment demands the authentic honoring of father and mother. Children owe just obedience, respect, gratitude, assistance, and the repaying of love for love to their parents. Parents have the responsibility of caring for their children's physical and spiritual needs, fostering a vocation, and teaching them to serve and follow God above all. The family forms the foundation for societal and ecclesiastical life.

The fifth commandment is an affirmation of the dignity of life. Being created in the image and likeness of God, the human person is sacred from conception to natural death. Murder is a violation of the dignity of the person and the creator. Unjust war, direct abortions, intentional euthanasia, abortion-causing contraceptives, and suicide are forbidden by this commandment.

The sixth commandment is a command that demands fidelity. Any act which is contrary to the dignity of chastity, such as fornication, adultery, polygamy, divorce and remarriage (without an annulment), open or free marriages, same-sex marriages or unions, homosexual and bisexual acts, masturbation, contraceptive use, pornography, prostitution, incest and rape are forbidden. Artificial insemination and the use of a surrogate uterus are forbidden. The sixth commandment is a call to authentic sexual integration, authentic life and love.

The seventh commandment is a prohibition against stealing. Stealing is characteristic of a lack of charity and injustice. Often stealing is done in subtle ways: For example, on the part of employers in a business a violation of the seventh commandment is often exemplified by business fraud, ignorance of contracts, and the mistreatment of workers through unfair wages and lack of health and retirement benefits. On the part of the employee this injustice and lack of charity is often seen in acts of laziness and all forms of lack of effort in the work environment. The seventh commandment forbids social relationships based solely on economic factors, as opposed to the nature of the human person. It acknowledges that the goods of creation are for the entire human family. The "author, center, and goal of all economic and social life is the human person." The seventh commandment demands the tithing of one's talent and treasure to God.

The eighth commandment is a prohibition against bearing false witness against one's neighbor. Lying, duplicity, hypocrisy, boasting, dissimulation (hiding under a false appearance), rash judgment (assuming without reason the moral fault of another), detraction (disclosing another's faults to someone who did not know them), betrayal of confidences, calumny (character assassination), and slander (a false statement that damages a person's reputation) are all acts contrary to the dignity of persons.

The ninth commandment is a prohibition against coveting one's neighbor's wife. It prohibits moral permissiveness, and seeks the purification of the social moral climate. This commandment calls one to live a life of decency, chastity and modesty. It is a call for purity of heart, intention, and vision.

The tenth commandment is a call to avoid coveting another's goods. It is a call to avoid greed, envy, and all immoderate desires. It is a call to desire a detachment from all that is contrary to the glory and honor of God. One is called to desire God above all.

Discernment of Spirits[199]

> Beware of false prophets, who come to you in sheep's clothing but inwardly are ravenous wolves (Mt. 7:15).

The discernment of spirits is guided by acquired and infused prudence and the gift of counsel. In the purgative stage, the spirit of the world or nature predominates. In the illuminative stage, the Spirit of God takes a hold of a person's spiritual journey. The spirit of the devil is identifiable and slowly being destroyed.

The Spirit of the Devil
The spirit of the devil is marked by pride, discouragement, despair, scrupulosity, boasting, dissension, hatreds, false humility, presumption, fear of correction, self-infatuation, bitter zeal, forgetfulness of God, lack of obedience, and an intense dislike for mortification. All that is contrary to the honor and glory of God is found in the influences of the devil.

The Spirit of the World
The spirit of the world bears a lot in common with the spirit of the devil. However, the spirit of the world does not bear the extreme evil that is indicative of the ways of the devil. In this phase, a person has very little regard for the infused virtues of faith, hope, and love. A person in this stage is pleasure and self-oriented. One is easily irritated and discouraged. One is indifferent to the glory and honor of God. One is indifferent to the love of God and the love of neighbor. There is no zeal in such a person. Tepidity, mediocrity, and false moderation are indicative of a person's spiritual life. People influenced by the spirit of the world (or nature) are people who are more social workers than disciples. They are the ones who at the first sign of difficulty in the spiritual life, abandon it, and go to their former way of life. They are people who are evangelized more by the world than the Gospel.

The Spirit of God

> But the fruit of the Spirit is love, joy, peace, patience, kindness, goodness, faithfulness, gentleness, self-control; against such there is

---

[199] Cf. Ignatius, *Spiritual Exercises*, 4th week.

no law. And those who belong to Christ Jesus have crucified the flesh with its passions and desires (Gal. 5:22-24).

All that is of the spirit of God is directed toward the honor and glory of God. Those who live in this manner bear the marks of faith, hope, and love. They are people of true, authentic humility bearing profound self-knowledge and a zeal for God. They are a people marked by interior joy and forgetfulness of self. They embrace suffering, the sweetness of the cross, and mortification. They have no regard for the world's standards of success or the world's scorn.

Authentic mortification takes place in those embraced with the Spirit of God. That which is of the Spirit of God in terms of mortification is always marked by respect for the body as the temple of God. Mortification that flows from the grace of God is moderated by discretion and obedience. A person engaged in mortification does not seek to attract attention, and he or she does not seek to damage his or her health. Rather, authentic mortification is directed toward purifying the heart and the will for the honor and glory of God.

The illuminative stage is exemplified by a person's ability to discern the spirits and to persevere in the Spirit of God. As St. John Climacus states:

It is characteristic of the [profoundly holy] that they always know whether a thought comes from within themselves, or from God, or from the demons.... The eyes of the heart are enlightened by discernment to things seen and unseen....[200]

Perceiving Christ in Others

Carryll Houselander, while traveling on a crowded underground train during rush hour in London, experienced this profound sense of seeing all people as Christs.

I was in an underground train, a crowded train in which all sorts of people jolted together, sitting and strap-hanging—workers of every description going home at the end of the day. Quite suddenly I saw with my mind, but as vividly as a wonderful picture, Christ in them all. But I saw more than that; not only was Christ in every one of them, living in them, dying in them, rejoicing in them, sorrowing in them—but because He was in them, and because they were here, the whole world was here too, here in this underground train; not only the world as it was at that moment, not only the people in all the countries of the world, but all those people who had lived in the past, and all those yet to come. I came out into the street and

---

[200] John Climacus: The Ladder of Divine Ascent, 255.

walked for a long time in the crowds. It was the same here, on every side, in every passer-by, everywhere—Christ.[201]

This sense of the everywhere of Christ is expressed in a prayer ascribed to St. Patrick:

Christ be with me, Christ within me, Christ behind me, Christ before me, Christ beside me, Christ to win me, Christ to comfort me and restore me, Christ beneath me, Christ above me, Christ in the hearts of all that love me, Christ in the mouth of friend and stranger.

Patrick sought to experience a world engulfed in Christ.

Prayer in the Illuminative Stage—Meditation to Contemplation

What began in the passive purification of the senses continues more profoundly in the illuminative stage of spirituality. Meditation is being transformed into contemplation. If one perseveres in the meditative life, meditation slowly becomes more simplified to such an extent that the various experiences and acts involved in meditation begin to fuse into a single act. The person's core being has been made docile to the workings of the Holy Spirit. The person's experience of prayer is raised to that of contemplation.

Contemplation is a mutual sharing among friends, a mutual presence, an inter-indwelling, a gaze on the guest within (Cf. 1 Jn. 4:16).[202] It is a pure, supernatural gift, an inflaming of love.[203] The Song of Songs in the Scriptures is the perfect analogy for the experience that occurs in the silence of the soul in contemplation. One who experiences contemplation is transformed into a person of great virtue, into a person of profound works (Mt. 7:20). The following are key aspects of the fruits of contemplation:[204]

- Peace, quietude, calm, repose, serenity, and rest beyond all understanding (Cf. Phil. 4:4-7).
- A knowledge of realities that transcend the natural means of knowing.
- A deepening, wounding, inflaming, engulfing, inflowing, longing love that is caused by God's self-communicating triune nature.
- Transformation into the image and likeness of God.

Contemplation is an act of the intellect that is superior to reasoning. It is a simple glance at truth, which springs from love. It is an act that proceeds from faith and is enlightened by the gifts of the Holy Spirit, especially wisdom and understanding. In the beginning, contemplation can be prepared for by the

---

[201] Caryll Houselander, A Rocking-Horse Catholic (New York: Sheed and Ward, 1955), 137-138.
[202] Life, Ch. 8, no. 5 and Ch. 10, no. 1; Way, Ch. 27.
[203] Ibid., Ch. 23, no. 5; Ch. 24, nos. 7-8; Ch. 39, no. 23.
[204] Ibid., Ch. 27, no. 4; Ascent, BK II, Chs. 12-15; Dark Night, BK I, no. 1, and Chs. 5, 8-13, 17; Spiritual Canticle, St. 39, no. 12.

reading of sacred Scripture, meditation, prayers of petitions, and centering prayer. This helps to prepare the person to experience contemplation. With time, however, these preparatory acts will not be necessary.[205] At this stage, God himself will teach and refresh the core of the person without meditation or any active effort.[206] Contemplation thus becomes, in the words of St. John of the Cross, the "science of love," which is an infused knowledge of God.[207]

Degrees of Prayer in the Illuminative Stage
    St. Teresa of Avila and St. John of the Cross describe most profoundly the various degrees of prayer in the illuminative way:[208]

1. The discursive meditations that survive the passive purification of the senses continue to transform the person as that person continues to grow in the virtues. As one progresses in the spiritual journey, meditation will give way to initial infused contemplation.

    a. St. John of the Cross sets a threefold guideline in determining when to progress from meditation to contemplation. First, one should experience no comfort in the imagination or the senses in one's attempts at meditation. Second, the memory that lingers on in prayer is one that is filled with anxiety, with a sense that makes one feel that one is going backwards or not serving God. Finally, one is consciously aware of an inability to meditate or engage in reflections, or to excite the imagination.[209]

2. The second degree of prayer in the illuminative way can be pictured as a pump or water-wheel that draws up water. This second degree requires much less effort and yields much more water, much more spiritual fruit. This is the stage of prayer that Teresa calls the "prayer of quiet."[210] It is that level of prayer where the will is seized and held.[211] This "prayer of quiet" has three distinct phases: In the first phase, the person's will experiences a sweet and loving sense of being absorbed by God. In the second phase the person experiences a sense of quiet tranquility because the will is now not only absorbed by God but it is now captivated by God. In the third phase, the will is still captivated and the person's ability to understand what is happening to his or her soul is no longer perceivable. The virtues flower, and the soul is docile in responding to the gift of piety. Yet, in this "prayer of quiet" the person is still susceptible to distractions in prayer, for the

---

[205] IIa IIae, q. 180, a.3, 4, 6, 7 ad 1um; IIa IIae, q. 8, a.1, 2, 4, 6, 7; q. 45, a.1, 2, 5, 6;
[206] *Dark Night*, BK I, Ch. 14.
[207] Ibid., BK II, Ch. 18.
[208] Cf. *Life*, Chs. 11-19.
[209] *Dark Night*, BK I, Ch. 9.
[210] *Life*, 14f.
[211] *Interior Castle*, 5th mansion, Ch. 1.

intellect, the memory and the imagination still continue to enter into the prayer experience.[212] Centering prayer becomes very good at this stage of the spiritual journey.

3. The third degree in the prayer life in the illuminative stage can be described in a way similar to a person who irrigates his or her garden with running water. Another image used is that of water overflowing unto a riverbank and washing up onto a garden. This is the type of prayer that is often referred to as the "prayer of simple union." God's self-communicating presence at this stage is such that the interior faculties at the core of the person are now put to sleep. It is a time where the intellect is seized and held, and it is a time when the exterior senses and the imagination "fall asleep." It is often an ecstatic state.[213] God is the object of all the activities of the inner core of the person. There is no longer any wandering. A person's will, thought, imagination and memory are captivated and absorbed by God. All things are calmed. There is no more restlessness.[214]

4. There is a fourth degree of prayer in the life of a person that is called the "prayer of union." It is, however, that degree of prayer that is reserved to those who reach the highest stage of the spiritual journey, the unitive stage. It is the prayer of the mystics.[215] This is the stage in the spiritual journey that is marked by the prayer of "transforming union" or "mystical union."[216] It is like a gentle, abundant rainfall that nourishes a garden completely. The person does nothing to water the garden. It is all God's doing.[217] This reality is described by St. Bernard of Clairvaux in his *Sermon 74*:

I remember afterwards that he had been with me; sometimes I had a presentiment that he would come, but I was never conscious of his coming or his going. And where he comes from when he visits my soul, and where he goes, and by what means he enters and goes out, I admit that I do not know even now.... The coming of the Word was not perceptible to my eyes, for he has not color; nor to the ears, for there was no sound; nor yet to my nostrils, for he mingles with the mind, not the air; he has not acted upon the air, but created it. His coming was not tasted by the mouth, for there was not eating or drinking, nor could he be known by the sense of touch, for he is not tangible. How then did he enter? Perhaps he did not enter because he does not come from outside? He is not one of the things which

---

[212] *Life*, Chs. 14 and 17; *Interior Castle*, 4th mansion, Ch. 2.
[213] *Interior Castle*, 5th mansion, Ch. 1.
[214] *Life*, Ch. 18f.
[215] Cf. Ibid., Ch. 18f.
[216] *Interior Castle*, 7th mansion, Ch. 3.
[217] *Life*, Ch. 11, no. 7.

exist outside us. Yet he does not come from within me, for he is good, and I know there is no good in me. I have ascended to the highest in me, and look! the word is towering above that. In my curiosity I have descended to explore my lowest depths, yet I found him even deeper. If I look outside myself, I saw him stretching beyond the furthest I could see; and if I looked within, he was yet further within. Then I knew the truth of what I had read, "in him we live and move and have our being." And blessed is the man in whom he has his being, who lives for him and is moved by him.[218]

The Our Father[219]

[This] prayer, the Our Father, contains the fullness of perfection. It was the Lord Himself who gave it to us as both an example and a rule.... It lifts them up to that prayer of fire known to so few. It lifts them up, rather, to that ineffable prayer which rises above all human consciousness with no voice sounding, no tongue moving, no words uttered. The soul lights up with heavenly illumination and no longer employs constricted, human speech.[220]

In the *Our Father* Jesus teaches us how to pray. Since he experienced all things we experience, except sin, he knows well our needs (cf. Heb. 4:15). Jesus in the *Our Father* teaches us the summary of the whole Gospel, the summary of what new life in God is all about. In this prayer one is empowered by the Spirit to cry out "abba," "Father" (cf. Jn. 6:63; Gal. 4:6)! In the Lord's Prayer one is brought into the presence of the Father, of the Trinity. In the *Our Father* one enters a prayer of "straightforward simplicity, filial trust, joyous assurance, humble boldness, and certainty of being loved"[221] (cf. Eph. 3:12; Heb. 3:6; 4:16; 10:19; 1 Jn. 2:28; 3:21; 5:14). As a prayer the *Our Father* reveals the Father and reveals one's own innermost being: It enlightens one to the Father and to one's core self.

Our Father
By saying "Our Father" one is saying that one is entering a relationship. He is our God and we are his people (cf. Jn. 1:17; Hos. 2:21-22; 6:1-6). One accepts the reality that one has also entered a relationship that implies not individualism but a sense of communion, of membership. One is a member of God's Body, the Church, the community of faith (cf. Acts 4:32; Jn. 11:52). One

---

[218] *Bernard of Clairvaux: On the Song of Songs IV*, trans. Kilian Walsh, O.C.S.O (Kalamazoo: Cistercian Publications, 1980), Sermon 74.
[219] See CCC 2777-2856.
[220] *John Cassian: Conferences*, Trans. Colm Luibheid (Mahwah: Paulist Press, 1985), Conference 9, n. 25.
[221] CCC 2778

recognizes that the communion between the three Persons of the Trinity must be modeled by God's people, who were and are created in the image and likeness of God. Prayer is always therefore a community-oriented experience. Even in what appears to be private prayer, one is in prayer with the unknown and with the angels and saints.

Who art in heaven

> "Our Father who art in heaven" is rightly understood to mean that God is in the hearts of the just, as in his holy temple. At the same time, it means that those who pray should desire the one they invoke to dwell in them.[222]

The phrase "who art in heaven" is not primarily a reference to a place because heaven is not a "place" as commonly understood. Heaven is a place in the sense that it is a dimension beyond space and time: Heaven is another dimension of reality. Consequently the phrase, used in the context of this prayer, is primarily a reference to God's majesty and his presence in the hearts of the just. Heaven, "the Father's house, is the true homeland toward which we are heading and to which, already, we belong."[223]

Hallowed be thy name

The phrase "Hallowed be thy name" is a phrase that conjures up the holiness, preciousness, and majesty of God (cf. Ps 8:5; Isa. 6:3). It reminds one that God is worthy of all praise and thanksgiving (cf. Ps 111:9; Lk. 1:49).

Thy Kingdom Come

God's kingdom became present in the first coming and will find its fulfillment in the second coming (cf. Tit. 2:13). As a follower of Christ one is called to help bring about the fulfillment of this kingdom. A person is called upon to help build the kingdom of God here on earth, a kingdom of love.

Thy will be done on earth as it is in heaven

This phrase is an affirmation that
5) all are called to be saved and come to the truth (cf. 1 Tim. 2:3-4; 2 Pet. 3:9; Mt. 18:14).
6) all must love one another (Jn. 13:34; cf. 1 Jn. 3; 4; Lk. 10: 25-37).
7) one must do all things according to God's will (Eph. 1:9-11).
8) all are called to imitate Christ in his obedience and surrendering to the Father's will (Heb. 10:7; Lk. 22:42; Jn. 4:34; 5:30; 6:38; 8:29; Gal. 1:4).

---

[222] St. Augustine, *De serm. Dom. In monte* 2, 5, 18: PL 34, 1277.
[223] CCC 2802

Give us this day our daily bread
This statement is an expression of God's goodness, a goodness that transcends all other goodness. The "Our" reminds one that one is a member of a community, a community built upon the foundation of solidarity. It is a call in trust and in a spirit of surrender to God; it is a call for God to meet the individual and the community's material and spiritual needs. It is a call to responsibility and justice (cf. Lk. 16:19-31; Mt. 25:31-46).

Another aspect of this phrase reminds the individual of the most important food of all, the Word of God and the Eucharist, the Body, Blood, Soul and Divinity of Christ. Without this food, Christian life is impossible, for it is the food of immortality. As St. Augustine and St. Peter Chrysologus point out, respectively:

> The Eucharist is our daily bread. The power belonging to this divine food makes it a bond of union. Its effect is then understood as unity, so that, gathered into his Body and made members of him, we may become what we receive.... This also is our daily bread: the readings you hear each day in church and the hymns you hear and sing. All these are necessities for our pilgrimage.[224] The Father in heaven urges us, as children of heaven, to ask for the bread of heaven. [Christ] himself is the bread who, sown in the Virgin, raised up in the flesh, kneaded in the Passion, baked in the oven of the tomb, reserved in churches, brought to altars, furnishes the faithful each day with food from heaven.[225]

And forgive us our trespasses as we forgive those who trespass against us
Love of God and love of neighbor are one reality. Any authentic love of God implies the love of neighbor, and any authentic love of neighbor implies an authentic love of God. How can a person love God if he or she does not love his or her neighbor (cf. 1 Jn. 4:20; Mt. 5: 43-44; 6:14-15; 5:23-24; 18:23-35; Mk. 11:25)? How can an individual ask for God's forgiveness if that individual is unwilling to forgive those whom God loves?

And lead us not into temptation
This petition is a call to be set free from the snares of evil. The spirit of discernment and strength become intrinsic to this petition. The Spirit guides one to determine between temptations, trials and tribulations that are for one's personal growth in the life of God (cf. Lk. 8:13-15; Acts 14:22; Rm. 5:3-5; 2 Tim. 3:12) and those temptations, trials and tribulations that lead to sin and death (cf. Jas. 1:14-15). One discerns the difference between being tempted (which is not sinful and in fact can lead to great spiritual growth) and

---

[224] St. Augustine, *Sermo* 57, 7: PL 38, 389.
[225] St. Peter Chrysologus, *Sermo* 67: PL 52, 392; cf. Jn. 6:51.

consenting to temptation. The Spirit helps discern and unmask the lies behind the temptations (cf. Gen. 3:6) and helps one to persevere through them to become strong in God (cf. 1 Cor. 10:13; Rev. 16:15).

But deliver us from evil

This is a petition that asks for protection from the cunning of the devil (cf. Jn. 17:15). The devil seeks to distort God's providential plan and seeks to destroy people in the process under the guise of doing good for them (cf. Jn. 8:44; Rev. 12:9). One finds confidence in this petition in that just as one has been delivered from evil in the past, one will be delivered from the evil one in the present and in the future if one perseveres in the spiritual battle.

> The Lord who has taken away your sin and pardoned your faults also protects you and keeps you from the wiles of your adversary the devil, so that the enemy, who is accustomed to leading into sin, may not surprise you. One who entrusts himself to God does not dread the devil. "If God is for us, who is against us?"[226]

VII

The Second Dark Night
The Passive Purification of the Spirit
(or Passive Purification of the Spiritual Soul)

> For a short time he allows us to taste how sweet he is, and before our taste is satisfied he withdraws; and it is in this way, by flying above us with wings outspread, that he encourages us to fly and says in effect: See now, you have had a little taste of how sweet and delightful I am, but if you wish to have your fill of this sweetness, hasten after me, drawn by my sweet-smelling perfumes, lift up your heart to where I am at the right hand of God the Father. There you will see me not darkly in a mirror but face to face, and "your heart's joy will be complete and no one shall take this joy away from you"....[227]

Guigo II

At the end of the illuminative stage of the spiritual life, one encounters the second *dark night*, the passive purification of the spirit. The passive

---

[226] St. Ambrose, *De Sacr.* 5, 4, 30: PL 16, 454; cf. Rm. 8:31.
[227] *Guigo II: The Ladder of Monks*, quoted in Egan, 211.

purification of the spirit is a "mystical death" to self that takes place within the person.

During the illuminative stage God has given the person, in a sense, a rest from the pain of the first *dark night*, the purification of the senses. Now God desires to complete the purification that began in the very beginning of the spiritual journey. While a person at this level of the spiritual journey is a person who is clearly a saint, a person at this level is still in need of fine-tuning.

In the passive purification of the senses that beginners often experience, the person is purified of sensible consolations that he or she might find his or her being excessively attached to. In the passive purification of the spirit one is being divested of any remaining stains of superficial knowledge in matters pertaining to God. The remaining defects in the will and the intellect, and the remaining weaknesses of intellectual and spiritual pride still need to be conquered. In the *dark night* of the senses the main battle that took place was over temptations against chastity and patience. In the dark night of the spirit, the main battle is over the temptations against faith and hope.

God at this stage is stripping the person to the core. Every aspect of the person, particularly the person's ways of thinking and praying, are being made anew. One feels at this stage deprived of God's divine illumination, his divine light. Darkness appears. One is experiencing a pain worse than martyrdom. The suffering at this stage is the ultimate purifier. As St. John of the Cross puts it:

> God divests the faculties, affections, and senses, both spiritual and sensory, interior and exterior. He leaves the intellect in darkness, the will in aridity, the memory in emptiness, and the affections in supreme affliction, bitterness, and anguish by depriving the soul of the feeling and satisfaction it previously obtained from spiritual blessings.[228]

This is a time of great sadness. "My God, my God, why have you forsaken me?" is the cry of the person in this predicament. One feels alone, abandoned, lost, no longer loved, on the verge of despair. One feels as if he or she is being ripped apart, torn down. One becomes painfully aware of one's wretchedness and one's need for God. The only thing that keeps the person going is the grace-driven hunger for God and the desire of being purified for him. The call is to walk in pure faith, in pure hope, and in pure love, which is pure darkness for the faculties of the person.[229]

---

[228] *Dark Night*, BK II, Ch. 3,3.
[229] Ibid., BK II, Chs. 4; 5; 8f.

Why the Suffering? Why the Darkness?

> Truly, truly, I say to you, unless a grain of wheat falls into the earth and dies, it remains alone; but if it dies, it bears much fruit. He who loves his life loses it, and he who hates his life in this world will keep it for eternal life (Jn. 12:24-25).

At this stage of the spiritual journey one enters into darkness not because of a lack of God's light, but because of an excess of God's divine light, his divine presence. The divine presence is so powerful that it transcends the capacity of the person's being to contain it. This blindness can be compared to looking into the sun directly. The sun is so bright that it blinds the sight.[230]

This divine light inevitably causes suffering, for its goal is to purify the soul of all that is not for the honor and glory of God. It is a suffering caused by the purification of any impurities still left in the core of the person's being. A purifying light, a spiritual fire is ridding the person's inner being of all its stains, of all that is contrary to love, faith and hope, of all aspects of ignorance, self-infatuation, half-truths, inordinate desires for consolations, and imperfections of any kind. It is an earthly purgatory. The cleansing words of the Scriptures come alive here: "The Lord our God is a devouring fire...(Dt. 4:24). From on high he sent fire; into my bones he made it descend...(Lam. 1:13). [Like] gold in a furnace he tried [me], and like a sacrificial burnt offering he accepted [me]" (Wis. 3:6).[231]

In this purifying fire of grace, God is healing the inner being. He is transforming the person into Christ by detaching him or her of all so that all he or she can see is God himself. The person is being prepared for intimacy with God. The person is being prepared for a "mystical death," a death to self and a new birth in the splendor of God. One is becoming nothing so that one can become everything!

What must one do to get through this stage?

One must heed the words of St. John of the Cross: "God teaches the soul secretly and instructs it in the perfection of love without its doing anything or understanding how this happens."[232] Because of this reality one must be completely abandoned to the divine will and to divine providence (Rom. 4:18).[233] One must pray for perseverance, and live by faith, hope and love. One must carry one's cross and unite oneself with Christ's passion (Cf. Rom. 1:17). One must abandon oneself to God's mercy and pray for the intercession of the saints, and particularly the intercession of the Blessed Mother. One must

---

[230] Ibid., Chs. 5 and 12.
[231] Ibid., Chs.5, 10, and 12; *Treatise*, BK II, Ch. 1.
[232] *Dark Night*, BK II, Ch. 5, 1.
[233] Treatise, BK IX, Chs. 3-6; 12-16.

cry out in the words of the Psalmist, "Thou art holy, enthroned on the praises of Israel. In thee our fathers trusted; they trusted and thou didst deliver them" (Ps. 22:3-4).

The Precious Outcome of the Burning Flame

The theological virtues of faith, hope, and love, with the help of the Spirit's gifts of understanding, knowledge, and piety are elevated to heights previously unknown. Because of this reality, one becomes a new creation in Christ. There are no longer any vestiges of spiritual and intellectual pride, no vestiges of selfish attraction to one's own way of seeing, feeling, and willing, and no vestiges of rudeness, impatience, bitter zeal, jealousy, slander, discord, delusions, or unconscious egoism.

One who comes out of the *dark night of the spirit* has entered the unitive stage of spirituality. The person has become an open treasure chest to God's love. One is living in a new realm. One seeks to be nothing, so that God may be everything, and by so seeking nothing one becomes everything. One seeks to love God for simply being God, as opposed to loving God for what he can give. Love truly becomes as strong as death for such a person (Song of Songs 8:6). One begins to see the world the way Christ sees the world; that is, to see the world the way the world truly is. Guided by the gifts of knowledge and understanding, one delves into the mysteries of God that transcend the limits of human reason.[234]

After a long journey in this *dark night* one can say with St. Therese of Lisieux:

[In] the crucible of trials from within and without, my soul has been refined, and I can raise my head like a flower after a storm and see how the words of the Psalm have been fulfilled in my case: "The Lord is my Shepherd and I shall want nothing."[235]

VIII
The Unitive Stage
A Taste of Heaven

There is no other path than through the burning love of the crucified…. For no one is in any way disposed for divine contemplation that leads to mystical ecstasy unless like Daniel he is a man of desires (Dan. 9:23).[236]

St. Bonaventure

---

[234] Cf. *Dark Night*, BK II, Chs. 2, 5, 9; IIa IIae, q. 8, a.1, 8.
[235] St. Therese, *Story of a Soul*, 3.
[236] Bonaventure, *The Soul's Journey into God*, trans. Evert Cousins (Mahwah: Paulist Press, 1979), n. 5.

The unitive stage of spirituality is the realm where the mystics live. This is the stage where a new transformation has taken place within the very core of the person. A new life begins here, a life like nothing ever before, a life that will only be surpassed in its bliss by the experience of heaven itself.

It is a stage where one has entered the ultimate sphere of being dissolved in God.[237] It is a realm where the Spirit's gifts of wisdom, understanding, counsel, fortitude, knowledge, piety, wonder and awe come to their fullest expression. It is where the fruits of the Spirit such as charity, joy, peace, patience, benignity, goodness, mildness, faith, modesty, and chastity are enjoyed. It is where the capital sins of pride, covetousness, lust, anger, gluttony, envy, sloth are non-existent.

The unitive stage is the stage of heroes. It is the stage where heroic virtue is lived out in its ultimate expression.[238]

The Heroic Theological Virtues

Faith

I am never afraid. I am doing my work with Jesus, I'm doing it for Jesus, I'm doing it to Jesus, and therefore the results are His, not mine. If you need a guide, you only have to look to Jesus. You have to surrender to Him and rely on Him completely. When you do this, all doubt is dispelled and you are filled with conviction.[239]

Mother Teresa

Faith at this stage in the spiritual journey is exemplified by its penetration, firmness, and promptness. A person of such profound faith is a person capable of penetrating the deepest mysteries of divine revelation. Such a person lives life contemplating all things in light of God's will. Reality is seen the way it really, authentically is: It is seen the way God sees it. Because of this deep penetration and firmness of faith, a person at this level of faith adheres not only to the great mysteries of the faith, but also to the most obscure aspects. There are no "cafeteria" Catholics at this stage of the faith. Promptness in decisions regarding one's eternal destiny and the eternal destiny of others becomes paramount. The great insight acquired at this level of life makes the rejection of errors easy, for all that is not of God screams emptiness. A person in the unitive stage of spirituality can be said to have a contemplative faith.[240]

---

[237] Cf. IIa IIae, q. 24, a.9.
[238] Cf. Ia IIae, q. 61, a.5, q.69.
[239] *Mother Teresa: A Simple Path,* compiled by Lucinda Vardey (New York: Ballantine Books, 1995), 44.
[240] Cf. IIa IIae, q.8, a.1,3.

Hope

There is a complete surrendering to God's will and his providence at this level of hope. Aided by the Spirit's gift of wisdom a person can live out the heroic life of hope in such a way that all the trials and tribulations of life are responded to with the words, "I can do all things in him who strengthens me" (Phil. 4:13). One firmly chants: "If God is for us, who [can be] against us" (Rom. 8:31)? Trust in God at this plateau is unequalled. The words of Luke 11:9-10 become reality: "Ask, and it will be given you; seek, and you will find; knock, and it will be opened to you. For every one who asks receives, and he who seeks finds, and to him who knocks it will be opened."

At this plateau in the spiritual life, hope becomes transformed into a sense of invisible trust, abandonment, and firmness in one's eternal destiny, life with God in heaven. While heaven is never assured on this earthly journey, for God's love always requires a response, the sense of one's eternal destiny attains a firmness that makes turning away from God almost impossible. In a sense, a person feels that he or she has reached the *point of no return*. One feels that to turn back would be a loss of such catastrophic proportions that one would cease to exist.

Love

Love of God and love of neighbor become experienced beyond anything that has ever been experienced before. One loves God completely for just being God. No more is there a longing for what I can get from God or what I can get from my neighbor by loving him or her. One loves God completely for just being God. One loves one's neighbor for simply being the image of God. As Evargrius Ponticus, the desert Father mentions, "Happy is the...[person] who considers all [people] as god—after God."[241]

At this stage the love of God and the love of neighbor become for all practical purposes a single reality. To authentically love God one needs to authentically love one's neighbor and to authentically love one's neighbor one has to authentically love God.

The person at this stage of love grasps the mystery of the intimacy of Christ's human will with his divine will. The human will of Jesus was in complete conformity with his divine will. One who experiences the heights of heroic love experiences a taste of this mystery of wills. While it is true that a person does not have two wills, nor two natures like the God-man Jesus Christ, a person's single, human will and God's will can become, because of love, one. While God's nature and the nature of the human spiritual person are distinct realities, that human spiritual person can grow in response to God's grace to such a level of love that that person's every desire and action can become in

---

[241] Evargrius Ponticus, *The 153 Chapters on Prayer*, 123, in Harvey Egan, *An Anthology of Mysticism* (*Collegeville*, The Liturgical Press, 1991), 52.

conformity with God's. Two truly become spiritually one. One truly becomes, as the Fathers of the Church so often echoed, *divinized*.

Consequently, love of the cross reaches its apex in the unitive stage of love, for within the cross is the mystery of Christ's love.

> Let's fix our eyes on the cross. What do we see? We see his head bent down to kiss us. Look at his hands. They say, "I love you!" We see his arms stretched out on the cross as if to embrace us. We see his heart opened wide to receive us. That is the cross, which is represented by the crucifix that most of us have in our homes. Each time we glance at it, it should help us to fall in love with Christ. It should help us to love him with sincerity of heart. What greater love is there than God's love for each of us? ....[242]

> Suffering—pain, humiliation, sickness and failure is but a kiss of Jesus. Suffering is a gift of God, a gift that makes us most Christ-like. People must not accept suffering as a punishment.... Any who imitate Jesus to the full must also share in his passion. Suffering is meant to purify, to sanctify, to make us Christ-like.[243]

> *Mother Teresa*

The Heroic Moral Virtues
Humility

In the unitive stage humility is experienced as never before. Humility is essentially self-knowledge. To know oneself the way one truly is is what humility is all about. The person is now seeing himself or herself the way God sees him or her. Self-knowledge at this stage is now uncluttered by inordinate self-infatuation. It is uncluttered from all things that hinder self-knowledge and the powerful imitation of Christ and the majesty of God reflected in all creatures.[244]

Humility finds its greatest expression at this stage in a person's ability to take ridicule, abasement, and humiliation without any concern for one's own self. Such persons see these assaults as opportunities to share in the cross of Jesus Christ.

This stage is a period of extraordinary modesty. There is no conceit or vanity in such a person.

Meekness

"Blessed are the meek, for they shall inherit the earth" (Mt. 5:5). One who is meek is patient and gentle. This is the stage of a person's walk in grace

---

[242] Mother Teresa, *One Heart Full of Love*, 95.

[243] Mother Teresa, *Words to Love By...* (New York: Walker and Company, 1983), 61-67.

[244] Cf. IIa IIae, q. 160, a.1, 2; q. 161, a.1, 3, 6 ad 3um.

that leads to perfect self-mastery—as perfect as is possible on this earthly journey. One does not return evil with evil. One dominates one's passions, particularly the passion of unjustified anger. A person finds no disturbance in being injured; rather, one experiences great empathy and compassion for the one doing the injuring.[245] St. Francis of Assisi exemplified the reality of this heroic virtue in his legendary prayer of gentleness:

> Lord, make me an instrument of your peace.
> Where there is hatred, let me sow love.
> Where there is injury, pardon.
> Where there is doubt, faith.
> Where there is despair, hope.
> Where there is darkness, light.
> Where there is sadness, joy.
> O Divine Master,
> grant that I may not so much seek
> to be consoled as to console;
> to be understood as to understand;
> to be loved as to love.
> For it is in giving that we receive;
> it is in pardoning that we are pardoned;
> and it is in dying that we are born to eternal life.

Fortitude

There are always souls to enlighten, sinners to pardon, tears to dry, disappointments to console, sick to encourage, children and youngsters to guide. There is, there ever shall be, [people] to love and save, in Christ's name! This is your vocation; it ought to make you happy and courageous.[246]

Pope John Paul II

Here the moral virtue of fortitude or courage is magnified by the Spirit's gift of fortitude. A person at this stage of his or her life is able to pursue in an extraordinary way that which is very difficult to do but which is very necessary to do. Fear, danger, fatigue, criticism, and so forth, are dominated and mastered. All that one undertakes is taken with great courage, from the simplest task to the most difficult.

---

[245] Cf. IIa IIae, q. 157, a.1, 2, 4.
[246] John Paul II, *Prayers and Devotions* (New York: Viking, 1994), 299.

Magnanimity

Closely associated with the gift of fortitude is the gift of magnanimity—the ability to endure trials for extended periods of time with patience and courage. Martyrdom is the quintessential expression of this grace-elevated virtue.[247] In the spiritual diaries of St. John de Brebeuf one reads the following account of the spirit of this virtue:

> For two days now I have experienced a great desire to be a martyr and to endure all the torments the martyrs suffered.
>
> Jesus, my Lord and Savior, what can I give you in return for all the favors you have first conferred on me? I will take from your hand the cup of your sufferings and call on your name. I vow before your eternal Father and the Holy Spirit, before your most holy Mother and her most chaste spouse, before the angels, apostles and martyrs, before my blessed fathers Saint Ignatius and Saint Francis Xavier—in truth I vow to you, Jesus my Savior, that as far as I have the strength I will never fail to accept the grace of martyrdom, if some day you in your infinite mercy should offer it to me, your most unworthy servant.
>
> I bind myself in this way so that for the rest of my life I will have neither permission nor freedom to refuse opportunities of dying and shedding my blood for you, unless at a particular juncture I should consider it more suitable for your glory to act otherwise at that time. Further, I bind myself to this so that, on receiving the blow of death, I shall accept it from your hands with the fullest delight and joy of spirit. For this reason, my beloved Jesus, and because of the surging joy which moves me, here and now I offer my blood and body and life. May I die only for you, if you will grant me this grace, since you willingly died for me. Let me so live that you may grant me the gift of such a happy death. In this way, my God and Savior, I will take from your hand the cup of your sufferings and call on your name: Jesus, Jesus, Jesus![248]

Prudence

Prudence at this level is exemplified by the perfect acting out of that which is best for one or another's eternal destiny. It is the unique moral virtue that enables a person to determine a reasonable milieu between excess and deficiency. Inconsideration, indecision, inconstancy, or rashness is non-existent at this point. A person at this point recognizes the true good and is able to direct the other virtues to accomplish this good. Prudence at this stage is powerfully engulfed by the Spirit's gift of counsel to such an extent that one

---

[247] Cf. IIa IIae, q. 123, a.6.

[248] *The Jesuit Relations and Allied Documents* (Cleveland: The Burrow Brothers, 1898), 164, 166.

inevitably experiences a supernatural sense or intuition of what ought to be done or not done. The hunger for truth is the focus of this stage in the experience of the virtue of prudence.[249]

Justice

> Immense distress moves us to launch a cry of alarm. Where is love for those who have been refused the right to live? For those who have been killed, mutilated, or imprisoned because they roam the streets? For those who have been exploited at an early age in forced labor or the commerce of perversion? For those whom famine has thrown on the roads of exile? For those who have been made to carry arms? Where is love for those who have been left without a school education and have been condemned to illiteracy? Where is love for those whose family has been destroyed and displaced?[250]
>
> *Pope John Paul II*

Justice is the upholding of what is right and fair. In the unitive stage justice takes on the heroic aspect of radically rendering to each person that which he or she is due as a child of God. Theft, fraud, lying, hypocrisy, calumny, slander, derision, simulation, raillery, and so forth, are non-existent in the person. One at this stage avoids any aspect of injustice with miraculous fervor.

This fervor, however, is accompanied by the perfect living out of *epikeia*, the spirit of the law. The person who lives the life of heroic justice is a person who, as Evargrius Ponticus describes, "considers himself one with all men because he seems constantly to see himself in every man."[251]

The Heroic Evangelical Councils
Poverty

> It would be a shame for us to be richer than Jesus, who for our sake endured poverty.[252]
>
> *Mother Teresa*

"Blessed are you poor, for yours is the kingdom of God" (Lk. 5:20). The focus of the mystic at this stage is on living on the bare minimum. Imitation of Christ's poverty is the desire of such a person. The mystic experiences a holy fear for those whose souls are at risk because of comfort and wealth. The contrast between the wealthy and the dying

---

[249] Cf. IIa IIae, q. 47, a.7.
[250] John Paul II, *Papal Wisdom* (New York: Dutton, 1995), 62.
[251] Evargrius Ponticus, *The 153 Chapters on Prayer*, 125.
[252] Mother Teresa, *Heart of Joy*, 137.

poor becomes a source of pain in the mystic. It becomes a sharing in the cross of Jesus Christ.

Chastity

Chastity becomes the great liberating gift of God at this juncture. No longer are the distractions of the flesh a hindrance to the spiritual life. In the married person, chastity enables a person to give his or her being fully, without doubt or reservation, to his or her spouse. Authentic conjugal love at its ecstatic apex takes place at this level of the relationship. For the celibate, freedom becomes the all-encompassing reality of existence. One is free to be fully, without doubt or reservation, a person that is radically for others.

Obedience

Self-centeredness is replaced by other-centeredness. The concern is with doing all that is for the glory and honor of God. There is an abnegation of self-will at this level. This is easily seen in the life of a holy religious. The brother or sister in a religious congregation is obedient to all orders, even the most difficult orders, even the most misguided orders, as long as they do not contradict God's will, honor, and glory. Obedience at this stage is the radical following of Christ's Way. It images the Son's obedience to his Father.

Degrees of the Unitive Life

The lover asked his Beloved if there was anything remaining in him which was still to be loved. And the Beloved answered that he still had to love that by which his own love could be increased.[253]

Ramon Lull

In the *passive purification of the spirit* a person encounters the experience of *arid mystical union*.[254] In the unitive stage, the person, the mystic, progresses to experience an *ecstatic union* with God and for the very few a *transforming union* in God. For the great mystics, the *transforming union*, the highest form of union with God on earth, is attained. These are the *divinized*.

Ecstatic Union

I am wounded by love. Love urges me to speak of love. Gladly do I give myself up to the service of love.... Do you not feel as if sometimes you were shot through the heart when the fiery dart of this love penetrates the inmost mind of man, pierces his affections

---

[253] Ramon Lull, *The Book of the Lover and Beloved*, trans. E. Allison Peers (Mahwah: Paulist Press, 1978), n. 1.

[254] *Interior Castle*, 4th and 5th mansions and chapter 1 of the 6th mansion.

so that he can in no way contain or hide the burning of his desire. He burns with desire, his affections are stirred, he is in fever and gasps, sighing deeply and drawing long breaths.... Thus, the fever of love, often waning but always returning more acutely, gradually weakens the spirit, wears down and exhausts the strength, until it completely conquers the soul and lays it low.[255]

Richard of St. Victor

Ecstasy is the suspension of the exterior senses, the loss of the use of the senses. It is a movement of the entire person's being, body and soul, toward God. It is an experience that may last a few moments, a few minutes, or at times for an entire day or days.[256] A vision at times is the prelude to this experience. But at all times, the person experiencing this ecstasy swoons as he or she becomes ravished and absorbed in the purity of God's love. The body is wounded with the wound of love. Ecstasy ends with an awakening whereby the person slowly recovers the use of the senses.[257]

Rapture

The spiritual experience of rapture is one that is experienced by some, yet it need not be experienced by all who progress toward the *transforming union*.[258] The person who experiences a rapture is a person who senses his or her very core being seized by God and carried away into another dimension of reality, a new divine region.[259] This rapture adds something to ecstasy; it adds a certain impulsive, intense, turbulent, jarring, jolting, fervent aspect to the experience.[260] It is as if the person's core is inebriated with the overabundance of God. The person's being is overwhelmed by a rushing flood of God's presence. It is not unusual to see the process toward the *spiritual marriage--* which we will take up in the next section--end in rapture.[261]

The Effects of the Ecstatic Union

The primary effect of the *ecstatic union* is the purification of love. By purifying the person's love, the person is prepared to enter in response to grace into the *transforming union*. The mystic at this level has reached the pinnacle of detachment, the pinnacle of sorrow for sin. The person has reached the apex of avoiding all that separates him or her from God. Crosses

---

[255] *Richard of Saint Victor: Selected Writings on Contemplation*, trans. Clare Kirchberger (New York: Harper and Brothers, 1957), 213-233.
[256] *Interior Castle*, 6th mansion, Ch. 6.
[257] Ibid., Ch. 2; Life, Ch. 20, par. 2; Treatise, Bk. VII, Ch. 4f.
[258] Ibid., Ch. 9.
[259] Ibid., Ch. 5.
[260] IIa IIae, q. 175, a.2 ad ium.
[261] *Interior Castle*, 6th mansion, Ch. 4.

are no longer feared but embraced as a sharing in the life of the Savior. Suffering becomes a precious gift.[262]

Transforming Union

> Resemblance to God is the whole of man's perfection. To refuse to be perfect is to be at fault.[263]
>
> *William of St. Thierry*

Once the person has progressed past the *ecstatic union*, the person reaches the summit of the mystical life, the *transforming union*. At this juncture of the mystical life one experiences the ultimate luminous, sweet, and penetrating experience of grace, of God. It is the culmination of the development of the life of grace.[264]

The essential nature of the *transforming union* is marked, as a rule, by the cessation of ecstasies. The person's very being has developed beyond this point in the spiritual journey. One's entire faculties are drawn to the very core of one's being, where the Trinity dwells.[265]

Spiritual Betrothal and Spiritual Marriage

The summit of union on this earthly journey ends in the *spiritual marriage* between a person and his or her Creator. As with every relationship that ends in marriage, there is a time of *betrothal*, a transitory time of union that awaits the *spiritual marriage*, that perfect, continuous union of life and love.[266] In the *spiritual marriage* one becomes so intimately united with God that one becomes, as St. John of the Cross so powerfully explains, God by participation:

> The spiritual marriage is incomparably greater than the spiritual betrothal, for it is a total transformation in the Beloved, in which each surrenders the entire possession of self to the other with a certain consummation of the union of love. The soul thereby becomes divine, God through participation, insofar as is possible in this life…. It is accordingly the highest state attainable in this life.[267]

Effects of the Transforming Union

The virtues and the Spirit's gifts have received their full development, as full as is humanly possible on this earthly journey. Sin for all practical purposes is no longer possible, not even venial sins. One has become in a sense deified.

---

[262] *Life*, Ch. 29; *Dark Night*, BK II, Ch. 11f; *Living Flame*, St. 1, v. 2-4; St. 2, v. 1-3.
[263] *William St. Thierry: The Golden Epistle*, n. 259.
[264] *Living Flame*, St. 2; *Spiritual Canticle*, Part III, St. 22f.
[265] *Living Flame*, St. 2.
[266] *Spiritual Canticle*, St. 14-15; *Interior Castle*, 7th mansion, Ch. 2.
[267] Ibid., St. 22,3.

One has become God by participation. For William of St. Thierry, "man becomes through grace what God is by nature."[268] And as St. John of the Cross so eloquently puts it:

[When one has reached the top of the mountain] the soul will be clothed in a new understanding of God in God (through removal of the old understanding) and in a new love of God in God, once the will is stripped of all the old cravings and satisfactions. And God will vest the soul with new knowledge when the other old ideas and images are cast aside (Col. 3:9). He causes all that is of the old self, the abilities of one's natural being, to cease, and he attires all the faculties with new supernatural abilities. As a result, one's activities, once human, now become divine.[269]

The Spiritual Senses

God be in my head and in my understanding. God be in my eyes and in my looking. God be in my mouth and in my speaking. God be in my heart and in my thinking. God be at my end and my departing.
Sarum Primer

One who has reached the level of the unitive stage experiences reality in a completely different light. One experiences what has often been referred to as the spiritualization of the senses or what is referred to as the *mystical senses*, whereby all of reality is seen differently. "It is no longer I who live" (Gal. 2:20). The person is in the sphere of spiritual sensitivity and discernment. A person enters a sphere where he or she has, in a manner, as St. Gregory of Nyssa mentions, "two sets of senses, one corporeal and the other spiritual..."[270] As Origen, one of the great ecclesiastical writers of the second century states:

Since Christ is a "fountain" and rivers of living water flow from him" (cf. Jn. 7:38), and since he is "bread" and gives "life," it should not seem strange that he is also "nard" and "gives forth fragrance" and is the "ointment" (cf. Cant. 1:12) by which those who are anointed themselves become Christ, as it says in the Psalm: "Touch not my Christs" (Ps. 105:15). And perhaps, according to what the Apostle says, in those "who have their faculties trained by practice to distinguish good from evil (cf. Heb. 5:14), each one of the senses of the soul becomes Christ. For that is why he is called the "true light"

---

[268] *William of St. Thierry: The Golden Epistle*, n. 263.
[269] Ascent, BK 1, Ch. 5, 7.
[270] From *Glory to Glory: Texts from Gregory of Nyssa's Mystical Writings*, ed. and intro. Jean Danielou, S.J., trans, and ed. Herbert Musurillo, S.J. (New York: Charles Scribner's Son's, 1961), 156.

394

(cf. 1 Jn. 2:8) so that the souls might have eyes with which to be illumined; and why he is called the "Word" (cf. Jn. 1:1), that they might have ears with which to hear; and why he is called "bread of life" (cf. Jn. 6:35), that the souls might have a sense of taste with which to taste. So too is he called "ointment" or "nard" so that the soul's sense of smell might receive the fragrance of the Word. And so too is he called perceivable, and touchable by hand, and the "Word became flesh" (cf. Jn. 1:14), so that the inner hand of the soul might be able to make contact with the Word of Life.... What do you think they will do when the Word of God takes over their hearing and sight and touch and taste? and when he gives to each of their senses the powers of which they are naturally capable? So that the eye, once able to see "his glory, glory as of the only Son from the Father" (Jn.1:14), no longer wants to see anything else, nor the hearing want to hear anything other than the "Word of life" (1 Jn. 1:1)..., nor will the taste, once it has "tasted the goodness of the Word of God" (Heb. 6:5) and his flesh...(Jn. 6:33, 52-58), be willing to taste anything else after this.... For just as in the body there are different senses of tasting and seeing, so are there...divine faculties of perception.[271]

Through the spiritual senses one sees reality through the eyes of God.

In Conclusion

The Christian of the future will either be a mystic or nothing at all. These are the words of the great twentieth century theologian and Jesuit priest Karl Rahner.[272] We are all called to be mystics. To the extent that one responds to God's grace is the extent that one will enter into the realm where a taste of heaven can be acquired even here on earth, where a taste of perfect happiness, peace and contentment can be found. May we all seek to become saints. May we live the words expressed by the prayer of Karl Rahner:

Son of the Father, Christ who lives in us, you are our hope of glory. Live in us, bring our life under the laws of your life, make our life like to yours. Live in me, pray in me, suffer in me, more I do not ask. For if I have you I am rich; those who find you have found the power and the victory of their life. Amen.[273]

---

[271] From *Origen, Spirit and Fire: A Thematic Study of His Writings*, by Hans Urs von Balthasar, trans. Robert J. Daly, S.J. (Washington, D.C.: The Catholic University of America Press, 1984), 220-221.
[272] Rahner, *Theological Investigations*, vol. 7, *Further Theology of the Spiritual Life*, trans. David Bourke (New York: Herder and Herder, 1971), 15.
[273] Rahner, *Everyday Faith*, 210-211.

APPENDIX 7
TRADITIONAL PRAYERS AND DEVOTIONS

Apostles' Creed

I believe in God, the Father Almighty, Creator of Heaven and earth; and in Jesus Christ, His only Son Our Lord, Who was conceived by the Holy Spirit, born of the Virgin Mary, suffered under Pontius Pilate, was crucified, died, and was buried. He descended into Hell; on the third day He rose again from the dead; He ascended into Heaven, and sitteth at the right hand of God, the Father almighty; from thence He shall come to judge the living and the dead. I believe in the Holy Spirit, the holy Catholic Church, the communion of saints, the forgiveness of sins, the resurrection of the body and life everlasting. Amen.

Sign of the Cross

In the name of the Father, and of the Son, and of the Holy Spirit. Amen.

Our Father

Our Father, Who art in heaven, hallowed be Thy name; Thy kingdom come; Thy will be done on earth as it is in heaven. Give us this day our daily bread; and forgive us our trespasses as we forgive those who trespass against us; and lead us not into temptation, but deliver us from evil. Amen.

Hail Mary

Hail Mary, full of grace. The Lord is with thee. Blessed art thou amongst women, and blessed is the fruit of thy womb, Jesus. Holy Mary, Mother of God, pray for us sinners, now and at the hour of our death. Amen.

Glory Be

Glory be to the Father and to the Son and to the Holy Spirit, as it was in the beginning, is now, and ever shall be, world without end. Amen.

Hail Holy Queen

Hail, Holy Queen, Mother of Mercy, our life, our sweetness and our hope! To thee do we cry, poor banished children of Eve. To thee do we send up our sighs, mourning and weeping in this valley of tears! Turn, then, O most gracious Advocate, thine eyes of mercy toward us, and after this, our exile, show unto us the blessed fruit of thy womb, Jesus. O clement, O loving, O sweet Virgin Mary.

V. Pray for us, O holy Mother of God.
R. That we may be made worthy of the promises of Christ.

Anima Christi *(Abbreviated Version)*

Soul of Christ, sanctify me;
Body of Christ, save me;
Blood of Christ, inebriate me;
Water from Christ's side, wash me;
Passion of Christ, strengthen me;
O good Jesus, hear me.
Amen.

Come Holy Spirit

Come, Holy Spirit, fill the hearts of Thy faithful and enkindle in them the fire of Thy love.

V. Send forth Thy Spirit and they shall be created anew.
R. And Thou shalt renew the face of the earth.

Let us pray.
O God, Who didst instruct the hearts of the faithful by the light of the Holy Spirit, grant us in the same Spirit to be truly wise, and ever to rejoice in His consolation. Through Christ our Lord. Amen.

Memorare

Remember, O most gracious Virgin Mary, that never was it known that anyone who fled to thy protection, implored thy help, or sought thine intercession was left unaided. Inspired by this confidence, I fly unto thee, O Virgin of virgins, my mother; to thee do I come, before thee I stand, sinful and sorrowful. O Mother of the Word Incarnate, despise not my petitions, but in thy mercy hear and answer me. Amen.

Prayer to One's Guardian Angel

Angel of God, my guardian dear, to whom God's love commits me here, ever this day, be at my side, to light and guard, rule and guide. Amen.

St. Michael the Archangel Prayer

St. Michael the Archangel, defend us in battle. Be our defense against the wickedness and snares of the Devil. May God rebuke him, we humbly pray, and do thou, O Prince of the heavenly hosts, by the power of God, thrust into hell Satan, and all the evil spirits, who prowl about the world seeking the ruin of souls. Amen.

Act of Contrition

O my God, I am heartily sorry for having offended Thee, and I detest all my sins, because I dread the loss of heaven, and the pains of hell; but most of all because they offend Thee, my God, Who are all good and deserving of all my love. I firmly resolve, with the help of Thy grace, to confess my sins, to do penance, and to amend my life. Amen.

Prayer of St. Francis of Assisi
The Peace Prayer

Lord, make me an instrument of Thy peace;
Where there is hatred, let me sow love;
Where there is injury, pardon;
Where there is error, truth;

Where there is doubt, faith;
Where there is despair, hope;
Where there is darkness, light;
And where there is sadness, joy.
O Divine Master,
Grant that I may not so much seek
To be consoled, as to console;
To be understood, as to understand;
To be loved as to love.
For it is in giving that we receive;
It is in pardoning that we are pardoned;
And it is in dying that we are born to eternal life. Amen.

St. Teresa of Avila Prayer for Serenity
Let nothing disturb you,
Let nothing frighten you,
All things are passing away:
God never changes.
Patience obtains all things
Whoever has God lacks nothing;
God alone suffices.

Praying the Rosary
How do we pray the Rosary

I. Make the Sign of the Cross.
II. Holding the Crucifix, say the *Apostles' Creed*.
III. On the first bead, pray an *Our Father*.
IV. Pray three *Hail Marys* on each of the next three beads.
V. Pray the *Glory Be*
VI. For each of the five decades, announce the Mystery, then pray the *Our Father* (on the bead that has more space between it than the other beads)
VII. For each closely tied bead pray a *Hail Mary* while meditating on the mystery of the rosary. Then pray a *Glory Be*. (After finishing each decade, some say the

following prayer: "O my Jesus, forgive us our sins, save us from the fires of hell, lead all souls to Heaven, especially those who have most need of your mercy.")

The repetition in the Rosary is meant to lead one into a meditative prayer related to the life of Christ. The gentle repetition of the words help to guide the duration of the meditation on each mystery of Christ's life.

Let us look at the mysteries you will meditate upon:

The **Five Joyful Mysteries** are traditionally prayed on Mondays and Saturdays (and Sundays of Advent).

1.   The Annunciation (Luke 1:28)
2.   The Visitation (Luke 1:42)
3.   The Nativity (Luke 2:7)
4.   The Presentation in the Temple (Luke 2:28)
5.   The Finding in the Temple (Luke 2:46)

The **Five Sorrowful Mysteries** are traditionally prayed on Tuesdays and Fridays (and Sundays of Lent)

1.   The Agony in the Garden (Mark 14:35)
2.   The Scourging at the Pillar (Mark 15:15)
3.   The Crowning with Thorns (Mark 15:17)
4.   The Carrying of the Cross (John 19:17)
5.   The Crucifixion and Death (Luke 23:33)

The **Five Glorious Mysteries** are traditionally prayed on Wednesdays (and Sundays outside of Lent and Advent)

1.   The Resurrection (Mark 16:6)
2.   The Ascension (Mark 16:9)
3.   The Descent of the Holy Spirit (Acts 2:4)
4.   The Assumption (Revelation 12:1)
5.   The Coronation of Mary (Revelation 12:1)

The **Five Luminous Mysteries** are traditionally prayed on Thursdays:

1. The Baptism of Christ in the Jordan (Matthew 3:13-17)
2. The Wedding Feast at Cana (John 2: 1-11)
3. Jesus' Proclamation of the Coming of the Kingdom of God (Mark 1:15; Matthew 5:1-11)
4. The Transfiguration (Matthew 17:1-8)
5. The Institution of the Eucharist (Matthew 26: 26-30)

After saying the five decades, pray the "Hail, Holy Queen, followed by the concluding dialogue and prayer:

Hail, Holy Queen, Mother of Mercy, our life, our sweetness and our hope! To thee do we cry, poor banished children of Eve. To thee do we send up our sighs, mourning and weeping in this valley of tears! Turn, then, O most gracious Advocate, thine eyes of mercy toward us, and after this, our exile, show unto us the blessed fruit of thy womb, Jesus. O clement, O loving, O sweet Virgin Mary.

V. Pray for us, O holy Mother of God.
R. That we may be made worthy of the promises of Christ.

Let us pray: O God, whose Only Begotten Son, by his life, Death, and Resurrection, has purchased for us the rewards of eternal life, grant, we beseech thee, that while meditating on these mysteries of the most holy Rosary of the Blessed Virgin Mary, we may imitate what they contain and obtain what they promise, through the same Christ our Lord. Amen.

Chaplet of the Divine Mercy

Optional Opening Prayer
You expired, Jesus, but the source of life gushed forth for souls, and the ocean of mercy opened up for the whole world. O Fount

of Life, unfathomable Divine Mercy, envelop the whole world and empty Yourself out upon us.

O Blood and Water, which gushed forth from the Heart of Jesus as a fountain of Mercy for us, I trust in You!

Begin with the Our Father, the Hail Mary and the Apostles' Creed:

Then, on the large bead before each decade pray:

Eternal Father,
I offer you the Body and Blood,
Soul and Divinity,
of Your Dearly Beloved Son,
Our Lord, Jesus Christ,
in atonement for our sins
and those of the whole world.

On the ten small beads of each decade, pray:

For the sake of His sorrowful Passion,
have mercy on us and on the whole world.

Conclude with the following (Pray 3 Times):

Holy God,
Holy Mighty One,
Holy Immortal One,
have mercy on us
and on the whole world.

Optional Closing Prayer

Eternal God, in whom mercy is endless and the treasury of compassion inexhaustible, look kindly upon us and increase Your mercy in us, that in difficult moments we might not despair nor become despondent, but with great confidence submit ourselves to Your holy will, which is Love and Mercy itself.

Scriptural Stations of the Cross

Opening Prayer:
Leader:
God of power and mercy,
in love you sent your Son
that we might be cleansed of sin
and live with you forever.
Bless us as we gather to reflect
on his suffering and death
that we may learn from his example
the way we should go.
We ask this through that same Christ, our Lord.

All:
Amen.

Leader:
We adore you, O Christ, and we bless you.

All:
Because by your holy cross you have redeemed the world.

First Station: Jesus in the Garden of Gethsemane
Reader:
Then Jesus came with them to a place called Gethsemane, and he said to his disciples, "Sit here while I go over there and pray." He took along Peter and the two sons of Zebedee, and began to feel sorrow and distress. Then he said to them, "My soul is sorrowful even to death. Remain here and keep watch with me." He advanced a little and fell prostrate in prayer, saying, "My Father, if it is possible, let this cup pass from me; yet, not as I will, but as you will." When he returned to his disciples he found them asleep. He said to Peter, "So you could not keep watch with me for one hour? Watch and pray that you may not undergo the test. The spirit is willing, but the flesh is weak."

(Matthew 26:36-41)

Leader:
Lord, grant us your strength and wisdom, that we may seek to follow your will in all things.

All:
Lord Jesus, help us walk in your steps.

Leader:
We adore you, O Christ, and we bless you.

All:
Because by your holy cross you have redeemed the world.

Second Station: Jesus, Betrayed by Judas, is Arrested
Reader:
Then, while [Jesus] was still speaking, Judas, one of the Twelve, arrived, accompanied by a crowd with swords and clubs, who had come from the chief priests, the scribes, and the elders. His betrayer had arranged a signal with them, saying, "the man I shall kiss is the one; arrest him and lead him away securely." He came and immediately went over to him and said, "Rabbi." And he kissed him. At this they laid hands on him and arrested him. *(Mark 14: 43-46)*

Leader:
Lord, grant us the courage of our convictions that our lives may faithfully reflect the good news you bring.

All:
Lord Jesus, help us walk in your steps.

Leader:
We adore you, O Christ, and we bless you.

All:
Because by your holy cross you have redeemed the world.

Third Station: Jesus is Condemned by the Sanhedrin
Reader:
When day came the council of elders of the people met, both chief priests and scribes, and they brought him before their Sanhedrin. They said, "If you are the Messiah, tell us," but he replied to them, "If I tell you, you will not believe, and if I question, you will not respond. But from this time on the Son of Man will be seated at the right hand of the power of God." They all asked, "Are you then the Son of God?" He replied to them, "You say that I am." Then they said, "What further need have we for testimony? We have heard it from his own mouth."
(Luke 22: 66-71)

Leader:
Lord, grant us your sense of righteousness that we may never cease to work to bring about the justice of the kingdom that you promised.

All:
Lord Jesus, help us walk in your steps.

Leader:
We adore you, O Christ, and we bless you.

All:
Because by your holy cross you have redeemed the world.

Fourth Station: Jesus is Denied by Peter
Reader:
Now Peter was sitting outside in the courtyard. One of the maids came over to him and said, "You too were with Jesus the Galilean." But he denied it in front of everyone, saying, "I do not know what you are talking about!" As he went out to the gate, another girl saw him and said to those who were there, "This man was with Jesus the Nazorean." Again he denied it with an oath, "I do not know the man!" A little later the bystanders came over and said to Peter, "Surely you too are one of them; even your speech gives you away." At that he

began to curse and to swear, "I do not know the man." And immediately a cock crowed. Then Peter remembered the word that Jesus had spoken: "Before the cock crows you will deny me three times." He went out and began to weep bitterly.
(Matthew 26: 69-75)

Leader:

Lord, grant us the gift of honesty that we may not fear to speak the truth even when difficult.

All:

Lord Jesus, help us walk in your steps.

Leader:

We adore you, O Christ, and we bless you.

All:

Because by your holy cross you have redeemed the world.

Fifth Station: Jesus is Judged by Pilate
Reader:

The chief priests with the elders and the scribes, that is, the whole Sanhedrin, held a council. They bound Jesus, led him away, and handed him over to Pilate. Pilate questioned him, "Are you the king of the Jews?" He said to him in reply, "You say so." The chief priests accused him of many things. Again Pilate questioned him, "Have you no answer? See how many things they accuse you of." Jesus gave him no further answer, so that Pilate was amazed.... Pilate, wishing to satisfy the crowd, released Barrabas... [and] handed [Jesus] over to be crucified.
(Mark 15: 1-5, 15)

Leader:

Lord, grant us discernment that we may see as you see, not as the world sees.

All:

Lord Jesus, help us walk in your steps.

Leader:
We adore you, O Christ, and we bless you.

All:
Because by your holy cross you have redeemed the world.

Sixth Station: Jesus is Scourged and Crowned with Thorns
Reader:
Then Pilate took Jesus and had him scourged. And the soldiers wove a crown out of thorns and placed it on his head, and clothed him in a purple cloak, and they came to him and said,"Hail, King of the Jews!" And they struck him repeatedly.
(John 19: 1-3)

Leader:
Lord, grant us patience in times of suffering that we may offer our lives as a sacrifice of praise.

All:
Lord Jesus, help us walk in your steps.

Leader:
We adore you, O Christ, and we bless you.

All:
Because by your holy cross you have redeemed the world.

Seventh Station: Jesus Bears the Cross
Reader:
When the chief priests and the guards saw [Jesus] they cried out, "Crucify him, crucify him!" Pilate said to them, "Take him yourselves and crucify him. I find no guilt in him." ... They cried out, "Take him away, take him away! Crucify him!" Pilate said to them, "Shall I crucify your king?" The chief priests answered, "We have no king but Caesar." Then he handed him over to them to be crucified. So they took Jesus, and carrying the cross himself he went out to what is called the Place of the Skull, in Hebrew, Golgotha.

(John 19: 6, 15-17)

Leader:
Lord, grant us strength of purpose that we may faithfully bear our crosses each day.

All:
Lord Jesus, help us walk in your steps.

Leader:
We adore you, O Christ, and we bless you.

All:
Because by your holy cross you have redeemed the world.

Eighth Station: Jesus is Helped by Simon the Cyrenian to Carry the Cross

Reader:
They pressed into service a passer-by, Simon, a Cyrenian, who was coming in from the country, the father of Alexander and Rufus, to carry his cross.
(Mark 15: 21)

Leader:
Lord, grant us willing spirits that we may be your instruments on earth.

All:
Lord Jesus, help us walk in your steps.

Leader:
We adore you, O Christ, and we bless you.

All:
Because by your holy cross you have redeemed the world.

Ninth Station: Jesus Meets the Women of Jerusalem
Reader:

A large crowd of people followed Jesus, including many women who mourned and lamented him. Jesus turned to them and said, "Daughters of Jerusalem, do not weep for me; weep instead for yourselves and for your children, for indeed, the days are coming when people will say, 'Blessed are the barren, the wombs that never bore and the breasts that never nursed.' At that time, people will say to the mountains, 'Fall upon us!' and to the hills, 'Cover us!' for if these things are done when the wood is green what will happen when it is dry?
(Luke 23: 27-31)

Leader:

Lord, grant us gentle spirits that we may comfort those who mourn.

All:

Lord Jesus, help us walk in your steps.

Leader:

We adore you, O Christ, and we bless you.

All:

Because by your holy cross you have redeemed the world.

Tenth Station: Jesus is Crucified
Reader:

When they came to the place called the Skull, they crucified him and the criminals there, one on his right, the other on his left. [Then Jesus said, "Father, forgive them, they know not what they do."]
(Luke 23: 33-34)

Leader:

Lord, grant us merciful hearts that we may bring your reconciliation and forgiveness to all.

All:

Lord Jesus, help us walk in your steps.

Leader:
We adore you, O Christ, and we bless you.

All:
Because by your holy cross you have redeemed the world.

Eleventh Station: Jesus Promises His Kingdom to the Good Thief

Reader:
Now one of the criminals hanging there reviled Jesus, saying, "Are you not the Messiah? Save yourself and us." The other, however, rebuking him, said in reply, "Have you no fear of God, for you are subject to the same condemnation? And indeed, we have been condemned justly, for the sentence we received corresponds to our crimes, but this man has done nothing criminal." Then he said, "Jesus, remember me when you come into your kingdom." He replied to him, "Amen, I say to you, today you will be with me in Paradise."
(Luke 23: 39-43)

Leader:
Lord, grant us perseverance that we may never stop seeking you.

All:
Lord Jesus, help us walk in your steps.

Leader:
We adore you, O Christ, and we bless you.

All:
Because by your holy cross you have redeemed the world.

Twelfth Station: Jesus Speaks to His Mother and the Disciple

Reader:
Standing by the cross of Jesus were his mother and his mother's sister, Mary the wife of Clopas, and Mary of Magdala. When Jesus saw his mother and the

disciple there whom he loved, he said to his mother, "Woman, behold, your son." Then he said to the disciple, "Behold, your mother." And from that hour the disciple took her into his home.
(John 19: 25-27)

Leader:
Lord, grant us constancy that we may be willing to stand by those in need.

All:
Lord Jesus, help us walk in your steps.

Leader:
We adore you, O Christ, and we bless you.

All:
Because by your holy cross you have redeemed the world.

Thirteenth Station: Jesus Dies on the Cross
Reader:
It was now about noon and darkness came over the whole land until three in the afternoon because of an eclipse of the sun. Then the veil of the temple was torn down the middle. Jesus cried out in a loud voice, "Father, into your hands I commend my spirit"; and when he had said this he breathed his last.
(Luke 23: 44-46)

Leader:
Lord, grant us trust in you that when our time on earth is ended our spirits may come to you without delay.

All:
Lord Jesus, help us walk in your steps.

Leader:
We adore you, O Christ, and we bless you.

All:
Because by your holy cross you have redeemed the world.

Fourteenth Station: Jesus is Placed in the Tomb
Reader:
When it was evening, there came a rich man from Arimathea named Joseph, who was himself a disciple of Jesus. He went to Pilate and asked for the body of Jesus; then Pilate ordered it to be handed over. Taking the body, Joseph wrapped it [in] clean linen and laid it in his new tomb that he had hewn in the rock. Then he rolled a huge stone across the entrance to the tomb and departed.
(Matthew 27: 57-60)

Leader:
Lord, grant us your compassion that we may always provide for those in need.

All:
Lord Jesus, help us walk in your steps.

Closing Prayer:
Leader:
Lord Jesus Christ, your passion and death is the sacrifice that unites earth and heaven and reconciles all people to you. May we who have faithfully reflected on these mysteries follow in your steps and so come to share your glory in heaven where you live and reign with the Father and the Holy Spirit one God, for ever and ever.

All:
Amen.

Eucharistic Prayers

Act of Spiritual Communion

My Jesus, I believe that you are present in the Blessed Sacrament. I love you above all things and I desire you in my soul. Since I cannot now receive you sacramentally, come at least spiritually into my heart. As though you were already there, I embrace you and unite myself wholly to you; do not permit me to ever be separated from you.

Prayer before Mass
By St. Thomas Aquinas

Almighty and ever-living God, I approach the sacrament of your only-begotten Son our Lord Jesus Christ. I come sick to the doctor of life, unclean to the fountain of mercy, blind to the radiance of eternal light, and poor and needy to the Lord of heaven and earth. Lord, in your great generosity, heal my sickness, wash away my defilement, enlighten my blindness, enrich my poverty, and clothe my nakedness. May I receive the bread of angels, the King of kings and Lord of lords, with humble reverence, with the purity and faith, the repentance and love, and the determined purpose that will help to bring me to salvation. May I receive the sacrament of the Lord's body and blood, and its reality and power. Kind God, may I receive the body of your only-begotten Son, our Lord Jesus Christ, born from the womb of the Virgin Mary, and so be received into his mystical body and numbered among his members. Loving Father, as on my earthly pilgrimage I now receive your beloved Son under the veil of a sacrament, may I one day see him face to face in glory, who lives and reigns with you for ever. Amen.

Thanksgiving after Mass
By St. Thomas Aquinas

Lord, Father all-powerful and ever-living God, I thank you, for even though I am a sinner, your unprofitable servant, not because of my worth but in the kindness of your mercy, you have fed me with the precious body and blood of your Son, our Lord Jesus Christ. I pray that this holy communion may not bring me condemnation and punishment but forgiveness and salvation. May it be a helmet of faith and a shield of good will. May it purify me from evil ways and put an end to my evil passions. May it bring me charity and patience, humility and obedience, and growth in the power to do good. May it be my strong defense against all my enemies, visible and invisible, and the perfect calming of all my evil impulses, bodily and spiritual. May it unite me more closely to you, the one true God, and lead me safely through death to everlasting happiness with you. And I pray that you will lead me, a sinner, to the banquet where you, with your Son and holy Spirit, are true and perfect light, total fulfillment, everlasting joy, gladness without end, and perfect happiness to your saints. Grant this through Christ our Lord. Amen.

Benediction

Exposition: *After the people have assembled, a song may be sung while the minister comes into the sanctuary. Wearing a humeral veil he brings the Blessed Sacrament from the place of reservation. It is placed in a monstrance, with candles on the altar, an altar cloth, and a purificator. The following song may be sung:*

O salutaris Hostia
Quae caeli pandis ostium
Bella premunt hostilia
Da robur fer auxilium.

Uni trinoque Domino
Sit sempiterna Gloria
Qui vitam sine termino,
Nobis donet in patria.
Amen.

During the song, or shortly after, the priest incenses the Blessed Sacrament.

Adoration: *During the exposition there can be prayers, songs, and readings directed toward instilling a greater worship of Christ the Lord. A homily may follow. Religious silence is also highly recommended.*

Benediction: *The priest or deacon goes to the altar, genuflects, and kneels. While kneeling, the minister incenses the Blessed Sacrament in the monstrance. The following song may be sung during this time:*

Tantum ergo Sacramentum
Veneremur Cernui;
Et Antiquum documentum
Novo cedat ritui;
Praestet fides supplementum
Sensuum defectui

Genitori Genitoque
Laus et iubilatio
Salus, honor, virtus quoque
Sit et benedictio:
Procendenti ab utroque
Compar sit laudatio.
Amen.

V.   You have given them Bread from heaven. Alleluia.

R.   Having within it all sweetness. Alleluia.

Minister rises, sings or says:

Let us pray. Lord, Jesus Christ, you gave us the Eucharist as the memorial of your suffering and death. May our worship of this sacrament of your body and blood help us to experience the salvation won for us and the peace of the kingdom where you live with the Father and the Holy Spirit, one God, for ever and ever. Amen.

The humeral veil is placed on the priest or deacon. He goes to the altar, genuflects, and takes the monstrance and elevates it over the people, making the sign of the cross. Afterwards, the divine praises may be said:

Blessed be God.
Blessed be His Holy Name.
Blessed be Jesus Christ, true God and true man.
Blessed be the Name of Jesus.
Blessed be His most Sacred Heart.
Blessed be His most Precious Blood.
Blessed be Jesus in the Most Holy Sacrament of the Altar.
Blessed be the Holy Spirit, the Paraclete.
Blessed be the great Mother of God, Mary most holy.
Blessed be her holy and Immaculate Conception.
Blessed be her glorious Assumption.
Blessed be the name of Mary, Virgin and Mother.
Blessed be St. Joseph, her most chaste Spouse.
Blessed be God in His angels and in His saints.
Amen.

Reposition:_ *The Blessed Sacrament is replaced in the Tabernacle and the priest genuflects. Meanwhile, the people may sing or say an acclamation, and the minister then leaves.*

O Sacrament Most Holy
O Sacrament Divine,

All praise and thanksgiving
Be every moment Thine,
Be every moment Thine.

Song

Holy God, we praise thy name,
Lord of all, we bow before thee,
All on earth thy scepter claim,
All in heaven above adore thee,
Infinite thy vast domain,
Everlasting is thy reign.

Infinite thy vast domain,
Everlasting is thy reign.

APPENDIX 8
GENERAL INFORMATION QUESTIONNAIRE

The following questionnaire is to help us get to know you and serve you better. If you feel uncomfortable with any of the questions, you can discuss any sensitive issue with a member of the parish's clergy. The following will be reviewed by the Pastor in order to understand your particular situation and needs as you explore your possible entrance into the Catholic faith.

Full Name:_____

Address:_____

_____

Home Phone:_____

Marital Status (circle the appropriate answer)
  Single (If single, were your previously married): Yes   No
  Married
  Widow/Widower
  Divorced

Marriage History:
Were you previously married prior to your current marriage?
            Yes   No

Has your spouse been married before? Yes   No

In what denomination were you married? Were you married by a

civil court?_____

Present Religious Affiliation:_____

Have you been baptized? If yes, in what denomination were you baptized?

_____

Please cut out page with scissors and return to RCIA director. Thank you.

53530478R00233

Made in the USA
Lexington, KY
08 July 2016